The Structured Credit Handbook

The Structured Credit Handbook

ARVIND RAJAN
GLEN McDERMOTT
RATUL ROY

BICENTENNIAL
1807
WILEY
2007
BICENTENNIAL

John Wiley & Sons, Inc.

Published by John Wiley & Sons, Inc., Hoboken, New Jersey.
Published simultaneously in Canada.

Wiley Bicentennial Logo: Richard J. Pacifico.

Library of Congress Cataloging-in-Publication Data:

Rajan, Arvind.
   The structured credit handbook / Arvind Rajan, Glen McDermott, Ratul Roy.
      p. cm.—(Wiley finance series)
   Includes bibliographical references and indexes.
   ISBN 978-0-471-74749-9 (cloth)
   1. Credit derivatives.   2. Credit—Management.   3. Default (Finance).
   I. McDermott, Glen, 1968–   II. Roy, Ratul, 1964–   III. Title.
      HG6024.A3R35 2007
      332.7—dc22

                                                        2006019227

Printed in the United States of America.

10 9 8 7 6 5 4 3 2 1

*To the memory of my dad, V. Varadarajan (1921–2002),
whose faith in my potential
still inspires me.*

—A.R.

*This book is dedicated to Gail B. McDermott
and to the memory of
Maurice and Claire McDermott
and John F. Brennan.*

—G.M.

*To my parents, Tapan and Uma, for their
love and faith in me.*

—R.R.

Contents

CHAPTER 2
Credit Default Swaptions   **39**

Arvind Rajan and Terry Benzschawel

CHAPTER 5

Matt King and Michael Sandigursky

PART TWO

Portfolio Credit Derivatives

CHAPTER 6

Single-Tranche CDOs 149

Jure Skarabot, Ratul Roy, and Ji-Hoon Ryu

PART THREE

Collateralized Debt Obligations

CHAPTER 10

CHAPTER 11
ABS CDOs   **335**

Ratul Roy and Glen McDermott

CHAPTER 12
CDO Equity   **371**

Glen McDermott and Alexei Kroujiline

Acknowledgments

This book is the culmination of many months of work by numerous people and we are especially grateful to Gaurav Bansal, David Park, and Jon Sondag, our research analysts—without them, this book would never have made it to press. We would also like to extend a special thank you to Adela Carrazana, K.K. Kua, Norma Lana, Cecilia Sarmas, Christopher Saunders, and Andrew Weissman for their tireless and careful work in preparation of this manuscript. Our thanks also to Charles Earle and Jeanne Campbell for resolving the myriad of compliance and legal issues which surround the publication of a book of this type.

This book evolved from a number of product primers and other research reports written by Citigroup's Global Structured Credit Research team for the benefit of fixed-income investors. We would like to acknowledge the following people who contributed to these research reports while they were at Citigroup, and who are no longer at the firm: Rohan Doctor, Madhur Duggar, Pradeep Kumar, David Li, Matt Mish, Jeff Prince, David Shelton, and Etienne Varloot. Their efforts are gratefully appreciated.

Finally, we would like to thank the professionals at Wiley, including senior editor Bill Falloon as well as his staff, especially Emilie Herman, Laura Walsh, and Mary Daniello for their hard work and patience during the long process of bringing this book to completion.

Arvind Rajan
Glen McDermott
Ratul Roy

About the Authors

Dr. Arvind Rajan is Managing Director in the Relative Value Group of Citigroup's Global Fixed Income Division, where he engages in proprietary trading of Credit, Structured Credit, and Emerging Markets. For the past 13 years, Arvind has held a number of senior positions at Citigroup and Salomon Brothers, including Co-head of US Fixed Income Strategy (2004–2005), Global Head of Structured Credit Research and Strategy (2003–2005), and Global Head of Emerging Markets Quantitative Strategy (1997–2003). Arvind was twice ranked first and once second in the All-America Fixed Income Research poll conducted annually by *Institutional Investor* magazine. In all, Arvind has two decades of experience in modeling and quantitative analysis, including a stint at Bell Laboratories and as a faculty member in the Mathematical Sciences Department at Rice University. He holds a Ph.D. and M.S. in Operations Research from Northwestern University, and a bachelor's degree from the Indian Institute of Technology, Chennai (Madras), India.

Glen McDermott, J.D., is a Director in the Structured Credit Sales Group at Citigroup Global Markets, Inc., where he sells credit derivatives and collateralized debt obligations to a wide array of institutional fixed income clients. Previously, Glen was a highly ranked research analyst and Global Head of CDO Research and Strategy at Citigroup (2000–2005), where he led a five-person team dedicated to analyzing a multitude of structured credit products, both cash and synthetic. Prior to joining Citigroup, Glen worked for 6 years (1994–2000) at Standard & Poor's Ratings Services where he analyzed many structured finance asset classes including mortgage-backed securities, credit card ABS and CDOs. Glen's work has been published in numerous scholarly journals, including *The Journal of Portfolio Management*, *The Journal of Fixed Income*, and *The Journal of Structured Finance*. He is also a contributor to Salomon Smith Barney Guide to Mortgage-Backed and Asset-Backed Securities (John Wiley & Sons, 2001). Glen received his B.A. degree from the College of the Holy Cross and his J.D. from Fordham University School of Law.

Ratul Roy is head of CDO Strategy for Citigroup Global Markets. Before taking on his current role in 2005, Ratul was head of European CDO

Strategy—a position he occupied in 2003 after spending the prior seven years in structuring or analyzing CDOs and other structured credit products. This included positions in UBS Capital Markets (1995–1997), Chase Manhattan Bank (1997–1999), Standard and Poor's (1999–2000), and finally, as a cash CDO structurer in Citigroup's London office (2000–2003). Ratul has a Ph.D. in chemical engineering from Cambridge University, England.

About the Contributors

Gaurav Bansal is a Sales and Trading Associate at Citigroup. Prior to this, he has spent a year each in Mortgage Research and Credit Derivatives Strategy at Citigroup. He has an M.S. in Management Science and Engineering from Stanford University and a B. Tech. in Chemical Engineering from IIT Bombay.

Terry Benzschawel heads the Credit Modeling group within US Fixed Income Strategy, Citigroup Global Markets. Terry holds a Ph.D. in experimental psychology and has held post-doctoral fellowships in optometry, ophthalmology, and engineering prior to embarking on a career in Finance. His financial career began in 1988 with Chase Manhattan Bank modeling corporate bankruptcy and his focus since then has been on risky debt of consumers, sovereign nations, and corporations. Terry joined the fixed income arbitrage group at Salomon Brothers in 1992 focusing on pricing models and risk management of emerging market cash and synthetic obligations until 1998 when he moved to fixed income strategy. Since then, his main focus has been on U.S. corporate debt, with recent emphasis on credit models as applied to structured products, credit derivatives, and capital structure arbitrage.

William Deitrick is a Director in the Loan Analysis and Strategy group within Citigroup's loan sales and trading business. Mr. Deitrick serves as the group's loan strategist and as the senior analyst covering corporate loans in the cable, media, and technology industry sectors. In 2006, Mr. Deitrick's team was ranked number one in *Loan Market Week*'s annual poll. In 2006, Mr. Deitrick was also selected to be a co-author of *The Handbook of Loan Syndications and Trading*, which was published by the Loan Syndications and Trading Association. Prior to joining Citigroup in 2000, Mr. Deitrick held similar positions at J.P. Morgan (1999–2000) and Bank of America (1997–1999). Mr. Deitrick holds BA and MA degrees in International Relations from the Johns Hopkins University. Following graduation, Mr. Deitrick served as a Foreign Service Officer with the U.S. Department of

State (1994–1997), where he was awarded a Fascell Fellowship and held various posts in Belarus, Slovakia, and the Czech Republic.

Matt King is a Managing Director and Head of Quantitative Credit Strategy at Citigroup in London. He aims to provide advice to clients on any aspect of credit portfolio management, from the latest views on the € and £ cash markets through to valuation and risk management techniques, and spanning the whole range of credit instruments from cash, to CDS, to CDOs. *Euromoney* ranked his team #1 in 2004, 2005, and 2006 for Credit Strategy and #1 for Credit Derivatives in 2006. Prior to joining Citigroup, Matt was Head of European Credit Strategy at J.P. Morgan, where his group was also ranked #1 (Euromoney 2003). Before shifting into credit strategy, he spent three years as a government bond strategist. Mr. King is British, and a graduate of Emmanuel College, Cambridge, where he read Social & Political Sciences.

Alexei Kroujiline is a Vice President on the CDO Secondary Trading Desk at Citigroup where he trades cash and managed synthetic CDOs across all asset types and currencies. Prior to his current position, Mr. Kroujiline spent three years in the CDO Research group at Citigroup where he co-authored several publications, among them *Diversifying Credit Risk Using a CDO Equity Fund* (2004), and *Optimizing Selection of Credit Portfolios* (2003). Mr. Kroujiline holds an M.A. degree in Astrophysics/Applied Mathematics from Moscow Institute of Physics and Technology and an M.S. in Economics from Southern Illinois University at Carbondale.

Robert Mandery is an Associate in the Loan Analysis and Strategy group within Citigroup's loan sales and trading business. Mr. Mandery serves as the group's senior analyst covering corporate loans in the airlines, health care, and packaging sectors. Prior to joining Citigroup in 2003, Mr. Mandery held similar positions at J.P. Morgan (2000–2002). Mr. Mandery holds a B.B.A. from Hofstra University.

Olivier Renault is a credit derivative structurer for Citigroup, based in London and was formerly in charge of European structured credit strategy. He is a regular speaker at professional and academic conferences and is the author of a book and many published articles on credit risk. Prior to joining Citigroup, Olivier was responsible for portfolio modeling projects at Standard & Poor's Risk Solutions and was a lecturer in finance at the London School of Economics where he taught derivatives and risk. He was also a consultant for several fund management and financial services companies. He holds a Ph.D. in financial economics from the University of Louvain (Belgium) and a M.Sc. from Warwick University (UK).

Ji Hoon Ryu is an associate at Citigroup, working on capital structure arbitrage trading models in Citigroup Equity Derivatives. Previously, he has worked in Credit Derivatives Strategy focusing on synthetic credit. Ji Hoon has an Electrical and Computer Engineering degree from Caltech.

Michael Sandigursky, CFA, is a Vice President in Quantitative Credit Strategy at Citigroup in London. He specializes in quantitative elements of credit derivatives and structured credit. Previously, Michael worked for a number of years in Citigroup Corporate Bank in London and Russia. Michael holds an M.B.A. from London Business School, and degrees from the University of Economics and Finance and the University of Electronics in St. Petersburg, Russia.

Jure Skarabot heads Citigroup's Credit Derivatives Strategy team in the New York office. His emphasis is on structured credit portfolio products, primarily focusing on synthetic markets. He joined Citigroup after completing his Ph.D. in Finance at Haas School of Business, University of California–Berkeley. His dissertation work was based on structural models of credit risk. He also holds a Ph.D. in Mathematics from the University of Wisconsin–Madison in the area of harmonic analysis.

Darrell Wheeler established Citigroup's CMBS Strategy and Analysis team in 1999. With more than 18 year of experience in commercial real estate, Darrell's research provides CMBS investors with unique, ground level insight into borrowers, real estate markets, and collateral performance. Citigroup's CMBS research has been the first to deliver a CMBS default model, provide strong coverage of the CMBS synthetic products, and is known for uncovering many relative value trends. As a result his CMBS team has been ranked first in the Institutional Investor poll for the past four years (2003 to 2006).

Introduction: A Roadmap of the New World of Structured Credit

Credit is probably almost as old as civilization itself. Certainly it has greased the wheels of commerce for several thousand years. For example, Hammurabi's code[1] (circa 1790 BCE) makes reference to terms of debt repayment. Although commerce has been transformed by successive waves of innovation and development in the past few centuries, it was not until the last decade of the twentieth century that financial technology began to revolutionize the world of credit. In the past ten years, there has been a virtual explosion on a global scale in the application of structured credit technology, and this has resulted in a qualitative transformation of credit markets and a huge expansion in the use of structured credit products. Traditional buyers of credit and new categories of investors such as credit hedge funds have begun to adopt structured credit solutions using a full spectrum of products, both cash and synthetic. Popular cash products include credit-linked notes (CLNs) and collateralized debt obligations (CDOs). CDOs come in many varieties based on the underlying collateral: asset-backed securities (ABS) CDOs, leveraged loan collateralized loan obligations (CLOs), middle-market loan CLOs, commercial real estate CDOs, and emerging market CDOs. Synthetic products, often generically referred to as credit derivatives, range from single-name default swaps to indexes like the CDX and iTraxx to custom synthetic CDO tranches. Prior to the arrival of mathematical and structuring techniques, the world of credit was a straightforward and quintessentially human one: It was all about the lender getting comfortable with the borrower. The changes being wrought by structuring, then, could be compared to those that occurred during the industrial revolution, when manufacturing moved from the hands of skilled artisans to factories.

As a result, the global credit landscape is being irrevocably changed, and this book is a road map to this new world. Written by practitioners with the new investor in mind, it is dedicated to explaining and demystifying these products and broadening their adoption by traditional credit investors. Each chapter introduces the reader to a new product and the technology used to

1

create it. It also uses case studies to illustrate the application of each product in a concrete market setting.

HOW STRUCTURED CREDIT COMPLETES MARKETS

We live in a time of low worldwide inflation and historically low yields and spreads. This, combined with the tremendous growth of Asia (and other emerging markets) and the cash generated by the commodities boom spurred by this growth, has led to a large pool of cash seeking securities to invest in. This demand for assets is heavily bifurcated, with the demand concentrated at the two ends of the safety spectrum. On the safe end, the accumulation of assets by fixed-income investors seeking a high level of safety of principal has spurred demand for highly rated assets, preferably AAA or AA, and yielding as much as possible. Exemplifying the safe end are the Asian central banks, who have been accumulating dollars at a staggering pace in the past few years. At the other end of the spectrum, the disappointing recent returns in equities precipitated by the collapse of the technology boom in the year 2000 have resulted in a glut of global assets seeking equity-like (that is, 10+ percent) returns. For example, there is now over a trillion dollars of hedge fund capital alone. Thus, the demand for assets is split between money seeking absolute safety of principal and money seeking high returns.

Prior to the securitization boom, the universe of fixed-income instruments issued tended to cluster around the BBB rating, offering neither complete safety nor sizzling returns. For example, the number of AA- and AAA-rated companies is quite small, as is debt issuance of companies rated B or lower. Structured credit technology has evolved essentially in order to match investors' demands with the available profile of fixed-income assets. By issuing CDOs from portfolios of bonds or loans rated A, BBB, or BB, financial intermediaries can create a larger pool of AAA-rated securities and a small unrated or low-rated bucket where almost all the credit risk is concentrated. For example, if a BBB-rated corporate bond portfolio were tranched, up to 90 percent of the tranches constructed would likely be rated AAA, and another 3 percent would likely be rated AA. Of course, since total credit risk has to be conserved, the remaining 7 percent of tranches of the CDO would have to have lower credit than the original portfolio. Thus, the CDO tranching process creates both higher and lower credit quality financial instruments from the original portfolio, but in highly unequal proportions. Thus, the structuring process serves to complete the financial market by creating high-credit-quality securities that would otherwise not exist in the market.

ENABLING TECHNOLOGY

The introduction of structured credit products has been accelerated by technology borrowed from two separate streams. The first is securitization, which was pioneered in the mortgage market in the early 1980s and has since also become the key technology behind asset-based securities. Applied to credit, this technology led naturally to the development of CDOs. The second important technology is the modeling of derivatives, pioneered by mathematicians such as Fischer Black, Myron Scholes, and Robert Merton, which was further developed and adopted by practitioners in the interest-rate and stock markets. Modified and applied to credit, this technology led naturally to the theory and practical analytics used by credit derivatives traders.

Over the past few years, the derivatives and securitization streams have merged to create the exciting product known as a synthetic CDO. Synthetic CDOs differ from cash CDOs in that the portfolios that provide the cash flow to service their liabilities consist of credit default swaps (CDSs) rather than bonds or other cash securities. The rules governing the cash flows of synthetic CDOs tend to be simpler than those of cash CDOs, and hence more amenable to mathematical modeling. The models used to value CDOs are called default correlation models. Their introduction has led to a huge focus of academic and practitioner interest in credit portfolio modeling, and model-based trading and hedging of default correlation and credit volatility are now widespread in the credit markets. However, because credit models are still evolving, it will be many years before they are dependable and stable, much in the way that it took several years for interest-rate derivatives markets to converge on common models and hedging methodologies.

IMPROVED LIQUIDITY, TRANSPARENCY, AND CUSTOMIZABILITY

Like any evolving technology, if structured credit is to be widely adopted, it needs to be more than just available and useful, and some of the key missing components are now falling into place. Perhaps most important are the dramatic rise in the liquidity of the single-name CDS market; the rapidly rising trading volumes of CDS indexes such as CDX and iTraxx, along with index sectors and tranches; new two-way markets in credit volatility through bond options, index options, and default swaptions; and increased secondary trading in cash CDOs. This increased liquidity has given the dealer community an incentive to standardize trading conventions and index products, which in turn has led to increased transparency, evidenced by daily two-way markets in single-name CDSs, tranches of CDX and iTraxx indexes, bond and index options, and so on. The wide adoption of so-called correlation models has also helped standardize synthetic CDO pricing. Recently, the preceding developments have emboldened investors to seek customized solutions, exemplified by the popularity of single-tranche transactions with substitution. Such customization can address the five key client-specific choices of portfolio composition (including both long and short positions), leverage (specified via the attachment point and thickness of a CDO tranche), currency, tenor, and dynamic management of positions, while allowing dealers to pool and thus more efficiently manage rate, credit, volatility, and correlation risk.

GROWTH OF STRUCTURED CREDIT MARKETS

The structured credit markets have grown dramatically in the first few years of the twenty-first century. The confluence of two factors, market demand stoked by global liquidity and product innovation and standardization spurred by this demand, has led to a so-called network effect in structured credit, the phenomenon whereby a service becomes more valuable as more people use it, thereby encouraging ever-increasing numbers of adopters. This recent expansion in structured credit has occurred in several dimensions: expansion into new underlying asset classes, development of new product lines, penetration of new geographical markets, and involvement of new market participants. Each dimension has added richness, complexity, and utility to the market.

Asset Classes

Structured credit technology was originally applied to corporate credit and has since expanded its reach to new underlying products. The first expansion was from investment-grade credit to high yield, followed by loans and asset-backed securities. Figure I.1 shows the breakdown of recent issuance of cash CDOs by asset class and demonstrates that activity has been particularly strong in the institutional leveraged loan and home equity loan asset-backed securities (HEL ABS) markets, and is picking up in commercial real estate (CRE) bonds. Other assets appear to have come full circle after a dip in structuring activity. For example, emerging market bonds and loans, which had been popular CDO assets prior to the emerging market crisis in 1998, are popular once again.

Products

The development of new structured products has been the main driving force behind the structured credit revolution. This is probably the most practical

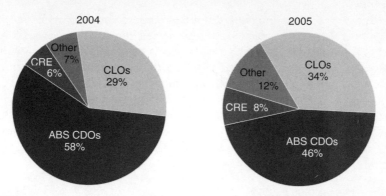

FIGURE I.1   Recent Breakdown of Cash CDO Issuance by Underlying Asset Class
Source: Citigroup.

way to present the development in structured credit, so we have organized this book along product lines. The three main product lines are single-name products (for example, credit default swaps and default swaptions), indexes (such as iTraxx and CDX default swap indexes), and portfolio products (such as CDOs and CDO-squareds or CDO^{2}s).

Figures I.2 through I.5 show the growth in cash CDO issuance, credit derivatives traded volumes, the growth in tranches based on credit indexes (primarily CDX and iTraxx), and the issuance of bespoke CDS tranche markets. As the figures show, issuance in all these markets has been healthy. The 2003-2004 British Bankers' Association (BBA) survey projected that the total notional amount in the various credit derivatives contracts is likely to exceed $8 trillion in year 2006.

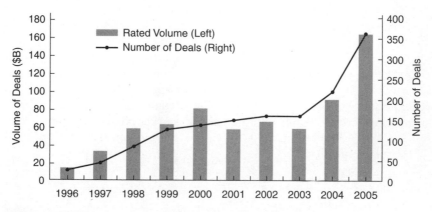

FIGURE I.2   Growth of U.S. Cash CDO Issuance (by Year)

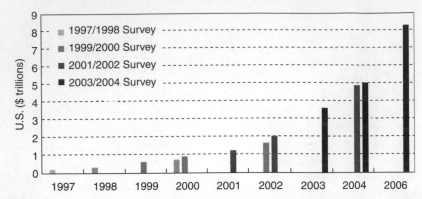

FIGURE I.3 Growth of Credit Derivatives Volumes (Notional Amount)

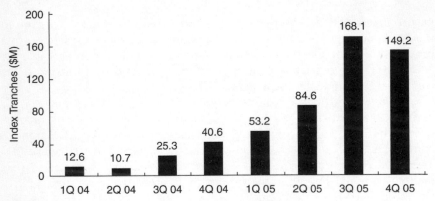

FIGURE I.4 Growth of Index-Based Tranche Markets

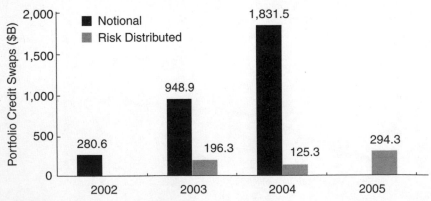

FIGURE I.5 Growth of Bespoke Tranche Market

Participants

The credit derivatives market began with European banks trying to lay off credit risk by buying default protection. Today, while banks still account for almost half of all credit default trades outstanding, the list of participants has grown to include broker-dealers, mutual funds, insurance and reinsurance companies, pension funds, and corporations from every part of the world. These participants trade a broad array of structured products from CDSs to CDOs, making markets deeper and more liquid. In the early days, banks were primarily protection buyers and other types of institutions were protection sellers. But nowadays most institutional categories, including banks, are buyers as well as sellers of default protection (see Figures I.6 and I.7).

Apart from becoming popular with new categories of investors, the use of structured credit products has become more widespread in a geographical sense as well. Initially, North America and Europe were the main markets for credit default swaps and other derivatives. Recently, these products have begun trading in Asia, Japan, and a number of emerging markets as well, although it remains to be seen whether the synthetic correlation and volatility products that have been introduced in Asia and other emerging markets will prove to be as popular there as in the broader and deeper European and North American markets.

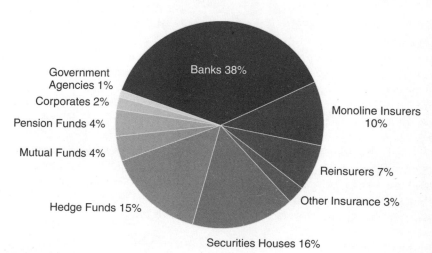

FIGURE I.6 Sellers of Protection
Source: BBA Survey 2004.

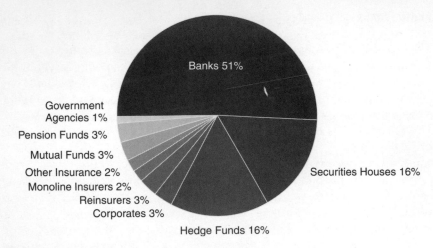

Banks 51%

Government Agencies 1%

Pension Funds 3%

Mutual Funds 3%

Other Insurance 2%
Monoline Insurers 2%

Reinsurers 3%

Corporates 3%

Securities Houses 16%

Hedge Funds 16%

FIGURE I.7 Buyers of Protection
Source: BBA Survey 2004.

CORE USES OF STRUCTURED CREDIT

Structured credit technology fulfills a number of useful functions. Here we outline some of the most important applications, which will be further illustrated by detailed examples throughout the book.

Nonrecourse Leverage

We have already pointed out the first key use of structured credit: allowing investors to get access to products whose spread would otherwise be either too high or too low for their needs. Structuring technology can be used to lever or delever according to the need. For example, an investor looking for A-rated risk can lever AAA assets (by choosing a junior tranche backed by AAA collateral) or delever BB assets to a single-A rating level (by buying a senior tranche backed by BB assets) in the structured credit market. While an investor can always leverage an investment by borrowing, a key attribute of CDOs is the nonrecourse nature of this leverage. The term *nonrecourse*, in contrast to recourse leverage or investing on margin, means that one cannot lose more than 100 percent of the initial investment. Another advantage is that a CDO investor can lock in the leverage for the term of an investment, whereas margin borrowers can rarely borrow to term.

Diversification

Traditional bond investors have historically used derivative products to diversify exposure away from their large and concentrated holdings in plain-vanilla credit and interest-rate product classes. The credit default market grew at first because of the need that banks had to reduce their concentrated exposures to certain counterparties with whom they had strong business relationships. Investors now use these same default swaps to add names to portfolios that they could not access previously. For example, an investor who cannot trade a bond traded in a foreign country's local bond market can now use a derivative contract to gain exposure to that bond.

Customization of Risk Profiles

Creditors such as banks and pension funds are often looking not just to mitigate their long-term risk exposure but also to tailor it in a way that maximizes the use of their economic capital. Because some credits are highly correlated while others add diversity to a portfolio, a great deal of customization and optimization is required to achieve an appropriate risk profile. Such customization can now be easily executed with credit derivative contracts involving so-called bespoke, or customized, CDO tranches.

Separating Legal from Beneficial Ownership

Another use is providing access to nontraditional assets by separating legal and beneficial ownership, so that yield-hungry investors can now tap into the remaining pockets of cheap assets with previously limited ownership profiles. The origin of such ownership limitations could be regulatory, for example, when certain investors can only invest in funded vehicles and ask for a CDS (unfunded) to be converted to a CLN (funded); jurisdictional, as is the case when certain investors can only invest in Japanese yen assets, requiring a currency swap to be bundled with a U.S. dollar/euro-denominated instrument; or driven by convenience, as is the case with pro rata loans, a type of revolving bank loan facility that is inconvenient to administer for most bond investors other than banks, but whose value can be unlocked with a CLO.

Separating Funding from Risk Transfer

Furthermore, structured credit solutions can tease funding apart from risk transfer, allowing cheap sources of funding such as the commercial paper (CP) market to be used to monetize the value in cheap AAA- and AA-rated assets that are otherwise subject to trading at a minimum yield insisted upon by traditional bond investors. For example, the proceeds of a CP transaction can be used to partly fund the purchase of such cheap assets, and the risks can then be parceled out using a standard CDO structure, allowing the differential in spread between the cheap AAA asset and the CP to be captured and leveraged. Separating funding from risk promotes market efficiency, and it can be used to give nonexpert investors safer access to new asset classes. It can also provide term nonrecourse financing to investors who have the expertise and risk appetite but lack favorable funding.

Isolating and Hedging Risk

Finally, structured credit technology is used to separate or combine credit-related and other risks. Until the arrival of such technology, an investor who bought a bond or a loan was forced to carry the entire basket of risks that it entailed. Today's tools enable investors to separate the various components of credit risk and pick and choose which ones they wish to be long or short and which ones they wish to hedge. Some of the types of risk that credit can now be decomposed into (and the measures used to quantify them) include default risk (jump-to-default), market risk (CR01), credit volatility (credit gamma and vega), and correlation risk (correlation skew or portfolio loss measures). Some of the most popular structured products are designed to separate the elements of credit risk from each other or from other financial risks. For example, credit default swaps remove the interest rate risk implicit in fixed-rate corporate bonds. Credit options tease apart credit volatility from outright credit exposure in the same way that stock options separate equity volatility as a distinct risk. Tranched products, including CDOs, synthetic tranches, and index tranches, separate spread and default risk. Contingent credit default swaps allow investors to remove the credit risk inherent in other types of exposure—those embedded in interest rate or commodity contracts, for example.

Once the elements of credit risk have been isolated, investors can choose which ones they want to be exposed to and hedge out the others. Derivative contracts are naturally two-sided and thus allow long and short positions to be taken on each element of credit risk.

Representative Examples of Structured Credit Solutions

Table I.1 illustrates some ways in which structured credit has been applied to take advantage of a market opportunity to fulfill certain investor needs. The examples are chosen to be representative and illustrate the use of instruments and markets described in the book. The examples will give the reader a flavor of how structured credit might be beneficially applied to his or her own portfolio, and they illustrate the practical importance of the products introduced in this book.

WHO SHOULD READ THIS BOOK?

We have written this book with three constituencies in mind. The first is the financial professional seeking an introduction to structured credit products. This includes buy-side professionals considering structured credit securities as a part of their portfolios, as well as sales, structuring, trading, and research personnel in investment banks. The second category is university students interested in learning about the fast-expanding product set that is creating a number of career opportunities globally. With regard to this group, the book is written to make it a suitable textbook in a semester-long course on structured credit as part of a business or finance curriculum at the advanced undergraduate or graduate level. Finally, the intelligent, financially savvy layperson can use the book to get a deeper understanding of the CDO and credit derivatives markets.

A feature of this book that we are particularly proud of, and which should make it very useful to students and financial professionals, is the rich set of case studies included on each product. Each case study, rather than being constructed as a hypothetical example, is based on a real-life application in a specific market environment that has actually arisen in the credit markets. Thus, the data on prices, spreads, hedge ratios, returns, and so forth used in the examples are far more realistic than in a typical stylized textbook example. These case studies can serve as useful adjuncts to the basic material in a classroom. For the financial professional, they ground the descriptive material about the products in an extremely practical context.

Unlike many other books on credit derivatives and CDOs, the book does not require a high level of proficiency in mathematical finance or structuring technology. The book assumes some familiarity with financial markets; in addition, some basic knowledge of fixed-income markets—that is, an elementary-level understanding that can be readily picked up from any introductory book on fixed-income products—is useful.

HOW THIS BOOK IS ORGANIZED

As we have seen, the story of structured credit can be thought to have multiple dimensions: product development, geographic usage, risk measures, and strategic application. We have chosen to lay this book out by product, from single-name building blocks to complex portfolio products. The book is divided into three parts containing chapters devoted to specific products. The first part describes and analyzes credit default swaps, default swaptions, and default swap indexes. The second part covers portfolio credit derivatives, with chapters devoted to single-tranche CDOs, correlation

TABLE I.1 Examples of Structured Credit Applications

Goal	Product Category	Fulfillment of Market Need	Structured Credit Opportunity	Investor Types	Instance of Implementation
Gain access to nontraditional fixed-income assets.	Cash CDOs	Provides global savings safety, yield pickup, and diversification, while addressing concern about owning unfamiliar assets without downside protection.	Access to cheap pockets of assets, management expertise, and loss protection (depending on tranche).	Asset managers	Buy a mezzanine tranche in a European leveraged loan managed cash CDO.
Leverage cheap asset class trading at low yields.	First-to-default (FTD)	Satisfies the belief that credit risk of certain AA or AAA names is minimal, but absolute spreads are too low.	FTD protection on baskets of names often trade at a spread that is a high percentage of the sum of the constituent names.	Asset managers, long/short investors, and hold-to-maturity investors.	Sell FTD protection on a basket of highly rated names, thereby levering AA or AAA assets up to spreads typical of A bonds.
Express credit views through tranched product.	Synthetic index tranches	Enables investors to express credit-specific overweight and underweight views.	Tranches provide leveraged way to express credit-specific overweight and underweight views.	Asset managers	Sell protection on 6%–9% or on 9%–12% tranche based on European Citigroup model portfolio.

Express cross-sector views efficiently.	CDX sectors	For when investors view (for example) the financial sector as being overvalued.	Liquid sector indexes make execution of directional views and hedging market risk simple and inexpensive.	Long/short investors, asset managers	Buy protection on financial sector of CDX, sell protection on CDX.
Obtain yield enhancement without triggering FAS133 derivative MTM rule.	Short-dated bond options	Enables hold-to-maturity accounts to enhance income on bond holdings believed to be near yield bottoms.	Short-dated options are now liquidly traded on several corporate bonds, default swaps, and iBoxx indexes.	Hold-to-maturity investors and asset managers	Sell covered calls on selected names to short horizons. This strategy generates positive alpha in a wide range of outcomes.
Diversify credit risk associated with CDO equity.	Fund-of-funds equity	Gives investors the high-risk/high-reward profile of CDO equity while mitigating asset-class-specific concentration risk.	A fund of funds diversifies risk among various assets such as ABSs, loans, and investment-grade and high-yield bonds.	Alternative investment managers and asset managers comfortable with high-risk investments	Sell protection on a portfolio of CDO equity tranches with active management. This approach can be shown to reduce the negative tail of the return distribution.

market technicals, CDO-squareds, and constant proportion portfolio insurance (CPPI) products, or credit CPPIs. The last section is devoted to cash CDOs, and includes chapters on collateralized loan obligations (CLOs), asset-backed CDOs, CDO equity, and commercial real estate CDOs.

Each chapter includes a primer on the product, covering the structure, cash flow characteristics, market application, and investment considerations that apply to the product. Each of these primers is followed by one or more examples or case studies illustrating a practical application of the product in the marketplace—as an investment, hedging vehicle, or other usage. The sophistication of these applications varies depending on the typical usage of the product. While the book occasionally addresses complex products or applications, the writing is designed throughout to be accessible to an investor who is familiar with the basics of bonds and fixed-income investing.

Each section is designed to be self-contained, and so are most of the chapters. The main exceptions to this rule are the chapters describing complex instruments such as default swaptions or CDO-squareds. In these cases, the reader may find it useful to review the material on the simpler products, which would be the chapters on default swaps and CDOs, respectively. Overall, the organization should make it possible for the reader to treat the book either as a comprehensive product introduction or as a reference book to be consulted as the need arises. To sum up, we hope we have provided a critical mass of information to give the reader a useful introduction to this exciting new technology and its main uses.

One

Index and Single-Name Products

CHAPTER 1

A Primer on Credit Default Swaps

Arvind Rajan

A credit default swap (CDS) is a contract in which the buyer of default protection pays a fee, typically quarterly or semiannually, to the seller of default protection on a reference entity, in exchange for a payment in case of a defined credit event[1] such as default (see Figure 1.1). Default swaps allow credit risk to be isolated and traded between investors. In a sense, they are synthetic bond equivalents, where the buyer of default protection has a position equivalent to shorting a bond, and the seller is in effect being long the bond. However, default swaps introduce counterparty risk. In particular, the buyer of protection is exposed to the seller contingent on the credit event. The intent of this chapter is to provide a basic understanding of the single-name CDS product and its practical implementation in the credit derivatives marketplace.

THE MARKET FOR CREDIT DEFAULT SWAPS

The market for CDSs originated with banks looking to hedge credit risk in their loan portfolios. This market has grown exponentially since 1997, exceeding the expectations of market participants, and the pace of its growth shows little sign of abating (see Figure 1.2). The set of participants has expanded as well, as more players are seeking credit hedges or yield (a pickup over conventional cash instruments). Banks, insurance companies, corporations, and hedge funds actively trade in the default swap market, which is expected to grow substantially in coming years.

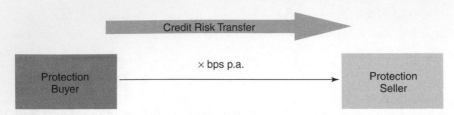

FIGURE 1.1 Cash Flow in a Credit Default Swap Transaction
Source: Citigroup.

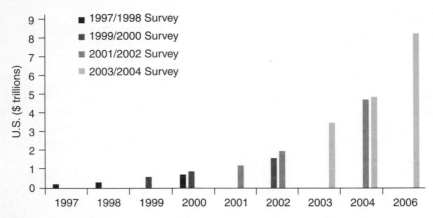

FIGURE 1.2 Credit Derivatives Market Growth, 1997 to 2006E
Source: BBA Surveys.

The amount of CDSs outstanding is more than doubling every year, according to the data provided by two industry sources, the International Swaps and Derivatives Association (ISDA)[2] and the British Bankers' Association (BBA).[3] According to the BBA, the credit derivatives market stood at a mere $180 million in 1997, measured by total outstanding notional. From this humble beginning, ISDA figures document that the market grew to more than $1 trillion by the end of 2001, to $8.42 trillion by the end of 2004, and to $12.43 trillion by the middle of 2005. This represents a growth rate of 123 percent in 2004 and 48 percent during the first six months of 2005. In its recently published 2003/2004 Credit Derivatives Report, the BBA continues to estimate close to 100 percent projected growth for the market.

The spate of debt restructurings, defaults, and high-profile bankruptcies in 2001 and 2002 also increased the awareness for the need to manage credit exposure. CDSs received a further boost in liquidity in 2003 when a broad consortium of dealers got together and began to trade investment-grade, high-yield, and emerging market CDS indexes under the CDX and iTraxx names. These indexes typically consist of baskets of 100 to 125 liquid default swaps, equally weighted. We discuss these indexes and their applications more fully in Chapter 4. Finally, regulatory factors, shareholders demanding higher returns, the ability to customize the maturity of the desired credit exposure (a feature not available in the cash market), and the standardization of default swap contracts have all played important roles in popularizing CDSs.

Credit derivatives have been tested on several occasions through various triggering credit events. In the first few years of the twenty-first century, there have been several high-profile corporate credit events or defaults, including WorldCom, Parmalat, Marconi, Railtrack, British Energy, Charter Communications, Calpine, Delphi, Dana, Delta Airlines, and Northwest Airlines. After most major bankruptcies, settlements caused only a minimal level of dispute. In a few cases, disputes and difficulties arising due to credit events caused the language in CDS contracts (particularly pertaining to restructuring) to be modified to reflect the experience. Overall, the experience so far has enhanced the robustness of the product and the enforceability of the contract.

Single-name CDSs constituted approximately half of all outstanding credit default contracts in 2003, but their market share was expected to fall to about 40 percent by 2006, primarily as a result of the rise in popular usage of index and index-linked products. In addition to CDSs, a range of products has accompanied the growth in the market, including synthetic portfolio/CLO products, credit-linked notes, total return swaps, basket products, and credit spread options (see Figure 1.3). Innovations in synthetic structures will continue to develop, and industry participants expect index and ABS and loan-based credit derivatives products to increase in market share over the next few years. However, in this chapter we discuss CDSs based solely on corporate credit.

The composition of market participants has also changed over the past few years. According to its 2003/2004 Credit Derivatives Report, the BBA found that banks and securities houses were still the main buyers of credit protection. Banks constituted 51 percent of the buyers' market share in 2003. This share is expected to decrease to 43 percent in 2006 as more players enter the credit derivatives market. Securities houses constituted

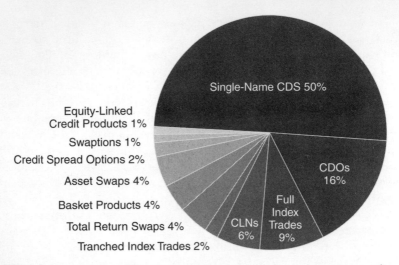

FIGURE 1.3 Breakdown of Credit Derivative Products by Current Outstanding Notional (Year 2003)
Source: BBA Survey 2004.

16 percent of the market share in 2003, and their share is expected to drop to 15 percent in 2006 with the advent of new entrants. The biggest recent change is the emergence of hedge funds as buyers of credit protection. In 2003, hedge fund market share was at 16 percent, equal to that of securities houses, whereas in 2001 it had been only 12 percent. The increase in hedge fund market share follows from the fact that hedge funds are active buyers of default swaps as well as the first-loss tranche in synthetic securitization deals. It is projected that hedge funds will maintain their market share in the future and potentially even replace securities houses as the second-biggest market participant on the buy side. The rest of the market is distributed among insurance companies, corporations, mutual and pension funds, and others (see Figure 1.4).

On the sell side of the credit protection market, banks still held the largest market share in 2003 at 38 percent, but their share is expected to drop to 34 percent in 2006 as the market continues to eveolve. Monoline insurance companies and reinsurers were second with a combined 17 percent share in 2003, and they are expected to retain their market share through 2006. The sell-side market share of securities houses and hedge funds has remained steady in recent years at about 15 percent and will probably stay

Buyers

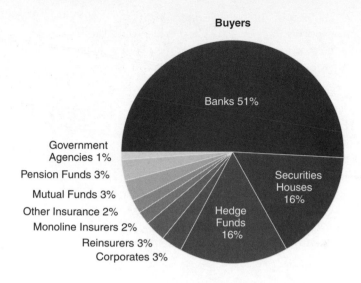

Sellers

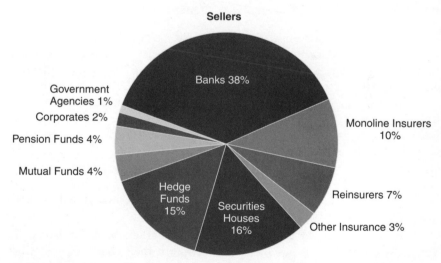

FIGURE 1.4 Credit Derivatives Market—Buyers and Sellers Breakdown (Year 2003)
Source: BBA Survey 2004.

at the same levels. The rest of the market participants are not expected to capture a substantial portion of the sell-side market for default protection (see Figure 1.3). In the next section, we describe the product in greater detail and outline the operation of the basic default swap transaction.

TRANSACTION TERMINOLOGY AND MECHANICS

Although a CDS is one of the simplest forms of credit derivative, there are nonetheless some mechanical details that are important to the practitioner desiring to participate in the CDS market. In this section, we describe some of the details of a CDS confirm, explain what happens if a credit event actually takes place, discuss how such transactions can be unwound, and introduce the market conventions regarding the spread between CDS and cash instruments.

Prerequisites for Credit Derivatives Transactions

Before entering into a transaction, both parties in the default swap usually have a signed ISDA confirmation document in place. This is an agreement that sets forth the rights and duties of the two parties under all swap contracts. Early credit derivative contracts suffered from the ambiguity surrounding the documentation of the agreements. Since 1999, the ISDA has provided a standard template to document a default swap transaction between the two parties. These contracts are governed by a set of common rules and definitions published by the ISDA. Before a CDS is executed, credit lines between the counterparties must be in place because each party is taking on credit exposure to the other.

The terms of a CDS contract are flexible and are negotiated between the buyer and seller of protection. Some key terms are:

- *Reference entity* is the obligor on which protection is being either bought or sold (e.g., ABC Corporation).
- *Reference obligation* is an obligation of the reference entity that is referred to in the default swap contract. The characteristics of the reference obligation often provide a basis on which to compare any obligation that may be delivered to the protection seller (a "deliverable obligation") if a credit event occurs. These characteristics typically require that any deliverable obligation be pari passu with the reference obligation in the priority of payments of the debt of the reference entity.

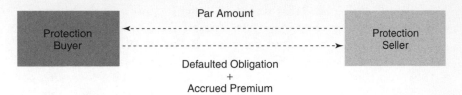

FIGURE 1.5 Cash Flow in a Credit Default Swap Transaction in Case of a Credit Event
Source: Citigroup.

- *Notional amount* (also referred to as *floating-rate payer calculation amount*) of the default swap is the amount of exposure to a particular credit (the reference entity) for which protection is being either bought or sold for a particular period of time.
- *Tenor for which risk is being transferred* is the period for which the protection under the default swap will remain effective (typically five years).
- *Credit events* are the circumstances that must occur for the protection buyer to exercise its right to exchange a deliverable obligation with the protection seller for a payment of par. For CDSs on corporate entities, these events typically include failure to pay, bankruptcy, and restructuring. For CDSs on sovereign entities, obligation acceleration and moratorium/repudiation are also considered credit events.
- *Default swap premium* is the premium (fixed rate) that the buyer agrees to pay the seller in exchange for the transfer of credit risk. The U.S. market convention is to pay quarterly on an Actual/360 basis.

What Happens in Case of a Credit Event?

If no credit events occur during the term of the default swap, the swap expires unexercised. If a credit event on the underlying reference entity should occur, the CDS is designed to unwind in an orderly manner. Figure 1.5 shows the typical exchange of cash flow that takes place when a credit event occurs. The following sequence of events is generally executed upon a credit event:

Occurrence of Credit Event Is Established A credit event is often documented in local newspapers, business magazines, or other publications that are publicly available. The recording of such an event allows the buyer to exercise the right to put the deliverable obligation to the seller at par. There are typically two options for settlement—physical and cash settlement—and the contract will specify which one applies to the specific situation.

Credit Event Notice Is Delivered by Either the Buyer or the Seller One of the counterparties (buyer or seller) delivers the "credit event notice" to acknowledge the occurrence of the event. A "notice of publicly available information" concerning the credit event must also be delivered (either as part of the credit event notice or separately). This notice cites the sources of information confirming the occurrence of the credit event. When both the notices are effective, the settlement period is initiated.

Buyer Delivers Notice of Intended Settlement to the Seller This notice is an expression of the buyer's intent to physically settle the CDS contract. The notice also contains a detailed description of the type of deliverable obligations that the buyer reasonably expects to deliver to the seller.

Physical Settlement: Buyer Delivers a Deliverable Obligation to the Seller and Receives Par If the contract calls for physical settlement, the protection buyer receives $N \times 100$ from the seller, where N is the notional amount, and gives the seller N units of a deliverable obligation. These are obligations of the reference entity that may be delivered, per the CDS contract, in connection with physical settlement. A deliverable obligation must typically be a bond or a loan and must meet certain characteristics. Investors should see the ISDA credit derivatives definition documents for details, but in the most common version of CDS, the deliverable obligation must be pari passu with senior unsecured obligations of the reference entity.

Cash Settlement: Seller Pays Par Minus Recovery Value to the Buyer If the contract is cash settled, a market value is determined for the reference obligation and the protection seller makes a cash payment to the protection buyer for the implied loss on that obligation. Specifically, the protection seller pays the buyer $N \times (100 - R)$, where R is the price of the reference security after the credit event (recovery value) and N is the notional amount.

As an example of a cash settlement, in a $10 million notional transaction, when the defined credit event occurs, assume that the market value of the reference security is 15 percent. The swap is then terminated, and the seller pays the buyer a redemption amount of $(100 - 15\%) \times 10,000,000 = \$8.5$ million.

If the settlement were physical, the seller would pay $10 million to the buyer, while the buyer would deliver to the seller the deliverable obligation with a face amount of $10 million (current market value of $1.5 million). Occasionally, the settlement may give one of the counterparties the choice of cash or physical settlement, or the cash settlement may be for a predetermined amount. In either case, the buyer owes the seller the accrued fraction of the default swap premium up to the credit event. The swap then terminates.

Unwinding Default Swap Transactions

When market conditions dictate, an investor may wish to terminate the swap prior to the final maturity of the default swap—for example, when the investor wants to book a profit. In such a situation, the investor will unwind the default swap contract at the current market value of the swap. Suppose the investor buys protection today on Acme Corporation credit (i.e., short Acme Corporation credit risk) at a spread of, say, 100 basis points (for five years). Now suppose Acme Corporation credit deteriorates and default spreads steadily widen. Assume that one year after having entered into the transaction the investor finds that protection on Acme Corporation credit is worth 400 bp, and the investor can book a profit by unwinding the transaction (typically with the dealer from whom the investor bought protection). Unwinding the transaction reduces to "selling" protection on Acme Corporation for the remaining life of the original default swap transaction—that is, four years. In practice, however, a transaction is unwound by way of a tear-up, where the dealer effectively tears up the original contract after agreeing to pay (in this case) an amount that represents an investor's profit on the trade. In this example, the investor receives either (1) a running coupon representing the difference between the two positions (i.e., the premium received from selling protection, or 400 bp per annum, minus the premium paid for buying protection, or 100 bp per annum) or (2) the present value of 300 bp per annum, running for four years discounted for the likelihood of Acme Corporation defaulting during the next four years. The discounting referred to here is the same that is used to price a CDS transaction after its inception and is described mathematically in the appendix after Chapter 4. The value of a default swap contract at a certain maturity T, per basis point, is referred to as the Spread01 at that maturity. Many examples of the sensitivity of default swaps to credit changes may be found in this chapter's case study and also in Chapter 5.

The DV01 of a Credit Default Swap

Taking exposure to a company for two years is very different from taking credit exposure for ten years. Quantifying the exposure of a default swap to changes in the company's credit quality is done using the concept of DV01, defined as the change in value of the swap for a 1 bp shift in the credit curve. Closely related to the spread DV01 of a credit-risky bond, the DV01 of a default swap is essential to quantifying the mark-to-market risk of an investor. For example, the value of default protection for five years in an investment-grade corporate will increase by approximately \$4,400 per \$10 million per basis point.

The Default-Cash Basis

While default swaps are quoted as a spread premium, corporate bonds are often quoted as a spread to Treasuries. Because most cash bonds are issued as fixed-rate instruments and because most investors fund on a London Interbank Offered Rate (LIBOR) basis, it is necessary to convert the Treasury spread to a spread to LIBOR[4] so that a comparison between default swap spreads and the spreads on the corresponding-maturity cash instruments is possible.

Default swap spreads, which are often leading indicators of deteriorating credit quality in addition to being more volatile than cash spreads, will typically be slightly wider than the spreads of comparable-maturity cash bonds (to LIBOR)—that is, the default-cash basis is generally positive. Many technical and fundamental factors affect the level of the default-cash basis, but the most important is the fact that default swaps have slightly greater risk than bonds or loans for a particular reference entity. An investor who buys a bond or loan knows exactly what obligation she holds in the event of a credit downturn, but the protection seller can only estimate that he will hold a senior unsecured bond or loan that meets the criteria of a deliverable obligation. He will not know the specific bond or loan he will receive until there is a credit event.[5]

SOME USES OF DEFAULT SWAPS

The following is a summary of the most common applications of default swaps, and illustrations with examples of trades are provided when appropriate. Investors can choose different recovery values based on their views on the credits involved.

Buying a Note versus Selling Default Protection

The cash flow of a (funded) cash instrument such as a corporate bond can be replicated using a CDS. In this sense a default swap is a synthetic substitute for a bond and provides investors an alternative to investing in cash instruments for essentially the same risk.

As an example, consider a trade in which an investor is faced with the choice of either buying the cash instrument or selling protection as described in Table 1.1.

The investor has the alternative of earning 205 bp per annum by selling ABC protection or earning a spread of 200 bp by buying the corresponding ABC notes. Some considerations in making an investment in the credit risk of ABC Corporation are highlighted in Table 1.2.

Note that the default-cash basis was implicit in the investor's choice.

TABLE 1.1   ABC Corporation—Cash or Derivative Exposure?

Buy 8 Percent ABC Notes 1/15/11	Sell Five-Year ABC Protection
Indicative bid/offer spread of 260 bp/250 bp to five-year Treasury.	Indicative bid/offer of 205 bp/215 bp in default swaps.
At +250 bp, with midmarket swap spreads of 50 bp, the notes asset swap to LIBOR + 200 bp.	Unfunded position, so seller receives 205 bp per annum.
If financing cost is LIBOR flat, net spread on the five-year trade is 200 bp per annum.	

Source: Citigroup.

TABLE 1.2   Investor Considerations in the Cash Versus Default Trade

Buy ABC Corporation Cash Bond	Sell Protection on ABC Corporation
Investor holds a specific bond.	If a credit event occurs, the protection seller will receive the cheapest ABC bond or loan (within certain parameters) at par.
LIBOR + funding costs results in lower spread pickup.	Larger benefit for investors who fund at LIBOR +.

Source: Citigroup.

Freeing Up or Using Bank Credit Lines

Banks with a mismatch between their credit lines and their desired portfolios often use the default swap market to close the gap. In fact, this was one of the very first applications of default swaps and the key reason that the CDS market got going. For example, an American or European bank with an unused credit line to a particular corporate name could use the default swap market to create a synthetic asset that pays it for taking on risk against that name, something that may not be possible if that corporation has not issued cash bonds or if existing bonds are illiquid or of an inappropriate maturity. In this case, the bank would effectively sell default protection. Alternatively, a bank wishing to reduce concentrated exposure to a particular corporation (e.g., a deteriorating credit with which it has a long-standing and extensive credit relationship) could buy default protection from a third party to effectively defease some of the credit risk.

Filling a Maturity Gap

Many credits do not have a full yield curve, and even when some bonds exist, they could be illiquid and rarely traded. This is particularly true for off-the-run credits, which often have just a couple of traded instruments. The default swap market offers an additional venue for taking a credit position for maturities different from those of the outstanding cash instruments. A short-maturity default swap allows the investor to take an almost pure credit position on default, effectively decoupling the credit risk from the spread duration risk inherent in longer securities. The investor looking to get short credit risk has the additional advantage of not having to short an illiquid bond, thus avoiding the risk of volatile repurchase agreement (repo) rates and short squeezes.

For example, in January 2006, General Motors Acceptance Corporation (GMAC), a General Motors (GM) subsidiary, traded at distressed spreads because of the travails of GM, but many investors felt that GMAC was likely to be spun off or bought and eventually return to investment-grade status. These investors expressed that view by selling six-month or one-year default protection in GMAC, even though short-dated GMAC bonds were not available.

Expressing Curve or Forward-Rate Views

A variant on the theme of expressing a cross-credit view is that of expressing a view that a particular part of a credit curve is too steep or too flat, or to synthetically express a view on the forward curve, where the forwards are not traded directly. For example, let us say the investor feels that ABC Corporation's credit curve between the 5- and 10-year point is too flat—in other words, that the implied probability of default between 5 and 10 years is lower than justified by the fundamentals. If the investor expects the spread between 5-years and 10-year CDs to steepen, the investor would sell 5-year protection on \$X million and buy 10-year protection on \$Y million (X and Y are chosen in a spread DV01-neutral ratio, (typically 1.3:1 to 1.8:1) such that the trade is neutral to parallel shifts of the spread curve) to express this view. This is a DV01-neutral curve steepener. Furthermore, the investor could capture the benefit of the (usually) positive carry of the trade and of the likely sharp roll-down in the under-five-year part of most credit curves (roll-down between 5 and 10 years is typically lower). Note that the investor is net long default risk on ABC to the tune of \$X–\$Y.

Now consider another investor who is bullish on ABC Corp, but who believes that the spread of the 10-year CDS is too wide relative to the 5-year CDS. Such an investor might be expecting a rally in ABC as well as a flattening of ABC's 5 to 10s spread, and therefore might wish to be long duration as well as a flattener. Selling $10 million of 10-year default protection and buying $10 million of 5-year default protection (equal notional amount) is a credit-neutral but long-duration trade. This investor would be immune to default for the first five years, and would benefit from a curve flattening and/or a parallel spread curve rally, but would be exposed to a credit sell-off in a mark-to-market sense, as well as to further steepening of the 5- to 10-year CDS spread.

Other types of curve trades, such as. DV01-neutral flatteners, forward credit shorts, etc. are possible. The analysis and application are similar to the examples above.

Barbell-Bullet Trade

A third version of the CDS curve trade is one where the investor believes, as in the preceding trade, that the slope of ABC's 5s to 10s CDS curve is too steep, but he is not bullish on the credit. Such an investor would enter a DV01-neutral curve flattener. This would be the exact opposite of the DV01-neutral curve steepener, and thus would involve selling $Y amount of 10-year protection and buying $X amount of 5-year protection, resulting in a negative carry. Notice that in this case, the investor is short $X–$Y of ABC credit, but may not believe that ABC has significant risk of suffering a credit event.

In this type of duration-matched relative-value curve trade (whether involving cash or CDS instruments), investors can neutralize themselves to the default event while improving the negative carry by selling an appropriate amount of short-maturity default protection. Thus, the investor can sell 1-year protection in addition to the 5- and 10-year legs. This trade is referred to as a barbell-bullet or butterfly.

Taking Advantage of Tight Repo Levels without Financing

Certain bonds may trade at tight ("special") levels in the repo (financing) market. That is, an investor long the bond and using it as collateral to borrow against would be charged a lower interest rate than normal (the so-called general collateral or GC rate). The yields of bonds that are trading special are usually slightly lower to reflect their repo advantage. Yet, many asset managers do not finance and usually face the unpleasant alternatives of not buying in that maturity range or putting up with inferior yields.

However, through the default swap market they can realize at least a part of the financing advantage. For example, while in early 2006 the Republic of Brazil 12.5% of 2016 bond was trading more than 100 basis points tight to general collateral in repo, the investor could purchase a note tied to a default swap of similar tenor with the Republic of Brazil as the reference entity that paid a spread of about 50 bp higher than the LIBOR spread of the bond.

Since the spread earned on a default swap can be as long as the maturity of the bond, it has the effect of monetizing the implied repo curve for the full life of the security. In contrast, the repo market itself does not normally make financing available for terms longer than a few months to a year.

CASE STUDY: RELATIVE VALUE—CASHING IN ON THE CURVE STEEPNESS IN TELECOMS

The following case study illustrates many advantages of CDSs described earlier in the chapter. By providing an opportunity to short credit risk, the CDS lets the investors express specific views about various parts of the credit curve. In October 2004, the curves in the telecom market were very steep and sophisticated investors could position for flattening by playing in the CDS and the cash market at the same time. The case study, taken from Citigroup's "Bond Market Strategy" publication, demonstrates our recommendation at the time on how this strategy could be implemented.

How to Blend CDs and Cash in Long-Maturity-Curve Trades

We have highlighted in our recent research the continued steepening in credit curves across most sectors of the market, particularly in higher-beta sectors such as autos and telecoms. Persistent portfolio-related selling of protection (i.e., buying credit) has helped fuel a significant rally in the short end of the curve, while the rally in Treasuries has evoked stronger expectations for a healthy backup in rates and, hence, investors seeking to shed longer-duration securities. Credit curves in the telecom sector specifically have been influenced by the buying back of some short-dated paper (Sprint is a case in point), further exacerbating the steepness across many curves; for example, many 10s/30s credit curves that we monitor are at their 100th percentiles.

To put the steepness among telecom credit curves into perspective, Table 1.3 depicts a list of benchmark nonfinancial issuers, the five-year CDS spread, the corresponding on-the-run long bond asset swap spread, and the differential (on an absolute and relative basis) between them. Telecoms (in boldface) account for five of the top seven steepest curves on an absolute basis. We also highlight that the majority of names are BBB-rated, higher-beta credits (excluding Cingular and Verizon), and for many the significant upward-sloping credit curve partly reflects strong short-term liquidity but potential concerns over credit quality going out more than a few years.

While market participants more often examine curves within either the CDS or cash markets, instead of both, we focus on these differentials across both the 5-year CDS and

TABLE 1.3 Steepness of 5/30s Credit Curves Across Select Benchmark Issuers (5-Year CDS, 30-Year Cash), October 2004

Issuer	Ratings	Coupon (%)	Maturity	Par ASW	Five-Year CDS (bp)	ASW—CDS (bp)	Ratio[a]
AT&T Corp.	Ba1/BB+	8	2031	378	225	153	1.7
Sprint Capital Corp.	Baa3/BBB−	8.75	2032	164	60	104	2.7
DaimlerChrysler	A3/BBB	8.5	2031	168	65	103	2.6
AT&T Wireless	Baa2/BBB	8.75	2031	134	33	100	4.0
Georgia Pacific Corp.	Ba3/BB+	8.875	2031	219	127	92	1.7
Cingular Wireless	A3/A	7.125	2031	109	29	81	3.8
Verizon Maryland	Aa3/A+	5.125	2033	112	35	77	3.2
Amerada Hess	Ba1/BBB−	7.125	2033	138	64	74	2.2
Devon Energy Co.	Baa2/BBB	7.95	2032	112	43	69	2.6
GMAC	A3/BBB	8	2031	241	173	68	1.4
Kroger Co.	Baa2/BBB	7.5	2031	115	48	66	2.4
SBC Communications	A1/A	6.45	2034	102	39	63	2.6
Safeway Inc.	Baa2/BBB	7.25	2031	121	58	62	2.1
May Dept. Stores	Baa2/BBB	6.9	2032	119	60	58	2.0
BellSouth Corp.	A1/A	6.55	2034	94	37	57	2.6
Valero Energy	Baa3/BBB	7.5	2032	112	57	55	2.0
Norfolk Southern	Baa1/BBB	7.25	2031	85	32	53	2.7
Walt Disney	Baa1/BBB+	7	2032	93	42	51	2.2
AOL Time Warner	Baa1/BBB+	7.7	2032	115	64	51	1.8
Kellogg Co.	Baa2/BBB−	7.45	2031	61	23	38	2.7
Comcast Corp.	Baa3/BBB	7.05	2033	105	67	37	1.6
Wyeth	Baa1/A	6.5	2034	109	74	34	1.5
Ford Motor Co.	Baa1/BBB−	7.45	2031	227	198	29	1.1
Boeing Co.	A3/A	6.125	2033	53	26	27	2.1
Wal-Mart Stores	Aa2/AA	7.55	2030	44	18	26	2.4
Caterpillar Inc.	A2/A	7.3	2031	48	25	24	2.0
Sara Lee Corp.	A3/A+	6.125	2032	43	24	19	1.8
Target Corp.	A2/A+	6.35	2032	40	23	17	1.7
Viacom Inc.	A3/A−	5.5	2033	70	53	16	1.3
IBM	A1/A+	5.875	2032	38	22	16	1.7
Procter & Gamble	Aa3/AA−	5.8	2034	26	14	12	1.9

[a]Ratio = Par ASW/five-year CDS.
Source: Citigroup.

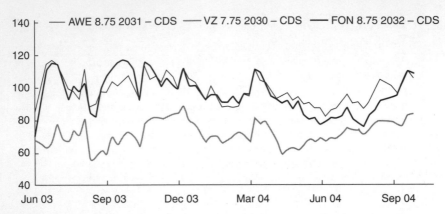

FIGURE 1.6   AWE, FON, and VZ 5s/30s Credit Curves: At Their Steepest Levels Year to Date
Source: Mark-It Partners and Citigroup.

30-year cash markets for a few reasons. First, liquidity in the five-year bucket of the CDS market is robust and allows investors to go long protection (short credit) more efficiently vis-a-vis the cash market. Second, there is no liquidity in the 30-year CDS bucket and limited liquidity in the 10-year bucket. A sizable amount of credit curve trading occurs in the CDS market, but in many instances the all-in transaction costs of 5 to 10 basis points in the single-name space (with the exception of 8 to 10 specific issuers, including Ford, GM, and AT&T) diminish the widespread application of such trades at this stage of the market's maturity. Third, we believe that the lack of focus on examining opportunities across the entire credit curve in the cash and CDS markets offers some new, interesting opportunities.

In Figure 1.6 we highlight these relationships across three selected telecom names, depicting the absolute spread differentials between AT&T Wireless (AWE), Sprint (FON), and Verizon (VZ) long bonds and five-year CDS spreads, which are all approaching year-to-date widest levels. On closer examination we find that the recent widening has been driven by the tightening in 5-year CDS spreads more than by a sell-off in 30-year bond spreads, whereas in March 2004 when the relationships traded at similar levels the large differential was driven primarily by a widening in long bond spreads, as expectations for interest rate hikes rose substantially.

In our view, the current rally in the CDS market has largely run its course, particularly for these arguably higher-quality, low- or mid-beta names that are trading well inside of historic averages. For example, Sprint has rallied about 45 to 58 bp (mid), AT&T Wireless has tightened over 20 to 33 bp (mid), and Verizon has tightened about 14 to 31 bp (mid) versus a tightening of 7 to 55 bp (mid) on the CDX.IG Series 2 index. We believe that at current levels, spreads are approaching a floor, and thus buyers of protection face limited downside risk.

We foresee two plausible scenarios:

1. **Higher-probability scenario**. The overall credit environment remains supportive of five-year CDS spreads, and these credits find a floor a few basis points inside of current levels. Long bond spreads begin a gradual grind tighter as investors become increasingly comfortable with the outlook for interest rates, and seek extra spread pickup in credits with constructive outlooks. Our telecom analyst Henry Mitchell carries an overweight recommendation on AWE and FON and a slight overweight on VZ.
2. **Lower-probability scenario**. The overall credit environment turns sour, as a result of weaker-than-expected third-quarter earnings/guidance, rising oil prices, or problems in Iraq, and five-year CDS spreads begin unwinding the large gains accumulated over the past few months, outpacing the more modest widening that would likely occur in long bond spreads.

We suggest a trade strategy for each of these views in the next section.

Implementing Credit Curve Flatteners—Two Basic Approaches

Implementing credit curve trades across either the investment-grade cash or CDS markets is generally accomplished in one of two ways: equal-weighted notional or spread-DV01 neutral. A third method is default neutral, but given our overall market view and individual credit views on these telecom names over the next six months, this is not a relevant strategy because we do not anticipate FON, AWE, or VZ to default.

Depending on which of the two scenarios outlined earlier is accorded a higher probability by the investor, he or she will pursue one of two strategies.

For the higher-probability (i.e., more optimistic) scenario, the credit bull flattener, implementing the trade equal notional (e.g., buying $10 million of five-year protection and $10 million notional of bonds) would be appropriate. This strategy can be dissected into two trades (for clarification purposes); an investor is explicitly long the flattener and long outright credit risk due to the larger duration of the long bond relative to CDS. These trades generate a positive payoff if spreads tighten in a parallel shift, or if the curve flattens; these trades generate a negative payoff if spreads were to widen in a parallel shift or if the curve were to steepen.

Table 1.4 illustrates the payoff of the equal notional trade, where an investor buys US$10 million notional of AWE 8.75 percent of 2031 at 130.7 and buys US$10 million of AWE five-year protection. Note the payoffs depict only the credit risk component of the trade; the interest rate component can be eliminated by putting on an asset swap—swapping the fixed-rate cash flows received from buying the bond into floating-rate cash flows.

There are two other (secondary) components that will affect the payoff of the trade: transaction costs and cost of carry. Assuming an average bid/offer cost of 6 bp all-in (3 bp bid/offer for CDS, 3 bp for the bond), transaction costs will total approximately US$61,000. In the case of the AWE example, the trade actually results in positive carry of US$98,000 per annum. If we assume an investor holds the position for six months (i.e.,

TABLE 1.4   Equal Notional Strategy

Strategy 1 Buy $10 million AWE 8.75 2031 at +141 bp over 30-year
            government (130.7, dollar price)

            Buy $10 million AWE five-year CDS at +32 bp

SCENARIO ANALYSIS — PROFIT AND LOSS PARALLEL SHIFT — AWE CREDIT CURVE (**AWE** TIGHTENS, WIDENS UNIFORMLY)			SHIFT IN AWE 8.75 2031 ONLY (**AWE** CURVE FLATTENS, STEEPENS)		
	−20 BP	+20 BP		−20 BP	+20 BP
Bond leg	320,175	−308,518	Bond leg	320,175	−308,518
CDS leg	−92,455	92,455	CDS leg	0	0
Net P&L	227,720	−216,063	Net P&L	320,175	−308,518

Source: Citigroup.

US$49,000), the transaction costs minus the positive carry results in a slightly negative payoff of—US$12,000. In this example breakeven for the trade will be about a 1 bp flattening in the curve.

For the lower-probability (i.e., less optimistic) scenario, the credit bear flattener, implementing the trade spread-DV01 neutral would be more appropriate. In this strategy an investor is explicitly long the flattener but neutral credit risk due to the matched duration of the long bond with the CDS. That is, an investor will generate a positive payoff if the curve flattens but is indifferent if spreads either tighten or widen in a parallel shift; these trades generate a negative payoff if the curve steepens.

Table 1.5 illustrates the payoff of the spread-DV01-neutral trade, where an investor buys US$10 million of AWE 8.75 percent of 2031 and buys approximately US$33 million of AWE five-year protection. We estimate transaction costs for this trade at approximately US$92,000 and positive carry of US$24,000 per annum. If we assume that an investor holds the position for one-half year (e.g., USD$12,000), the transaction costs minus positive carry totals roughly US$80,000. In this example breakeven for the trade will be about a 5 bp flattening in the curve.

The structure of the payoff profiles in general will be similar across the telecom names listed in Table 1.3. However, we like implementing the trade in AWE given the significant degree of curve steepness in the name and, as a result the positive carry offered in either strategy (more so in the equal notional trade). Most spread-DV01-neutral trades of a similar nature—that is, buying protection and buying long bonds—will result in negative carry because the trade requires buying about 3.3 times as much CDS for a given amount of long bonds. Therefore the ratio of the par ASW spread to the CDS spread would have to be greater than 3.3:1 to result in a positive carry trade (as it is in this case).

One alternative to the AWE trade(s) described earlier, either equal-weighted notional or spread-DV01 neutral, would be to put the trade on by buying Cingular (CNG) CDSs as opposed to AT&T Wireless (AWE) CDSs, as the CNG CDS trades about 3 to 4 basis points

TABLE 1.5 Spread-DV01-Neutral Strategy

| Strategy 2 | Buy $10 million AWE 8.75 2031 at +141 bp over 30-year government (130.7 dollar price) |
| | Buy $33 million AWE five-year CDS at +32 bp (Spread-DV01 neutral) |

Scenario Analysis — Profit and Loss Parallel Shift — AWE Credit Curve (AWE Tightens, Widens Uniformly)			Shift in AWE 8.75 2031 Only (AWE Curve Flattens, Steepens)		
	−20 BP	+20 BP		−20 BP	+20 BP
Bond leg	320,175	−308,518	Bond leg	320,175	−308,518
CDS leg	−302,358	302,358	CDS leg	0	0
Net P&L	17,817	−6,160	Net P&L	320,175	−308,518

Source: Citigroup.

inside the AWE, meaning that the CNG is a cheaper short. As the AWE-CNG merger is completed at a future date[6] we would expect AWE and CNG CDS to converge, so we would prefer to be short the tighter of the two credits. We also recommend that investors consider putting on the trade in VZ and FON, referenced earlier as credits with very steep credit curves (and generally constructive fundamental outlooks).

APPENDIX: EQUIVALENCE OF A BOND SPREAD AND DEFAULT SWAP PREMIUM

Here we show how one may price a default swap using the market spread of a bond issued by the same reference entity. Our approach will be first to derive expressions for a simplified default swap and then to add correction terms to bring the pricing closer to reality. We assume the following simplified default swap as a starting point:

- The swap is written on a single par floater and initiated on a coupon date.
- There is no payment of the accrued default swap premium to the seller of protection in case of default.
- The swap has no transaction costs and financing specialness.
- Termination payments are made by physical settlement at the coupon date immediately after the credit event.

Now consider a portfolio consisting of the following:

- A short position in default protection (you have sold default protection) where you receive a premium U and in case of default you receive a security worth R and make a payment of 1.
- A long position in a risk-free floater that pays L on coupon dates of the risky bond.
- A short position in the risky security issued by the reference entity that requires payments of $L + S$ on coupon dates.

If there is no default, the net cash flow is zero, because both the risky and risk-free bonds mature at par. If a default event does occur, the portfolio is liquidated at the coupon date immediately after the event. In this case the long position in the floater brings a cash flow of +1, the contingent payment results in a cash flow of $-(1 - R)$, and covering the short position $-R$, which again net out to zero. So, to prevent arbitrage, the intermediate cash flows must be zero, and we have $U + L - (L + S) = 0$, or $U = S$. We will now examine the other factors that affect the pricing and attempt to relax some of the simplifying assumptions.

Specialness of the Underlying

Assume the underlying risky security is special in repo, with specialness Y. In this case, the intermediate cash flows are U from the default swap premium, L from the long position in the risk-free security, and $-(L + S) - Y$ from the short position. These cash flows must all add up to zero, so that $U + L - (L + S) - Y = 0$, or $U = S + Y$. In practice, it is difficult to estimate the effective specialness Y because default swaps typically run much longer than available term repos.

Effect of Accrued Default Swap Premium

The market convention is that the buyer of protection must pay the accrued default swap premium that has accrued since the last coupon date. The expected difference between the time of the credit event and the previous coupon is approximately half of the coupon period, so given that a default has occurred, the expected advantage to the writer of protection is half a coupon, or U/4 assuming semi-annual coupons, where U is the default swap premium rate. Assuming semiannual coupons, if the semiannual probability of default is q, for a one-period par bond we have

$$\frac{(1-q)[1+(r+s)/2]+qR}{1+r/2} = 1$$

so that

$$q = \frac{s/2}{1+(r+s)/2-R} \tag{1.1}$$

where s is the spread over the risk-free rate r, and therefore equals the arbitrage-free default swap premium rate U for a par floater under the same simplifying assumptions as before. The annualized probability of default is given by $q_a = 1-(1-q)^2$. Therefore, the advantage to the seller of protection is approximately:

$$v = \frac{U}{4}q_a = \frac{s}{4}q_a = \frac{s}{4}[1-(1-q)^2] \tag{1.2}$$

To illustrate the orders of magnitude involved, assume the risk-free rate is $r = 6\%$, the spread is $s = 5\%$, and the recovery value is $R = 20\%$. Using Equations 1.1 and 1.2 we get $q = 2.94\%$, $q_a = 5.76\%$, and $v = 7.2$ bp. This is a benefit to the writer of protection, and so reduces the default swap premium.

Accrued Interest on the Underlying Risky Security

Similarly, the writer of protection does not owe accrued interest on the underlying risky security in case of default. There is a benefit to the writer of protection, which is given by:

$$v' = \frac{c}{4}q_a$$

where c is the coupon on the risky security.

Accrued Interest on the Underlying Risk-Free Security

As we argued for the starter case, the protection seller has a net cash flow of $-(1-R)$ with the protection buyer and $(1-R)$ from liquidating the positions, which add up to zero. However, this calculation ignores the accrued interest on the risk-free security. The expected value of this accrued interest conditional on default is $L_{avg}/4$, assuming semiannual compounding, where L_{avg} is the average future value of the default-free forward rate L

through maturity. In spread terms, this is equivalent to the unconditional expected value $w = q_a \cdot L_{avg}/4$). If the average value of the risk-free forward rate is L_{avg}, $q_a = 5.76\%$ from the earlier example, we have $w = 10$ bp. This is a benefit to the writer of protection, and so reduces the default swap premium.

CHAPTER 2

Credit Default Swaptions

Arvind Rajan
Terry Benzschawel

A credit default swaption, as the name suggests, is an option on a credit default swap (CDS), typically labeled either a payer or a receiver. As trading activity in CDSs increases, traditional credit market participants often find themselves confused by the meaning of "payer" and "receiver" options on CDSs. The purpose of this chapter is to provide an introduction to these products and show how they can be used to express directional views on credit.

Like most directional derivative instruments, credit swaptions come in two basic forms that may be either bought or sold. Therefore, they have a number of similarities with equity options, but there are a number of differences as well. One important difference is market maturity. While one-off trades certainly traded earlier, the CDS options *market* began to trade actively in 2003. Initial activity in single-name CDS options was followed shortly thereafter by trading in options on indexes. Volume picked up during 2004 and 2005, and today the CDS options market, though still young, has firm footing. We estimate that of the total notional CDS option market volume, three-quarters is tied to CDX indexes. By number of trades, we estimate that half are tied to indices and the remainder tied to single-name credits. Currently, only a few single-name CDS options may be considered liquid, with bid/ask spreads of 4 to 6 vols.[1] Another several dozen single-name credits trade with bid/ask spreads of 7 to 11 vols and the remainder with bid/ask spreads of 12 to 20 vols. Many of the CDS indexes and subindexes trade at levels comparable to those of the liquid single names (i.e., bid/ask spreads of 4 to 6 vols).

PAYER OPTIONS

Figure 2.1 shows four positions using options. A payer option is the right to buy CDS protection at a specified rate at some date in the future. If an investor buys a payer option, he makes money if CDS spreads widen between now and expiry of the option contract.[2] Buying a payer is therefore a bearish view on credit: If spreads widen (the credit deteriorates), the investor makes money. If spreads tighten (the credit improves), the most he can lose is the premium.

    Typically, investors think of a payer as a put option on credit because as credit quality deteriorates the option becomes more valuable. Alternatively, a payer option can be viewed as a call option on spreads. An investor buys the right to purchase credit default protection at a prespecified strike. As credit quality deteriorates, the CDS spread widens, and profit rises. One reason for using the term *payer* option as opposed to put or call is that a payer option is an option to pay a prespecified rate for credit protection.

	Bullish	**Bearish**
Less Risk	**Buy Receiver** *Own Call on Credit* Make money if CDS narrows. Maximum loss is premium.	**Buy Payer** *Own Put on Credit* Make money if CDS widens. Maximum loss is premium.
More Risk	**Sell Payer** *Short Put on Credit* Keep premium if CDS narrows. Maximum loss is notional.	**Sell Receiver** *Short Call on Credit* Keep premium if CDS widens. Maximum loss is price value of the strike – premium.

FIGURE 2.1   Bullish and Bearish Views on Credit Using Options (Payoffs Assume No Default)
Note: See Figure 2.4 for payoffs in the event of default. Maximum loss on selling a payer option depends on whether there is a knockout provision. The maximum loss on selling a payer would be less than the notional if (1) there were a knockout provision, or (2) there were no knockout provision, but positive recovery value.
Source: Citigroup.

Example—When to Buy a Payer

Suppose that an investor sold five-year credit default protection on Sprint (FON) in late November 2003, when it was trading around 140 basis points (see Figure 2.2, top). As of April 7, 2004, with Sprint trading at about 85 bp, the profit would be 55 bp times the DV01. The investor believes that Sprint will continue to tighten but wants to hedge against the risk that credit

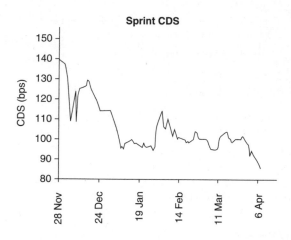

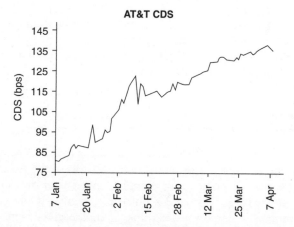

FIGURE 2.2 Five-Year CDS Spread on Sprint, November 28, 2003, to April 7, 2004, and AT&T, January 7, 2004, to April 7, 2004 (in basis points)
Source: Bloomberg.

spreads could widen. The investor buys a three-month at-the-money payer option. Thus, if Sprint widens, the losses from having sold the CDS will be offset by the gains from having bought the payer option, less the premium. If Sprint's spread narrows, the investor also benefits, less the premium. Thus, buying a payer allows the investor to capture most of the upside but provides protection from the downside risk.

Similarly, selling a payer is a bullish view on credit. Exposure to the underlying credit is the opposite of that in the case of buying a payer, and the payoffs are opposite as well. If the CDS spread tightens, the option expires out-of-the-money and the investor keeps the premium. By contrast, if the CDS spread widens, the investor loses money, and the maximum loss is limited only by the recovery value in default.

Example — When to Sell a Payer

Suppose an investor bought five-year credit default protection on AT&T (T) in early January 2004, when it was trading at about 80 bp (see Figure 2.2, bottom). As of April 7, 2004, AT&T is trading at about 135 bp, so the profit would be 55 bp times the DV01. Assume also that the investor thinks that AT&T has room to widen a bit further, but is concerned that it might tighten. In this case, the investor should consider selling a slightly out-of-the-money payer option on AT&T, say at 140 bp. If AT&T widens more than 5 bp plus the spread value of the premium, the gains from having bought the CDS will be more than offset by having sold the payer option. The investor should be comfortable with locking in the upside, given his belief that AT&T spreads will widen only a bit further. If CDS spreads on AT&T tighten, the investor is protected so long as the premium received for selling the payer exceeds the losses on having bought the CDS. (If AT&T tightens significantly, he will still lose money.) In selling a payer option, the investor has extra cushion on the downside.

RECEIVER OPTIONS

Another way to express a bullish view on credit is to buy a receiver option. A receiver option is the right to sell CDS protection in the future at a given spread, in exchange for an up-front premium. A receiver option is, in effect, both a call (on credit quality) and a put (on spreads). If the CDS level on the underlying credit narrows, the value of the receiver option increases. A receiver option can also be viewed as a put on spreads because if credit quality improves, spreads narrow, and the receiver option becomes more valuable.

Example—When to Buy a Receiver

Assume again that the investor buys protection on AT&T and made a profit as spreads widened. He thinks that AT&T might widen further but wants to protect his previous gains, so he considers buying a three-month at-the-money receiver option. Should the CDS on AT&T widen, the profit would remain the same as that from the original CDS, minus the premium paid for the option. By contrast, should AT&T tighten, the losses on the CDS would be offset by the increase in the value of the receiver, less the premium paid. Thus, going long a receiver option allows the investor to continue to capture most of the upside, while protecting against downside risk.

If the investor sells a receiver, he is expressing a bearish view on credit. The payoffs are the exact opposite of the case when one buys a receiver. Should the CDS widen, the investor keeps the premium, because the buyer of the receiver option does not exercise. (If the investor were to exercise, he would receive a worse-than-market level for selling credit default protection.) However, should the CDS tighten, the seller of the receiver loses money, with the maximum loss being the price value of the strike, minus the premium. By price value of the strike, we are referring to the price change if the spread were to tighten to zero. This is what the strike of the option is worth when converted from spread (basis points) to dollars, or the strike times the forward DV01 of the credit.[3] This brings us to the following point.

Effect of DV01 on Credit Swaption Payoffs

Although the payoff at expiry for an equity option depends only on the difference between the underlying asset (i.e., the stock) price and the strike, credit swaption payoffs are dependent on the DV01 of the underlying CDS. This is because the option is struck in spread terms rather than on price, and the DV01 upon the expiry of the option (the "forward DV01") converts from spread terms to dollar value. For example, suppose the investor buys an at-the-money June 2004 payer option for a premium of 40 basis points. If the DV01 of the five-year credit default swap in June 2004 is 4.5 ($4,500 per basis point for a $10 million notional), then the investor makes money if the single-name CDS widens by more than 40 bp divided by 4.5, or about 9 bp. Thus, if the underlying spread were 70 bp today, then the investor makes money if spreads widen to more than 79 bp.

Alternatively, suppose that the investor were to sell an at-the-money June 2004 receiver option struck at 65 bp for a premium of 15 bp and the underlying credit default swap were to tighten all the way to zero. The amount that the investor would lose is 65 bp times the 4.5 forward DV01 minus the 15 bp premium, or about 278 bp.

Those familiar with options on corporate (cash) bonds may wonder why the DV01 conversion is not necessary on those options. This is because options on corporate bonds trade in dollar price, not spread, so no conversion is necessary.[4]

Example—When to Sell a Receiver

Consider again the Sprint example, in which the investor is short protection and spreads have rallied from 140 to 85. The investor thinks that Sprint is unlikely to tighten more than 10 bp and that there is only a small chance that it will widen back out. The premium from selling a slightly out-of-the-money receiver option struck at 75 bp (the current 85 bp, minus the 10 bp you think Sprint has left to tighten) immediately adds to the profits. Should Sprint tighten more than 10 bp, the receiver would be exercised, and the gains from having sold the CDS would be capped by having sold the receiver, but the investor would retain the swaption premium. Conversely, should Sprint widen, the swaption premium would provide a cushion and further opportunity to liquidate the position without suffering losses.

Why should an investor consider selling an option (a more risky strategy), rather than buying one? First, because buying an option has a cost. In selling an option, the investor receives an up-front premium, at the cost of only partial downside protection. Provided the investor is attentive to the credit, hedging a CDS by selling an option may provide sufficient cushion to unwind the position before it loses money.

Second, selling an option expresses a different view on potential spread movement than buying one. If the investor sells a receiver option, he has taken an implicit view that spreads will not tighten dramatically. If they do, the investor can suffer large losses, as shown in the payoff diagram in the bottom left panel of Figure 2.3 for a short receiver on Ford Motor Credit Corporation (FMCC). Similarly, a slight narrowing in spreads for an at-the-money option provides the same upside as a significant narrowing in spreads: The most the investor can earn is the option premium. So the upside is capped, while the downside is extensive. In short, investors who sell options should believe that spreads will trade in a narrower range than investors who buy options.

Figure 2.3 presents payoff profiles versus spread levels for long and short payer and receiver swaptions on CDSs for FMCC. We assume a notional amount of $10 million and show the profit or loss in thousands of dollars. The horizontal lines show profits or losses for cases in which the swaptions expire out-of-the-money. The diagonal lines show gains or losses for in-the-money spread levels. Notice that the payoff on the diagonal line is not one-for-one. This is because of the DV01 conversion from spread terms into dollar terms and the convexity of the price-yield relationship.

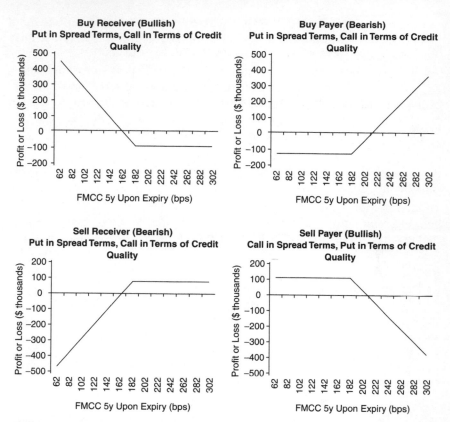

FIGURE 2.3 Payoffs from At-the-Money (182 bp) Payer and Receiver Options on Five-Year Ford Motor Credit Corporation (FMCC) CDS Based on a Notional of $10 Million, April 7, 2004
Source: Citigroup.

We do not go into a detailed discussion of convexity here because of its complexity, and also because for small spread moves convexity is not particularly important. Including convexity would reduce the payoff for significant spread widening on buying a payer option and increase the payoff for significant spread tightening on buying a receiver option.

- If you were to buy a receiver option on FMCC, struck at 182 bp, and spreads on option expiry (June 21, 2004) had narrowed to 82 bp, the actual value of your position would be $360,347 per $10 million, rather than the DV01 approximation of $350,000, for a difference of $10,347. If you were to buy a payer option and spreads on option expiry had widened to 282 bp, the actual value of your position would be $289,405, rather than the DV01 approximation of $325,000, for a difference of $35,595.

- The asymmetry (the smaller difference for 100 bp of spread tightening than for 100 bp of spread widening) is because the actual spread DV01 would be $4,700 per $10 million notional if spreads were to tighten 100 bp—close to our approximation of $4,500. But this figure would be just $4,000 if spreads were to widen 100 bp.

We emphasize that for smaller spread moves convexity is far less important.

CREDIT SWAPTION PAYOFFS IN DEFAULT

The payoffs described in Figure 2.1 are altered somewhat in the event of default as shown in Figure 2.4. That is, a single-name receiver option becomes worthless in default. The buyer of the receiver option loses the premium paid to the seller. The seller of the option keeps that premium. That is, it makes no sense for the buyer of the receiver option to exercise, as he would sell protection on a credit default swap on which he would owe par (due to default).

	Bullish	Bearish
Less Risk	**Buy Receiver** Lose premium.	**Buy Payer** If no knockout, earn (100 − Recovery)% × notional − premium. If knockout, lose premium.
More Risk	**Sell Payer** If no knockout, lose (100 − Recovery)% × notional − premium. If knockout, keep premium.	**Sell Receiver** Keep premium.

FIGURE 2.4 Payoffs on Single-Name Options in the Event of Default
Source: Citigroup.

There are two possibilities for a single-name payer option in default. If the option carries a *knockout in default* provision, the option contract terminates out-of-the-money, with the buyer of the payer option losing the premium paid to the seller. However, if the payer option has *no knockout provisio*n, the option buyer will exercise, which entitles him to (100—recovery) percent times the notional amount of the contract. That is, although the investor is out the option premium, in buying protection he receives par in exchange for delivering a cash bond. Because the payoff for the seller is exactly the opposite, the seller loses (100—recovery) percent times the notional but keeps the original premium.

The difference in price between a swaption with a knockout provision and a swaption without a knockout provision is simply the up-front (or present value) cost of the CDS until expiry of the option. In practice, knockout provisions have been more common, as they are not as sensitive to short-end CDS rates. Moreover, for short-dated options, investors are often comfortable with assuming that the underlying credit is unlikely to default within, say, the three-month term of the contract.

Credit Swaption Implied Volatility

The higher the volatility of a CDS spread, the greater the likelihood that an option written on that spread will finish in-the-money. Investors who have a view on CDS spread volatility, but no directional view, may wish to consider buying a *straddle*. Figure 2.5 shows payoff profiles for long and short straddles. A buyer of a straddle takes a view that underlying CDS volatility will be greater between now and expiry of the option contract than implied by its cost. In practice, if the CDS spread moves up or down by more than the premium divided by the forward DV01, then the buyer of an at-the-money straddle makes money. Conversely, a seller of a straddle believes that a firm's CDS spread will be less volatile than the current implied volatility between now and expiry of the option contract.

CONCLUSION

We have presented an overview of payer and receiver options and provided examples of how investors can use these credit swaptions to express bullish and bearish views on credit and spread volatilities. We have also explained how the DV01 of the underlying CDS is important in calculating option payoff and touched on the effect of convexity on option value. Finally, we presented swaption payoffs in the event of default.

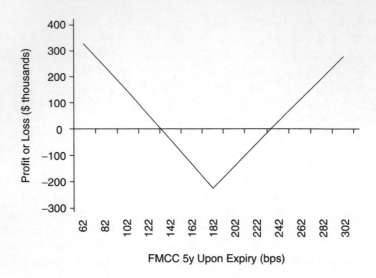

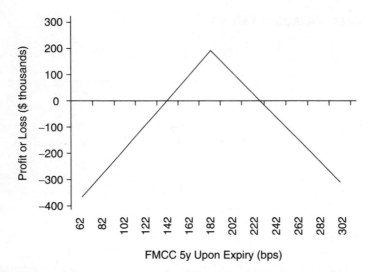

FIGURE 2.5 Payoffs from Buying (top) and Selling (bottom) At-the-Money (182 bp) Straddles on Ford Motor Credit Corporation (FMCC) Based on a Notional of $10 Million, April 7, 2004
Note: For the simplicity of an introductory piece, we ignore the effect of convexity.
Source: Citigroup.

To recap:

- Single-name CDSs offer a way to express directional views on credit or to hedge existing positions.
- A payer option is the right to buy CDS protection at a specified rate at some date in the future. Buying a payer is a bearish view on credit—investors make money if spreads widen.
- A receiver option is the right to sell CDS protection at a specified rate at some date in the future. Buying a receiver is a bullish view on credit—buyers of receivers make money if spreads tighten.
- "Knockout" and "no knockout" provisions in default affect option payoffs differently.
- Straddles offer investors a way to express a view on CDS volatility.

CASE STUDY: ARE TIGHT SPREADS GIVING YOU BUTTERFLIES?

As we discussed, credit swaptions can have many uses, from taking directional views on the market to positioning for credit volatility. Combining different options, one can create a customized payoff profile to suit a particular view under specific market conditions.

Our case study, written in August 2004, pertains to one such application: The credit market had rallied and this provided an opportunity to express the view that the market and some particular entities would experience a modest sell-off going forward. The study shows how a butterfly payer option could be constructed for this purpose and how it could be customized to reflect the expected timing and severity of the sell-off.

Introduction

Corporate bond and loan default rates had fallen precipitously over the prior two years, causing spreads to tumble as well. Quarterly default rates for high-yield bonds dropped from a peak near 5 percent in the third quarter of 2002 to 0.19 percent for the second quarter of 2004 to sit well below the historical dollar-weighted average annual rate of 5.35 percent over the 1971 to 2003 period.[5] Meanwhile, speculative grade spreads to Treasuries had fallen from 9.7 to 4.6 percent over the same period.[6] The story was similar for investment-grade bonds: Improving credit conditions and a lack of credit blowups allowed spreads to rally from their third-quarter 2002 peak of 233 to 100 bp in mid-2004.[7] Recent quarterly default rates and spreads are shown in Figure 2.6.

All of this good news caused some investors to wonder whether the credit rally was overdone, however. Increasingly aggressive lending standards, rising oil prices, impending rate hikes, more aggressive growth, and leverage strategies—mergers and acquisitions (M&A), leveraged buyouts (LBO), share buybacks—and election-year uncertainty gave some investors pause. While generally bullish on credit fundamentals, these investors were slightly bearish on spreads. Our butterfly trade idea, using credit swaptions, was directed at investors who shared this view.

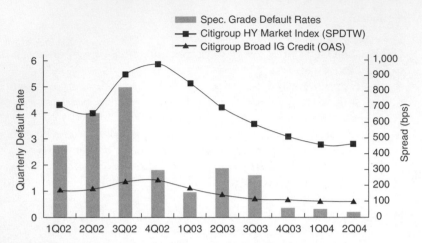

FIGURE 2.6 Corporate Issuers—Recent Default Rates and Spreads
Source: Citigroup.

For others, who might not share such a dubious view of market spreads on the whole, we recommended several single-name trade opportunities as well. Our credit analysts had recently identified these names as likely to widen 10 to 20 bp by the end of 2004.

Float Like a Butterfly, Sting Like a Bee

As described in the examples in this chapter, CDS swaptions can be used to express simple directional credit views.[8] However, more subtle credit views may be expressed as well by combining CDS options in more elaborate ways. For investors who may be only *slightly* bearish or who wish to minimize the up-front premium payment, we steal a page from the equity derivatives playbook to demonstrate how investors can profit from only a slight backup in spread (mildly bearish credit view) of a credit index or single name. Commonly called a *butterfly* trade because of the shape of its payoff diagram, this investment has a positive payoff within a spread range selected by the investor and a negative payoff (loss of premium) outside of this range (see Figure 2.7).[9] Therefore, this trade is most applicable to investors who have views on the level of credit spreads, not simply the direction of spread movement. If constructed correctly, this trade will provide a sizable payoff for relatively modest spread widening and will limit the downside if spreads tighten or, conversely, widen too much.

Butterfly Versus Payer

For investors with moderately bearish credit views, a butterfly trade compares favorably to a payer or payer spread because it has a lower cost (much lower when compared with a stand-alone payer option). The price advantage of a butterfly trade is a direct result of *limiting* the payoff for spread moves beyond the second strike point, K_2, and *eliminating* the payoff

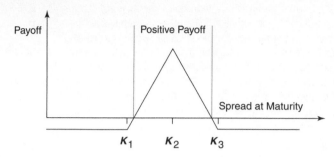

FIGURE 2.7 Simple Butterfly Trade Payoff Diagram
Source: Citigroup.

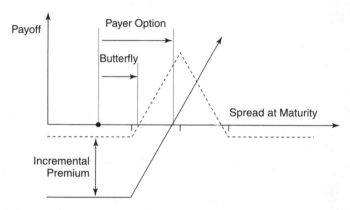

FIGURE 2.8 Butterfly Payoff versus Payer Option Payoff
Source: Citigroup.

for moves beyond the third strike point, K_3. Both of the other strategies maintain a positive payoff under these circumstances—but at a price. Therefore, while the butterfly cost is cheaper, one must be more precise in one's views of spread movement. The cost and payoff difference between a simple payer option strategy and a butterfly strategy is highlighted in Figure 2.8. One result of a cheaper price is that the spread movement required to break even is much lower for a butterfly trade (assuming that the position is out-of-the-money initially).

Trade 1: General Market Widening   For investors who anticipate a marketwide backup in spreads, we suggest a trade based on the CDX High Volatility Index (CDX.NA.IG.HVOL, SEP09). Other liquid indexes, such as the CDX.IG, could be selected as well but they are not as likely to achieve the 10 to 20 bp move that we need. For our recommended butterfly trade, all three option legs expire on December 20, 2004, and are tied to CDSs that end on

September 20, 2009. The three swaption components are described in Table 2.1. The net cost for this trade was approximately $16,500 as of August 6, 2004.

The payoff diagram for this transaction is shown in Figure 2.9.

Therefore, a 3 bp upward move in the CDX.HV2 index is required to break even and the maximum payout, $44,500, occurs when the spread is 145 bp. While this may seem like a significant jump, the CDS market seems to anticipate a spread of 140 bp based on the current credit curve (i.e., at-the-money forward = 140 bp). The butterfly trade turns negative once the CDX.HV2 spread moves above 156 bp. The maximum loss for the trade is $16,500,

TABLE 2.1 Three Swaption Components of the Butterfly Trade for CDX.HV2

	Swaption 1	Swaption 2	Swaption 3
Buy/sell	Buy	Sell	Buy
Payer/receiver	Payer	Payer	Payer
Expiration date	12/20/04	12/20/04	12/20/04
Underlying	CDX.HV2	CDX.HV2	CDX.HV2
End date	9/20/09	9/20/09	9/20/09
Strike (bp)	130	145	160
Notional	$10,000,000	$20,000,000	$10,000,000
Cost (bp)[a]	87	57	43.5
Implied vol (%)	37	39.1	44.8

[a]Cost when buying swaptions as part of a package and therefore not available for individual swaptions.
Assumes current CDX.HV2 spread of 131 bp and December 20, 2004, expiry.
Source: Citigroup.

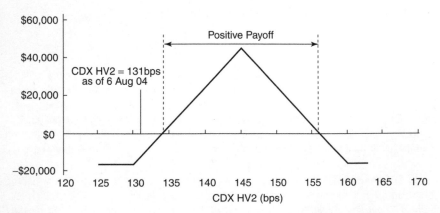

FIGURE 2.9 CDX.HV2 Butterfly Payoff Diagram, as of August 6, 2004
Source: Citigroup.

which compares favorably to the potential loss of $87,000 for a simple payer option strategy. Of course, the maximum payout ($44,500) for the butterfly trade is also lower.

Trade 2: Single-Name Trades A similar trade may be executed on single-name CDSs as well. For investors who have a particular view on certain credits, this could be an excellent avenue to express a mildly bearish view. For example, a moderately bearish butterfly trade for Eastman Kodak (EK) has the properties illustrated in Table 2.2.

The payoff diagram for this transaction is shown in Figure 2.10.

TABLE 2.2 Eastman Kodak Swaption Components and Butterfly Payoff Diagram, as of August 6, 2004

	Swaption 1	Swaption 2	Swaption 3
Buy/sell	Buy	Sell	Buy
Payer/receiver	Payer	Payer	Payer
Expiration date	12/20/04	12/20/04	12/20/04
End date	9/20/09	9/20/09	9/20/09
Strike (bp)	190	205	220
Notional	$10,000,000	$20,000,000	$10,000,000
Cost (bp)[a]	124.2	89.5	73.4

[a]Cost when buying swaptions as part of a package and therefore not available for individual swaptions.
Note: Assumes current spread of 186.5 bp and December 20, 2004, expiry.
Source: Citigroup.

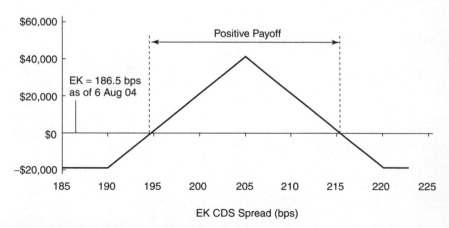

FIGURE 2.10 Eastman Kodak Butterfly Payoff Diagram
Source: Citigroup.

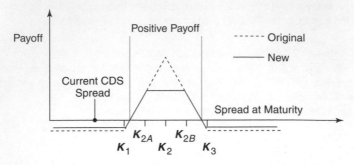

FIGURE 2.11 Alternative to the Simple Butterfly Trade
Source: Citigroup.

Variations

Variations of the butterfly trade may also be considered. For example the short payer position with strike K_2 can be replaced with two separate short positions with strike spreads, K_{2A} and K_{2B}, that straddle the original so that the payoff profile peak is a bit lower and flatter but the cost (potential loss) is lower as well. Conceptually, the new payoff diagram is shown in Figure 2.11 alongside the original butterfly trade.

Details of Butterfly Construction

A simple butterfly trade is made up of three components: a long payer position with strike K_1 and notional N, a short payer position with strike K_2 and notional $2N$, and a long payer position at K_3 with notional N, where $K_3 > K_2 > K_1$. By layering each component, or leg, we can see how the composite payoff diagram is constructed. See Figure 2.12.

Conclusion

The CDS option market began in earnest toward the end of 2003, and now it is on firm footing. CDS swaptions can be used to express simple directional credit views or more subtle ones. As corporate default rates have plunged so have spreads. Some investors are concerned that spreads may change course and widen modestly. We show how a butterfly trade using CDS options may be used inexpensively to hedge (or profit from) such an occurrence. Butterfly trades may be executed on single-name CDSs as well.

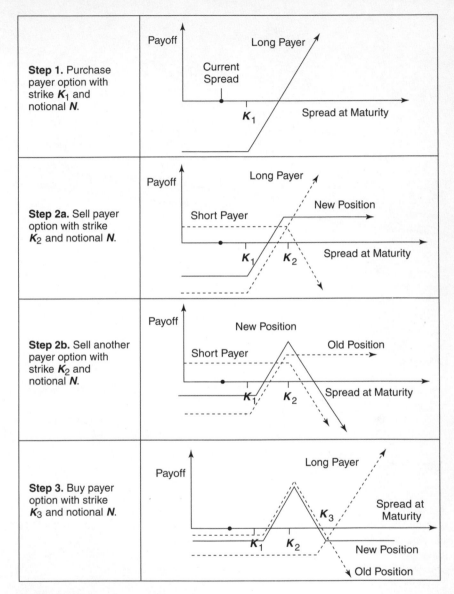

FIGURE 2.12 Butterfly Construction
Source: Citigroup.

CHAPTER 3

Constant Maturity Credit Default Swaps

Olivier Renault
Ratul Roy

Constant maturity credit default swaps (CMCDSs) are a new kind of credit derivative that provides a natural extension to traditional credit default swaps (CDSs). While a CDS offers default protection in exchange for the payment of a fixed premium, the premium on a CMCDS is reset periodically at the prevailing CDS rate. Thus, CMCDSs can be seen as floating premium CDS contracts. The qualification "constant maturity" stems from the fact that the premium of a CMCDS is indexed to a CDS rate with fixed maturity—for instance, five years.

To a large extent, the motivations of investors for buying or selling CMCDSs are the same as for regular CDSs. Protection buyers want to hedge their credit exposures to individual names or to an index and are willing to pay an insurance premium for that protection. Protection sellers are comfortable with bearing the default risk and are looking for positive carry.

Key differences of CMCDSs, compared to regular CDSs, however, are that they have lower mark-to-market volatility and they provide an opportunity to separate spread risk away from default risk when combined with an equivalent CDS. This chapter reviews the main features of the CMCDS and describes several trades that can be implemented using a CMCDS, either for short-term horizons or for hold-to-maturity strategies.

BASICS OF CMCDSs

CMCDSs are contracts to exchange a conditional payment in default (default leg) for a stream of floating premiums indexed to a CDS rate

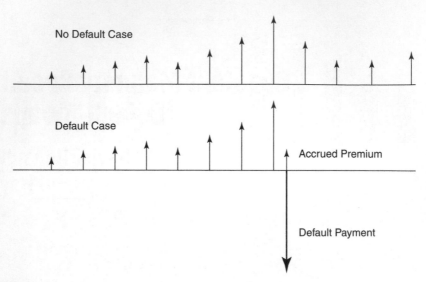

FIGURE 3.1   Schematic Payoff Structure of CMCDS Protection Seller
Source: Citigroup.

(premium leg). Figure 3.1 illustrates the payments and receipts of a CMCDS protection seller. The default leg is identical to that of a regular CDS and simple arbitrage arguments imply that the present value (PV) of the floating premiums of the CMCDS should equal that of the expected fixed CDS premium with the same maturity. This equality is achieved through the use of a scaling factor, called the *participation rate*.

PARTICIPATION RATE

The participation rate is the variable that equates the cash flows of a CMCDS with an equivalent traditional CDS. When the credit underlying the CMCDS has the usual upward-sloping spread curve, this implies that the market expects its CDS spreads to increase. Given that on average CDS and CMCDS discounted premiums should be equal, CMCDS protection sellers should receive only a fraction of future CDS spreads. The participation rate should therefore be lower than one. In the case of an inverted spread curve, the market implies that CDS spreads are expected to fall. CMCDS sellers should therefore receive more than 100 percent of CDS spreads; that is, the participation rate should be greater than one.

Figure 3.2 illustrates the participation rate graphically. First, we compute the CDS forward spreads for all reset dates until the maturity of the

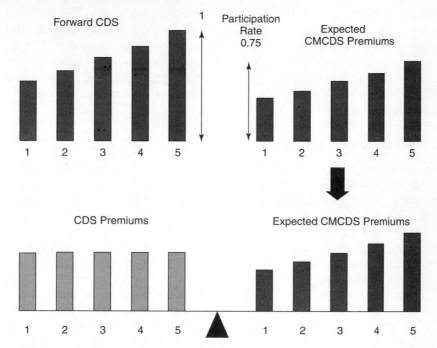

FIGURE 3.2 Computing the Participation Rate
Source: Citigroup.

CMCDS, using an entire term structure of CDS spreads. Here we assume that there are five annual reset dates (top left of figure). These spreads are rescaled such that the expected CMCDS premiums balance the fixed CDS rates. The participation rate is the ratio of this rescaling, or 75 percent in our example.

CMCDSs are quoted in terms of participation rate; that is, a broker's quote for a CMCDS may be 72/75, which would be interpreted as a bid of 72 percent of the equivalent CDS premium and an offer of 75 percent of the CDS. The appendix at the end of this chapter explains how the participation rate is calculated.

BEHAVIOR OF CMCDSs

A comparison of a CDS with a CMCDS shows that the shape of the spread curve is the most important determinant of the participation rate. Once this rate is fixed, any change in the level and slope of the curve will impact the CMCDS. While regular CDS prices are affected only by changes in spreads for maturities up to the CDS tenor (T), CMCDS premiums are impacted by spreads up to $T + m$, where m is the tenor of the CDS to which the CMCDS is indexed. For example, a CMCDS with five years to maturity ($T = 5$), indexed to a 5-year CDS rate ($m = 5$), will be sensitive to changes in the spreads up to 10 years. Therefore, in that example, the CMCDS combines 5-year default risk with exposure to spreads up to 10 years. Spread volatility also plays an important role in the pricing of the CMCDS.

Impact of Spread Level

Investing in or hedging with CMCDSs is essentially taking a view on forward rates. By construction, a CMCDS will provide the same discounted payoff as would a CDS if forwards are realized. A CMCDS, if realized CDS premiums exceed forward rates when the investor entered the contract, will outperform an equivalent CDS from the point of view of the protection seller.

Figure 3.3 shows the value of long CMCDS and CDS protection positions as spreads widen in parallel, assuming zero spread volatility. The widening is assumed to take place instantaneously. An increase in spread is associated with increasing default probability. The default leg (which is identical for CDS and CMCDS) therefore increases with the spread level. The premium leg of the CMCDS also increases (in absolute value) as spread widening leads to higher future premiums. However, the increase is not as fast as that of the default leg, since the spread increase is only reflected partly in the CMCDS rate (because of the participation rate). In contrast to the CMCDS, the premium leg of the CDS falls as spreads increase because the premiums are fixed and the probability of receiving the premiums falls as spreads increase. Overall, a parallel spread widening affects the CDS much more than the CMCDS.

Similarly, a spread tightening would have a moderate positive impact on the CMCDS holder and a much larger impact on the equivalent CDS. In short, the mark-to-market volatility of CMCDSs is reduced compared to that of CDS positions for parallel shifts in the spread curve.

CMCDSs are, however, more exposed than CDSs to changes in slope of the spread curve. We need to distinguish between two cases: When the steepening/flattening occurs beyond the maturity of the CDS/CMCDS (long end) or when it occurs before (short end). CDSs are insensitive to spread changes beyond their maturity, while CMCDSs will be affected by them through changes in forward spreads. A steepening of the long end of the spread curve will benefit sellers of protection, as they will receive higher premiums without bearing more default risk. Obviously, the opposite would be the case for flattening spreads. A steepening of the short end would also benefit CMCDS sellers as it implies higher forward rates, but would not affect CDSs.

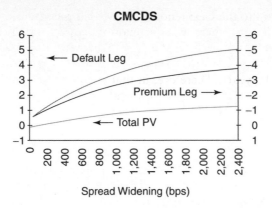

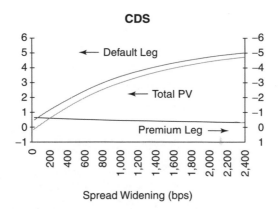

FIGURE 3.3 Present Value of €10 Million Long CMCDS and CDS Protection Positions (euros in millions)
Source: Citigroup.

Figure 3.4 illustrates the impact of a parallel shift, a steepening and a flattening in the spread curve on a hypothetical CDS and an equivalent CMCDS. The CMCDS has a five-year maturity and is indexed to an equivalent CDS with a current spread of 120 basis points. The CMCDS has a participation rate of 63.1 percent and we take the position of a protection seller on €10 million notional. The parallel shift of the curve by 1 bp leads to a loss of €4,600 on the CDS and only €1,200 on the CMCDS. The steepening of the curve by 1 bp, as shown in the figure, generates a gain of €2,050 for the CMCDS but has no impact on the CDS.

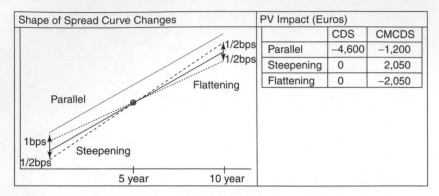

FIGURE 3.4 Impact of Spread Curve Changes on CDS and CMCDS Present Value
Source: Citigroup.

TABLE 3.1 Comparative Sensitivity of CDS and CMCDS to Spread Curve
Changes

Change in PV For Protection Seller	Parallel Curve Shift		Slope Change (Short End)		Slope Change (Long End)	
	Widen	Tighten	Steepening	Flattening	Steepening	Flattening
CDS	−	+	0	0	0	0
CMCDS	−	+	+	−	**+**	−

Short end = all tenors up to but not including the maturity T of the CDS/CMCDS; long
end = all maturities beyond T.
Boldface means larger impact. All changes are assumed to occur instantaneously.
Source: Citigroup.

The various spread scenarios discussed so far are summarized in
Table 3.1.

How would a CDS perform versus a CMCDS in real life? Taking IBM
as an example in Figure 3.5, we compare the two for a trade starting in
September 2001. Over the subsequent three years, the IBM spread curve
experienced more parallel shifts than steepenings and flattenings. This
would have led to a much reduced marked-to-market volatility for holders
of CMCDSs compared to CDS investors.

Spread curves often do not move so cleanly as Figure 3.5 suggests. It is
necessary to understand the sensitivity of a CMCDS to specific parts of the
spread curve. This will then enable us to understand the risks and also to
construct an appropriate hedge using a CDS if necessary. The sensitivities
of the PVs of both legs of the aforementioned CMCDS to 1 bp changes
in spreads of various maturities are shown in Figure 3.6. The default leg

We have constructed a hypothetical CMCDS example using historical IBM spreads to show what could have happened had the CMCDS market existed in 2001: First, spreads rose dramatically until mid-2002 before tightening substantially to reach lows of 15 bps, in September 2004. CDS payments would have been flat at $8,000 (= 10M x 32bps/4), while CMCDS payments would have tracked three-year CDS rates with a three-month lag, with a peak premium payment of $12,000 in December 2002 and a trough of $3,800 in April 2004. Overall, CMCDS payments would have been significantly lower than those of the equivalent CDS.

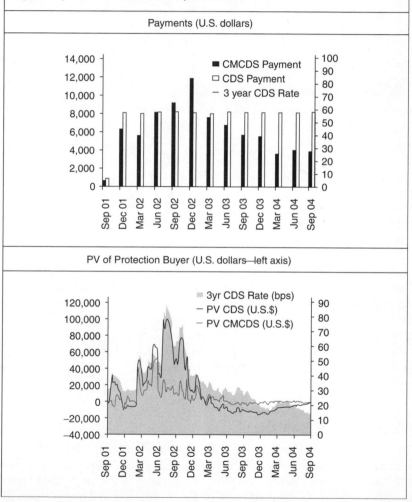

FIGURE 3.5 Three-Year IBM CDS and Three-Year/Three-Year CMCDS Payments and Present Value (Hypothetical)—Notional of US$10 Million, Participation Rate: 74.2 Percent
Source: Citigroup.

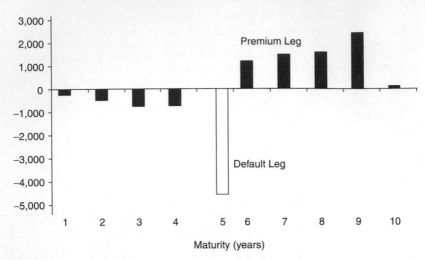

FIGURE 3.6   Spread01 of CMCDS Legs—10 Million Notional—Present Value of the Protection Seller (euros in millions)[a]
[a]Spread01 is change in value due to 1 bp change in spread at specific maturity, all other spreads unchanged.
Source: Citigroup.

is predominantly affected by spread moves at the exact maturity of the trade (five years). A 1 bp widening of the five-year spread translates into a loss of €4,500. The premium leg, as we have discussed, is sensitive to changes in spreads of all maturities up to 10 years. An increase in spreads at a point before the maturity would flatten the short end of the curve and trigger a loss. An increase in spreads beyond the five-year maturity implies a steepening and an increase in PV. At the five-year horizon, the Spread01 of the premium leg would be almost zero because losses from the flattening of the 5- to 10-year region would be offset by gains generated by the steepening of the 0- to 5-year area.

Impact of Spread Volatility

Until now, in our examples, we have considered the volatility of spreads to be zero. In reality, increases in spread volatility would translate into lower participation rates. If CDS rates followed a deterministic path, then forward spreads would be exact predictors of future spreads and the participation rate would be fully determined by the forward spreads. Uncertainty about future CDS rates requires an adjustment of forward rates as spot CDSs may substantially overshoot the forwards. This is reflected in steeper expected CDS rates and therefore in a lower participation rate.

TABLE 3.2 Impact of Spread Volatility on Participation Rate

Spread Volatility	Participation Rate
0%	59.5
30	59.1
60	57.3

Source: Citigroup.

Table 3.2 reports the participation rates for a name with a spread curve coinciding with the iTraxx Europe index (assume spread levels at 5 years = 37.5 bp, and at 10 years = 53 bp). The spread volatility adjustment (called a *convexity adjustment*) is quite small for low levels of volatilities and becomes more significant as volatility increases above 50 percent. The current iTraxx implied volatility is around 35 percent.

In Figure 3.3, we assumed that spread volatility was zero. Setting it to a more realistic value of 50 percent amounts to increasing expected future CDS rates. The default leg is therefore unaffected, but the premium leg is now much increased in absolute terms (see Figure 3.7). After a certain

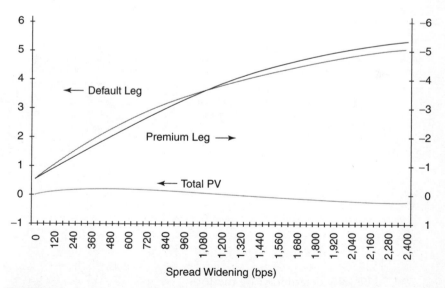

FIGURE 3.7 Present Value of € 10 Million Long CMCDS Protection Position with Spread Volatility (euros in millions)
Source: Citigroup.

level, the PVs of the two legs cross and the total PV of the CMCDS becomes negative (creating a different profile from the left-hand diagram in Figure 3.3). In all cases, the change in PV arising from parallel shifts remains small, as discussed previously.

CAPPED CMCDS

Most CMCDS rates are capped at a given level, for example, 800 bp. While this may appear a harmless assumption for most investment-grade credits that trade below 100 bp, it can substantially reduce the payoff in cases of credit blowup. The value of this cap can be seen as a portfolio of payer credit swaptions struck at the level of the cap and with maturities corresponding to the reset dates (see Figure 3.8). The value of these options is reflected in a higher participation rate for capped CMCDS compared with uncapped CMCDS.

To illustrate the impact of a cap on a real-life example, assume that an investor sold five-year protection on Ahold on January 2, 2003, when the CDS premium was 200 bp. Assuming that a market for CMCDSs existed at the time, the investor could have entered a CMCDS contract with a participation rate of around 77.7 percent. The corresponding 800 bp

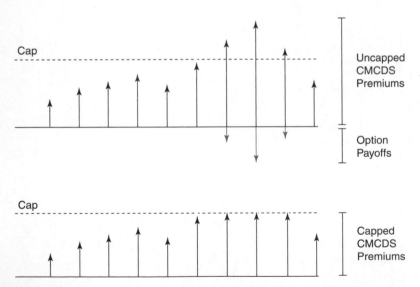

FIGURE 3.8 Capped CMCDS as Uncapped CMCDS Plus Portfolio of Payer Options
Source: Citigroup.

capped CMCDS would have had a higher participation rate for the reason described earlier, in this case 81.3 percent, assuming market volatility levels.

Figure 3.9 shows Ahold's CDS rate and the premiums that would have been paid for the first two years after the inception of the contract. CMCDS protection sellers would have benefited from selling the capped

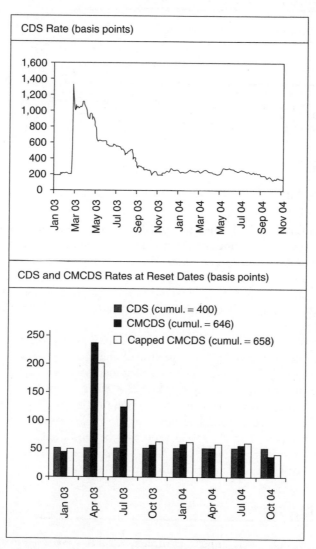

FIGURE 3.9 Ahold Five-Year CDS and CMCDS Performance (Hypothetical)
Source: Citigroup.

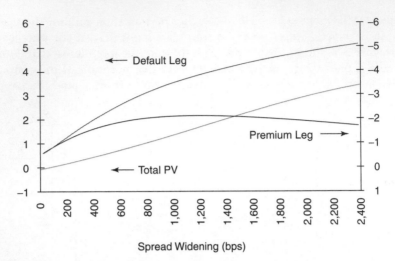

FIGURE 3.10 Present Value of Capped CMCDS for €10 Million Nominal (euros in millions)
Source: Citigroup.

CMCDS compared with the uncapped (because of higher participation for the former) for all but the second period. Selling CMCDS protection would also have outperformed CDS protection. The drop in spreads would, however, have led the fixed CDS premium to exceed both capped and uncapped CMCDS payoffs. For credit blowups that eventually lead to default or remain at high spreads for a long time, capped premiums would benefit the protection buyer.

As a final remark on the impact of the cap, it is interesting to return to the changes in value associated with spread changes. In Figure 3.3, we saw that both the coupon leg and the default leg increased with spread, with the default leg progressively diverging. Figure 3.10 is a similar plot obtained for a capped CMCDS. The value of the default leg is the same as in the noncapped case. The coupon leg, however, no longer rises continually with spread but reaches a cap. As spreads increase beyond the CMCDS premium cap, the premium stops increasing but the probability of receiving future premiums drops, thereby creating a hump-shaped curve.

HEDGING CMCDSs

Hedging CMCDSs can appear complex, as doing so requires in theory taking CDS positions corresponding to all CMCDS reset dates. Looking back at Figure 3.6, we see that a short CMCDS protection position has positive Spread01 for spreads before the tenor and negative Spread01 from the tenor and beyond, where Spread01 is change in value due to 1 bp change in spread at specific maturity, all other spreads unchanged. This is in contrast to DV01, which is the change for a parallel shift in the spread curve. In practice, most investors in CMCDSs hedge them using two CDS: one corresponding to the tenor of the CMCDS (for instance, 5 years) and one with long maturity (for instance, 10 years).

In the preceding example (long €10 million protection in Ahold five-year/five-year CMCDS), the DV01 of the CMCDS was €1,000 for €10 million notional. A DV01-neutral position would consist of selling 5-year CDS protection on Ahold with DV01 of −€4,500 and buying 10-year CDS protection with DV01 of €7,400. The resulting position retains some spread risk (risk of nonparallel shifts as shown earlier), but is hedged against parallel shifts in the spread curve and default risk before five years (see Table 3.3).

An alternative strategy consists of hedging the CMCDS against changes in the short end and the long end of the spread curve. To do so, we compute the sensitivity (DV01) of the CMCDS and CDS to 1 bp changes in spreads in the short end (zero- to five-year maturities) and long end (above five years) of the spread curve. Hedge ratios are then determined to offset the DV01s of the CMCDS (see Table 3.4). This hedge provides better protection against spread moves than the previous one (which only covers against parallel shifts) but retains some default risk.

For the most liquid names, a similar strategy can be adopted with more maturity buckets hedged with a greater number of CDSs.

TRADING STRATEGIES WITH CMCDSs

Selling CMCDS Protection

One of the main reasons for the recent interest in CMCDSs lies in the current low spread and low default environment. While most investors are still bullish on credit fundamentals and do not expect many defaults to occur

TABLE 3.3 Hedging a €10 Million Long CMCDS Protection—Parallel Shift and Default Hedge

	5-Year/5-Year CMCDS	5-Year CDS	10-Year CDS	Hedged Position
Notional (euro)	€10,000,000	−€22,000,000	€12,000,000	0
DV01 (euro)	€1,000	−€9,900	€8,900	0
Jump to default (euro)[a]	€6,000,000	−€13,200,000	€7,200,000	0

[a]Assumes 40% recovery rate.
Source: Citigroup.

TABLE 3.4 Hedging a €10 Million Long CMCDS Protection—Change in Spread Curve

	5-Year/ 5-Year CMCDS	5-Year CDS	10-Year CDS	Hedged Position
Notional (euro)	€10,000,000	−€13,300,000	€6,600,000	−€6,700,000
DV01 for 0- to 5-year maturities (Euro)	€6,000	−€6,000	0	0
DV01 for 5- to 10-year maturities (Euro)	−€5,000	0	€5,000	0

Source: Citigroup.

in the short to medium term, some take the view that spreads may widen substantially from their current lows. Selling default protection via CMCDS can fit this view as doing so amounts to going long default risk and positive carry and would benefit from any increase in spread at future reset dates.

Buying CMCDS Protection

As discussed earlier, forward spreads are the key determinants of the participation rates. CMCDSs can therefore be used to take a view on the level of forward rates. Do current forward rates overestimate or underestimate future CDS rates?

An investor wishing to hedge a credit exposure by buying default protection can now include his or her views on future CDS spreads. Some hedging may, for example, have to be carried out to reduce economic or regulatory capital held by a bank, although the portfolio manager may be fundamentally bullish on the credit. A CMCDS can achieve both objectives by protecting against outright default but lowering the cost of protection if spreads indeed narrow. As we saw in our IBM example, a hedger may reduce the cost of the hedge by buying CMCDS protection if he or she believes that spread curves are too steep and that forwards will not be realized.

Combination Trades and Index CMCDSs

So far, we have dealt only with plain-vanilla CMCDSs. The products were exposed to single-name credits and were indexed to a CDS with identical underlying name and maturity. In this section, we look at slightly

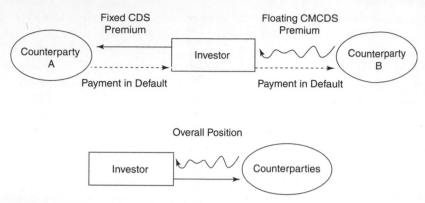

FIGURE 3.11   Creating a Credit Spread Swap
Source: Citigroup.

more exotic products, allowing for maturity mismatch, and also consider combinations of floating and fixed CDSs.

Floating-Fixed Premium Swap   A typical combination trade would combine a position in a CMCDS with an opposite position in a CDS with the same maturity and underlying credit. This is illustrated in Figure 3.11, where we assume the investor has bought protection in the CDS market and sold protection in CMCDS. The resulting net position (assuming no counterparty risk) is a floating-fixed premium swap, which should enable the investors to profit from spread widening on a given name without bearing default risk.

Taking naked positions in CDSs and CMCDSs requires investors to be comfortable with the default component and with the spread component of these instruments. The premium swap enables one to isolate default from spreads and therefore to take pure positions in spreads. The swap allows, for example, investors to take a bearish view on spreads without incurring as much negative carry as that associated with being long CDS protection.

However, although a floating-fixed premium swap should not suffer from any loss on the default legs of the CDS and CMCDS, it is still exposed to jump-to-default risk on the premium legs. In case of default by the underlying credit, premium payment would cease. If default were to occur early in the life of the trade and the forward spread curve is steep, the CMCDS holder would have received only low premiums and would lose its expected higher future cash flows, hence incurring a loss. The opposite is true for downward-sloping curves.

Mismatch Combinations   A CMCDS is not necessarily indexed to a CDS with the same maturity. One could, for example, structure a three-year CMCDS on IBM indexed to the five-year IBM CDS premium. Combinations of CMCDSs can then be created to express direct curve views without bearing any default risk. For example, an investor could buy protection using the IBM CMCDS just described and simultaneously sell protection on a more conventional three-year/three-year CMCDS, thereby creating a flattener.

Note that a more traditional trade involving two CDSs (short three-year protection, long five years) would be exposed to default risk between year 3 and year 5 and is therefore not a pure spread position. The CMCDS position, in contrast, has offsetting default risk positions and is therefore exposed mainly to spread risk.

This Is Just the Beginning   Index CMCDSs are also available. In this case, an additional technical difficulty arises from the roll in indexes (i.e., the periodic changes in index constituents).

The market is already expanding to more exotic structures and more likely will follow. Possible extensions include partly fixed/partly floating CMCDSs. For example, the contract might initially pay a fixed spread that is replaced with a floating premium at some predefined time. The switch between fixed and floating may be left to the choice of one of the parties or may be obligatory.

The development of CMCDSs also paves the way for constant maturity collateralized debt obligations (CMCDOs), that is, synthetic CDOs backed by floating-premium CDSs and paying floating spreads.

CONCLUSION

CMCDSs are a new kind of credit derivative by which investors can exchange a stream of floating premiums against a contingent payment on default. CMCDSs exhibit lower mark-to-market volatility from parallel shifts in the spread curve but are quite sensitive to curve steepening.

Combined with regular CDSs, CMCDSs enable investors to separate spread risk from default risk and to take pure credit spread positions. The market for CMCDSs is still relatively new, but quotes are available for many single-name credits and indexes for which the CDS curve extends to 10 years. Most of the liquidity is on three- to five-year tenors indexed to three- to five-year CDSs.

CASE STUDY: TAKING CURVE VIEWS WITH CMCDSS

As discussed in the chapter, CMCDSs allow investors to take exposure to floating credit spreads. They can use the instrument to take curve views and separate spread risk from default risk. The following case study, written in November 2004, identified opportunities at that time to benefit from the flattening or steepening of various credit curves.

Features of CMCDSs

CMCDSs are floating-rate CDSs that enable investors to express credit curve views. In this article, we propose several specific CMCDS trade ideas.

Before proposing our trades based on CMCDSs, it is useful to recall some of the main features of this product:

- The participation rate is the multiplication factor that equates the expected discounted cash flow on a CMCDS with that of an equivalent CDS. CMCDS prices are quoted in terms of the participation rate.
- The participation rate is lower for steeper curves and higher for flatter curves. It is less than one for upward-sloping credit curves and more than one for downward-sloping curves.
- Curve steepening benefits CMCDS protection sellers and flattening benefits protection buyers.
- Parallel shifts in the spread curve affect CMCDSs less than an equivalent CDS.
- Combining a CMCDS with an opposite CDS position enables one to offset most of the default risk and results in a straight spread position.

Trade Ideas

Marks and Spencer (M&S) Although CDS spreads have come down dramatically since the failed takeover bid, M&S's curve has continued to steepen with the 10-year CDS trading at 36 bp above the 5-year CDS. Investors seeking protection on M&Ss may buy CMCDSs at a participation rate of around 74 percent rather than purchase equivalent CDSs, creating less negative carry today (see Figure 3.12).

This position would benefit from a possible flattening of the curve, as shown in Table 3.5. The table shows the change in PV of the CMCDS trade on a nominal of £10 million and that of an equivalent CDS trade, for various scenarios with a six-month horizon. Should the curve go back to its pretakeover levels, the CMCDS hedge would also have a positive profit and loss (P&L), while the CDS protection would exhibit a large MTM loss. The trade is, however, exposed to curve steepening, which is likely to occur in the case of a leveraged buyout (LBO). Although speculation will subside only gradually, we think such action is now unlikely.

Ahold Ahold CDS spreads have rallied considerably since their highs in 2003. We are still relatively bullish on that name although a lot of good news is probably priced into current spreads. The Ahold curve is still very flat in the 5- to 10-year region. If Ahold's credit quality improves, it should start behaving more like an investment-grade credit and its curve should steepen. We therefore recommend selling protection on Ahold using a five-year/five-year CMCDS, at a participation rate around 69 percent (see Figure 3.13).

Table 3.6 shows the change in PV of the CMCDS trade on a nominal of € 10 million and that of an equivalent CDS trade, for various scenarios with a six-month horizon.

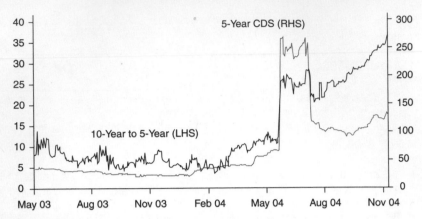

FIGURE 3.12 Marks and Spencer's 5-Year CDS Spread and 5- to 10-Year Slope
Source: Citigroup.

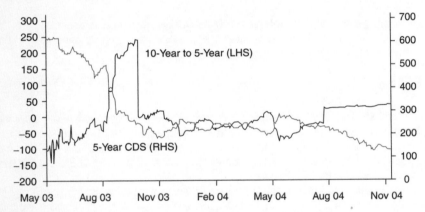

FIGURE 3.13 Ahold 5-Year CDS Spread and 5- to 10-Year Slope
Source: Citigroup.

Sainsbury's Sainsbury's 5- and 10-year slope and 5-year CDS levels have moved in parallel over the past 18 months (see Figure 3.14). Although the company is not yet out of trouble, we believe the market has priced a lot of bad news into current spreads and that LBO risk is overestimated. We expect spreads to narrow in coming months; this should be associated with a flattening of the credit curve. We therefore recommend the following combination trade: Buy five-year CMCDS protection at around 73 percent participation rate versus selling CDS protection on Sainsbury's in order to hedge out default risk and obtain a pure curve position.

Table 3.7 shows the change in PV of the CMCDS/CDS combination trade on a nominal of £10 million, for various scenarios with a six-month horizon.

TABLE 3.5 Marks and Spencer CMCDS and CDS (Long Protection)—£10 Million Nominal, Five Year/Five Year

Scenario	CMCDS Change in PV	CDS Change in PV
Spreads unchanged	−£9,633	−£27,635
Spread back to six months ago	£73,877	−£265,049
Curve steepens by 30 bp between 5- and 10-year	−£96,811	−£27,635
Curve flattens by 30 bp between 5- and 10- year[a]	£76,972	−£27,635

[a]We think this scenario is most likely to occur.
Source: Citigroup.

TABLE 3.6 Ahold CMCDS and CDS (Short Protection)—€10 Million Nominal, Five Year/Five Year

Scenario	CMCDS Change in PV	CDS Change in PV
Spreads unchanged	€13,708	€25,877
Parallel shift down 30 bp	€45,341	€151,342
Parallel shift up 30 bp	−€17,090	−€96,723
Curve flattens by 30 bp between 5- and 10-year	−€67,666	€25,877
Curve steepens by 30 bp between 5- and 10-year[a]	€96,070	€25,877

[a]We think this scenario is most likely to occur.
Source: Citigroup.

TABLE 3.7 Sainsbury's Long CMCDS/Short CDS Protection—10 Million Nominal, Five Year/Five Year

Scenario	Combination Change in PV
Spreads unchanged	£16,818
Spread back to six months ago	£433,427
Curve steepens by 30 bp between 5- and 10-year	−£69,107
Curve flattens by 30 bp between 5- and 10-year[a]	£102,307

[a]We think this scenario is most likely to occur.
Source: Citigroup.

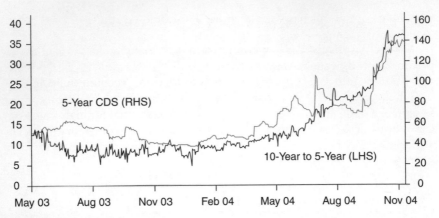

FIGURE 3.14 Sainsbury's 5-Year CDS Spread and 5- to 10-Year Slope
Source: Citigroup.

APPENDIX: COMPUTING THE PARTICIPATION RATE

The participation rate is the multiplication factor that equates the current CDS premium to a fraction of future expected CDS rates. It is the key determinant of CMCDS prices.

Let $S(t, m)$ be the reference spread at time t and with tenor m. $D(t)$ is the discount factor and $Q(t)$ is the cumulative probability of default up to time $t(D(0) = 1, Q(0) = 0)$. There are n reset dates until maturity.

The participation rate PR satisfies the condition that the present value of the premium leg on CMCDS equals that of the premium leg on CDS that is,

$$\sum_{t=0}^{n} PR \times E_{t=0}[S(t, m)]D(t)[1 - Q(t)] = S(0, m) \sum_{t=0}^{n} D(t)[1 - Q(t)]$$

where $E[\ ]$ denotes expectation as of the inception of the contract, and thus:

$$PR = \frac{S(0, m) \sum_{t=0}^{n} D(t)[1 - Q(t)]}{\sum_{t=0}^{n} E_{t=0}[S(t, m)]D(t)[1 - Q(t)]}$$

This equation assumes implicitly that there are n discrete cash flow dates and that default can occur only on those dates. Default can, of course, occur on a continuous basis and the formula should be adjusted for accrued premium in default.

Expected spreads are key determinants of participation rates. While forward spreads can be seen as the market's expectation of future CDS spreads, they need to be adjusted upwards to take into account the volatility of CDS premiums. This is known as *convexity adjustment*. For most names the convexity adjustment is small, but it may be substantial for high-volatility names or for long-maturity trades. The upward adjustment of forward CDS rates leads to a lower participation rate when volatility increases.

CHAPTER 4

Credit Derivatives Indexes

Jure Skarabot
Gaurav Bansal

Credit derivatives indexes are default swap products referenced to portfolios of single-name credits. Since their introduction, they have developed into the most liquid instruments in the credit market.

The most popular credit derivatives indexes are members of the Dow Jones CDX/iTraxx credit derivatives index family, trading under standardized rules.

Both leveraged and real-money investors are users of indexes; strategies applied include long/short trades, relative value positions, expressing directional views, and hedging.

Credit derivatives indexes provide building blocks for structuring portfolio products such as index-linked tranches and index swaptions.

The importance of credit derivatives indexes should continue to grow, as index structures are expected to develop in other asset classes.

INTRODUCTION

The introduction of credit derivatives indexes has been a milestone for the credit markets. They have made the credit markets more transparent and liquid, but also potentially more volatile. They have revolutionized the scope of investment strategies available to credit investors and led to the development of various structured credit products. Credit derivatives indexes were originated as younger siblings of established cash credit indexes, but their suitability as a trading instrument and the overall rapid growth of derivatives markets quickly brought them into the front line. The generic structure of credit derivatives indexes is simple. They are default swaps based on an equally weighted portfolio of a relatively small number of liquid names in a specific credit default market. The indexes trade under standardized rules and they are, for the most part, aggregated in the Dow Jones CDX/iTraxx credit derivatives index family. They are supported by a large number of market makers through liquid trading in both on-the-run and off-the-run maturities. CDX/iTraxx indexes are used in a variety of applications, but most important, they allow investors to quickly put on long or short positions in the credit markets. Although they are not designed as a benchmark for cash credit investors, they are a good indicator of the activity of liquid names in the default markets.

Credit indexes have gained popularity across a variety of investor segments. In addition to leveraged investors, real-money investors have also found credit derivatives indexes very useful. Indexes are used to quickly express market views, for directional and relative value trades, to leverage credit investments, and to take short positions.

Furthermore, indexes are an important hedging tool in the credit space, especially to hedge marketwide spread moves. They are also an essential building block for a variety of structured credit products.

FAMILY OF CREDIT DERIVATIVES INDEXES

Since 2001, dealers have been trying to develop tradable credit indexes. There has been strong interest for such products, as investors have searched for means to quickly and efficiently put on aggregate positions in credit markets. Several credit indexes were created, but initially they lacked the required liquidity to become fully embraced by investors. After various index products eventually merged into the CDX/iTraxx index family, credit derivatives indexes finally came into their own (see Table 4.1).

A key factor that contributed to the success of credit derivatives indexes was the growth and improved liquidity in single-name credit default swap (CDS) markets.[1] With the general acceptance of single-name credit default swaps, it became clear that this structure could be a suitable platform for developing tradable credit indexes. To enhance their simplicity and liquidity, launched credit indexes were designed as portfolio credit default swaps based on equally weighted pools of liquid names in the CDS markets. The credit derivatives indexes became a success story after dealers realized the utility of forgoing their proprietary versions in favor of collaborating on the development of standard indexes owned and sponsored by a group of dealers. The success of the merger between iBoxx CDX and Trac-X that led to the CDX/iTraxx index family has shown that the market prefers liquidity rather than supporting competing indexes at the same time.

TABLE 4.1 Evolution of Credit Derivatives Indexes

2001–2003	Separate Credit Indexes for Different Asset Classes (e.g., Hydi, Tracers, Jeci, Emdi, iBoxx)
2003	Hydi, Jeci, Tracers merge to form Trac-X family.
	Dealers consortium launches iBoxx CDX index family (IG and HY, EM).
	Indexes have independent administrators (iBoxx, Dow Jones).
	Launch of Trac-X Asia and CJ50 (Japan) indexes.
2004	Dow Jones Trac-X and iBoxx CDX dealers agree to merge their indexes into iTraxx (Europe) and Dow Jones CDX (North America) index family.
	Unification of Asian indexes into iTraxx Asia index family.
2005	Launch of iTraxx EM Diversified index.
	Expansion of iTraxx Asia indexes.
	Dow Jones CDX Crossover index introduced for the U.S. market.
	Introduction of price fixings for credit derivatives indexes.

Source: Citigroup.

Trading volume in CDX/iTraxx indexes has been increasing[2] and liquidity has been improving as the standard documentation has allowed investors to efficiently execute trades across a large number of market-making dealers.

Over a short time, CDX/iTraxx indexes have become leading indicators for the credit markets, reacting quickly and efficiently to market changes. Thus, even though they are not as comprehensive as some bond indexes and therefore might be less useful as tracking tools, they have become the best benchmark to follow the credit market movements.

STRUCTURE OF THE CDX/iTRAXX INDEX FAMILY

The current set of CDX/iTraxx credit derivatives indexes can be divided into five major categories, as shown in Table 4.2. All but DJ CDX EM have an equal weighting for the different components. Although trading and liquidity is greatest in the five-year tenor, other tenors, especially the seven- and ten-year maturity, are becoming popular as well.

Starting in 2003, each CDX index has been rolled every six months (see Table 4.3). With each roll, the maturity of the on-the-run CDX/iTraxx indexes is advanced by six months.[3] Note that six-month rolls have no effect on the existing indexes, as the old index continues to trade based on the same reference portfolio—except for defaulted credits. Investors who want

TABLE 4.2 Dow Jones CDX/iTraxx Credit Derivatives Indexes, January 2006

Index	Number of Components at Inception
North America—Investment Grade	
DJ CDX NA IG	125
DJ CDX NA HVOL	30
North America—High Yield and Crossover	
DJ CDX NA HY	100
DJ CDX NA HY BB	All BB-rated names in HY CDX
DJ CDX NA HY B	All B-rated names in HY CDX
DJ CDX NA XO	35
Emerging Markets	
DJ CDX EM	14
Europe	
iTraxx Europe	125
iTraxx Europe HiVol	30
iTraxx Europe Crossover	40
Asia	
iTraxx CJ (Japan)	50
iTraxx Asia ex-Japan	50

Source: Dow Jones and iTraxx.

TABLE 4.3 Existing DJ CDX Index Series and Their Maturities, January 2006

	Series	Five-Year Maturity	Ten-Year Maturity
Dow Jones CDX.NA.IG	5	12/20/10	12/20/15
Dow Jones CDX.NA.IG	4	6/20/10	6/20/15
Dow Jones CDX.NA.IG	3	3/20/10	3/20/15
Dow Jones CDX.NA.IG	2	9/20/09	9/20/14
Dow Jones CDX.NA.IG	1	3/20/09	3/20/14
Dow Jones CDX.NA.HY	5	12/20/10	
Dow Jones CDX.NA.HY	4	6/20/10	
Dow Jones CDX.NA.HY	3	12/20/09	
Dow Jones CDX.NA.HY	2	9/20/09	
Dow Jones CDX.NA.HY	1	3/20/09	
Dow Jones CDX.EM	4	12/20/10	12/20/15
Dow Jones CDX.EM	3	6/20/10	6/20/15
Dow Jones CDX.EM	2	12/20/09	
Dow Jones CDX.EM	1	6/20/09	

Source: Markit Group.

TABLE 4.4 Overlap of Names in CDX Indexes, Dow Jones CDX IG 1–CDX IG 5

	CDX IG 1	CDX IG 2	CDX IG 3	CDX IG 4	CDX IG 5
CDX IG 1	125	119	115	113	106
CDX IG 2		125	120	118	110
CDX IG 3			125	122	114
CDX IG 4				125	116
CDX IG 5					125

Source: Citigroup.

to stay in the on-the-run contract can choose to roll from the old index into the new one.

The roll process and the substitution of the credits are governed by transparent rules. In most cases, defaults, rating downgrades or upgrades, and corporate reorganizations force credits out from the specific index. Sometimes names are also substituted based on liquidity objectives, although dealers try to minimize the use of this rule to keep the indexes as stable as possible. We provide a more detailed explanation of the roll process in the appendix at the end of this chapter.

Eventually, the composition of on-the-run indexes changes through the rolls. For example, there is only 80 percent overlap between the CDX IG 1 and CDX IG 5 series (see Table 4.4). The maturity gap between CDX IG indexes is six months, except between the CDX IG 3 and CDX IG 4 series, which are three months apart (refer back to Table 4.3).

ADMINISTRATION OF INDEXES

Markit Group and International Index Company (IndexCo) administer the Dow Jones CDX and iTraxx indexes, respectively. They conduct the voting for choosing the credits to be included in a new index. They also collect the levels for all of the indexes and publish historical spreads. The reference portfolio for the CDX and iTraxx indexes can be found at www.markit.com. Dow Jones Indexes[4] is responsible for branding, licensing, and marketing these indexes, and continues to oversee and approve the creation of new indexes.

BASKET OF CREDIT DEFAULT SWAPS

A CDX/iTraxx credit derivatives index is a default swap referenced to a portfolio of single-name credits. For almost all of the indexes, the single-name credits have equal weights in the portfolio. Typically the portfolio has 100 or 125 credits, but some specialized indexes reference fewer credits because of a limited number of liquid names.

Similar to single-name credit default swaps, buying and selling protection on a credit derivative index is identified by a start date, an end date, the premium spread, and the notional. It is important to note that once the portfolio is formed, it remains static through the life of the contract and only a credit event results in the removal of a name (along with the reduction of the notional). There cannot be any additions to the reference portfolio after origination. A new index series is created every six months. If investors want to roll their index positions, they need to unwind the old contracts and enter into new ones.

Trading Example — The Index

DJ CDX IG (Series 5) five-year index is a basket of credit default swaps on 125 names from the U.S. investment-grade market. Each name has a weight of 0.8 percent. The index matures on December 20, 2010. Thus, buying protection on $125 million notional of this index is essentially equivalent to buying protection on $1 million notional of each of the 125 single names for the period from the date of purchase to December 20, 2010.[5]

UP-FRONT AND RUNNING PAYMENTS

As shown in Figure 4.1, for the life of the contract, the protection buyer makes premium payments to the protection seller. All the indexes in the CDX/iTraxx family, except for the Emerging Markets Index, have quarterly premium payments. DJ CDX EM has semiannual premium payments.

CDX/iTraxx indexes trading in the market have fixed running spreads (coupon) that are determined at each roll. When the trade is originated, the protection buyer makes or receives an up-front payment depending on the prevailing protection premium quoted in the market. This payment is equal to the present value of the difference between the current spread (as quoted in the market) and the running spread (coupon) over the life of the contract. Note that the cash flows are risky as they depend on the defaults in the reference portfolio of the index. Therefore, payment calculation requires a valuation model.[6] The practice of paying/receiving a standard running spread complemented by an up-front payment makes it efficient to offset contracts when dealers take opposite positions.

Similar steps are followed in calculating the mark-to-market of an existing index contract after the change in index spreads. CDX IG and iTraxx indexes are quoted on a spread basis, while the CDX HY and EM

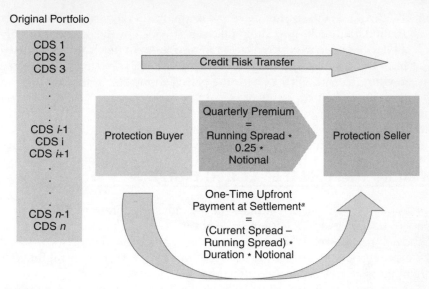

Original Portfolio

FIGURE 4.1 Mechanics of Credit Derivatives Index (Before the Credit Event)
[a]One-time up-front payment at settlement is made from protection buyer to protection seller or vice versa, depending on whether the current spread is higher or lower than the running spread. Payment also includes accrued.
Source: Citigroup.

indexes are quoted on a dollar price basis (see the chapter appendix for further details).

Trading Example—Premium Payments

Let us suppose that on December 1, 2005, a market maker quotes 49 basis points for selling protection on the five-year DJ CDX IG (Series 5) index. An investor buys protection on $125 million notional of the index.

The running spread on the index is 45 bp. Therefore, the investor will be making 21 quarterly premium payments of $140,625 (one-quarter of 45 bp of $125 million; note that the CDX/iTraxx indexes follow an Actual/360 convention) starting December 20, 2005, and the last payment on December 20, 2010.

In addition to quarterly payments, the investor will also make an up-front payment to account for two factors:

1. The contract is settled on 49 bp and the investor is paying only 45 bp running; therefore, the investor must make an up-front payment equivalent to the 4 bp running premium.

2. The investor will be making a whole quarterly payment on December 20, 2005, but will enjoy the protection provided by the product for only 20 days of the quarter; thus, the accrued amount needs to be deducted from the up-front payment. Following the ACT/360 convention, the investor deducts $110,937 for the period from September 21, 2005, to December 1, 2005.

The net up-front payment is calculated as $108,888.[7]

WHAT HAPPENS IN CASE OF A CREDIT EVENT?

In case of a credit event of a name in the index, the protection seller pays the protection buyer the settlement to cover the loss. The defaulted credit is removed from the index. Going forward, the protection buyer pays a spread on a proportionally reduced notional amount and, therefore, the buyer's premium payments are reduced (see Figure 4.2).

Credit events are defined in a similar way to single-name CDS, although DJ CDX indexes are trading under no restructuring (No-R). That means, in the case of CDX indexes, only bankruptcy and failure to pay are considered as credit events and restructuring is excluded. That represents a difference from U.S. investment-grade single-name CDS contracts, which usually trade under a modified restructuring (Mod-R) provision (see Table 4.5).

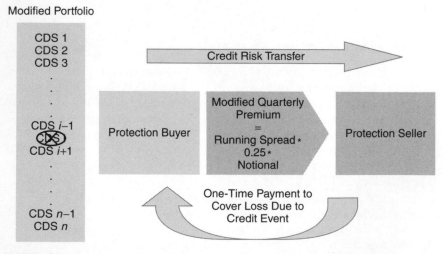

FIGURE 4.2 Mechanics of Credit Derivative Index (After the Credit Event)
Source: Citigroup.

TABLE 4.5 Restructuring Clause for Major CDX Indexes and the Corresponding Reference Single-Name CDS

Index	Restructuring Clause—Index	Restructuring Clause—Reference CDS
North America—Investment Grade (DJ CDX IG)	No restructuring	Modified restructuring[a]
North America—High Yield (DJ CDX HY)	No restructuring	No restructuring[a]
North America—Crossover (DJ CDX XO)	No restructuring	No restructuring[a]
Emerging Markets (DJ CDX EM)	Not applicable (all sovereign entities)	Not applicable (all sovereign entities)
Europe (iTraxx)	Modified restructuring	Modified modified restructuring
Asia (iTraxx)	Restructuring	Restructuring

[a]A majority of reference CDS contracts trade with the specified restructuring clause.
Source: Citigroup.

Trading Example—Credit Event

Suppose an investor bought protection on $125 million notional of five-year DJ CDX IG (Series 5) index on December 1, 2005, and one of the names in the index defaults on January 15, 2006. Since the investor bought protection on $125 million notional of the index, it includes protection on $1 million notional of the defaulted name. Assuming a physical settlement, the investor will get $1 million from the seller of protection and deliver $1 million face value of deliverable reference obligation for the defaulted credit. The index contract will be reduced to $124 million and the defaulted credit will be removed from the reference portfolio. Since the next premium payment (on March 20, 2006) will be only $139,500 (a quarter of 45 bp of $124 million), the investor will have to make an accrued premium payment of $312.50 to cover for the protection on $1 million of the defaulted credit for the period from December 21, 2005, to January 15, 2006.

SETTLEMENT PROCESS AFTER CREDIT EVENT

Under standard documentation, indexes are settled using a physical settlement. In a physical settlement, the protection buyer delivers to the protection seller a deliverable obligation[8] for the amount of the defaulted reference entity in the index contract. In return, the protection seller pays the protection buyer the par value for that portion of the contract.[9]

There are several key elements in the settlement process (see Table 4.6). A credit event notice references a credit event that occurred on or after the effective date and on or prior to the scheduled termination date. A notice of publicly available information cites publicly available information confirming the occurrence of the credit event. The event determination date is the first date that both the credit event notice and the notice of publicly available information are effective after being delivered by the protection buyer or the protection seller.

Physical Settlement (Indexes and Tranche Products)

In case of physical settlement, the buyer delivers the Notice Of Physical Settlement (NOPS) to the seller and it confirms that the buyer will require performance in accordance with the physical settlement method. The NOPS contains detailed information and the amount of the deliverable obligations that the buyer will deliver to the seller. The NOPS must be effective on or before the 30th calendar day after the event determination date. The date on which the buyer delivers the deliverable obligations is the delivery date. For bonds, the market standard is to deliver on or before the third business day after the NOPS is delivered.

Cash Settlement (Tranche Product Only)

In case of cash settlement, the valuation date is the third business day following the delivery date. On the valuation date, an auction is conducted by the calculation agent using the standard auction method: The final price is the highest bid obtained when the calculation agent attempts to obtain full quotations from five or more dealers.

RECENT DEFAULTS IN CDX INDEXES

In the recent past, the International Swaps and Derivatives Association (ISDA) conducted a cash settlement process that has been established as an alternative option to the settlement process as specified under the standard documentation.

To simplify the operational burden associated with the settlement of index and index-linked products, ISDA, in collaboration with the dealers community, has evolved separate CDS Index Protocols to deal with credit events. These protocols establish an auction process to set a recovery rate for each credit event. The protocols provide investors with an option to cash settle their transactions based on the outcome of auctions. In that way,

TABLE 4.6 Time Line for the Settlement After the Credit Event

Event	Description	Restrictions
Credit event date	The date on which the event (failure to pay, bankruptcy, restructuring, etc.) takes place.	Date has to lie between the trade date and the scheduled termination date of the contract.
Event determination period starts	Time for one of the counterparties to acknowledge the event by delivering notices to the other party.	
Event determination date	Final date on which both the credit event notice and the notice of publicly available information are effective.	Cannot exceed 14 calendar days after the scheduled termination date, grace period extension date (if applicable), or repudiation/moratorium evaluation date (if applicable).
Settlement period starts	The parties are ready for initiating the settlement process as soon as the event is determined.	
Last date for notice of physical settlement	If the protection buyer desires a physical settlement, it needs to be conveyed to the counterparty by this date.	Cannot exceed 30 calendar days after the event determination date.
Physical settlement period starts	Once the notice of physical settlement is delivered, the counterparties work to meet the conditions of settlement.	
Physical settlement date	Last day of the longest physical settlement period after the conditions of settlement are met.	If all deliverable obligations are delivered on or before this date, this date will be the termination date.
Start of settlement fallbacks	In case settlement is not complete, alternate measures are adopted.	Starts five business days after physical settlement date.

Source: ISDA and Citigroup.

TABLE 4.7   Recent Defaults Affecting DJ CDX Indexes, January 2006

Name Defaulted	CDX Indexes Affected	ISDA Auction Recovery Price
Winn Dixie Stores	DJ CDX.HY.1	—
Collins & Aikman Products Co.	DJ CDX.HY.1, DJ CDX.HY.2, DJ CDX.HY.3, DJ CDX.HY.4	43.625
Delta Airlines Inc.	DJ CDX.HY.1, DJ CDX.HY.2	18
Northwest Airlines	—	28
Delphi Corp.	DJ CDX.IG.1, DJ CDX.IG.2, DJ CDX.IG.3, DJ CDX.HY.4, DJ CDX.HY.5	63.375
Calpine	DJ CDX.HY.1, DJ CDX.HY.2, DJ CDX.HY.3, DJ CDX.HY.4, DJ CDX.HY.5	19.125

Source: ISDA and Citigroup.

protection buyers and sellers can choose to avoid any potential operational difficulties and market short squeezes when they search for or dispose of the deliverable obligations. Recent CDS Index Protocols for Collins & Aikman, Delta, Northwest, Delphi, and Calpine (see Table 4.7) have been processed without any serious problems. A substantial number of investors have opted for the settlement based on the CDS Index Protocols.[10]

In addition to greater efficiency, time, and cost savings, established protocols have improved the process by which the index and tranche market work through settlement difficulties after credit events. As this settlement option simplifies settlements and potentially avoids a short squeeze in deliverable obligations, it could become a preferred settlement process in the future.

INDEX VERSUS INTRINSICS

Because buying protection on the credit derivatives index is equivalent to buying protection on each underlying name, the spread on the index closely follows the average—simple and duration-weighted[11]—of the CDS spreads on the underlying names. The intrinsic average does not exactly match the index spread. There are fundamental and technical factors that lead to the basis between the index spreads and the intrinsic average. For example, the difference between the DJ CDX IG index, which trades under "No Restructuring", and the majority of underlying single-name CDSs in the U.S. investment-grade market, which trade under Mod-R provisions (Table 4.5) should lead to a lower breakeven spread for the index versus the intrinsics, as restructuring triggers a credit event for the single-name CDS, but the index would not be affected. However, the key drivers for the basis are the technicals in the market. Indexes react differently to the market signals than the single-name CDSs do. As the indexes are being used as a delta hedge for other structured credit products, changes in the issuance of structured credit products will affect the indexes more than the single-name market.

Index-intrinsics spreads often get out of line during extreme moves in the market and at the time of index rolls. Although it seems that market fluctuations in the index-intrinsics basis may sometimes lead to arbitrage opportunities, it is often difficult to capitalize on them.[12] The bid-ask spreads on the individual names are wider than the index bid-ask, which can make the economics of the trade less appealing. Also, it might be difficult to get efficient execution on a hundred or so single-name CDS positions at the same time. However, the basis between two series of indexes is easier to trade against intrinsics since there are only a few nonoverlapping names.

INVESTMENT STRATEGIES WITH CREDIT DERIVATIVES INDEXES

As CDX/iTraxx indexes gained popularity, they began to be used in various ways. Because of their liquidity and transparency, they react quickly to new market information, especially during sell-offs. But more important, they are an efficient tool to quickly gain access to specific credit asset classes and sectors. Although many single-name CDSs are liquid, it is more efficient to use the indexes when trying to quickly gain or reduce the exposure to the market. This property is important for investors trying to rebalance, diversify, or hedge their existing portfolios, particularly during volatile periods.

Key applications include the following:

- **A quick way to take long or short market positions.** Investors can use credit derivatives indexes to express credit macro views.
- **Portfolio diversification and rebalancing**. Indexes allow investors to access asset classes that are harder to obtain in cash or single-name form. That property is especially important for portfolio managers who want to diversify or rebalance their portfolios.
- **Asset ramp-up.** Many of the structured finance collateralized debt obligations (CDOs)include synthetic buckets. Using credit derivatives indexes, CDO managers can quickly fill a core position in those lines.
- **Hedging.** Credit derivatives indexes are an efficient tool to take short positions in the market and are commonly used to hedge marketwide spread risk inherent in credit portfolios. An index hedge can be fine-tuned using additional selected positions in single-name CDS.

- **Relative value trading.** A rich family of CDX/iTraxx credit derivatives indexes provides relative value players with a variety of potential strategies. Liquidity in the indexes accommodates efficient executions of relative value trades. Examples of relative value trades are the following:
  - **Index versus index trades.** The CDX/iTraxx family provides a variety of relative value trades between different indexes, composite indexes, and their subindexes and index series with different maturities.
  - **Index versus intrinsics trades.** Although harder to execute, indexes sometimes trade at a substantial spread compared to the intrinsics. Index-intrinsics relative value trades are suitable for the indexes with a lower number of credits in the portfolio or for indexes where the reference CDSs are less liquid.
- **Trades around the index roll.** Around the roll, technicals can play a significant part. Under normal conditions, investors are more likely to roll their short positions than the long positions. Rolling the short positions allows staying in the on-the-run product and providing a more liquid hedge. These trends lead to potential relative value opportunities around the roll time.
- **Curve trades.** Increased liquidity across the credit curve allows for various index curve trades.

Investors

Credit derivatives indexes and index-linked products used to be primarily in the domain of leveraged accounts, such as credit hedge funds and proprietary desks. But real-money investors have also started actively participating in credit derivatives markets and using CDX/iTraxx indexes for a variety of reasons, especially as the indexes can be structured in the form of credit-linked notes.

Although credit derivatives indexes are gaining in popularity among real-money investors, mark-to-market accounting rules and regulations are one of the main roadblocks for wider acceptance. This is because a significant proportion of credit positions held by banks and insurance companies are in hold-to-maturity books that are not marked to market. But regulations governing credit derivatives, for the most part, do not allow them to be held in such books.

Index-Related Structured Credit Products

Indexes are one of the main products in credit derivatives markets, but other index-related structured credit products are also playing a significant role. Among index-related products, the most important are index-linked tranches and index swaptions. Both of these market segments have experienced substantial growth over the past few years that could not have been possible without the liquidity in the underlying index markets. Dealers and mark-to-market accounts use indexes to delta-hedge their positions in index tranches and swaptions. Index-linked tranches represent one of the strongest market segments among structured credit products. As synthetic structures have replaced cash CDOs that reference investment-grade and high-yield corporate credit collateral, index tranches represent approximately half of the issued synthetic tranche volume today.

Structured credit has also affected the indexes. As the trading volume in tranches and swaptions increased, hedging needs affected the index trading and improved liquidity. Overall, we could say that one of the main factors for the growth of credit derivatives indexes has been the strong activity in the synthetic tranche space.

Issues and Concerns

Although credit derivatives indexes have contributed significantly to the growth of structured credit markets, some investors might worry about risks and potential problems when considering index trades. Credit indexes, just like other credit derivatives instruments, increase liquidity and transparency in the credit markets. However, high-volume index trading could potentially make these markets more volatile. As the indexes trade in an unfunded form, they can amplify market moves, especially during sell-offs. Liquid credit indexes have accommodated the development of other structured credit products, as they are used as a hedging tool. But as the indexes are closely linked with other products, there is a risk that market shocks could be transmitted from structured credit products back to other credit markets. For example, spread moves in tranche space require that mark-to-market accounts rebalance their hedge positions. Such rebalancing would transfer tranche spread volatility into index space. Finally, there is always concern about how the defaults of names in indexes will affect the market and to what extent the settlement process could break down. Unforeseen events that have not been properly addressed in the index documentation could shake investor confidence in index products. Although these concerns are justified, the settlement process that was put into place by ISDA and the dealers community indicates that so far credit events have been handled without any significant problems.

CONCLUSION

Overall, credit derivatives indexes have been a success story in credit markets. Their liquidity, transparency, and overall support from the dealers community contributed to their growth and expansion. Credit derivatives indexes are now firmly anchored in the structured credit product lineup. They play an essential role in the development of related structured credit products, such as index tranches and index swaptions. We expect the presence of index products to increase as synthetic derivatives indexes are being introduced to other asset classes.

CASE STUDY: DJ CDX HY AND DJ CDX EM—CONVERSION OF PRICE LEVEL INTO A SPREAD LEVEL

The CDX HY and EM indexes are quoted on a price basis. In terms of cash flows, a price implies that the protection buyer will make an up-front payment equal to the difference between the price and par, in addition to making the periodic premium payments based on the fixed running spread of the index. Thus, suppose the five-year DJ CDX HY (Series 5) index is trading at $99.25 and an investor buys protection on $10 million notional; the investor will make an up-front payment of $75,000 ($0.75 per $100 times $10 million) besides making quarterly payments of $98,750 (a quarter of 395 bp of $10 million; note that the five-year DJ CDX HY 5 running spread is fixed at 395 bp). However, if the index is trading at $101, the investor buying protection on $10 million will get $100,000 up front and will then pay $98,750 every quarter.

To convert a market price level into a market spread level, the up-front payment of the difference between the price and par has to be converted into an equivalent running spread over the length of the contract and then added to the fixed running spread. On the CDSW page of Bloomberg, investors can choose the "Calculate Par CDS Spread" mode in the calculator. They can then specify the details of the contract, the fixed running spread, and the price to get the equivalent market spread. It is most convenient to pull up the CDSW page on the standard indexes by browsing through the CDSI page, since in this case the contract details are already filled in.

CASE STUDY: USING ITRAXX TO REPLICATE BOND PORTFOLIOS

As a practical application of the credit derivatives indexes, the following case study examines the use of iTraxx to replicate bond portfolios. Specifically, it shows how to effectively replicate the performance of the 579-instrument, 248-issuer Euro Broad Investment-Grade (EuroBIG) index (EBIG) using iTraxx and single-name CDSs. Tracking error was found to be similar to that of an 80-name cash tracker.

Motivation

Credit default swap indexes and selected single-name credit default swaps (CDSs) can be used to efficiently track cash indexes.

iTraxx and five single-name credit swaps can effectively replicate the performance of the 579-instrument, 248-issuer EuroBIG index. Tracking error is similar to that of an 80-name cash tracker.

CDSs work equally well as a temporary market hedge.

Many cash bond portfolio managers have resisted using credit swap indexes in volume because their mandates often tie them to cash indexes. As a result, they are not taking advantage of the increased liquidity and low transaction costs in the credit swap market. For example, bid-offer spreads on on-the-run iTraxx are only half a basis point, substantially less than those for most cash instruments. Using the Citigroup EuroBIG index (EBIG) as our case study of an accepted cash index, we propose a replication scheme using interest rate swaps and futures, the iTraxx index and small portfolio of single-name CDSs. Finally, although we discuss index replication in this piece, the same analysis can be used by someone looking for an efficient credit hedge for a portfolio (e.g., to lock in today's spreads or to reduce future exposure to credit risk).

In this piece, we first break the risk of the EBIG into its major constituents: interest rate risk and credit risk. We then use interest rate swaps and futures to replicate the interest rate exposures and a combination of iTraxx and five single-name CDSs to replicate the credit exposures.

Typical Portfolio Risks

A typical fixed-income portfolio comprises domestic and foreign sovereign debt, agency debt, and corporate debt. A good example of that type of portfolio is the Citigroup EuroBIG index (see Table 4.8). Broadly, the risks of such a portfolio can be decomposed into four major factors:

1. Government curve reshaping (interest rate risk).
2. Swap spread (interest rate risk).

TABLE 4.8 EBIG Index—Government Risk and Swap Risk Breakdown, August 2004

Portfolio	Issues	Issuers	Market Value (%)	Asset Swap Spread (bp)	Weighted Duration (Years)	1–5.5 Years	5.5 Years–11 Years	11+ Years
Government (EGBI)	245	11	65	−3	3.72	0.87	1.29	1.56
Agencies and Collateralized	694	152	23	7	0.99	0.37	0.53	0.09
Corporates (EBIGCorp)	579	248	12	41	0.55	0.20	0.28	0.06
EBIG	**1,518**	**411**	**100**	**2**	**5.25**	**1.45**	**2.10**	**1.71**

Source: Citigroup.

3. Broad credit market (credit risk).
4. Single-name credit (credit risk).

Investors who want to replicate an index such as the EBIG need to build a replicating portfolio.

Replicating Interest Rate Risks

To replicate the first two noncredit risks, we use government bond futures and swaps. A well-established approach is to match the partial durations of the portfolio across the two curves. We suggest using three swaps to cover the full maturity exposure[13] (5-, 10-, and 25-year swaps, for example), and two futures to hedge the government exposure (at least for the part of the government curve below 10 years). The only interest rate–related risks that cannot be replicated that way are:

- The very long-term swap spread.
- The individual government, sovereign, and agency-specific asset swap spread risks.

To fund our tracker, we invest in two liquid bonds, the European Investment Bank's 2012 (to get a return close to LIBOR) and the long on-the-run Bund[14] (to achieve a return close to the Euro government return). A long Bund is necessary because of the lack of long-dated futures. Table 4.9 provides an example of such a replicating portfolio in both funded and unfunded form.

Such a tracker would have 70 bp annual tracking error versus the EBIG (using historical back-testing). Most of the residual risk is the result of broad market and single-name credit risk, which we replicate using iTraxx and a few single-name default swaps, as we discuss next.

Using iTraxx to Replicate Broad Credit Market Risk

The iTraxx offers a liquid instrument to replicate the broad credit market risk of EBIG Corp (EBIGC): Bid-offer spreads are currently only half a basis point and daily traded volume is more than €1 billion. Alternative strategies—for example, customized portfolios of default swaps or iTraxx Corp—could offer a closer fit to EBIG (iTraxx has only 125 names and is equally weighted), but we would be giving up the low transaction costs. For example, bid-offer spreads on single-name default swaps are typically 3 to 4 bp, and the iTraxx Corp trades much less often.

We have shown elsewhere[15] that the best way to capture credit market risk is to compute the beta of the portfolio we are holding versus its benchmark, and similarly the beta of the replicating instrument (here iTraxx Diversified CDS September 2009), then to match the weighted beta duration of both to duplicate the overall beta risk.[16]

Two approaches are possible for calculating the beta of iTraxx. One can either regress the iTraxx spread quote changes with the market spread changes or compute the weighted beta of the intrinsic portfolio[17] of 125 credit swaps by combining the risky DV01s and the issuer beta of its constituents. We prefer the second approach as we already compute very

TABLE 4.9 Portfolio Tracker for the Euro Broad Investment Grade Index (EBIG)—Government Curve and Swap Spread Risk: Unfunded and Funded, August 2004

Tracker—Unfunded	Coupon (%)	Maturity	Par	Sensitivity	EBIG Index	Sensitivity
Swap	3.623	02/08/2009	15	0.57	EBIG-Ex EGBI[a] 1–5 Yrs[b]	0.57
Futures	Bobl	13/09/2004	18	0.87	EGBI 1–5 Yrs	0.87
Swap	4.314	02/08/2014	11	0.81	EBIG-Ex EGBI 5–10 Yrs	0.81
Futures	Bund	13/09/2004	15	1.29	EGBI 5–10 Yrs	1.29
Swap	4.868	02/08/2029	11	1.71	EGBI 10+ Yrs	1.71
Portfolio			5.25			5.25

(continued)

TABLE 4.9 (continued)

Tracker—Funded	Coupon (%)	Maturity	Par	Sensitivity	Market Value (%)	EBIG Index	Sensitivity
Swap	3.623	02/08/2009	15	0.57	0	EBIG-Ex EGBI 1–5 Yrs	0.57
Futures	Bobl	13/09/2004	18	0.87	0	EGBI 1–5 Yrs	0.87
EIB[c]	5.375	15/10/2012	80	5.86	90.3		
Swap	4.314	02/08/2014	−66	−5.05	0	EBIG-Ex EGBI 5–10 Yrs	0.81
Futures	Bund	13/09/2004	15	1.29	0	EGBI 5–10 Yrs	1.29
Swap	4.866	02/08/2029	1	0.15	0	EBIG-Ex EGBI 10+ Yrs	0.15
Bund	4.75	04/07/2034	10	1.56	9.7	EGBI 10+ Yrs	1.56
Portfolio				5.25	100.0		5.25

[a]EGBI: European Government Bond Index.

[b]In practice, the breakdown is realized in effective DV01 terms because the concept of weighted duration does not actually exist for futures.

[c]EIB: European Investment Bank.

Source: Citigroup.

TABLE 4.10 Computation of the Hedge Ratio for the Corporate Part of the EBIG Corporates

	Spread	Duration	Beta	Mkv	WgtBeta
EBIGC	41	4.39	1.00	1.00	4.39
iTraxx	43	4.62	0.94	1.01	4.39
Tracker	2	0.27		0.01	0.00

MKV: Market Value. This can be justified by the historical fact that the credit market can be realistically reduced to a single market risk factor model.
WGTBETA: Weighted Beta.
Source: Citigroup.

precise issuer betas for our cash model portfolio. The average beta across the 125 issuers puts the current iTraxx beta at 0.94.[18] This then allows us to compute the current iTraxx hedge ratio of 1.01, as described in Table 4.10. The resulting hedged position has a slight positive carry of 2 bp per year.

Adjusting for Single-Name Risk through Default Swaps

Not surprisingly, the 125 names of iTraxx and their equal concentration do not completely match the 579-instrument, 248-issuer EBIG Corp. The differences relate not just to the names but also to the concentration of individual obligors. Single-name swaps need to adjust for this difference if we are to obtain effective replication. Without such adjustment, tracking error is a significant 57 bp per year.[19]

The construction rules of iTraxx Diversified allow only European issuers. In contrast, EBIGC includes corporates issuing in euros, regardless of country of origin. Therefore names like General Motors (GM) and General Electric (GE) occur in EBIGC but not in iTraxx. However, iTraxx includes sterling issuers like Sainsbury that do not qualify for inclusion in EBIGC. All in all, of the 125 issuers in iTraxx Diversified CDS September 2009, 100 qualify for EBIGC. Figure 4.3 shows the overlap.

In addition, EBIGC shows a high concentration of default risk to certain individual names. Figure 4.4 shows the risk concentration in the EBIGC index versus the similar risk concentration in the iTraxx CDS. The first 15 issuers of the EBIGC index constitute 31 percent of the total spread risk.[20] (The cumulative curve is achieved by adding up the percentage-weighted beta of each bond and/or CDS in their respective portfolios.)

Figure 4.5 illustrates the residual position from the beta-weighted replication in weighted beta terms. As expected, we end up with a massive short in all of the major issuers of the euro market (especially the U.S. names), and we also exhibit a collection of shorts consisting of names that were not in the index.

We now combine our iTraxx broad credit market hedge with single-name longs for which we had a major mismatch (see Figure 4.5). The intuition behind adjusting our first strategy of just using a beta-weighted notional iTraxx is to increase the risk-specific exposure

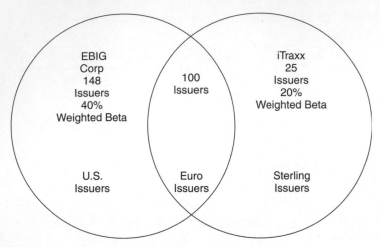

FIGURE 4.3   Issuer Overlap between iTraxx Diversified September 2004 and EBIG Corp 2004[a]

[a]One-time upfront payment at settlement is made from protection buyer to protection seller or vice versa, depending on whether the current spread is higher or lower than the running spread. Payment also includes accrued.

Source: Citigroup.

in all the major names by selling protection on specific credit default swaps and by selling less iTraxx CDS protection to stay weighted beta neutral. To keep the example simple and liquid, we use only five-year CDSs.

Table 4.11 presents the structure of the five-CDS hedge; the carry is slightly better than before at 3 bp (48 bp × 0.924 = 44 bp, a positive carry of 3 bp). We first evaluated the exposure in weighted-beta terms to the five major names in the index (net of the initial iTraxx hedge, i.e., GM, FRTEL, TITIM, DT, and F), and matched it with the correct amount of CDSs (taking into account that FRTEL, TITIM, and DT are also part of the iTraxx index) and finally sold protection on the correct amount of iTraxx to match the overall weighted beta of the index.

Performance

After this addition, the residual position is more satisfying than the previous replication in terms of risk. The maximum exposure in spread duration for a single name is reduced from 0.27 years (GM in Figure 4.5) to 0.09 years (VW in Figure 4.6),[21] and the *ex ante* tracking error of our residual position falls from 22 to 17 bp *ex ante* and from 57 to 38 bp ex post.

If we were to build a portfolio of 10 CDSs using the same approach, the *ex ante* tracking error would be reduced by two additional basis points. Our model seems to show that there is no further gain once the portfolio includes 15 CDSs or more, because of the structural difference between the EBIGC and the iTraxx (see Table 4.12). In addition, whereas picking

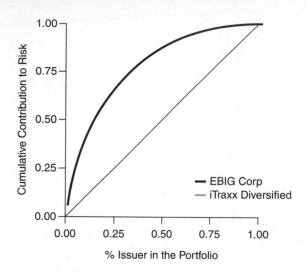

Cumulative Contribution to Total Spread Risk in EBIG Corp (%)

1. TITIM	4
2. FRTEL	8
3. DT	11
4. INTNED	13
5. GM	16
6. RWE	18
7. VW	20
8. GE	22
9. LYCE	24
10. AAB	25
11. AUTSTR	26
12. VIEFP	28
13. DB	29
14. EOAGR	30
15. ENEL	31

FIGURE 4.4 Issuer Cumulative Marginal Risk Contribution in the EBIG Corp and iTraxx Diversified
Source: Citigroup.

the first five CDS is straightforward, the choice of additional names is far more complex and requires the use of an optimizer.

We back-tested this replication with real CDS market data for the past four months, using the fixed hedge portfolio described previously (see Figure 4.7). We did not adjust the credit weightings over the period, even though the EBIGC slightly changes structure every month. We assumed the use of constant-maturity swaps to partially correct this effect.

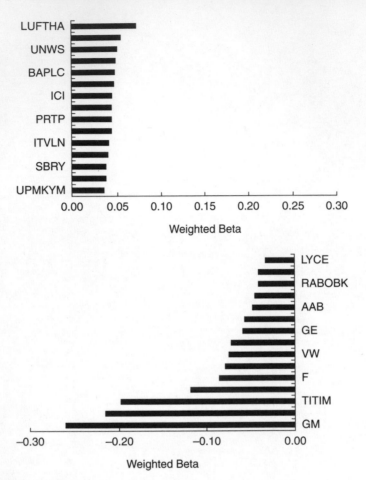

FIGURE 4.5 Portfolio Tracker for the EBIGC Index—Residual Top Long and Short in Weighted Beta Terms, August 2004
Source: Citigroup.

We tested the quality of the overall tracker and of the pure credit replication. For the overall tracker we observed a tracking error of 32 bp per year with a cumulative loss of 7 bp. Readjusting the curve DV01 bucketing on a monthly basis would greatly improve the result. For the credit replication itself we observed an excess return over swap tracking error of 38 bp per year with a cumulative loss of 3 bp. Both results are similar to what can be achieved using a portfolio of 60 to 80 credit bonds. The good results of our historical simulations confirm what our *ex ante* model predicted: The iTraxx CDS is so diversified that it really does capture the beta effect of the overall credit market and only needs to be slightly adjusted to replicate any benchmarked corporate portfolio.

TABLE 4.11 The Replicating Portfolio

	Spread	Duration	Beta	Mkv (%)	WgtBeta	WtgBeta-Ex[a]
iTraxx Five-Years	43	4.62	0.94	80	3.46	3.33
GM Five-Years	150	4.35	2.28	3	0.26	0.26
FRTEL Five-Years	56	4.57	1.60	3	0.23	0.28
TITIM Five-Years	60	4.56	1.45	3	0.21	0.25
DT Five-Years	49	4.58	1.46	3	0.13	0.17
F Five-Years	103	4.49	1.88	2	0.09	0.09
Hedge	48	4.61	1.04	92	4.39	4.39

	Spread	Duration	Beta	Mkv (%)	WtgBeta-Ex[a]
EBIGC-Ex[a]	38	4.46	0.89	84	3.33
GM	172	3.44	2.30	3	0.26
FRTEL	85	4.99	1.60	3	0.28
TITIM	77	4.59	1.45	4	0.25
DT	61	3.70	1.46	3	0.17
F	97	2.39	1.89	2	0.09
EBIGCorp	41	4.39	1.00	100	4.39

Mkv: Market Value.
WgtBeta: Weighted Beta.
[a]Ex means that with column redistributes the contribution of FRTEL TITIM and DT into the following lines and exclude them from the main index, either the iTraxx or the EBIG Index.
Source: Citigroup.

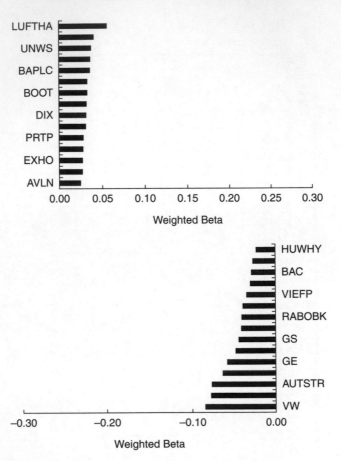

FIGURE 4.6 Portfolio Hedge for the EBIG Index—Residual Top Long and Short in Weighted Beta Terms After the Hedge, August 2004
Source: Citigroup.

Conclusion

A simple structure based on a basket of five CDSs and the iTraxx Diversified CDS affords efficient replication or hedging of a corporate or aggregate credit portfolio. The structure can be easily established, because it relies on simply matching the weighted beta contributions of the overall portfolio and its major positions on an issuer-by-issuer basis. *Ex ante* credit excess return to swap analysis as well as historical back-testing have shown tracking error results similar to that which can be achieved by an elaborate portfolio of single names.

TABLE 4.12 *Ex Ante* Credit Tracking Error as a
Function of the Structure of the Tracker

Tracker	Tracking Error (bp)
1.01 iTraxx	22
0.80 iTraxx + 5 CDSs	17
0.74 iTraxx + 10 CDSs	15
0.67 iTraxx + 15 CDSs	14
0.71 iTraxx + 20 CDSs	14

Source: Citigroup.

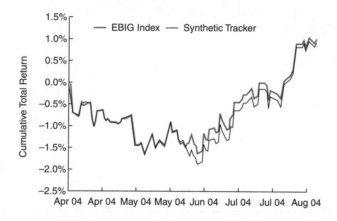

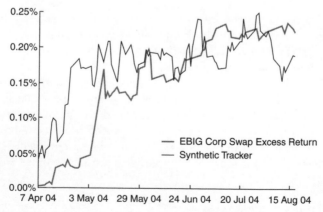

FIGURE 4.7 EBIG and Tracker—Cumulative Total Return
Source: Citigroup.

APPENDIX: DESCRIPTION OF THE ROLL PROCESS

The CDX indexes roll every six months, on March 20 and September 20. The process works as follows[22]:

1. No later than 10 days before each roll date, each of the consortium members submits: (1) a list of entities that have been downgraded below investment grade by either Standard & Poor's (S&P) or Moody's Investors Service; (2) a list of entities for which a merger or corporate action has occurred that makes the issuer unsuitable for the inclusion in the index; and (3) a list of entities for which CDS contracts have become significantly less liquid.
2. The administrator removes from the index all issuers that have been downgraded below investment grade by either S&P or Moody's. The administrator then removes entities that received a majority vote for deletion with respect to (2) and (3).
3. To replace deleted entities, no later than nine days prior to the roll the consortium members submit a list of new entities that they want added to the index (members submit twice the number of entities required after the elimination round). The administrator adds to the new index those entities that receive the highest number of votes, until the index reaches the full number of names. After the names are made public, consortium members submit votes for each fixed-rate coupon, and the median of submitted rates becomes the new coupon.

The roll process for the European iTraxx indexes is similar, but has some minor differences:

1. The 125 names in the portfolio are restricted to produce the following sector distribution: 10 names in autos, 30 in consumers, 20 in energy, 20 in industrials, 20 in TMT (Telecommunications, Media and Technology), and 25 in financials.
2. On the roll date, the various members submit to the administrator trading volumes for highly liquid names over the previous six months. Ineligible (downgraded, defaulted, changed sector, or merged) entities from the previous index are replaced by the next most liquid entity available from the same sector as the name being removed.
3. For Asian iTraxx indexes, 12 months of trading volume are used to measure liquidity.

Risky PV01 of a CDS Contract

Risky PV01, the risky present value of 1 bp of a CDS contract, is the present value of 1 bp of premium payment lasting until the maturity of the contract or until a credit event occurs associated with the reference obligation that terminates the contract, whichever comes first. In a hypothetical scenario, if the reference obligation is free of credit risk (implying that the CDS spread is zero), the Risky PV01 will simply be the present value of 1 bp paid over the premium schedule until the maturity of the contract. However, as the credit risk (and, therefore, the probability of a credit event) is nonzero, the expected life of the contract is less than the stated maturity of the contract. The premium payment leg is not expected to last until maturity and the present value of 1 bp of premium (the Risky PV01) is less than the value in the hypothetical zero credit risk scenario.

In fact, as the credit risk of the reference obligation goes up, the expected life of the contract comes down and so does the Risky PV01. Therefore, Risky PV01 is also a surrogate measure of the expected life of the CDS contracts and is sometimes even referred to as *duration* of a CDS contract.[23] Note that this also means that the Risky PV01 is inversely proportional to the CDS spread.

To calculate the Risky PV01 of a CDS contract, a model is needed to estimate the probability of a credit event. The most common approach to model the credit risk for this purpose is to use a flat-forward hazard rate.[24]

Once the survival probability curve is calculated, Risky PV01 can be determined as

$$RiskyPV01(t_v) = \sum_n [D(t_v, t_n) \times S(t_v, t_n) \times 1 \text{ bp}]$$

where

t_v = time of valuation

t_n = time of the nth payment according to the CDS contract schedule

$D(t_v, t_n)$ = risk-free discount factor from t_v to t_n

$S(t_v, t_n)$ = Survival probability of the reference obligation from t_v to t_n

$\sum_n$ = summation over the payment schedule of the CDS contract

Note that the formula is for demonstration purposes only and assumes that the time of valuation and the time of default coincides with one of the payment dates on the CDS contract schedule, therefore ignoring the complication of an accrued payment.

Calculation of Intrinsic Spread of the Index

Assume that the index refers to a portfolio of N single-name credits. The CDS spread for the ith name is given by S_i. How does the investor calculate an intrinsic spread $S_{Intrinsic}$ for an index as implied by the underlying single-name spreads?

To calculate the $S_{Intrinsic}$, the investor can use the Risky PV01 for each single-name credit. The intrinsic spread is defined as

$$S_{Intrinsic} = \frac{\sum_{i=1}^{N} S_i \cdot RiskyPV01_i}{\sum_{i=1}^{N} RiskyPV01_i}$$

The $RiskyPV01_i$ is a surrogate measure of the expected life of a CDS contract on the single-name credit i. For that reason, $S_{Intrinsic}$ is referred to as the duration-weighted average spread of index. Since the Risky PV01 of a CDS contract decreases as the CDS spread increases, the duration-weighted average spread of the index is lower than the simple average. Although market participants sometimes use the simple average as an approximation for the index-intrinsics spread, the duration-weighted average spread is a better measure because it accounts for the dispersion of spreads in the index portfolio.

Risky PV01 of an Index

Similar to the calculation of the intrinsic spread for the index, the Risky PV01 for an index could be estimated as the notional-weighted sum of the Risky PV01s of the underlying single-name CDS contracts. A simple approach is to equate the 1 bp change in the index spread with the 1 bp change in the underlying single-name CDS spreads, which leads to the estimation of the index Risky PV01 as the notional-weighted sum of the Risky PV01s of the underlying single-name CDS. However, this approach is only an approximation. The spread change of the index can be replicated in a number of ways using spread changes of the underlying CDS. Also, the index spread most likely differs from the duration-weighted intrinsic average spread.

It is important to note that the CDSW page on Bloomberg treats the index spread as a single-name spread while calculating the Risky PV01 and the mark-to-market amount.

Mark-to-Market Estimation of an Index Position

Suppose an investor bought protection on a notional amount N of an index at the spread of S_0. If the spread changes from S_0 to S_t, the investor would like to calculate mark-to-market (MTM) of the change.

Theoretically, MTM can be calculated using $RiskyPV01_{Index}$ as: $MTM = (S_t - S_0) \times RiskyPV01_{Index} \times N$.

When using the CDSW page on Bloomberg, both parties agree on the inputs (credit curve, recovery rate, valuation, and settlement date) and the "Market Value" field on the CDSW page determines the mark-to-market figure.

CHAPTER 5

The Added Dimensions of Credit—A Guide to Relative Value Trading

Matt King
Michael Sandigursky

Many investors think that credit trading is only about buying credit, earning carry, and making money as spreads tighten. During the bull phase of the credit cycle, they are, by and large, correct. Who cares about a few basis points made by relative value trading when you might make a killing simply by being long the cash credit indexes when they come screaming in as companies deliver?

Every party, though, comes to an end. When it does, we think it is relative value trading that will help you through the hangover. This involves exploring the pricing discrepancies and fundamental drivers behind the many other dimensions that credit has to offer: multiple durations, cross-currency opportunities, cash versus synthetics, interplays with equities, and the seemingly limitless field of structured credit.

In this chapter, we introduce a variety of cross-credit strategies that today's market offers: the added dimensions of credit.

OVERVIEW OF CURVE TRADES

The most obvious extra dimension in credit (over equities) is duration. Taking credit exposure to a company for two years is very different from taking credit exposure to a company for 10 years. It is this variation in a company's credit risk through time that curve trades try to monetize. Before we embark on how to potentially make money from curve trades, it is worth understanding why credit curves have the shape they do.

Learning Curves

Theory suggests that the spread curves of highly rated companies should be upward sloping, whereas those of very low-rated companies (high-yield) tend to be negatively sloping.

To see this, consider an AAA corporate. Its credit risk is one-sided—future ratings may only be lower. Moreover, the further in the future an investor looks, the less certain one can be of the company paying back its debt. Thus, the longer the tenor of the bonds investors buy, the more they should ask to be paid, making the credit curve slope upward. The combined likelihood and severity (in spread terms) of cumulative downgrades is, nevertheless, more severe for slightly lower-rated debt than for, say, AAAs: hence the greater steepness of the AA, A, and BBB curves (see Figure 5.1).

However, a company on the brink of default is in the opposite situation. Spreads are very high for the immediate maturities, to reflect the high risk of default. If it does survive, though, the chances are that it will have been upgraded or have otherwise improved its credit quality. Furthermore, there is a price effect that plays a big factor here. When default is imminent, all bonds, irrespective of maturity, trade close to their expected recovery value and not on the basis of yield to maturity. However, when this deeply discounted price is used to derive yields and spreads to maturity, it is a

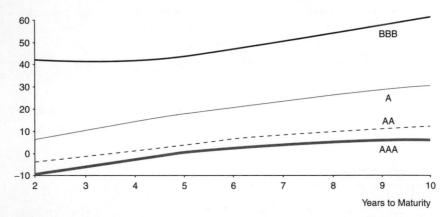

FIGURE 5.1 Typical Credit Curve for AAA to BBB Bonds in Euros (asset swap spreads in basis points)
Source: Citigroup.

mathematical inevitability that at equal prices bonds with longer maturities have lower yields and spreads than bonds with shorter maturities. As such, spreads in longer maturities are lower as a result, which causes an inverted curve.

These intuitions can be more formally expressed if we think of the curve shape as a strip of tradable forwards. In theory, the forward rate for a given year should correspond to the firm's creditworthiness during that year. In practice, forward-starting credit default swap (CDS) contracts that directly implement forward credit views do not trade. Nevertheless, cash-neutral curve trades result in almost the same position—again giving credit curves more or less the intuitive forms described earlier. That said, curves' behavior through time in practice is often quite a bit more complicated.

Drivers of Curve Steepness

In practice, we are more interested in what drives the steepness of a credit curve through time rather than the theoretical shape of the curve, such that one can monetize a steepening view with a steepener and a flattening view with a flattener. To this end, the spread curve can be split into two parts—3s10s and 10s30s—that behave quite differently, even for the same underlying credit. We suspect market segmentation is to blame. Buy-and-hold, yield-targeting investors, such as insurance companies and pension funds, account for a larger share of demand at the long end because of their liabilities. This causes the 10s30s[1] curve to move differently from the short end. See Figure 5.2.

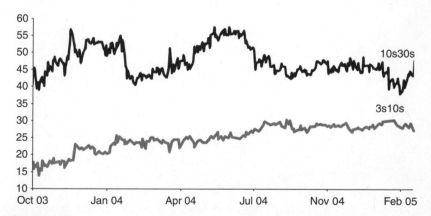

FIGURE 5.2 Example—Peugeot 3s10s and 10s30s Curves Behave Differently (basis points)
Source: Citigroup.

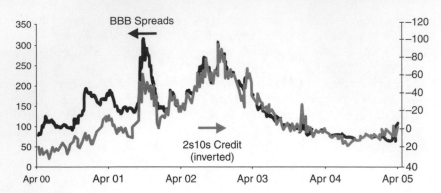

FIGURE 5.3 BBB Spreads versus 2s10 Slope for Citigroup's EuroBIG Corporate Index (basis points)
Source: Citigroup.

At the short end of the curve (i.e., 2s10s or 3s10s), curves steepen when spreads rally and flatten when spreads sell off. This behavior is visible at market level (see Figure 5.3), but frequently holds for long periods of time at single-name level as well.

The reason for this is that, more often than not, news on the corporate market—next quarter's earnings estimates, news of an asset disposal, share buyback, bond tender, mergers and acquisition (M&A), provision for bad loan, and such—is focused on the near future rather than the distant future, and consequently affects the short-term creditworthiness (and credit spreads) of a company more than the long term. If, for example, GM were to suddenly have a windfall gain, with enough cash to pay back all of its debt out to 2010, credit spreads for all its bonds maturing within the next few years would tighten dramatically, as there is very little chance GM would be unable to pay debt maturing before then.

GM's 2033 bonds would probably also rally on the news, but by a smaller amount, as a single cash windfall would probably not be sufficient to solve its longer-term problems.[2] This spread change at the short end would result in a bull steepening of the credit curve. Similarly, spread widening on bad news tends to cause short-term spreads to sell off more than long-term spreads, leading to bear flattening.

What, then, drives the slope at the long end? Well, the data suggest that the 10s30s credit curves steepen when government yields back up. Long-term investors, such as insurers and pension funds, tend to focus on absolute yield targets rather than spread changes. When government yields back up, investors are attracted to these high yields and sell out of their long credit positions. As a result, the credit curve steepens at the long end. Conversely, when government yields fall, investors' hunt for yield

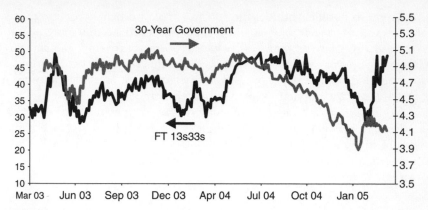

FIGURE 5.4 FT 13s33s Slope (basis points) versus 30-Year Treasury Yields (percent)
Source: Citigroup.

takes them into long-duration credit, causing the credit curve to flatten (see Figure 5.4).

All this said, individual bond movements do not always fit neatly into these broad patterns. The size of the issue, its availability in the repurchase agreement (repo) market, the proximity to CDS standard maturities, the way the bond was placed with investors at issue, its covenants or indentures, and its coupon size can all influence investors' preferences. This—together with the relative newness of the mere idea of credit curve trades—tends to make curve analysis in practice considerably more complex than the theory. At the same time, though, it can also be thought of as creating opportunities.

PUTTING ON A CURVE TRADE

There are two main methods of putting on a curve trade, which can yield very different returns.

A *cash-for-cash* trade involves buying and selling par-for-par in different maturities: literally buying one unit of the short-maturity bond for every unit of the long-maturity bond sold; for an upward sloping curve this results in positive carry on flatteners and negative carry on steepeners. Such positions are also highly exposed to parallel shifts in the curve, since the duration of positions in the long end is greater than that of the same amount of cash deployed in the short end.

A *duration-neutral* curve trade, where one buys or sells more of the short-maturity bond than the long-maturity bond, is designed to be indifferent to parallel shifts of the spread curve. Steepeners require the use of leverage, as one is buying more than one euro at the short end for every euro sold at the long end, which requires borrowing the shortfall. Conversely, duration-neutral flatteners can require large short positions at the front end.[3] These are more difficult to achieve in cash credit[4] than in CDSs—hence the popularity of CDSs in curve trades.

In addition, to take advantage of the relative steepness or flatness of one credit curve versus another, one can enter a box trade, where one has an outright steepener on one curve and an outright flattener on another. This is often structured such that there is minimal profit and loss on parallel shifts in either curve.

CROSS-CURRENCY TRADES

Companies often tap the global capital markets across a number of different currencies to get the cheapest possible funding.[5] Cross-currency trades try to monetize anomalies that exist among credit spreads to swaps in different currencies.

These trades typically involve buying a bond in one currency and selling a bond of the same credit in another currency. For example, switching between the Compass 2010 bond in sterling and the 2009 in euros would yield a carry pickup of about 8 bp (see Figure 5.5) and offers the potential to make money from any spread convergence of the euro bond relative to the sterling bond.

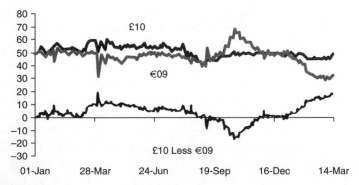

FIGURE 5.5 Example—A Cross-Currency Trade with Compass
Source: Citigroup.

Such trades require hedging out both currency and interest rate risk, the effects of which would otherwise swamp the small credit differences. This can be done using a cross-currency asset swap,[6] which uses a strip of FX forwards to collectively convert all the (in this example) dollar-denominated coupons into sterling-based cash flows.

Cross-Currency Opportunities in Bonds

A growing number of investors can now invest globally, but the majority in each market remain currency-constrained. As such, and especially in relatively small credit markets such as sterling, the markets are segmented by, for example, investment constraints that happen to dominate in that market, such as being a forced seller of high-yield or having a certain maturity target. Global investors not subject to the same constraints can frequently take advantage of the anomalies that such constraints create. Other barriers to entry, such as tax issues and unfamiliarity with foreign accounting, can also contribute to such anomalies.

Cross-Currency Trades in CDSs

Contrary to popular belief, CDSs in different currencies do trade at slightly different spreads. The first reason is called the *quanto effect*, where spreads and foreign exchange rates may be correlated and cause one CDS to outperform as the currency to which it is correlated appreciates. Dealers have to hedge these risks dynamically, and they charge for this accordingly.

Consider a scenario in which the euro/dollar exchange rate is at parity and a trader sells protection on €10 million of GM while simultaneously buying protection on $10 million of GM to remain credit neutral on GM. Now suppose the euro/dollar moves to 1.3. The trader may wish to buy a further $3 million of dollar-denominated protection to remain credit neutral. This extra $3 million of protection may be more expensive or less expensive with equal probability if there is no correlation between the foreign exchange (FX) rate and spreads. The trader may be willing to charge the same spread for euro and dollar protection as a result. However, the trader may feel that there is some correlation (i.e., GM does worse as dollar weakens) between GM credit spreads and the euro/dollar, and may well require some extra compensation if the situation creates a bias against his/her position. For this reason, the currency of a CDS can have an impact on the spread level, which stems from the assumed correlation between the credit spreads and the currency rate.

The second reason is that the CDS curves are based on global default probabilities but are discounted using the local swap curve of the currency in which they are quoted. As the swap curve in one currency steepens or widens versus the swap curve in another, the CDS spreads in the two currencies will diverge. This effect, however, is very small because CDS spreads are relatively insensitive to changes in interest rates,[7] as the expected CDS spreads and the expected loss on default are both discounted using the same interest rate curves, albeit with a small timing mismatch. Furthermore, CDS traded in the United States have modified restructuring (MR) language while in Europe they have modified modified restructuring (MMR) language, which can further add to differences in CDS spreads.

In practice, most investment-grade credits trade at very similar CDS spreads in G-7 currencies, although the width of bid-offer spreads may vary according to the liquidity of CDSs in that market. As a result, investors tend not to focus on cross-currency trades in CDSs.

BASIS TRADES

The cash-default basis is of mounting interest to investors thanks to two huge, but almost segregated, pools of money in credit: cash investors who focus only on bonds and structured credit investors who focus almost exclusively on CDSs. This creates opportunities for those investors, often hedge funds, who can use both bonds and CDSs to position in one market against the other. We think many real-money managers do have mandates to use CDSs but that back-office issues may stop such investors from being active in CDSs just yet. This should change with time. Meanwhile, the basis should be as choppy as ever and lead to opportunities for those who follow it.

Back to Basis

Basis trades can be a low-risk means of monetizing the difference between the price of credit in bonds and CDSs. The basis is broadly defined as the CDS spread minus the bond's asset swap spread. It is therefore negative when the bond spread is higher than the CDS spread and positive when the CDS trades wider than the bond (see Table 5.1). Investors enter negative basis trades, also known as *buying the basis*, when the basis is atypically negative, by buying the bond and buying cheap protection on that name, typically in notional terms. By contrast, a positive basis trade, also known as *selling the basis*, involves selling the bond and selling protection. Basis trades are generally credit neutral, as one leg of the trade is long credit while the other is short.

Basis trades, hence, give investors positive carry to the earlier of maturity or default of the bond. If investors can hold the trade to maturity, then this carry will indeed be their buy-and-hold profit. Most investors choose to

TABLE 5.1   The Basis Trade—A Guide to the Jargon

Basis = CDS Spread − Asset Swap (ASW) Spread

		Jargon	Trade	Carry	Capital Gain
Negative basis trade	CDS spread < Bond spread	"Buying the basis"	Buy the bond and buy protection on that bond.	The carry on a negative basis trade is the ASW − CDS.	Basis narrows (becomes more positive) when the CDS widens more than the bond (or the bond tightens more than the CDS).
Positive basis trade	CDS spread > Bond spread	"Selling the basis"	Short the bond and sell protection on that bond.	The carry on a positive basis trade is CDS − ASW.	Basis narrows (becomes more negative): When the bond widens more than the CDS (or the CDS tightens more than the bond).

Source: Citigroup.

asset swap the bonds so as to remove the interest rate risk and make them more directly comparable with CDSs.

A Negative Basis Trade   Many active investors, though (typically hedge funds and proprietary desks), tend to enter negative basis trades not for their carry but in the hope of a mark-to-market gain. To this end, we recommend a simple rule of thumb: Enter negative basis trades when you are negative on a name, and positive basis trades when you are positive on a name. Generally speaking, CDSs move more than bonds—in both directions. If spreads do widen dramatically, the fact that it is easier to short credit via CDSs than via bonds tends to make spreads on default swaps gap out further than on bonds, making the basis less negative/more positive and allowing the position to be unwound at a profit. Figure 5.6 shows the performance of the negative basis trades in various spread scenarios.

Such positions also work well in the event of LBO speculation, especially if there is any chance of the bonds being tendered for (e.g., because of their short maturities). Finally, note that a negative basis trade is also a means of effectively going long volatility (or long an option on the bond going special) as the cheapest-to-deliver option embedded in the CDS becomes more valuable to the protection buyer when volatility picks up.

So why does a negative basis exist in the first place? Negative basis packages tend to exist for bonds with high cash prices. Let us consider

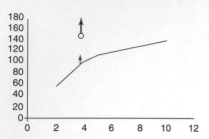

SPREADS WIDEN, YOU LOSE: When the bond widens more than the CDS, you lose more money by being long via bonds than you make by being short via CDSs.

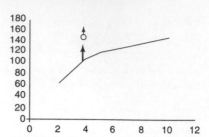

SPREADS WIDEN, YOU WIN: When the CDS widens more than the bond, you make more money by being short via CDSs than you lose by being long via bonds.

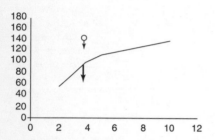

SPREADS TIGHTEN, YOU LOSE: When the CDS tightens more than the bond, you lose more money on being short via CDSs than you make by being long via bonds.

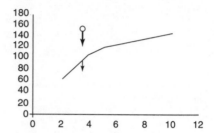

SPREADS TIGHTEN, YOU WIN: When the bond tightens more than the CDS, you make more money by being long via bonds than you lose by short via CDSs.

FIGURE 5.6 Example—Profit and Loss Legs of Negative Basis Trades under Various Spread Scenarios
Source: Citigroup.

an investor who buys the BT 8.125% of 2010 bond trading at £120 at a spread of LIBOR + 55 bp, and buys CDS protection to that date at 39 bp; so, the basis is CDS − ASW = 55 − 39 = 16 bp. In the event of a default, the investor would lose £20 as the CDS pays only £100 on delivery of the defaulted bond. So, in effect, the investor is getting 16 bp for taking on £20 of default risk in BT. The investor could buy more CDSs to hedge the £20 loss (i.e., buy CDSs of notional £120), but this will eat into the positive carry earned from the trade.

A Positive Basis Trade A positive basis is often a feature of a deteriorating credit, as it is much easier to take outright short positions via CDSs than bonds. Further still, cash bond spreads tend to become sticky as their liquidity dries up and bids become less available. Investors stand to make money via a narrowing basis if the credit improves thereafter, as CDS is likely to outperform because the CTD optionality reduces in value as spreads tighten. Conversely, if the credit spreads on the name are unchanged, the position will normally earn its carry unless some technical factor (such as the bid from money market funds for short maturities, or buybacks by corporates) causes bonds to rally more than CDSs. Figure 5.7 shows the performance of the positive basis trade in various spread scenarios.

Investors can, however, find it hard to enter positive basis trades, as shorting the bond (especially if it's trading "special") is often difficult and can vastly reduce the carry of such trades. This is one of the reasons why the positive basis exists in the first place.

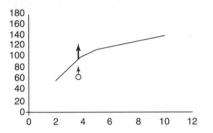

SPREADS WIDEN, YOU LOSE: When the CDS widens more than the bond, you lose more money by being long via CDSs than you make by being short via bonds.

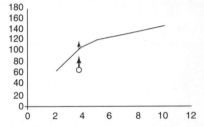

SPREADS WIDEN, YOU WIN: When the bond widens more than the CDS, you make more money by being short via bonds than you lose by being long via CDSs.

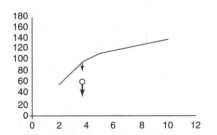

SPREADS TIGHTEN, YOU LOSE: When the bond tightens more than the CDS, you lose more money by being short via bonds than you make by being long via CDSs.

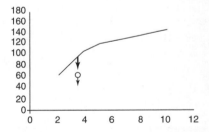

SPREADS TIGHTEN, YOU WIN: When the CDS tightens more than the bond, you make more money by being long via CDSs than you lose by being short via bonds.

FIGURE 5.7 Example—Profit and Loss Legs of Positive Basis Trades under Various Spread Scenarios
Source: Citigroup.

Drivers of Basis

There are two broad drivers of the basis: First, technical factors relating to the differing mechanics of CDSs and bonds; and, second, market factors, which relate to supply and demand. We have summarized these drivers in Tables 5.2 and 5.3, with the intention of providing a reference for investors trying to establish what key factors are driving a particular basis.

Why CDSs and Bonds Are Two Sides of the Same Coin

On a slightly more theoretical note, we spell out the link between CDSs and bonds that investors new to basis trading often question.

An investor is compensated for the default risk of the bond by receiving a certain spread over LIBOR. Similarly, a CDS protection seller is compensated for taking exposure to the default risk of a credit by getting paid a CDS spread. Both the bondholder and the CDS protection seller stand to lose "100 − recovery" if the credit defaults while they have exposure to it. They should both therefore also be paid the same spread during the period that they take this exposure. Investors nowadays think of bonds and CDSs in similar terms and simply as two different ways of getting rewarded for taking credit risk on a company.

To be more thorough, let us consider borrowing €100 at LIBOR flat to buy a floating rate note[12] (FRN) on a credit that pays a coupon of LIBOR plus a fixed spread B, and buying CDS protection over the life of that bond at spread C. In the event of default, the investor can deliver the defaulted FRN to the protection seller in return for par. This par amount is then used to repay the €100 borrowed. The net strategy is thus meant to be credit risk free, as the investor has no exposure to the default of the asset. So, the investor, having assumed no credit risk, earns an annual spread of $+(B − C)$ over LIBOR until the earlier of either maturity or default of the FRN. For this reason, the arbitrage-free relationship requires that $B = C$ (i.e., a basis of zero). This theoretical risk-free trading strategy can, to a lesser extent, be applied to fixed-rate bonds, which account for a larger proportion of the credit market than do FRNs. The strategy is much the same as the basis trade described earlier for floaters because an investor can asset swap a fixed-rate bond and convert it into a synthetic floater (Figures 5.8 to 5.11).

There are, however, some reasons why CDSs and bonds are not actually quite the same. First, there is a credit-contingent interest rate risk on the asset swap leg: In the event of default, the investor receives par in return for a defaulted bond, but still has to honor the off-market interest rate swap, which can be unwound at a profit or a loss, depending on the prevailing interest rate environment at that time. Default-contingent interest rate or FX risk can be eliminated by means of a "perfect" asset swap,[9] but these often

TABLE 5.2 Guide to Key Basis Drivers—Factors That Increase CDS Spreads and/or Decrease Asset Swap Spread Are Good for Negative Basis Trades and Bad for Positive Basis Trades

Technical Factors	
Cheapest-to-deliver option in CDS	The protection buyer is long an option to choose the cheapest out of a basket of deliverable assets to be delivered in the event of default. This is an advantage to the buyer and disadvantage to the seller, so CDS spreads paid by the buyer to the seller widen accordingly.
Extra default triggers in CDS	CDS may be triggered by events (for instance, late payment, restructuring) that do not constitute a full default on the corresponding cash asset. Protection sellers may demand a higher spread to compensate them for this risk.
Bonds trading below par	Other things being equal, the amount at risk on a bond is its dirty price, while for a CDS, the amount at risk is based on a notional of 100. This means that bonds trading below par have less cash at risk and hence a lower spread than equivalent CDS protection. This increases the CDS spread and tightens the bond spread, as the bonds begin to trade increasingly below par.
CDS spreads must be positive	Highly rated bonds can trade sub-LIBOR (i.e., better than LIBOR banks) but CDS spreads are always positive, as every credit has a positive probability of default, and the concept of being paid (that is, negative CDS spread) to receive protection makes little sense. So CDS spreads are typically higher than bond spreads for very high-quality issuers that trade sub-LIBOR.
Risky DV01 (the risky dollar value of a basis point)	Unwinding a default swap by entering into the offsetting transaction means that any profit/loss (P&L) is only realized at maturity or default, whereas the P&L on a bond can be immediately realized by selling it. This exposes the investor to default risk because there is a chance of default, albeit small, in which the remaining net spread payments terminate and any remaining P&L is lost. This is often referred to as the risky value of a basis point. For example, a 10 bp profit a year, due for four years, from buying protection at 40 and

(continued)

TABLE 5.2   (*continued*)

Technical Factors	
	selling it at 50 may be paid for only one year if the company defaults at the end of year 1. This implies that CDS investors would require a higher spread as compensation relative to cash investors, hence widening CDS relative to cash.
Convertible bond issuance and arbitrage	CDS are driven wider by convertible bond hedge funds looking to unlock cheap equity volatility by stripping convertible bonds into their debt and equity option components, which involves buying protection in the CDS market.

Market Factors	
Option to fund via repo market	Investors can fund a bond position using either normal on-balance sheet funding at the issuer's borrowing rate, or in the repo[a] market. The cheaper alternative is usually chosen. This is an advantage of cash over CDS (as CDS cannot be "repoed out") and so tightens bond spreads relative to CDS.
Easier to short credit via CDS market	A negative view in credit can be expressed in two ways: either short the bond or buy CDS protection. Due to the illiquidity of most corporate bonds, in the repo market, they can be hard to find and uneconomical to trade if the are "special" (i.e., if there is high demand to short). Hence, buying protection via CDS may be preferable, and this demand drives CDS spreads wider. Banks, in particular, buy large amounts of protection on companies to which they have loan exposures.
Liquidity	If bonds are perceived to be more liquid than the CDSs (i.e., huge amount outstanding or recently issued bonds) then bonds can trade tighter and CDS spreads can be wider as a result of liquidity premiums.

[a] *Repo* stands for repurchase agreement: An investor essentially borrows by agreeing to purchase the bond at a later stage for a slightly higher price (in line with a collateralized borrowing rate). If the bond is "general collateral," the cost is usually very close to LIBOR (and capped by the borrower's own funding rate). If, however, the collateral is in high demand (i.e., it trades "special"), it can have a sub-LIBOR repo rate (i.e., the bond lender gets rewarded for lending the collateral because it is in high demand).

Source: Citigroup.

TABLE 5.3 Guide to Key Basis Drivers—Factors that Decrease CDS Spreads and/or Increase Asset Swap Spreads Are Good for Positive Basis Trades and Bad for Negative Basis Trades

Technical Factors	
CDSs are funded at LIBOR flat	Most market participants fund above LIBOR. For such investors, selling protection (which implies LIBOR funding) is cheaper than buying the asset at a funding rate over LIBOR, and so helps tighten CDS.
CDS are off balance sheet	As CDS are unfunded transactions, they do not appear on the balance sheet. This makes them a more attractive way for some investors to take credit exposure (by selling protection) and drives CDS spreads tighter.
Counterparty risk	A cash bond is a direct agreement between the issuer and the bondholder, involving no other credit risk. A CDS, in contrast, is an over-the-counter bilateral agreement between two parties, deriving value from the creditworthiness of a reference entity. This adds counterparty credit risk to the transaction, which is disadvantageous to the protection buyer, who pays a lower premium as a result. The higher the correlation between the protection seller and the reference entity, the more counterparty risk and tighter the CDS spread will be. Note that this risk can be greatly reduced by using credit-linked notes rather than CDS.
Bonds trading above par[a]	Other things being equal, the risk on a bond is its dirty price, while for CDS, the notional at risk is based on 100. This means that bonds trading above par have more cash at risk and hence a higher spread than equivalent CDS protection. This decreases the CDS spread and widens the bond spread, as the bonds start to trade increasingly above par.
Credit-contingent interest rate risk	In an asset swap, the asset buyer is exposed to an unknown mark-to-market on the interest rate swap in the event of default. The buyer may demand a wider asset swap spread as compensation for this risk.
Market Factors	
CSO^b issuance drives CDS spreads tighter (as the Street covers its technical short[c])	The huge market for synthetic CDOs has resulted in an excess of protection sellers on a broad range of credits in the default swap market. This abundance of protection sellers (investors going long via portfolio products) causes CDS spreads to tighten.

(continued)

TABLE 5.3 (*continued*)

Market Factors	
Liquidity	If the CDS is perceived to be more liquid than the bond, then investors will accept a lower CDS spread for taking on the credit risk, driving CDS spreads tighter relative to bonds. Liquidity in default swaps is often better than that for cash at the standard three- and five-year maturities when comparing the same notional sizes, especially in some smaller names.
Cash funding risk	Cash positions funded by repos cannot usually lock in a repo rate for a considerable amount of time (for instance, for more than one month). This exposes the investors to new repo rates as they roll over each month. CDSs, however, are unfunded and implicitly lock in a LIBOR flat funding rate over the whole tenor of the CDS. Investors may be content going long with a lower CDS spread as a result.

[a]Furthermore, a par asset swap created from a premium bond has a higher asset swap spread because of the implicit leverage (funding the premium at LIBOR) in the structure.
[b]CSO = Synthetic CDO, a CDO structured using CDS rather than bonds.
[c]In the cash market, credit investors are typically long credit, and it is the issuing company on the other side of the transaction that is "technically short" the credit risk. In the OTC CDS market, for every investor that is short there is another that is long. For supply to meet demand, there is an equilibrium market price: If people want to go long credit, the spreads tighten, and if people want to go short credit the spreads widen. Recently, an increasing number of investors have been going long credit by buying tranches of synthetic CDOs. Due to the significant sizes of these transactions (typically in excess of 1 billion), a significant technical short is created within the community of issuing banks. In turn, these issuing banks fill this technical short by going long credit in the single-name market, and in doing so drive credit spreads tighter, until the supply meets demand.
Source: Citigroup.

cost more. Furthermore, the basis (CDS − ASW) is the level of carry for only those investors who can borrow at LIBOR flat, while most leveraged investors fund at LIBOR plus a spread, X, which reduces the carry of the trade to CDS − ASW − X.

Trading the Basis

When trading the basis, the investor has some alternatives on how to structure the trade: Default-neutral, duration-neutral, or par-for-par. All three are mutually exclusive in that you cannot be default-neutral and duration-neutral at the same time. Default-neutral is when the notional on

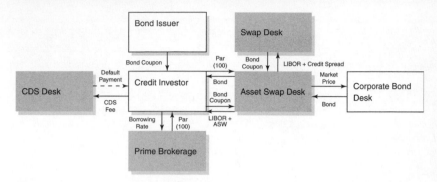

FIGURE 5.8 Sequence of Cash Flows Associated with Entering Unfunded Basis Trade on a Fixed-Rate Bond
Source: Citigroup.

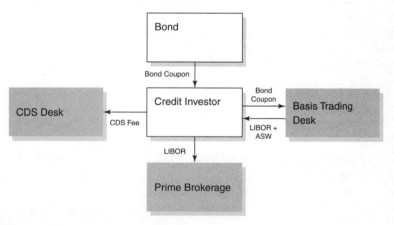

FIGURE 5.9 Hypothetical Cash Flows on Holding a Basis Trade to Maturity in a Nondefault Scenario
Source: Citigroup.

the CDS matches the full price of the bond and so in the event of default one loses nothing. Duration-neutral involves buying the correct ratio of notionals such that the package is insulated from parallel shifts in spreads. This weighting may offer positive convexity when the spread convexity of the bond is greater than the spread convexity of the CDS position. Par-for-par involves buying a bond at full price and buying a CDS on the corresponding amount of notional. This trade is not entirely default-neutral for bonds that trade away from par, but often has a higher carry for negative basis trades as explained earlier.

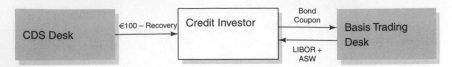

FIGURE 5.10   Default Scenario—Investor Receives €100 in Exchange for the Defaulted Bond but Must Honor Asset Swap Leg until Maturity or Sell the Asset Swap at the Current Market Price
Source: Citigroup.

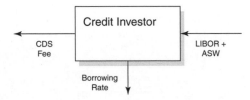

FIGURE 5.11   Net-Net the Investor Receives a Carry of CDS Minus ASW and Funding over LIBOR, to the Earlier of Default or Maturity
Source: Citigroup.

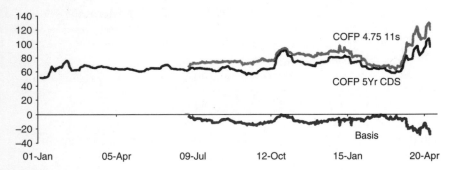

FIGURE 5.12   An Example of a Negative Basis Trade on Casino from Our Model Portfolio TotalCredit, April 21, 2005
Extract from *TotalCredit*, April 21, 2005 (Citigroup publication): "A negative basis! And, oddly, in a rather risky sector like French retail. While not on our list of LBO candidates, this is a name for which a merger or an LBO has been mooted as a possibility (Bloomberg, April 8). If this were to gain even the slightest credence, we would look for CDS to move sharply wider than the bonds: Buy five-year CDS protection on COFP at 87 bp versus buying COFP €4.75% 2011 at 94 bp."
Source: Citigroup.

A New Spread Measure: C-Spread

Investors often complain that when it comes to bonds trading significantly away from par, asset swap spreads cease to be a representative measure of credit risk. As such, the regular basis (CDS minus the asset swap spread) is misleading. To this end, a number of market participants have introduced a probability-adjusted basis, which compares bonds and CDSs in an entirely consistent fashion by directly comparing the default probabilities from the bond market with those from the CDS market. See Figure 5.12.

DEBT-EQUITY TRADES

Debt-equity trades, also somewhat misleadingly known as *capital structure arbitrage* trades, were first suggested by the theoretical link established by Robert Merton in 1974. Nowadays, either on the basis of a variant of his model or through a method of scenario analysis, these trades involve some combination of cash equities and equity options against credit spreads.

Meet the Models

The modeling of debt versus equity, even for some of the most complex models in the market, still involves only variants of Merton's original model. These models are collectively called *structural models* because they are formed on an economic framework rather than on no-arbitrage pricing assumptions. In such models, the value of a firm is considered to be the sum of the debt plus equity of the company, and the definition of default is the accountant's version: when the amount the company owes (debt) is greater than the company's market value (equity).

Hence, the firm's equity is viewed as a call option on the firm's assets with a strike at the face value of the outstanding debt. If the firm's asset value falls below the face value of the debt (default boundary) at maturity, the company defaults, with equity holders receiving nothing. Conversely, any market value in excess of the outstanding debt can be viewed as payoff for the equity holders. If we assume, as Merton did, that the firm's asset value follows a lognormal distribution,[10] the probability that the asset value crosses the default boundary (i.e., the probability of default) can be easily determined. This requires several inputs: equity price, leverage ratio (debt to equity), equity volatility, and the assumption that the capital structure does not change through time—hence the name *capital structure arbitrage*. Given these inputs, an equity-derived probability of default (and hence, albeit indirectly, credit spread) can be calculated. If this credit spread is out of line with market spreads, one can be traded against the other.

One of the main failures of Merton's original model is that the short-term default probabilities imputed by it are lower than historical default rates realized in the actual market. This is because the diffusion process is a function of the square root of time.

One approach to overcoming this is to try to improve on the assumption that default can take place only at maturity of the debt. Instead a default barrier (level of debt) is introduced with its own lognormal stochastic process, where the credit defaults as soon as the asset value touches the barrier. This approach does, however, require the volatility of the distribution to be calibrated to observed spreads. A well-known commercial model, CreditGrades, subscribes to this approach.

Another approach is to assume the firm's asset value follows a lognormal distribution but this time with an overlaid jump-to-default process. The jump-to-default process follows a Poisson distribution, such that whenever a random jump occurs, the company defaults, similar to randomness observed in real life. Again, one has to calibrate the frequency of these random jumps through an intensity parameter in the Poisson process equation. The few hedge funds that do subscribe to a model often use this one.

KMV-Moody's approach is the most popular of the commercial models. It uses a regular Merton model but with debt fixed at 100 percent of short-term debt and 50 percent of long-term debt. This leaves equity prices and equity volatility as the moving parts of the model. This is precisely what is needed to estimate default probabilities from the equity market's movements. The KMV-Moody method then maps the distance to default (number of standard deviations the asset value of the firm is from the default boundary) to historical default probabilities for companies in a certain distance-to-default bucket. This gives more realistic default probabilities, especially in the short term.

Citigroup takes yet another approach with the hybrid probability default (HPD) model. This model combines a Merton model with other financial information regarding a firm's ability to avoid default in times of economic stress, such as the size of the firm, its profitability, and the net income. This model has had slightly better results than KMV in accurately predicting defaults. For further details please see *HPD Models: A Practical Approach to Modeling Default Risk* by Sobehart and Keenan, Citigroup, October 2003.

The Debt-Equity Cycle

Most traders, though, do not follow their models slavishly. They complement the models either with scenario analysis or with some intuitive observations about the leverage cycle.

In general, credit spreads, equity volatility, and equity prices usually move together, except during periods of violent changes in leverage. This

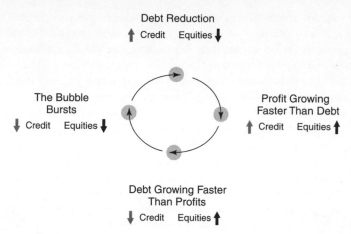

FIGURE 5.13 The Debt-Equity Cycle
Source: Citigroup.

can be easily understood through the concept of the leverage cycle (see Figure 5.13).

At 12 o'clock on the cycle, companies deleverage the hard way, by means of asset disposals and bond tenders, in an active attempt to mend their balance sheets. As a result, credit rallies as creditworthiness increases, while equities sell off as a result of the reduction in gearing. The most recent period of significant deleveraging was between October 2002 and March 2003.

Since then, the divergences between credit and equities have been short-lived as we enter the 3 o'clock phase of the cycle, where profits start growing faster than debt. In this phase, credit continues to rally as companies deleverage the easy way—by growing out of their debt as equities rally thanks to increased profits.

The worry, especially for credit investors, is that the next stop in the cycle is the 6 o'clock position, where companies start to lever up again (through debt-financed M&A, share buybacks, or capital expenditures) to boost prospects for future earnings. While equity investors reap the rewards of the higher gearing, credit spreads widen, reflecting the progressive deterioration of balance sheet quality.

The 6 o'clock phase of the credit cycle is clearly unsustainable, and sooner or later the bubble bursts, resulting in a sell-off in equities and credit at the 9 o'clock phase.

A Practical Hurdle or Two

Even taking account of the cycle, though, practical limitations tend to limit the usefulness of the pure models.

Options on *assets* do not exist, so they have to be proxied by options on equity. The volatility of a far out-of-the-money (OTM) option[11] is what Merton models associate with default probabilities, and hence makes comparable to the default component of credit spreads. This has two problems. First, the default component of a spread increases dramatically as one goes lower down the rating curve (crossover and high-yield names), which are often relatively illiquid. Second, liquidity of far OTM options is extremely poor, and the steep volatility smile makes these options expensive. These liquidity issues, together with the many theoretical objections to the models, make the original concept of capital structure trading difficult. Instead, investors tend to focus on volatilities at the 80 to 90 percent strike, knowing full well that these volatilities are less representative of default risk, as the options are far from the default barrier. Despite these necessary departures from the theory, many investors still feel that the opportunities are sufficient to justify debt-equity trading.

Debt-Equity Trading in Practice—Arbitrage or Mirage?

Roughly speaking, there are three distinct approaches to debt-equity trading.

Some investors whose mandates prevent them from trading equity products like to use debt-equity signals as early warning indicators. This approach is particularly popular among loan portfolio managers, where the debt-equity model serves as an alternative mark-to-market on names where accurate marks of the loans themselves will simply be unavailable. The trouble with this approach is that where debt and equity pricing diverge, it is seldom clear which market is right and which is wrong. Investors may sell a loan on the back of a debt-equity signal, only to find that loan spreads remain unchanged and that it is the equity (or equity volatility) market that rallies back instead. The two other approaches to trading therefore focus on trading relative value between the two markets, not on assuming that one or the other market is ahead.

The second approach relies on monitoring the debt and equity signals on a great many names, and trying to trade on discrepancies. But even here, one has always to dig deeper to understand why such divergences take place. For instance, the prospect of a company levering up for a debt-financed acquisition typically results in credit selling off, and equities potentially rallying, on the prospect of acquisitive growth (provided management has not overpaid for companies in the past). The credit and equity hence decouple. The art is to establish how much of the decoupling is due to the change in leverage and how much is not, whether it will continue to decouple and for how long. While models can help a great deal in answering these questions, they often depend heavily on fundamental inputs—such as forecasts of where leverage at a company may go—or assumptions about the level of volatility and the volatility smile.

The third approach is mainly event-driven and tends to work best around the time of possible corporate actions, such as acquisitions, takeovers, share buybacks, or leveraged buyouts (LBOs), where dramatic changes in leverage often send markets in opposite directions—thereby reducing the impact of inaccuracies in hedge ratio estimation. This approach does follow the spirit of the Merton model but not its mathematical detail. Some investors use a "scenario analysis" methodology to analyze the estimated relative prices of bonds, equities, and equity options under different circumstances. Sometimes the Merton calculations will not even feature in the analysis, with historical regressions frequently taking their place.

Deciding What to Trade

Deciding on what trade to put on is not a trivial exercise in this multiasset space. There are numerous combinations of bonds, convertibles, CDSs, and credit swaptions, all with a variety of maturities and subordination that can be traded against stocks, equity options, variance swaps, and equity default swaps, again with a variety of maturities and strikes.

To be very basic: A good premise for any trade is to structure it to maximize profit if you are right and simultaneously minimize loss if you are wrong. Depending on how strong the view, one can focus more on the former than the latter. For instance, in today's low-default environment, many debt-equity traders are willing to take on downside risk (tail risk) and trade debt versus cash equity, rather than buy downside protection on the equity leg through a call option.

There are others who still prefer to trade debt versus equity volatility (though not as OTM as Merton suggested) but, more often than not, fail to isolate the equity volatility by delta hedging the option, instead being happy to sit on a naked option position that will vary in value as stock price and equity volatility change (they are exposed to delta and vega risk). One reason behind this is that implied equity volatility is often asymmetric—a large downward move in stock price tends to cause implied volatilities to increase more than a large upward move in stock price. This makes some traders comfortable with selling CDS protection against buying a naked put. If the credit deteriorates, you lose money on the credit leg but can gain on the equity: first by the put being in-the-money, and second by the increase in implied volatility. Debt-equity traders have to battle constantly with the likely scenarios and multiple ways of putting on the same trade.

A Recovery Trade

A further trade that is worth mentioning because of its increasing popularity is the debt-equity recovery trade. As the name suggests, it is relevant for companies with a significant chance of default. It involves selling credit default protection today,[12] and using the entire proceeds, in present value terms, to buy out-of-the-money equity put options. There are two possible outcomes:

In the case of no default, the trade is zero carry from a present value perspective. There is a timing mismatch, in that all the money for the equity put options is spent up front, whereas proceeds from selling credit protection are received quarterly. That said, some dealers are willing to trade CDSs with points up front. Furthermore, there may be some upside even when there is no default if the equity option expires in-the-money due to a decline in stock price (without default). Otherwise, the investor breaks even from a present value perspective.

In the event of a default trigger, the investor owes the notional amount of CDS, less recovery on bonds delivered (for instance, €1 million notional minus recovery). The investor also receives the strike price on the equity put, less the actual stock price, times the number of puts, times 100 (a typical equity put contract has 100 shares). For example, if the stock price were to fall to 0.75[13] in default, the investor would receive the following: $(\text{strike} - 0.75)^{€} \times (\text{number of puts}) \times 100$. We then set the two cash flows equal to each other and solve for a break-even recovery rate as:

$$1\,\text{million} - \text{break-even recovery} = (\text{strike} - 0.75) \times (\text{number of puts}) \times 100$$

If recovery exceeds break-even, the investor makes money. If recovery is less than the break-even value, the investor loses money. Assuming a typical recovery value in the range of 40 to 55 percent, break-even recovery values in the mid-1930s or lower look attractive from the perspective of selling credit default protection and buying equity put options. Similarly, break-even recovery values above 70 percent look attractive for buying credit default protection and selling equity put options.

ITRAXX CREDIT INDEXES

The unified CDS indexes (resulting from merger between iBoxx and Trac-X) have been heralded as the most significant development in the credit markets since the invention of the credit default swap. Since their arrival in June 2004, Dow Jones iTraxx in Europe and Asia and Dow Jones CDX in the United States and emerging markets have become the most liquid credit products in the world, as evidenced by the collapse of bid-offer spreads.[14]

This boom in liquidity has, in part, been driven by the 19 largest investment banks participating as market makers for the standardized indexes, but also by strong two-way demand across a diversified set of end users. Today, iTraxx and CDX indexes are used by loan portfolio managers to (partially) hedge credit exposure, by correlation desks to control their spread risk, by corporate issuers to help lock in today's credit spreads, and most of all by credit investors, both to hedge existing cash credit exposures, and increasingly to take credit exposure at both the market and sector level. The indexes have also fueled significant growth in second-generation standardized credit derivatives such as index tranches, first-to-default (FTD) baskets, and options. Further still, the imminent arrival of the iTraxx futures contract and a daily market-standard fixing of credit spreads on indexes (similar to LIBOR fixing) are tipped to herald the final steps in the commoditization of the credit markets.

Truly Global

The global indexes are split into three regions—Europe, the United States, and Asia—as well as emerging markets. The participating banks that provide liquidity in these indexes are largely the same, but the indexes and traded subsectors do differ among markets.

In Europe, iTraxx Europe is now the main investment-grade index for CDSs (see Figure 5.14). It is an equiweighted index consisting of solely European names that are selected by a dealer poll based on volume rankings, and it requires a certain number of names in each sector: financials (senior and subordinated), nonfinancials, autos, consumer (cyclicals and noncyclicals), energy, industrials, and TMT (Telecommunications, Media, and Technology). The HiVol index comprises the 30 names in the Europe index with the widest credit default swap spreads. It was given the name HiVol based on the conjecture that a credit with a wider spread is likely to have higher spread volatility than one with a lower spread.

Lower down the rating spectrum, the iTraxx Crossover comprises the 35 most liquid nonfinancial European names rated BBB/Baa3 or lower and on "negative outlook."

A less popular European index that was introduced for the benefit of asset managers who wanted to track/hedge cash portfolios is the iTraxx Corporate index, which comprises the largest, most liquid nonfinancial names from the iTraxx European Corporate bond index, including non-European names. Unlike the other iTraxx indexes, which are equiweighted, the Corporate index names are the same weighted by the "duration value ×omething market value amounts"[15] that the issuers have in the iBoxx cash bond indexes.

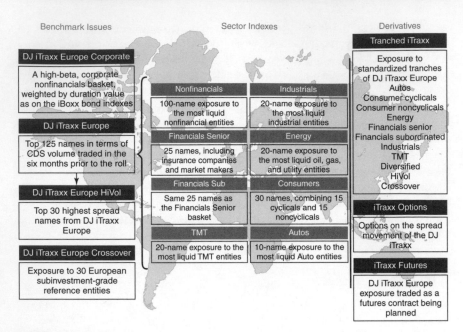

FIGURE 5.14 iTraxx Credit Indexes—The European Platform
Source: Dow Jones iTraxx.

For the most part, iTraxx indexes and sectors trade in an unfunded format with both 5- and 10-year maturities, with the exception of the Corporate index, which trades in a five-year maturity only. That said, for those who need it, funded notes are also available for five-year maturities for the DJ iTraxx Europe, Corporate, and Crossover indexes, and permit the taking of both long and short positions.

Details of the U.S. and Asia platforms can be found on www.iTraxx. com, which is an excellent (free) web site for anyone interested in the latest iTraxx constituents, historical spreads, and other information.

You've Got to Roll with It

As with all indexes, iTraxx indexes change their constituents on preset dates referred to as *roll dates*, which occur twice a year on March 20 and September 20.

On the roll, some names drop out and others take their place based on a dealer poll of the most liquid names. The old iTraxx series continues to trade, but is not seen as representing the credit landscape as well as does the new iTraxx series; as a result, liquidity builds up in the on-the-run index and falls in the just-off-the-run series.

On these roll dates, it is difficult to tell which names will replace others in the index, and therefore it is difficult to tell whether the index will trade tighter or wider than with the previous series. In contrast, most cash indexes change composition every month, based on a list of criteria (to do with rating, maturity, amount outstanding, and other factors) rather than a dealer poll. In general,[16] cash indexes tighten during this change of composition, as names that have lost their investment-grade rating or have defaulted drop out and no longer contribute their wide spread to the index. This effect can also occur for the iTraxx roll. However, during a period of no defaults or fallen angels, the liquid names that are added to the indexes tend to be wider credits than the less interesting, highly rated, low-spread credits that tend to drop out. So, the new series may trade wider than the new series purely due to compositional changes rather than any deterioration in the credit markets. Anecdotal evidence also suggests that net positions play a part. If investors are by and large short the old index, then rolling this short into the new index causes the new index to widen versus the old index, requiring a look at where iTraxx is trading versus its intrinsics.

iTraxx Intrinsics

Today, each iTraxx index trades like a commodity and has a price that depends on the supply-and-demand dynamics of the market. This can create opportunities, as the weighted-average spread of the constituent names of the index (we call this the intrinsic spread) does not necessarily have to equal the traded spread of the index. To this end, the spread to intrinsics (difference between the traded spread and theoretical intrinsic spread) is a useful indicator of positions, sentiment, and at times relative value opportunities.

When the index is trading wide to its intrinsic spread, it tends to signal that people have bought protection to hedge their single-name positions. This may indicate a net short position, and is thus a technical positive for the market: The difference between traded and intrinsic levels is mean reverting, and tends to move in the same direction as the market itself, that is, falling when spreads fall (rally) and vice versa.

In addition to being an overall market signal, the spread to intrinsics (others may call it the *skew*) for the various indexes and sectors can also be traded outright, by buying the "cheap" index versus selling the constituents when the index trades abnormally wide to intrinsics, and vice versa when it is abnormally tight. That said, the spread to intrinsics, although mean reverting for indexes such as iTraxx Europe, can often have significant volatility, making the mark-to-market on such trades far from the arbitrage it looks on paper. This is one of the reasons we think a finite spread to

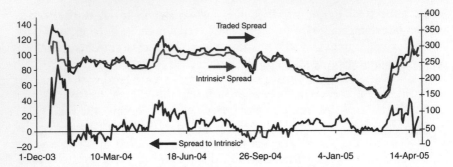

FIGURE 5.15 iTraxx Intrinsics[a] for the Crossover Index[b]

[a]iTraxx Intrinsics compares traded index spreads and theoretical spreads given the index constituents. To build up a history of traded spread to intrinsics, we use the three-month roll back into previous iBoxx/iTraxx contracts.

[b]Whenever one looks at a time series of iTraxx spreads, it is important to realize that on the roll dates spread changes can have large contributions from the change of constituents rather than genuine market movements.

Source: Citigroup.

intrinsics persistently exists. The Crossover index, for example, has almost always traded wide to its intrinsic value (see Figure 5.15), and has a larger absolute difference to intrinsics than the high-grade indexes (see Table 5.4). We suspect this is because in this part of the market investors like to choose their favorite "rising stars"—rather than buying the whole market—and

TABLE 5.4 iTraxx Spreads for the Indices and Sectors, Close of April 14, 2005 (basis points)

	Traded	Intrinsic[a]	Difference
iTraxx Europe	40.5	40.2	0.3
ITraxx Crossover	281.0	258.6	22.4
iTraxx HiVol	77.0	77.3	−0.3
iTraxx Autos	58.0	65.0	−7.0
iTraxx Industrials	48.0	47.2	0.8
iTraxx TMT	39.0	39.2	−0.2
iTraxx Energy	29.5	28.2	1.3
iTraxx Consumers	53.0	56.3	−3.3
iTraxx Financials	19.0	17.8	1.2
iTraxx Sub Financials	32.0	28.9	3.1

[a]Intrinsic spread = the weighted-average spread of the constituent names of the index.

Source: Citigroup.

because the higher bid-offers on these wider names make the difference harder to arbitrage.

What Happens When a Name Defaults?

An iTraxx contract can be purchased in an unfunded form (known as a CDS) or in a funded form (known as a note). If a name in the iTraxx index defaults, the resolution differs depending on which type of contract is involved.

In CDS form, settlement is physical. The protection seller has to pay the protection buyer the index weighting multiplied by the face value of the CDS in exchange for a deliverable obligation with the same face value. Going forward, the protection buyer pays a spread based on a smaller face value (the initial notional − notional of the defaulted name). It is worth noting that some names, such as Nokia, have no outstanding bonds, and hence a loan would have to be delivered into the contract.

In note form, settlement is by cash. Here, the protection seller has to pay the protection buyer (100 − recovery on a pari passu reference obligation on the credit) × the index weighting × the face value of the note.

Equiweighted or Not

Although the CDS indexes are generally perceived to be equiweighted in spread terms as well as default terms, the former is not strictly true. In actual fact, spreads on the iTraxx indexes are Risky DV01−weighted to account for the dollar value of a 1 bp move in the underlying CDS curve for each name. This has the effect of reducing the weighting of a credit when it trades at very high near-default spreads (for argument's sake, greater than 1,000 bp), such that the index is not ostensibly high because of one name trading at a very high spread. For most investment-grade spreads (roughly less than 400 bp), this DV01 weighting simply results in near equal weighting for all the names in the index—hence the general perception that they are equiweighted in spreads as well. A more apt description would be that they are equiweighted[17] in default and Risky DV01−weighted for spreads.

Second-Generation Products: iTraxx Tranches

One of the most startling effects of the advent of iTraxx indexes has been the resultant growth in the liquidity of CDO tranches, fueled by the iTraxx tranches now providing a standardized and liquid hedge for default correlation. Despite their greater complexity, index tranches have quickly moved into the mainstream of credit trading, and thanks to the numerous benefits they offer—from cheaper premium-to-spread exposure to the ability to separate default risk from spread risk—we think that popularity is here to stay.

Oddly enough, the mechanically simpler standardized FTD baskets have not been blessed with the same popularity; bespoke FTDs are still the most popular. These were designed for investors who want to go long particular credits and would like to enhance the spread they get by selling FTD protection on a basket, say, of five names. The trouble is, everyone has different views on the names they are comfortable with. The standardized tranches have, in fact, increased the trading volumes in FTDs as investors now know roughly what these products should cost by looking at the standardized prices. On the dealer side, FTDs are a great way for dealers to reduce exposure they have from bespoke tranches.

CREDIT OPTIONS

Just as the iTraxx indexes have greatly improved liquidity in the single-name and tranche markets, so iTraxx options have given a boost to the nascent credit options market. Options are an ideal tool for expressing views on the volatility of credit spreads and for leveraging exposure to single names.

The so-called credit option is actually a European swaption, as it is the right to enter a credit default swap at a specified spread (the strike) at a specified date (the expiry). Investors familiar with equity options may like to draw comparisons between credit and equity options by thinking of credit spreads as the underlying rather than the stock price.

A payer option is the right to buy CDS protection at a specified level at some date in the future. Buying a payer implies a bearish view on credit—investors make money if spreads widen.

A receiver option is the right to sell CDS protection at a specified level at some date in the future. Buying a receiver implies a bullish view on credit—buyers of receivers make money if spreads tighten. Figures 5.16 and 5.17 summarize how credit options are used to express views on spreads.

It's a Knockout

Perhaps surprisingly, most options on single names have a knockout provision,[18] which means that they terminate worthless if the underlying name defaults before the expiry date of the option. In high-grade, this is not so important, but in high-yield this could have serious implications. If you buy payers and they start to be seriously in-the-money, we suggest you make sure to sell them before any default!

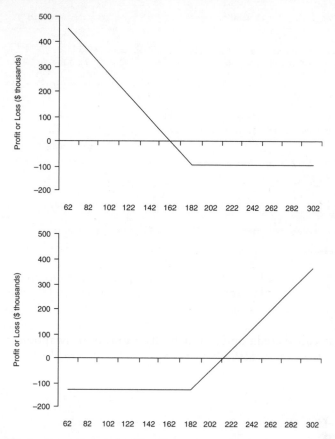

FIGURE 5.16 Buy Receiver (top) When Bullish and Buy a Payer (bottom) When Bearish
Source: Citigroup.

Index options, however, do not have a knockout provision. In the event that one of the names in the index defaults, recovery on that name is paid to the option holder if the option holder exercises the option at expiry. However, on exercise of the option, the spread-to-strike paid/received is based a smaller notional (i.e., the original notional minus the defaulted notional). See Figure 5.18.

Effect of Convexity on Credit Option Payoffs

Although the payoff at expiry for an equity option depends only on the difference between the underlying asset (i.e., the stock) price and the strike,

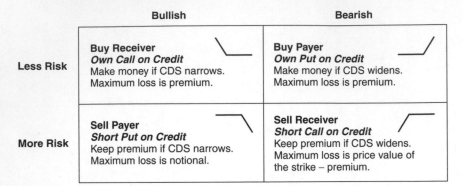

	Bullish	Bearish
Less Risk	**Buy Receiver** *Own Call on Credit* Make money if CDS narrows. Maximum loss is premium.	**Buy Payer** *Own Put on Credit* Make money if CDS widens. Maximum loss is premium.
More Risk	**Sell Payer** *Short Put on Credit* Keep premium if CDS narrows. Maximum loss is notional.	**Sell Receiver** *Short Call on Credit* Keep premium if CDS widens. Maximum loss is price value of the strike – premium.

FIGURE 5.17 Using Credit Options to Express Bullish and Bearish Views in Credit[a]

[a]One way to remember the names of these options is to relate them to a put or call on credit spreads. A *payer* is a call on credit spreads such that you have a positive payoff when you have the right to *pay* the strike spread even when the market requires a higher spread. A *receiver* is a put on credit spreads such that you have a positive payoff when credit spreads tighten below the strike, and you have the right to *receive* the credit spread at the strike.
Source: Citigroup.

	Bullish	Bearish
Less Risk	**Buy Receiver** Lose premium.	**Buy Payer** If no knockout, earn (100 – Recovery)% × notional – premium. If knockout, lose premium.
More Risk	**Sell Payer** If no knockout, lose (100 – Recovery)% × notional – premium. If knockout, keep premium.	**Sell Receiver** Keep premium.

FIGURE 5.18 Single-Name Option Profit/Loss in the Event of Default
Source: Citigroup.

credit swaption payoffs are dependent on the DV01 of the underlying CDS. This is because the option is struck in spread terms rather than on price, and the DV01 upon the expiry of the option (the "forward DV01") converts from spread terms to dollar value. For example, suppose the investor buys an at-the-money June 2004 payer option for a premium of 40 cents. If the DV01 of the five-year credit default swap in June 2004 is 4.5 (4,500 per $10 million notional), then the investor makes money if the single-name

CDS widens by more than 40 cents divided by 4.5, or about 9 bp. Thus, if the underlying spread were 70 bp today, then the investor makes money if spreads widen to more than 79 bp.

Alternatively, suppose the investor were to sell an at-the-money June 2004 receiver option struck at 65 bp for a premium of 15 cents and the underlying credit default swap were to tighten all the way to zero. The amount that the investor would lose is 65 bp times the 4.5 forward DV01 minus the 15-cent premium, or about 278 cents.

Those familiar with options on corporate (cash) bonds may wonder why the DV01 conversion is not necessary on those options. This is because options on corporate bonds trade in dollar price, not spread, so no conversion is necessary.

Delta-Exchange

When buying and selling options via a dealer, a concept called *delta-exchange* can make options a little cheaper. This involves buying the combined package of an option with a delta (D) amount of its underlying CDS at a cheaper cost than buying the two separately and paying the bid-ask each time. Dealers are generally happy to make tight markets when options are bought or sold with delta-exchange, as this does not leave them with a net long (or short) position as can be seen:

- Buy payer, sell protection on D percent. Sell payer, buy protection on D percent.
- Buy receiver, buy protection on D percent. Sell receiver, sell protection on D percent

Investors who buy or sell an option for a directional view would not want an option with delta-exchange. Nevertheless, a route that some investors are taking is to still buy the option with delta-exchange and "sell on" the unwanted protection.

Why Sell an Option (Riskier Strategy) Rather Than Buy One?

First, because buying an option has a cost. In selling an option, the investor receives an up-front premium for taking on some downside risk. Provided the investor is attentive to the credit, hedging CDSs by selling an option may provide sufficient cushion to unwind a position if need be before it loses money.

Second, selling an option expresses a view on potential spread movement that is different from buying one. If the investor sells a receiver option, he or she has taken an implicit view that spreads will not tighten dramatically. If spreads do tighten, the investor could suffer large losses, as shown in the payoff diagram in the bottom left of Figure 5.18. Similarly, a slight widening in spreads for an at-the-money option can provide upside similar to a significant widening in spreads: The most the investor can earn is the option premium. So the upside is capped, while the downside is extensive. In short, investors who believe that spreads will trade in a narrower range ought to sell options rather than buy them.

Option Strategies

Apart from taking leveraged views on credit spreads, options can also be used to take views on spread volatility and spread correlation (dispersion). The higher the volatility of a CDS spread, the greater the likelihood that an option written on that spread will finish-in-the money. Investors who have a view on CDS spread volatility, but no directional view, may wish to consider buying a straddle. Figure 5.19 shows payoff profiles for long and short straddles. A buyer of a straddle takes a view that underlying CDS volatility will be greater between now and expiry of the option contract than implied by its cost. In practice, if the CDS spread moves away from the strike by more than the premium divided by the forward DV01, then the buyer of an at-the-money straddle makes money. Conversely, a seller of a straddle believes that a firm's CDS spread will be less volatile than the current implied volatility between now and expiry of the options contract.

Dispersion trades, which are common in equities, involve trading spread volatility of index constituents versus the volatility of the index spread itself. If spreads on the constituent names move together (i.e., are highly correlated) then the volatility of the index as a whole will be quite large and comparable to the weighted-average volatility of the individual constituents. Conversely, when credit spreads of the constituents move in opposite directions (low or negative correlation) the spread movements cancel out each other, resulting in an index spread volatility considerably less than the weighted-average spread volatility of the individual constituents. Investors who buy index volatility versus single-name volatility are hence long spread correlation. Such trades are now becoming possible in credit, thanks to the growth in the single-name CDS options market and the advent of tradable iTraxx/CDX indexes. When the whole market sells off or rallies, the correlation in the market is very high, compared with periods when some names rally and some names sell off (see Figure 5.20). Entering a dispersion trade where one is long correlation for a three-month horizon could be a good strategy for monetizing the possibility of these markets moving together, without being long or short credit in the process.

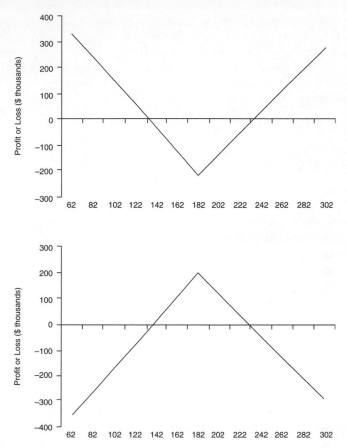

FIGURE 5.19 Buying a Straddle (top) and Selling a Straddle (bottom)
Source: Citigroup.

Strategies such as trading the skew (i.e., buying and selling spread volatility at different strikes or expiries) are possible but uncommon in the credit options market. This is because of a smaller number of expiries that trade (see Figure 5.21) and relatively few strikes that are liquid. This situation should change as the credit options market in Europe matures.

The 20th of March, June, September, and December are the standard expiry dates for options. At any given time, only options expiring at the closest expiry date (referred to as the front contract) and the one after that (the back contract) are liquid. Hence, the trader's run (sent in April 2005) gives quotes only for the June 2005 and September 2005 contracts. Furthermore, strikes are quoted at certain round figures, so even though the

FIGURE 5.20   Heat Map of a Market with High Positive Correlation (left) and
Low Correlation (right)
Each rectangle is a bond and collectively they make up the entire European credit
market. When the rectangle is lighter, bonds spreads are tightening, and when it is
darker, spreads are selling off. The picture on the left shows the whole market selling
off (that is, correlated) over the month of March 2005, while the picture on the
right shows some spreads rallying and others selling off, implying less correlation in
February 2005.
Source: Citigroup.

```
                          Recvr    Straddle   Payer
              --->          35         40       45    <--- strikes
Europe                      5/9      34/41    10/16    Jun05 (57/64% ATM implied vol;
spot @ 40    (Jun10)       8/13      49/58    22/29    Sep05 (51/58%)

              --->          70         80       90    <---
HiVol                     25/32      79/91    16/24    Jun05 (69/77%)
spot @ 73    (Jun10)      31/42    107/130    38/50    Sep05 (62/72%)

              --->         250        280      310    <---
Crossover                 62/81    264/300   95/115    Jun05 (70/77%)
spot @ 275   (Jun10)     84/110    367/425  176/209    Sep05 (61/69%)
```

All prices in cents up front, assuming delta-exchange at spot.

FIGURE 5.21   A Screenshot of a Credit Option Trader's Run on April 22, 2005,
at 3:51 P.M.
Source: Citigroup.

HiVol market is at 73 bp, which implies a three-month forward of 76 bp,
the at-the-money option the trader is making a market in has a strike of 80
in this instance. The at-the-money volatility of 69/77 percent refers to the
strike at 80. The trader is also offering options at the 70 and 90 strikes. To
buy a June 2005 receiver with a strike at 70 bp, on a notional of €10 million
would cost €32,000, assuming delta-exchange.

Portfolio Credit Derivatives

Single-Tranche CDOs

Jure Skarabot
Ratul Roy
Ji-Hoon Ryu

T he single-tranche collateralized debt obligation (STCDO) product represents one of the more recent examples of tranched credit products. It gives investors exposure to a customized slice of the credit risk of a reference portfolio, and also provides an opportunity for relative value players to put long/short trades often over short investment horizons. In this chapter we discuss the main risk measures of this product and outline the main strategies employed by investors in this product. The chapter concludes with two case studies, "Dispersion Trades and Tranches" and "Attractions of Hedged Mezzanines," which describe several relative value long/short strategies that STCDO technology allows.

OVERVIEW OF SINGLE-TRANCHE CDOs

An STCDO is a powerful and flexible vehicle for investors seeking credit exposure consistent with their risk/return preference. The STCDO gives investors exposure to one slice (tranche) of credit risk of a selected portfolio of preselected reference credits. Investors may choose the credit portfolio that they want exposure to as well as the specific part or tranche of the capital structure. Investors can also choose a customized subordination level and tranche size. Investors with a higher rating requirement and a lower yield target can choose a greater level of subordination and/or a larger tranche size. The flexibility of the product is enhanced by investors' ability to substitute underlying credits in the portfolio at the prevailing market prices during the life of the investment (see Figure 6.1 for the basic structure of the STCDO).

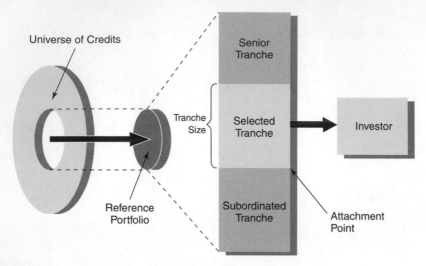

FIGURE 6.1 Basic Format of a Single-Tranche CDO
Source: Citigroup.

Advantages of Single-Tranche CDOs

STCDOs have several advantages over alternative investment products. First, the leveraged tranche structure often provides higher yields than a similarly rated corporate investment. Second, investors have the ability to customize trades in terms of portfolio selection, the choice of subordination level, and tranche size. STCDOs also provide efficient market access to credits that might be expensive and/or difficult to acquire in the underlying cash markets. STCDOs give investors the ability to easily and efficiently go short the selected portfolio, sectors, and specific tranches. Investors can dynamically manage their positions through substitution of credits in the reference portfolio through the life of the STCDO. Finally, using STCDOs, investors can more efficiently hedge their portfolios, separating the fundamental (default) risk from the marketwide risk factors.

Key Features of Single-Tranche CDO Transaction

The key value drivers of STCDOs are the credit quality of the underlying portfolio, the subordination level and tranche size, and the correlation structure among the credits in the portfolio. Other features, such as substitution rights, also play an important role. STCDO investors range from buy-and-hold investors who desire limited substitution rights and tend to hold the investment to maturity to correlation traders who use STCDOs to pursue various long and short strategies. However, traders are not the only ones who use STCDOs as defensive vehicles; for example, even traditional long-only investors can and do buy protection on STCDOs referenced to customized credit portfolios or the liquid CDX index[1] to hedge fundamental (default) risk in their portfolios or to protect against market-widespread sell-offs.

Dealers take on risk when selling STCDO transactions to investors because they are placing only a portion of the capital structure. Dealers mitigate this risk by hedging with single-name default swaps, with default indexes (e.g., CDX/iTraxx), or with other portfolio transactions. For example, "delta-hedging" offers dealers a way to manage their mark-to-market risk from underlying credit default swap (CDS) spread movement. There are other risks that dealers need to manage as well, such as the risk of individual credits defaulting, correlation risk, shortening of maturity, and convexity effects.

Description of the Product and Basic Structure

An STCDO is a financial contract between two parties that references a portfolio of credits. The parties are called *protection buyer* and *protection seller*. Once a reference portfolio is specified, a single tranche is commonly referred to as an *x excess y* tranche, where *x* is the tranche size and *y* the subordination level (attachment point). Equivalently, the tranche covers losses between the *y* and *x + y* parts of the total portfolio losses. Protection sellers can invest in a STCDO in either a funded note or an unfunded portfolio default swap format. For ease of exposition, for the remainder

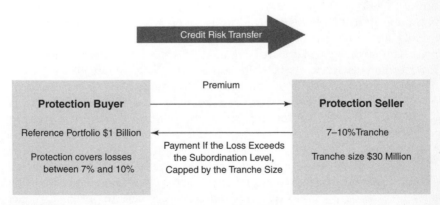

FIGURE 6.2 Mechanics of Single-Tranche CDO Transaction
Source: Citigroup.

of this chapter we generally use the term *investor* to denote the *seller* of protection, and we explicitly point out the instances where the investor is the buyer of protection.

Single-Tranche CDO—Unfunded Form   If the transaction is structured as a portfolio default swap, the investor receives a periodic premium usually expressed as a fixed percentage in basis points of the outstanding notional amount of the tranche. In return the investor provides protection for any loss more than subordination level, but the loss payment made by investors is capped by the tranche size; that is, the maximum loss for an investor is the tranche size.[2] Therefore, the cash flow exchanged between the two counterparties is default swap premium from protection buyer to the protection seller, and the loss payment, if any, from the protection seller to the protection buyer.

Single-Tranche CDO—Funded Form   Although the unfunded form is more typical, the same investment position can also be designed as a funded obligation through a credit-linked note. If structured in a funded note form, the notional amount the investor pays on closing is usually invested in high-quality, liquid assets such AAA-rated asset-backed securities. The note pays fixed rate or LIBOR plus a premium on the outstanding notional. At maturity, the investor is paid back the notional, unless the losses exceed the subordination level. If that occurs, the notional is reduced, and a portion of the collateral is liquidated and paid to the protection buyer.

Variations of the Standard Single-Tranche CDO Structure   There are several variations to the standard STCDO transaction. First, variations can be created on how the premium is paid. For instance, the protection seller may prefer to receive the present value of the premium up front or part of the premium up front (this is referred to as a *points up front* payment and is usually used in the equity tranches). Other protection sellers may prefer premium payments to be increasing or decreasing over time to mitigate or reverse time-decay effects (see the subsection "Single-Tranche CDO Risk Measures and Hedging"). So far, most of the transactions have been based on a horizontal slice of the portfolio as represented in Figure 6.1, but there is no practical difficulty for dealers to offer a vertical slice of a tranche, such as 50 percent of the "3 excess 7" tranche, where the premium is paid based on half of the underlying notional amount, but the loss is based on the full amount of the tranche. Such tranche specification offers additional leverage and could be particularly interesting for investors selling protection on a preexisting portfolio of credit obligations, where the original owner keeps the part of the vertical exposure in order to resolve potential adverse selection conflicts.

Second, the protection seller may want to have different parts of the investment exposed to different risk profiles. For example, the investor might want the final payoff of the investment principal to be linked to a single highly rated credit and the coupon payments to the junior STCDO tranche. Such variations, made possible by STCDO technology, are similar in principle to a principal-protected structure, which allows risk-averse investors to enjoy the upside in a risky investment.

Third, the flexibility of STCDOs allows investors to better manage their investments or exposures in conjunction with other business objectives. For example, a life insurance company might prefer to receive a decreasing premium payment scheme to increase its near-term earnings profile and better match its long-term asset/liability mix.

Ramp-Up Period for Single-Tranche CDOs   The STCDO structure resolves another structural conflict inherent in traditional CDO investments. Traditional cash CDOs or balance-sheet synthetic CDOs are basically supply-driven products because brokers and dealers drive the reference portfolio selection and the ramp-up process. Unless they wish to carry a substantial amount of risk, the originators of a synthetic CDO are forced to sell the entire capital structure to investors. This process can be time-consuming and costly, often implicitly resulting in a conflict of interest between senior and junior investors. With only two parties to a STCDO, the buyer of a tranche (seller of protection) takes on the tranche credit risk and the protection buyer hedges mark-to-market risk in the liquid CDS market. This dramatically reduces the transaction period. Supply and demand for different parts of the capital structure are resolved through differences in the levels of implied correlation.

Main Decision Steps for Investors

In a typical STCDO transaction, there are three main decision steps for potential investors:

1. Select a portfolio of credits to which they want exposure.
2. Choose a subordination level (attachment point) and a tranche size corresponding to their risk/return preference or yield target.
3. Dynamically manage their position and substitute credits in the collateral portfolio throughout the life of a STCDO.

Selection of Single-Tranche CDO Reference Portfolio   The first step in structuring a STCDO transaction is the investors' selection of the credits in the underlying reference portfolio according to their preferences. For example, investors can choose a portfolio of credits different from their current positions, and by selling the protection on those names they achieve further diversification of their overall credit exposure. They can also sell protection on the subset of names in their current portfolio in case they want to overweight certain credit or sectors. Alternatively, investors can designate the whole or a part of their portfolios as the reference pool, and by buying protection they hedge themselves against spread widening or individual defaults.

As a common alternative, investors choose as a reference portfolio the CDX/iTraxx default index, which is based on a diversified set of liquid names in the credit default market. The main reason for that choice is the liquidity and diversification of the index. The standard tranches on the CDX/iTraxx indexes also trade as liquid instruments in the broker-dealer market.

Selection of the Subordination Level and Tranche Size   Once a portfolio is selected, investors must choose a subordination level and tranche size. The tranche size and subordination level determine the degree of leverage and the required protection premium. Investors who are primarily concerned about the rating and want to have the tranche rated by rating agencies, such as Moody's and S&P, could choose the tranche size and subordination level so as to maximize the premium received for the selected rating. Other investors could choose a subordination level that would provide a total spread equal to some desired return target. This tranching of credit portfolio risk can provide any desired risk/return profile. The idea is similar to one used by insurers for many years; the subordination level is equivalent to the deductible in the insurance contract and the tranche size is analogous to the concept of insurance risk ceiling ("maximum amount of coverage"). Also, by choosing the position of a tranche on a capital structure of the STCDO, investors can separate their views on default risk from their views on market risk. We review such investment strategies later, in the Investment Strategies section.

Substitution of Credits in the Reference Portfolio   The third distinctive feature of STCDOs is investors' ability to dynamically manage their investment gain and loss by substituting credits in the portfolio. Because the credit risk of individual credits in the portfolio changes after the initial transaction, investors might wish to substitute certain names. They could, for example, eliminate issuers that they perceive as potential credit blowups and substitute less risky names. Following each change, the dealer will adjust the premium for the tranche, change the level of subordination, or settle through an up-front payment to offset the impact on the substitution on the mark-to-market of the tranche. Substitution rights are especially important for market participants who intend to use single-tranche synthetic CDO structures as an efficient hedging and portfolio-rebalancing tool to manage their existing credit portfolio. In case the portfolio has experienced losses and the subordination below the invested tranches has been decreased, investors can improve the rating of their tranche by increasing the subordination level, even if they do not alter the composition of the reference portfolio.

Role of Outside Managers   Although substitution rights are inherently in the hands of the investors, some market participants prefer the delegate these tasks to outside investors. Choosing a manager for an STCDO involves many of the same considerations that apply when picking a manager for a full capital structure synthetic CDO. In rating tranches managed by the third-party managers, the rating agencies pay special attention to the set of investment guidelines governing the managers' trading behavior. Investors should be careful to ensure that the guidelines and rules are set up to avoid a conflict of interest with the manager's fiduciary to the investor.

Key Issues in Modeling and Valuation

The cash flows of STCDOs depend only on the actual occurrence of defaults in the underlying credit portfolio. These cash flows are the overriding consideration for investors who are not subject to mark-to-market requirements and are expecting to hold the investment to maturity. However, investors who are subject to mark-to-market requirements are also affected by the day-to-day spread movements of individual credit default swaps as well as the market perception of default correlation among the credits within the portfolio. Therefore, these two categories of investors would emphasize different risks when investing in STCDOs.

Any STCDO pricing model has the following two essential parts:

1. A source of information that provides single-name default probability for the credits in the reference portfolio.
2. A mechanism for the introduction of default correlation among credits.

Single-Name Information   The most commonly used sources of information for single-name default analysis are:

- *Historical information based on rating agency default experience studies.* This is used for performance and risk measurement by net risk takers interested in long-term credit exposure. However, these investors will tend to require additional premium over and above the compensation based on expected loss derived from historical data. This additional premium, much like "risk loading" within the insurance industry, is based on a multiple of unexpected loss. This risk premium is associated with the investor's risk preference and appetite for unexpected losses.

- *Market- and rating-driven spreads for market-traded instruments such as credit default swaps.* Some investors use a combination of rating and spread such as a matrix of idealized credit spreads classified by rating and industry. Others may use historical default data, but rather than using the current rating of the credit, they may choose to work with the rating implied from current market spreads. Broker-dealers tend to use market information because they need to manage the composite trading book (portfolio transactions and single-name default swaps) in a consistent way.

- *Debt/equity-based measures of default probability—for example, Moody's/KMV EDF model of probability of default (PD) or Citigroup's internal HPD model.* Debt/equity-based information of default probability incorporates forward-looking credit measures of default expectation for a specific firm over a given time horizon. The default expectation is based on the Merton-type structural model of default risk. This framework is driven by two main inputs: the asset volatility and the leverage of the firm. The asset volatility of the firm is determined from market observables, such as equity price and equity volatility, and leverage information based on the firm's financial information. Commonly used debt/equity model measures are EDFs developed by Moody's/KMV.

Default Correlation   The information on single-name default risk alone is insufficient to characterize the default risk of a portfolio tranche. This is because of default correlation. Put simply, default correlation measures the degree to which the default of one asset makes the default of another asset more or less likely. The concept of correlation is conceptually related to the more widely understood concept of diversification in credit portfolios.

Intuitively, one can think of default risk as being driven by a set of factors shared to different degrees by the individual credits. These factors tend to tie all credits into a common set of economic risks, but to different degrees. A particular factor may be associated with the general economy, or a region, or a specific sector, or, more idiosyncratically, related to the specific credit itself. Due to the shared influence of certain factors, it is generally believed that default correlation is positive between companies, even if they operate in different sectors. The greater the influence of general factors on a particular company, the greater the correlation of the default risk of that company with the general market, and with other companies in the market.

Within the same sector we would expect companies to have an even higher default correlation because they have more factors in common.

Quantifying default correlation is a challenge because of scarce data, even though the standard analytical framework is well understood. This framework, which is based on copula analysis, requires the prediction of joint (i.e., correlated) survival times for all credits within a reference portfolio. Individual default probabilities only provide survival time for single credits. A copula function provides a method of obtaining a joint or multivariate distribution from a set of univariate distributions.

Model Implementation   Once a joint distribution of default times is obtained, a Monte Carlo simulation algorithm can be used to generate a large number of correlated default time scenarios. For each simulation scenario, we know exactly which credit defaults within the maturity of the transaction and exactly when that default occurs. By aggregating the results of all the scenarios, we estimate the loss distribution of the whole portfolio. The loss distribution of any particular tranche of a certain size with a subordination level can then be inferred from the portfolio's total loss distribution. The break-even spread for a tranche is defined as the premium that equates the present value of expected losses with the present value of premium payments for the tranche. This is the most common way of implementing the copula function approach to credit portfolio modeling. Alternative approaches that use fast Fourier transform, recursive calculation, or conditional analytical approximation can substantially reduce the computational time and noise inherent in the Monte Carlo simulation.

Role of Correlation   The expected loss of a portfolio of credits is the sum of the expected losses of each credit. This sum is not affected by portfolio diversity or default correlation.

However, while leaving its mean unchanged, default correlation does affect the shape of the portfolio loss distribution, particularly its variance and its tail. As tranches are exposed to a slice of the portfolio loss, they are particularly sensitive to properties of the corresponding range of the loss distribution. Thus, although the portfolio expected loss is indifferent, their expected loss is sensitive to correlation via its effect on the shape of the loss distribution.

Correlation estimates can be obtained from historical default analysis or they can be viewed as a parameter implied by quoted tranche prices. Intuitively, increasing correlation has the effect of making extreme events—very few defaults or very many defaults—more likely, thus increasing the loss variance and the loss tail.

The standard model that has been adopted by the market is the Gaussian copula model. In this version of the model, correlation is incorporated via a parameter that is approximately the correlation of issuers' asset returns.

Single-Tranche CDO Risk Measures and Hedging

Valuation models for STCDOs are important for more than just the pricing. They establish a platform to analyze the risks associated with the specific tranche investments. Based on the estimation of tranche risk sensitivities, buy-and-hold investors can estimate their mark-to-market exposure, and correlation traders can structure their hedging strategies. Note that different STCDO tranches on the capital structure can have a different direction and magnitude of sensitivity to each risk factor.

The buyer or seller of a STCDO should consider the following five risk measures (Greeks):

1. Credit spread sensitivity (delta).
2. Credit spread convexity (gamma).
3. Default sensitivity (omega).
4. Correlation sensitivity (rho).
5. Time-decay sensitivity (theta).

Credit Spread Sensitivity—Delta When the underlying credit spreads widen, the total portfolio expected loss will increase and correspondingly the expected loss of all tranches. A long position in tranches will thus see its mark-to-market decline and its break-even spread rise as underlying spreads increase. There are two forms of spread sensitivity: individual (or micro) spread sensitivity delta and sensitivity to a broad move in the portfolio spread, which is called the *Credit01*.

We define the (individual) credit spread sensitivity delta as the ratio of the mark-to-market value change (Δ MTM) of a tranche Tj to the mark-to-market value change of a single- name default swap when the spread of one individual credit *CDSi* moves by a small amount, typically one basis point.

$$\Delta_i^{Tj} = \frac{\Delta MTM(Tj)}{\Delta MTM(CDSi)}$$

Generally speaking, delta increases as we move down the capital structure, with the greatest delta (in absolute terms) in the equity tranche. In addition, spread delta for the equity tranche is higher for the individual credits with higher spreads, and spread delta for senior tranches is lower for the individual credits with higher spreads (see Figure 6.3). The reason is

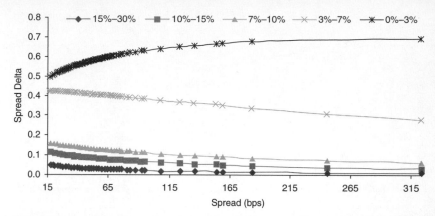

FIGURE 6.3 Individual Credit Spread Deltas as a Function of Individual Credit
Spread Levels
Source: Citigroup.

that when an individual credit spread is higher, the sensitivity of the senior
tranche to this credit is lower because the specific credit is more likely to
default and hit the equity tranche. For the same reason, spread delta for the
equity tranche is higher for the credits with higher spread.

In a similar fashion, we define the Credit01 as the mark-to-market
change in dollar value of a tranche if all the names in the portfolio widen by
1 bp in a parallel move. Credit01 is an aggregate spread sensitivity measure,
and is thus a suitable measure for estimating the hedge ratio when, for
example, delta-hedging a CDX tranche with the underlying CDX index.
Unlike an individual spread sensitivity, Credit01 of senior tranches increases
as all spreads widen in a parallel way and Credit01 of the equity tranche
decreases if all spreads widen in a parallel way (see Figure 6.4). With a
parallel spread shift, the senior tranches become more risky and therefore
more sensitive to spread widening, and the equity tranche becomes less
sensitive to additional spread widening.

Credit Spread Convexity—Gamma   Just as with spread sensitivity, spread
convexity comes in two flavors, macro and micro (idiosyncratic or credit-
specific).

Macro Spread Convexity   We define macro spread convexity as the additional
mark-to-market change on a tranche over that obtained by multiplying the
Credit01 by the parallel spread move for the underlying single-name credit
default swaps. In general the delta to the portfolio spread is greatest in
the equity tranche. However, if spreads widen on average, the expected

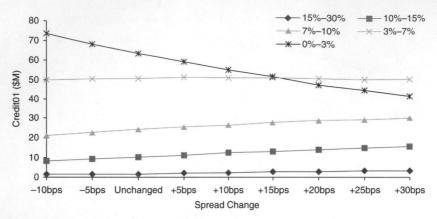

FIGURE 6.4   Credit01 versus Parallel Spread Changes
Source: Citigroup.

loss on the equity tranche draws nearer to the maximum loss it can sustain—tranche notional. For this reason, a long credit position in the equity tranche will have positive convexity (like a long bond position), and a long credit position in more senior tranches will have negative convexity. The best way to understand this is through an analogy with how simple options work. The tranche loss profile with respect to total portfolio loss resembles the payoff profile at expiration of a call spread with respect to the price of the underlying. Buying protection on a senior tranche is thus equivalent to owning an out-of-the-money call spread on default-driven losses in the underlying portfolio. The first few defaults do not affect the payout of tranche. As spreads go up, defaults become more likely, so the out-of-the-money option comes closer to becoming an at-the-money option, and the tranche sensitivity to spreads increases. Conversely, protection bought on a sufficiently junior tranche is either at-the-money or in-the-money. Thus an increase in spread reduces its sensitivity as it goes deeper in-the-money.

Idiosyncratic Spread Convexity   Perhaps against our intuition, the convexity of a senior tranche to the spread of an individual name in the portfolio is generally of the opposite sign to the convexity with respect to the average spread. But this makes sense if you consider how the sensitivity of the portfolio spread to the changes in the individual credit spread is distributed among tranches. We observe that wide credits have a greater impact on junior tranches, and tight credits have a relatively greater impact on senior tranches. As the spread of an individual credit widens, junior tranches receive a greater portion of the credit's delta and senior tranches receive less.

Thus a long credit position in a senior tranche will have positive convexity to an individual credit spread.

Default Sensitivity—Omega   Following a credit event in the portfolio, the seller of protection on the equity tranche will compensate the buyer of protection for the loss suffered by the credit, and the notional amount of the tranche will be decreased by the "1 minus the recovery rate" multiplied by the notional amount of the defaulted credit in the portfolio. The buyers of senior tranches will lose a portion of the subordination, and the tranches will become more risky. That will affect their mark-to-market positions.

We define Default01 as the mark-to-market change in the value of a tranche if one of the credits defaults (the defaulted credit is chosen to have the largest impact on the tranche). We observe that the equity tranche is allocated most of the Default01 risk in the portfolio, but its percentage share decreases as the spreads widen (see Figure 6.5).

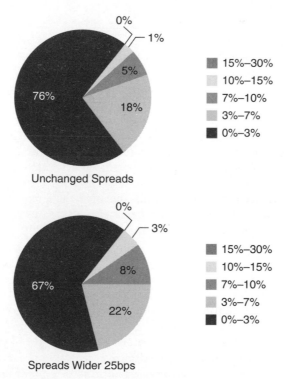

FIGURE 6.5   Distribution of Default 01 Risk Measure
Source: Citigroup.

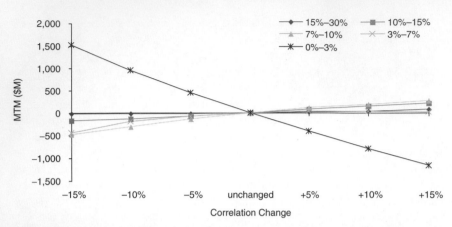

FIGURE 6.6 Protection Buyer's Mark-to-Market Value Change versus the Correlation Change
Source: Citigroup.

Correlation Sensitivity—Rho We understand that increased correlation makes more extreme events more likely. The increased likelihood of both good and bad extremes pushes expected loss out of junior tranches and into senior tranches, with the total expected loss unaffected. So, long equity tranche and short senior tranche credit positions have positive correlation sensitivity, and short equity tranche and long senior tranche credit positions have negative correlation sensitivity. Also, with senior tranches gaining risk and junior tranches shedding it, there will also be a region in the capital structure that is relatively insensitive to a change in correlation. In a tight spread environment, this is generally the junior mezzanine tranche (see Figure 6.6).

Time-Decay Sensitivity—Theta Theta measures the impact on the value of tranches as the remaining time to maturity decreases. When we price a tranche, the break-even spread is the spread that would make the value of tranche loss equal to the total premium on expectation at inception. But as time elapses this equality will no longer hold. The reason is that the premium received for each period does not necessarily exactly offset the loss for the tranche in that period. The graph in Figure 6.7 shows the periodic expected loss and the expected premium over each period for the next five years for the 3 to 7 percent tranche.

Figure 6.7 shows that at the beginning the protection buyers pay more than enough to cover the expected loss over each period for the first nine periods. However, that relationship reverses after the first nine periods. So the theta for this tranche from protection provider's perspective is initially negative. This means that a long credit position in this tranche will initially

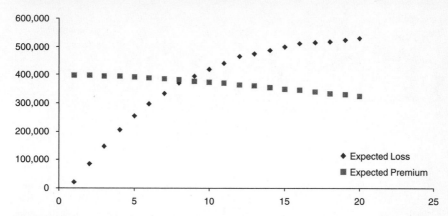

FIGURE 6.7 Periodic Expected Premium and Loss for Tranche (3 to 7 percent)
Source: Citigroup.

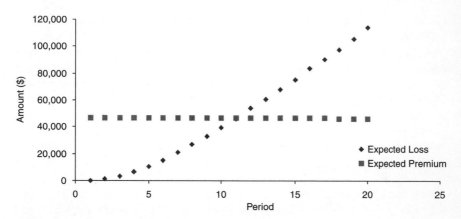

FIGURE 6.8 Periodic Expected Premium and Loss for Tranche (10 to 15 percent)
Source: Citigroup.

suffer negative mark-to-market, like a premium bond. Similar graphs for two other tranches, 0 to 3 percent and 10 to 15 percent, are shown in Figures 6.8 and 6.9.

For all senior tranches the periodic premium is flat, reflecting small incremental loss over each period while the expected periodic loss increases steadily. The equity tranche is the only tranche whose expected loss is larger than the expected premium at the origination of the transaction. In the preceding example (see Figure 6.9) the equity tranche premium is paid as the running spread. In most transacted cases, the market follows the "points

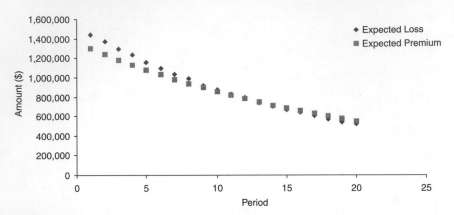

FIGURE 6.9 Periodic Expected Premium and Loss for Tranche (0 to 3 percent)
Source: Citigroup.

up front" convention, similar to the trading convention for the single-name CDSs on the distressed names. In this case, the protection on the equity tranche is paid as percentage of the notional up front and the fixed running premium (e.g., 500 bp annual). *Points up front* is defined as the difference between the present value of the expected loss on a tranche and the present value of the expected fixed running premium. Therefore, as time passes, the value of points up front decreases, just as a bond priced initially at a discount pulls to par.

Substitution of Credits

Advantage of Substitution When investing in static CDOs, the investor's knowledge on the underlying credit pool is used only at the time that the investor signs the contract. After that, the investor can merely hope for the best performance of the investment with no option to dynamically manage credit risk by replacing credits of the underlying portfolio. With the managed single tranche, in contrast, the investor is allowed to make a limited number of credit replacements per year. For example, an investor might be allowed to substitute 10 names per year, with a maximum change of 50 percent of the portfolio composition during the maturity period of five years for a single-tranche transaction with a reference credit pool of 100 names. This flexibility gives the investor freedom to manage the investment in a dynamic way.

Substitution Calculation Since the dealer needs to rehedge his position once a credit in the portfolio is replaced by another credit, the settlement of substitution has to be done in a mark-to-market way. The simplest way is to price the specific tranche with the replaced credit first and then with the replacing credit, the difference being the substitution cost or benefit. This approach requires both parties of the transaction to agree on the model used and also the parameters used in the model. This has become possible since the normal copula model has been accepted as the market standard for CDO pricing. The two parties usually agree on the pricing parameters, with a typical reference point being the current implied correlation embedded in the corresponding STCDO tranche. The cost of the substitution may be positive or negative—that is, paid by the tranche buyer to the dealer or by the dealer to the tranche buyer. The cost can be paid through any of the following three steps:

1. Up-front payment between the protection buyer and the protection seller.
2. The alteration of the subordination level below the STCDO.
3. Resetting the coupon payable to the STCDO up to the point where the coupon has been reduced to zero, followed by either step (1) or step (2).

Each of these methods of substitution settlement aims to offset the change in the mark-to-market value of the tranche before and after the substitution of the credit. The net effect on mark-to-market value of the credit substitution on one side and the cash payment, alternation of the tranche subordination, or change of the coupon on the other side should be zero. This mark-to-market change in tranche value can be captured by the net marginal credit factor (MCF).

Marginal Credit Factors The MCF for each name and for each tranche measures the impact on the tranche value when the credit changes from risky status to risk-free status. It is in contrast to jump-to-default (JTD), and may be called the *jump-to-paradise* risk measure. This jump-to-paradise risk measure allows us to compare two credits in a portfolio context. The difference of MCF between the replacing credit and replaced credit is the substitution cost. That difference—net MCF—is equal to the change in the mark-to-market value of the tranche as valued with the old and new reference portfolios of credits.

MCFs tend to decrease when trading into tighter names because the value of protection provided by tranche decreases as the spread tightens. In this case, substitution results in the protection seller owing the protection buyer. MCFs also depend on the correlation of the name with the rest of the credit portfolio. Trading into lower-correlated names increases the value of the protection provided by the equity tranche (and some lower mezzanine tranches), but decreases the value of protection by the senior tranche.

Approximate Substitution Cost Calculation   The problem with MCFs is that there is a need to have an agreement between dealer and investor on model, model parameters, and also other model inputs, such as those single-name default swap spreads that are not easily verifiable. This lack of transparency leaves tranche investors dependent on the dealer's interpretation of risk and model parameterization. A simple way to ballpark the effect of substitution is to consider the net impact of the substitution on the expected loss of the portfolio. We define the impact of substitution as the difference between the expected loss of the replaced credit and the replacing credit. Based on that calculation, we adjust the subordination level of each tranche to offset the net effect of substitution on the portfolio expected loss. For example, if we would like to replace a credit A with spread of x basis points by a credit B with spread of y basis points, then we calculate the difference in the present value of expected loss of credit A and credit B as a percentage of notional amount. After that, we reduce the subordination level of that tranche by that calculated percentage difference divided by the number of underlying credits in the portfolio. This approximation is based on the assumption that the net change of expected loss after substitution is deemed as if it is the actual loss incurred by the portfolio right away. Therefore, to make the adjustment for this net loss change, we lower the size of the equity tranche by this loss change, and make the same parallel adjustments in the subordination level of all other tranches on the capital structure.

This measurement ignores the difference in spread sensitivity of each tranche as well as the credit risk on the premium side. It usually underestimates the compensation required for the credit substitution. But the exact size and direction of the difference between the approximation approach and the mark-to-market approach depend on the various parameters, such as spread levels of the replaced credits, size and subordination of the tranche, and the overall spread levels in the portfolio. The advantage of this approximation approach is that investors can easily assess the substitution cost (in terms of substitution-level change) independently from a portfolio model output.

Single-Tranche CDO Market

Trading and liquidity in STCDOs has risen dramatically, since they have proven to be powerful and flexible structured credit products. The reason for their popularity is that investors can use them to execute a variety of customized investment objectives and solutions. Although these trading strategies are generally structured around the liquid market in CDX/iTraxx tranches, investors can apply the same strategies to customized portfolios in which they select the reference obligations of the STCDOs. As a combined

TABLE 6.1 IG CDX Tranches—Each Tranche Notional Size Is $10 Million, April 12, 2004

Tranche	Maturity	Implied Correlation (%)	Mid Spread (bp)	Credit01 ($000)	Default01 ($000)	Correlation01 ($000)
15%–30%	Sep 09	28.7	10.25	2.9	4.9	5.5
10%–15%	Sep 09	22.9	43.5	10.7	28.1	15.3
7%–10%	Sep 09	19.6	107.5	23.2	86.0	22.8
3%–7%[a]	Sep 09	—	295	45.5	282.9	0.7
0%–3%[b]	Sep 09	19.8	39%	65.4	1,395.9	−81.8
IG CDX[a]	Sep 09	—	54.5	4.9	47.5	0.0

Credit01 is the mark-to-market change in dollar value of a tranche if each of the names in the portfolio widens by 1 bp. Default01 is the mark-to-market change in the value of a tranche if one of the credits defaults (defaulted credit is chosen to have the largest impact on the tranche). Correlation01 is the mark-to market change in the value of the tranche if correlation changes by 1%. Risk figures are based on the implied correlation for each tranche.
[a]Tranche is correlation insensitive.
[b]0%–3% IG CDX tranche is quoted in points of up-front payment plus a fixed 500 bp running premium.
Source: Citigroup.

approach, investors can start with standard CDX portfolio and substitute certain number of handpicked names for which they have preference not to have them included in their STCDO portfolio. As a representative example of STCDOs, we present the liquid September 2009 IG CDX tranches (see Table 6.1). Each tranche trades at a different implied correlation, which is a market-driven factor in a standard copula model reflecting the demand and supply for the tranche protection. Implied correlation skew may also be due to copula model specifications and assumptions.

Investment Strategies

Investors can use STCDOs to structure various investment strategies to target their risk/return profiles or hedging needs. We classify the strategies as:

- *Leverage strategies.* Enhancing yield through leverage provided by tranching.
- *Market view strategies.* Expressing a long or short view on the market using the appropriate tranches.
- *Correlation strategies.* Expressing a view on implied correlation (equivalently, expressing a view on tranche technicals).

- *Relative value strategies.* Taking a view on the relative cheapness of old versus new CDX tranches, 5-year versus 10-year CDX tranche spreads, and so on.
- *Micro/macro hedging strategies.* Hedging individual default (micro) risk and/or market-spread (macro) risk.

Leverage Strategies   Leverage strategies of single-tranche CDOs are summarized in Table 6.2.

Long Position in Mezzanine or Senior Tranche Investors can take a long buy-and-hold position (sell protection) in mezzanine or senior tranches on the CDX index or in customized portfolios. This trade should appeal to investors who are looking for enhanced yield through leverage. The motivation for this bullish trade is to obtain a targeted degree of leverage on the underlying portfolio while picking up spread with respect to the CDX index or comparable corporate investments. Such buy-and-hold positions are often executed in an unfunded way, although investors can buy the credit through a funded credit-linked note, collateralized by AAA-rated paper.

Market View Strategies   Single-tranche CDOs that are referenced on CDX index products allow investors to separate their views on credit fundamentals (defaults) from their views on market and liquidity risk (spreads) and allow investors to take directional investment decision positions on defaults and spreads separately. Single-tranche trades are structured to be superior in terms of carry, leverage, and convexity to outright long or short

TABLE 6.2   Single-Tranche CDOs—Leverage Strategies

Strategy	Sample Trade	Motivation	Investors
Long position (sell protection) in mezzanine or senior tranche of CDX IG or customized portfolio.	Investor sells protection on $10 million Sep 09 7%–10% CDX IG tranche. Tranche spread (mid): 107.5 bp CDX IG spread (mid): 54.5 Date: 12 Apr 04	Investors who look for a buy-and-hold investment can obtain enhanced yield through leverage and express a bullish view.	Portfolio managers, CDO investors.

Source: Citigroup.

market positions on the CDX index or a portfolio of individual names (see Table 6.3).

Short Position in Senior Tranche Investors who are bearish on overall market-spread movements driven by global factors can take a short position (buy protection) in the senior CDX tranche. For example, we recommend buying protection on the 7 to 10 percent CDX IG tranche because this tranche requires a lower premium for protection per unit of spread risk than junior tranches or an outright short with the CDX IG index. This position offers leverage and positive convexity relative to a short on the CDX IG index, and it provides a low carry protection against the spread backup.

Long Position in Equity Tranche Investors who are bullish on the credit quality of a portfolio of names or about default rates risk in the market as a whole can go long (sell protection) the 0 to 3 percent tranche. This trade offers bullish investors a leveraged and positively convex position with a high carry. Of course, this trade is exposed to defaults and to spread widening. Depending on their fundamental views, investors can hedge certain individual credits in the reference portfolio by buying default protection on those names and reducing the idiosyncratic risk of the trade. After partially hedging against defaults, investors should still be left with a significant positive carry on the trade.

Carry- or Delta-Neutral Combinations of Short Senior Tranche and Long Equity Tranche Investors who are bearish on the possibility of spread sell-off and bullish on credit quality can combine a long position in the equity tranche with a short position in the senior tranche to pay for the negative carry. This carry-neutral trade captures the effect of positive convexity for senior and junior tranche and generates gains in the case of larger spread moves. A short senior and long equity tranche position can also be combined into a delta-neutral trade. Compared with directional trades, this delta-neutral combination generates lower, but still positive, gains in spread sell-off and spread rally scenarios.

Correlation Strategies Using a single-tranche synthetic CDO, investors can express their views on the implied correlation of tranches as different tranches can have opposite reactions to changes in correlation. Investors can choose the tranche subordination and size in line with their views on correlation. Note that the implied correlation is primarily a market-based factor, driven by the demand and supply of protection for each individual tranche. In most cases, correlation traders delta-hedge their positions against the spread risk. Name-specific spread risk (micro spread risk) can be delta-hedged with the single-name credit default swaps, and market-spread risk

TABLE 6.3 Single-Tranche CDOs—Market View Strategies

Strategy	Sample Trade	Motivation	Investors
Short position (buy protection) in senior 7%–10% CDX IG tranche.	Investor buys protection on $10 million Sep 09 7%–10% CDX IG tranche. Tranche spread (mid): 107.5 bp CDX IG spread (mid): 54.5 bp Date: 12 Apr 04	Investors who want to protect against spread backup can execute this leveraged, low-carry, positively convex position.	Portfolio managers, bearish investors who worry about a reversal in the corporate spread rally.
Long position (sell protection) in equity 0%–3% CDX IG tranche.	Investor sells protection on $10 million Sep 09 0%–3% CDX IG tranche. Tranche spread (mid): 39 points up front + 500 bp running CDX IG spread (mid): 54.5 Date: 12 Apr 04	Investors who are bullish about default rates and want to enter into a leveraged, positively convex, high-carry position.	Credit-savvy hedge funds.

Carry- or delta-neutral combination of short position (buy protection) in 7%–10% CDX IG tranche and long position (sell protection) in 0%–3% CDX IG tranche.	Delta-neutral trade: Investor buys protection on $28.2 million Sep 09 7%–10% IG CDX tranche. Investor sells protection on $10 million Sep 09 0%–3% CDX IG tranche. 7%–10% tranche spread (mid): 107.5 0%–3% tranche spread (mid): 39 points upfront + 500bps running CDX IG spread (mid): 54.5 Date: 12 Apr 04	Investors who are bearish on spreads and bullish on credit quality can structure carry-neutral or delta-neutral position and maintain positive convexity.
		Hedge funds and investors expressing view on global macro risk.

Source: Citigroup.

(macro spread risk) can be hedged by the appropriate position in the CDX index. In addition, correlation traders can also hedge a portion of the default risk with a set of selected single-name credit default swaps. Therefore, these trades allow correlation traders to take a view on market demand and supply for STCDOs, without taking on credit risk (see Table 6.4).

Short Position in Senior Tranche or Long Position in Equity Tranche (Long Correlation)   Investors who prefer to be long correlation can set up such a position by going short the senior tranche (buying protection) or going long the equity tranche (selling protection). A rise in senior tranche implied correlation would imply that increased demand for protection is pushing senior tranche spreads wider and, all else being equal, making the trade profitable. A rise in equity tranche implied correlation would imply that increased supply of protection is pushing equity tranche spreads tighter and, all else being equal, making the trade profitable.

Long Position in Senior Tranche or Short Position in Equity Tranche (Short Correlation)   Investors can choose a short correlation position by going long the senior tranche (selling protection) or going short the equity tranche (buying protection). A decrease in senior tranche implied correlation would imply that the senior tranche is trading at lower spreads, making the trade profitable, with all else being equal. A decrease in equity tranche implied correlation would imply that increased demand for protection is pushing equity tranche spreads wider, making the trade profitable.

Long or Short Position in Junior Mezzanine Tranche (Correlation Insensitive)   If investors are uncertain about default correlation levels and they do not wish to take correlation risk, they can invest (sell protection) in the tranche on the capital structure that is correlation insensitive. Typically, this tranche would be the junior mezzanine (second-loss tranche), but the exact attachment point and size depend on the characteristics of the collateral pool. Proactive investors can achieve a similar correlation-neutral position by investing in a more junior and a more senior tranche below and above the correlation inflection point. These two tranches have opposite sensitivities to the correlation, and investors can earn a higher spread with this position than investing in the correlation-insensitive mezzanine tranche alone. Although at origination the specific tranche can be correlation-insensitive, with time decay the correlation sensitivity will change.

Relative Value Strategies   Relative value strategies of single-tranche CDOs are summarized in Table 6.5.

Long/Short Position in On-the-Run CDX IG Tranches versus Short/Long Position in Matching Off-the-Run CDX IG Tranches   The rolls of the indexes provide a set of relative value trade opportunities in the single-tranche market. With the two-sided market in on-the-run and off-the-run CDX IG tranches, investors can now compare matching tranches referenced to similar underlying portfolios. Investors can focus on the implied correlation of new and old CDX IG single tranches and look for relative value opportunities at the same leverage level in the capital structure.

Long/Short Position in 5-Year CDX IG Tranches versus Short/Long Position in 10-Year CDX IG Tranches   Expecting that liquid market for 10-year IG CDX tranches will improve further, we believe that investors will be able to execute relative value trade strategies based on the comparison between the 5- and 10-year IG CDX tranches referenced to the same portfolio. Implied correlation skew surface should be an indicative cheap/rich measure for individual tranches.

Long/Short Position 3 to 100 Percent CDX IG Tranche with Short/Long Position in CDX IG Index versus Short/Long Position in 0 to 3 Percent CDXIG Tranche   Investors can combine a 3 to 100 percent CDX IG tranche and delta-hedge it with the IG CDX index to synthetically replicate the equity 0 to 3 percent tranche of the CDX IG index. Comparing the obtained spread premium with the market spread for the traded equity 0 to 3 percent equity tranche of the CDX IG index allows investors to enter into a relative value trade or execute the directional view by using a cheaper way to access the equity part of the CDX IG capital structure.

Micro/Macro Hedging Strategies   Micro/macro hedging strategies of single-tranche CDOs are summarized in Table 6.6.

Short Position in Equity Tranche   A short position (buying protection) in an equity tranche on a customized portfolio of names is an efficient way to hedge against default risk. Investors select names from their portfolio that, in their view, have high risk of default and the protection on the first-loss tranche of this portfolio. Usually, investors sell protection to the same counterparty on individual CDS names ("exchange the deltas"). Buying protection on the equity tranche of a customized portfolio is a cheaper way to hedge against default than buying protection on each individual name. In addition, investors who are comfortable with a certain number of defaults being unhedged can buy protection on the second-loss tranche. The higher attachment point of the tranche can substantially lower the cost of carry.

TABLE 6.4 Single-Tranche CDOs—Correlation Strategies

Strategy	Sample Trade	Motivation	Investors
Long Correlation Trade: Short position (buy protection) in senior tranche or long position (sell protection) in equity tranche. Delta-hedge with single-name CDS or CDX IG index.	Investor buys protection on $10 million Sep 09 7%–10% CDX IG tranche. Investor sells protection on $47.3 million Sep 09 CDX IG index Tranche spread (mid): 107.5 bp IG CDX spread (mid): 54.5 bp Date: 12 Apr 04	Investors who want to have long correlation exposure and expect implied correlation to increase. Positive carry.	Correlation traders (hedge funds, bank proprietary desks, and broker-dealers) with a positive view on implied correlation.
Short Correlation Trade: Long position (sell protection) in senior tranche or short position (buy protection) in equity tranche. Delta-hedge with single-name CDS or CDX IG index.	Investor sells protection on $10 million Sep 09 7%–10% CDX IG tranche. Investor buys protection on $47.3 million Sep 09 IG CDX IG index. Tranche spread (mid): 107.5 bp IG CDX spread (mid): 54.5 bp Date: 12 Apr 04	Investors who want to have short correlation exposure and expect implied correlation to decrease.	Correlation trades (hedge funds, bank proprietary desks, and broker-dealers) with a negative view on implied correlation.

174

| Correlation-Insensitive Trade: Long (sell protection) or short (buy protection) position in junior mezzanine tranche. | Investor sells or buys protection on $10 million Sep 09 3%–7% CDX IG tranche. Tranche spread (mid): 295 CDX IG spread (mid): 54.5 Date: 12 Apr 04 | Investors who are uncertain about correlation levels and don't want to take correlation risk, but want to invest in single-tranche CDOs to get leverage or take a directional market view position. | Investors who don't want to take exposure to changes in correlation. |

Source: Citigroup.

TABLE 6.5 Single-Tranche CDOs—Relative Value Strategies

Strategy	Sample Trade	Motivation	Investors
Long/short position in on-the-run CDX IG tranches versus short/long position in matching off-the-run CDX IG tranches.	Investor buys protection on $10 million Sep 09 7%–10% CDX IG tranche. Investor sells protection on $10 million Mar 09 7%–10% CDX IG tranche. Sep 09 7%–10% tranche spread (mid): 107.5 bp Mar 09 7%–10% tranche spread (mid): 112.5 bp CDX IG Sep 09 spread (mid): 54.5 bp CDX IG Mar 09 spread (mid): 56 bp Date: 12 Apr 04	Relative value trade opportunities at the same leverage level between the new Sep 09 CDX IG tranche and the old Mar 09 CDX IG tranche. Investors can focus on implied correlation as relative value measure.	Hedge funds, correlation traders, broker-dealers.
Long/short position in 5-year CDX IG tranches versus long/short position in matching 10-year CDX IG tranches.	Investor sells protection on Sep 09 7%–10% CDX IG tranche. Investor buys protection on Sep 14 7%–10% CDX IG tranche.	Relative value trade opportunities between the 5-year and 10-year CDX IG tranches. Investors use implied correlation skew surface as relative value measure.	Hedge funds, correlation traders, broker-dealers.

Long/short position in 3%–100% CDX IG tranches and short/long position in CDX IG index versus short/long position in 0%–3% CDX IG tranche.

Investor buys protection on $10 million Sep 09 3%–100% CDX IG tranche. Investor delta-hedges by selling protection on $6.8 million Sep 09 CDX IG index.

Tranche spread (mid): 20
CDX IG spread (mid): 54.5
Date: 12 Apr 04

Relative value trade opportunities between the traded 0%–3% CDX IG tranche and synthetically replicated equity piece using 3%–100% CDX IG tranche and CDX IG index.

Relative value hedge funds.

Source: Citigroup.

TABLE 6.6 Single-Tranche CDOs—Micro/Macro-Hedging Strategies

Strategy	Sample Trade	Motivation	Investors
Short position (buy protection) in equity tranche on a customized portfolio of names.	Investor buys protection on 0%–3% tranche of a customized portfolio. Investor sells protection to the same counterparty on individual CDS names (exchange the deltas).	Cheaper way to hedge against default risk than buying protection on each individual name.	Portfolio managers and bank loan portfolios.
Short position (buy protection) in equity tranche on a customized portfolio of names and long position (sell protection) in CDX IG tranche.	Investor buys protection on 0%–3% tranche of a customized portfolio. Investor sells protection on Sep 09 7%–10% CDX IG tranche.	Portfolio managers with a positive view on macro risk can compensate the cost of hedging by going long senior CDX IG tranche.	Portfolio managers or buy-and-hold investors who are not subject to mark-to-market accounting treatment.
Short position (buy protection) in senior CDX IG tranche.	Investor buys protection on $10 million Sep 09 7%–10% IG CDX tranche.	Investors who already hedged the most risky names against default and want to hedge against marketwide spread widening. This strategy is more efficient hedge than a short CDX IG position.	Portfolio managers or buy-and-hold investors with strong fundamental approach to portfolio selection.

Long position (sell protection) in senior IG CDX tranche.

Tranche spread (mid): 107.5 bp
IG CDX spread (mid): 54.5 bp
Date: 12 Apr 04

Investor sells protection on $10 million Sep 09 7%–10% CDX IG tranche.

Tranche spread (mid): 107.5 bp
IG CDX spread (mid): 54.5 bp
Date: 12 Apr 04

Portfolio managers who have bought default protection in single-name CDS market and want to protect their hedging portfolio against mark-to-market risk.

Bank loan portfolio managers.

Source: Citigroup.

Short Position in Equity Tranche and Long Position in Mezzanine Tranche   Hedging against default using individual credit default swaps or a short position in the equity tranche can be an expensive strategy. Investors who are less sensitive to market-spread widening or who have a positive view on the general macro risk factors but worry about defaults in their portfolios can compensate for their hedging cost by going long a senior tranche on the CDX IG index. The premium received on the senior tranche protection should lower the cost of protection on the equity tranche.

Short Position in Senior Tranche   Certain investors are searching for solutions that will protect them against general market-spread widening in their portfolios, especially if they have already hedged the most risky names against default or they trust in their selection of credits based on their fundamental views. For such investors, hedging with the CDX IG index is not the most efficient solution, because the outright market short does not separate default and spread risk protection. A more effective hedging strategy is to put on a short position (buy protection) in the senior tranche that has the highest Credit01-to-carry ratio. We estimated that the 7 to 10 percent CDX IG tranche provides investors with the most suitable hedge, after taking into account the liquidity component of traded CDX IG tranches.

Long Position in Mezzanine or Senior Tranche   A long position in mezzanine and senior CDX IG tranches is a leveraged position on marketwide spread movements. If investors, such as bank loan portfolio managers, have bought protection in the single-name CDS market against defaults in their portfolios, this hedging portfolio is exposed to mark-to-market risk driven primarily by macro factors. If investors want to protect against mark-to-market risk in their hedging portfolios, then a long position in the mezzanine or senior CDX IG tranche can provide the solution. Because the junior tranches take on relatively more default risk than senior tranches, they are much less suitable for such hedging purposes. In addition, a long position in the CDX IG index is a less efficient hedge against marketwide spread moves, because the index spread is affected as much by the systematic market risk as by the credit-specific events.

CASE STUDY: DISPERSION TRADES AND TRANCHES

Traditional Bull-Bear Trade

As seen from the previous section, STCDOs allow investors to place various leveraged positions in the credit market and efficiently execute their investment strategies. Most commonly recommended tranche strategies follow the standard "bull-bear" approach: selling protection in the equity tranche and buying protection in the more senior tranche.

The bull-bear strategy expresses the investor's view that default rates will stay low, but there could be a marketwide spread widening in the near future. As another practical example, the following section presents a different tranche strategy that benefits from individual credit spread widening and defaults.

Not Just Another Bull-Bear Tranche Trade

Tranche markets provide investors with a variety of different strategies. The market has expanded, but it seems that the majority of standard strategies is still a variation of the classic bull-bear trade. In this trade, investors sell protection on a junior tranche and buy protection on a senior tranche, expressing bullish views on default and bearish views on spreads.[3]

The bull-bear trade strategy is aligned with the common view that default rates should stay low, but there could be a marketwide spread widening in the near future. In 2006, we have seen a number of different variations of this strategy, and the low-default environment in 2004 has contributed to its popularity.

This bull-bear view on defaults and spreads is our baseline scenario for the coming months,[4] but it would be interesting to look at the alternatives. Although we see persistent interest for the classic long/short trade, investors are looking for new ideas in the tranche space. Improved liquidity in the tranche market offers opportunities for other tranche strategies. But are there any other tranche trades out there? What kind of credit views can be stated in the tranche space? What tranche strategies should investors be looking at in the future?

In this section we outline a dispersion strategy that is opposite to the standard bull-bear trade. With this tranche trade investors take a view on individual credit spread widening, while expecting that overall spreads stay range-bound over the next several months. Blowups should have a positive mark-to-market effect, but overall spread change for credits in the portfolio will hurt the trade. Furthermore, we suggest that the trade should be executed using CDX IG tranches.

Who's Afraid of Blowups?

Roll of CDX indexes every six months provides an opportunity to design a trade that expresses views on idiosyncratic spread blowups. We have observed interesting phenomena with previous CDX rolls. Not only has the dispersion of spreads in each new index increased relative to the existing ones (see Figure 6.10, top panel), there is a good chance of an individual spread blowup soon after the origination (see Figure 6.10, bottom panel). This trend is not surprising. For example, following the selection rules for the roll, lower-quality names that have been downgraded below investment grade are replaced by higher-quality, investment-grade names. We can expect that some of the credits in the on-the-run portfolio will eventually widen substantially. Such spread widening could be a stand-alone credit event (e.g., Citizens Communications in CDX IG 1 and Intelsat in CDX IG 2) or a spread blowup affecting the whole sector (e.g., insurance names in CDX IG 3).

Credit blowups are unexpected events, and it is hard to predict specific cases. Tranches are better suited to express views on blowups than single-name or index short positions. Tranches not only are referenced to portfolios, but also have different sensitivities to

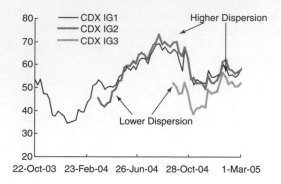

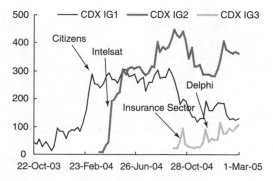

FIGURE 6.10 CDX IG Portfolios: Dispersion of the Individual Spread Levels (top panel), Widest Spread Widening from Inception for Names (bottom panel), October 22, 2003, to March 2, 2005
Note: Dispersion of the individual spread levels is defined as standard deviation of spreads in the CDX IG portfolio for a specific point in time. Widest spread widening from inception for names in the CDX IG portfolio is defined as the maximal spread difference across the names from the inception date to a specific point in time.
Source: Citigroup.

individual and parallel spread changes. Newly rolled indexes should be especially interesting because the quality on the names in the on-the-run CDX index is usually higher at inception. Therefore, there should be a higher likelihood of a blowup in the new portfolio than in the off-the-run indexes.

    The challenge for dispersion trades is that they are most likely some variation of short leveraged positions and therefore may have significant negative carry. Investors would probably want to implement strategies that are carry neutral or at least not too expensive. Tranches that are affected the most by single-name spread widening are junior tranches, while the senior tranches are relatively more exposed to marketwide spread changes.[5] Therefore a classic bull-bear trade[6] would not be suitable strategy to express views on individual blowups. We need to look for alternatives.

Buy Protection on 10-Year 3 to 7 Percent CDX IG Tranche, Sell Protection on 5-Year 10 to 15 Percent CDX IG Tranche

To achieve the potential benefit from the individual spread, but minimizing the cost of protection, we structure the dispersion trade as a short/long tranche position. We choose short position in the 10-year 3 to 7 percent CDX IG tranche. According to our analysis (see subsection "How to Choose the Most Efficient Tranches"), this tranche should have high mark-to-market change due to individual blowup relative to the tranche spread. We compensate the cost of protection by taking a long position in the five-year 10 to 15 percent CDX IG tranche. This tranche should have low sensitivity to the individual blowup relative to the tranche spread.

We recommend the following two variations of the dispersion trade.[7]

Credit 01 Neutral Dispersion Trade Buy protection on $10 million of the 10-year 3 to 7 percent CDX IG tranche, sell protection on $140.8 million of the 5-year 10 to 15% CDX IG tranche (see Table 6.7).

Carry-Neutral Dispersion Trade Buy protection on $10 million of the 10-year 3 to 7 percent CDX IG tranche, sell protection on $267.9 million of the 5-year 10 to 15 percent CDX IG tranche (see Table 6.8).

These two trades should benefit from the individual spread blowups. The mark-to-market gain on the short leg is higher than the mark-to-market loss on the long leg in case of individual credit spread widening. Furthermore, any defaults would generate even higher net mark-to-market gain on the whole trade. From a time-decay perspective, the negative theta effect on the short leg should be offset by positive time gain on the long position. But the strategies are negatively convex, and, therefore, large parallel spread moves will hurt the trade.

TABLE 6.7 Credit01 Neutral Dispersion Trade with CDX IG Tranches, March 7, 2005

	Maturity	Spread[a] (bp)	Delta	Tranche Duration	Notional ($)	Annual Carry ($)
Buy protection on 3%–7% tranche	10-year	442	11.5	7.30	10,000,000	(442,000)
Sell protection on 10%–15% tranche	5-year	16.5	1.3	4.58	140,838,342	232,383
Net						(209,617)

[a]Spreads are midlevel.
Source: Citigroup.

TABLE 6.8   Carry–Neutral Dispersion Trade with CDX IG Tranches, March 7, 2005

	Maturity	Spread[a] (bp)	Delta	Tranche Duration	Notional ($)	Annual Carry ($)
Buy protection on 3%–7% tranche	10-year	442	11.5	7.30	10,000,000	(442,000)
Sell protection on 10%–15% tranche	5-year	16.5	1.3	4.58	267,878,788	442,000
Net						

[a]Spreads are midlevel.
Source: Citigroup.

In summary, the suggested dispersion trade is a suitable strategy for investors who have a view that overall spreads in the CDX IG index should stay range-bound in the near future and think that there is a chance of a substantial spread widening in a few individual credits.

Effect of Blowups in CDX IG on the Dispersion Trade

Potential for spread blowups in the newly rolled CDX IG index is the main objective behind the recommended dispersion trade. As the trade is structured as a short/long tranche trade, individual blowup in the index portfolio will have opposite mark-to-market effect on each leg of the trade. To illustrate this effect, we present the instantaneous mark-to-market sensitivity to blowups (see Tables 6.9 and 6.10).
   Comparison of the two trades:

1. Credit01-neutral version of the dispersion trade is weighted more toward the short leg, and, therefore, it should have higher mark-to-market gain if a single-name credit widens (but for the cost of negative carry).
2. Carry-neutral version of the dispersion trade is balanced from the perspective of the cost, but the mark-to-market benefit after the spread blowup is lower because the trade is weighted more toward the long leg.

Trade Sensitivity Analysis

To address the risk associated with the recommended dispersion trades, we analyze their mark-to-market sensitivity to parallel spread changes, individual spread blowups, and defaults. The profit/loss (P&L) is estimated after six-month period.

TABLE 6.9 Instantaneous P&L of Credit01 Neutral Dispersion Trade, a Sensitivity to Blowups, March 7, 2005 (in dollars)

	Maturity	Notional	One Blowup	Two Blowups
Buy protection on 3%–7% tranche	10-year	10,000,000	240,166	475,023
Sell protection on 10%–15% tranche	5-year	140,838,342	(70,538)	(158,717)
Net			**169,628**	**316,306**

Model-based analysis. The P&L is based on spread change (blowup) for selected credits, with the rest of input parameters kept unchanged. Correlation skews are rescaled based on the expected tranche loss. Blowup is defined as spread widening of one credit for 400 bp.
Source: Citigroup.

TABLE 6.10 Instantaneous P&L of Carry-Neutral Dispersion Trade, a Sensitivity to Blowups, March 7, 2005 (in dollars)

	Maturity	Notional ($)	One Blowup	Two Blowups
Buy protection on 3%–7% tranche	10-year	10,000,000	240,166	475,023
Sell protection on 10%–15% tranche	5-year	267,878,788	(134,165)	(301,884)
Net			**106,001**	**173,139**

Model-based analysis. The P&L is based on spread change (blowup) for selected credits, with the rest of input parameters kept unchanged. Correlation skews are rescaled based on the expected tranche loss. Blowup is defined as spread widening of one credit for 400 bp.
Source: Citigroup.

Credit01 Neutral Trade The main characteristics of the Credit01-neutral dispersion trade are the following:

- Positive time gain if spreads widen moderately, but overall negative P&L of the trade in case of parallel spread tightening or widening (see Table 6.11).
- Positive P&L if one or two credits blow up after six months. Projected gain with one credit blowup should offset the P&L losses associated with a more pronounced parallel spread widening (see Table 6.12).
- Projected gain following one default should offset the P&L losses due to parallel spread tightening (see Table 6.13).

TABLE 6.11 Six-Month P&L of Credit01 Neutral Dispersion Trade, a Sensitivity to Parallel Spread Changes, March 7, 2005 (in dollars)

	Maturity	−10bp	−5bp	0bp	5bp	10bp	15bp	30bp
Buy protection on 3%–7% tranche	10-year	(1,251,209)	(857,768)	(451,439)	(34,485)	383,973	813,278	2,015,418
Sell protection on 10%–15% tranche	5-year	742,712	617,918	368,655	36,584	(342,005)	(823,559)	(2,049,695)
Net		(508,497)	(239,850)	(82,784)	2,098	41,968	(10,281)	(34,277)

Model-based analysis. The P&L is based on spread change (blowup) for selected credits, with the rest of input parameters kept unchanged. Correlation skews are rescaled based on the expected tranche loss. Blowup is defined as spread widening of one credit for 400 bp.
Source: Citigroup.

TABLE 6.12   Six-Month P&L of Credit01 Neutral Dispersion Trade, a Sensitivity to Blowups, March 7, 2005 (in dollars)

	One Blowup	Two Blowups
Net	92,289	260,696

Model-based analysis. The P&L is based on spread change (blowup) for selected credits, with the rest of input parameters kept unchanged. Correlation skews are rescaled based on the expected tranche loss. Blowup is defined as spread widening of one credit for 400 bp.
Source: Citigroup.

TABLE 6.13   Six-Month P&L of Credit01 Neutral Dispersion Trade, a Sensitivity to Defaults, March 7, 2005 (in dollars)

	One Default	Two Defaults
Net	403,924	963,424

Model-based analysis. The P&L is based on spread change (blowup) for selected credits, with the rest of input parameters kept unchanged. Correlation skews are rescaled based on the expected tranche loss. Blowup is defined as spread widening of one credit for 400 bp.
Source: Citigroup.

Carry-Neutral Trade   The main characteristics of the carry-neutral dispersion trade are:

- Positive time gain if spreads tighten, but significant negative P&L with parallel spread widening (see Table 6.14).
- Positive P&L if one or two credits blow up after six months. Projected gain with one-credit blowup should offset the P&L losses associated with moderate parallel spread widening (see Table 6.15).
- Projected gain following one or two defaults should offset the P&L losses due to more significant parallel spread tightening (see Table 6.16).

How to Choose the Most Efficient Tranches

We structured the recommended trade in a way that it should benefit the most from potential blowups at the minimal cost of negative carry. Normalized spread and blowup mark-to-market could be a measure, but actually the ratio of these two quantities is the main decision factor.

We observe that the 10-year 3 to 7 percent CDX IG tranche has the highest blowup mark-to-market (MTM)-to-spread ratio (see Table 6.17), whereas the 5-year 10 to 15 percent CDX IG tranche has the lowest blowup mark-to-market-to-spread ratio (see Table 6.18), not counting for the 0 to 3 percent equity tranches.[8]

TABLE 6.14 Six-Month P&L of Carry-Neutral Dispersion Trade, a Sensitivity to Parallel Spread Changes, March 7, 2005 (in dollars)

	Maturity	−10bp	−5bp	0bp	5bp	10bp	15bp	30bp
Buy Protection on 3%–7% Tranche	10-year	(1,251,209)	(857,768)	(451,439)	(34,485)	383,973	813,278	2,015,418
Sell Protection on 10%–15% Tranche	5-year	1,412,661	1,175,298	701,194	69,584	(650,503)	(1,566,434)	(3,898,581)
Net		161,452	317,530	249,755	35,098	(266,530)	(753,156)	(1,883,163)

Model-based analysis. The P&L is based on spread change (blowup) for selected credits, with the rest of input parameters kept unchanged. Correlation skews are rescaled based on the expected tranche loss. Blowup is defined as spread widening of one credit for 400 bp.
Source: Citigroup.

TABLE 6.15 Six-Month P&L of Carry-Neutral Dispersion Trade, a Sensitivity to Blowups, March 7, 2005 (in dollars)

	One Blowup	Two Blowups
Net	377,715	488,812

Model-based analysis. The P&L is based on spread change (blowup) for selected credits, with the rest of input parameters kept unchanged. Correlation skews are rescaled based on the expected tranche loss. Blowup is defined as spread widening of one credit for 400 bp.
Source: Citigroup.

TABLE 6.16 Six-Month P&L of Carry-Neutral Dispersion Trade, a Sensitivity to Defaults, March 7, 2005 (in dollars)

	One Default	Two Defaults
Net	642,900	1,090,389

Model-based analysis. The P&L is based on spread change (blowup) for selected credits, with the rest of input parameters kept unchanged. Correlation skews are rescaled based on the expected tranche loss. Blowup is defined as spread widening of one credit for 400 bp.
Source: Citigroup.

TABLE 6.17 Ten-Year IG CDX Tranches, Blowup MTM/Spread Efficiency, March 7, 2005 (blowup MTM in dollars)

	Spread[a] (bp)	Tranche Duration	Delta	Blowup[b] MTM ($)	Spread/ (Delta ∗ Duration)	Blowup MTM/ (Delta ∗ Duration)	Blowup MTM/ Spread
0%– 3%	1,773	4.35	8.0	205,694	51.2	5,944	116
3%– 7%	442	7.30	11.5	239,858	5.3	2,867	543
7%–10%	156.5	7.89	3.7	75,816	5.3	2,574	484
10%–15%	70.5	8.05	2.5	33,593	3.4	1,638	476
15%–30%	29.5	8.12	0.7	10,435	5.1	1,803	354

[a]Spreads are midlevel.The 0% to % tranche is quoted as equivalent running spreads with no points up-front payment.
[b]Blowup is defined as spread widening of one credit for 400 bp.
Source: Citigroup.

TABLE 6.18 Five-Year CDX IG Tranches, Blowup MTM/Spread Efficiency, March 7, 2005 (blowup MTM in dollars)

	Spread[a] (bp)	Duration	Delta	Blowup[b] MTM ($)	Spread/ (Delta * Duration)	Blowup MTM/ (Delta * Duration)	Blowup MTM/ Spread
0%– 3%	1,234	3.68	18.7	297,762	17.9	4,322	241
3%– 7%	149.5	4.51	8.1	76,936	4.1	2,101	515
7%–10%	49	4.57	1.6	18,450	6.9	2,593	377
10%–15%	16.5	4.58	1.3	5,011	2.8	847	304
15%–30%	6.5	4.59	0.1	2,463	12.3	4,656	379

[a]Spreads are midlevel. The 0%–3% tranche is quoted as equivalent running spreads with no points up-front payment.
[b]Blowup is defined as spread widening of one credit for 400 bp.
Source: Citigroup.

Again, note that choice of tranches has been made based on the CDX IG 3 index (with maturity March 2010/March 2015), but we expected that the roll should not affect our selection.

Conclusions

To summarize:

- This is not a bull-bear tranche trade.
- Liquid tranche markets across different maturities offer the opportunity to look for alternative strategies.
- The recommended strategy lets investors express views on dispersion of spreads in the CDX IG portfolio.
- Investors should benefit if an individual credit in the CDX IG blows up. Significant parallel spread moves hurt the trade.
- In the past, each CDX IG portfolio had credits that have widened significantly, although overall spread levels have been relatively range-bound.
- Looking forward, the new CDX IG portfolio with its improved credit quality should be a suitable reference pool for the implementation of the dispersion strategy.

CASE STUDY: ATTRACTIONS OF HEDGED MEZZANINES

The following is another practical application of STCDOs. Investors comfortable with default risk, but looking for carry and convexity, usually sell delta-hedged equity tranche protection. The case study focuses on selling delta-hedged mezzanine protection, which achieves the same goal yet leaves the investor exposed to less default risk for the same carry. Such a strategy can be more attractive for low-leverage fixed-income portfolios.

Motivation

Strong credit fundamentals and uncertainties about the direction of spreads have led investors to seek strategies in which they may bear some credit risk but benefit from positive carry and positive convexity. A typical strategy consists of selling protection on the equity tranche of a synthetic CDO and buying protection on the underlying names in the CDS markets.[9]

An alternative way to achieve the same exposure is to buy a credit portfolio and then to buy protection on a mezzanine tranche—that is, to short a mezzanine tranche delta-hedged. This still creates a position that is long default risk and long convexity, and is hedged against spread movements. Its main advantage is that it has lower default risk per unit of carry and is more attractive than the equity trade for low-leverage fixed-income portfolios. However, it can have a less attractive time-decay profile for low defaults.

In this section, we illustrate the risk/return profile of a hedged mezzanine trade and contrast it with an equity trade with a similar jump-to-default (JTD) risk.

The Trade

The trade that we propose consists of buying $16.7 million[10] of protection on the 3 to 6 percent tranche and selling protection on individual names via CDSs in a ratio of 1 to 10.9. Our example is based on a diversified portfolio that includes 100 global names and has an average spread of 55 bp. The ratio of 10.9 makes the tranche spread-neutral at current spread levels. An alternative would be to carry out the trade on an index portfolio (e.g., iTraxx).

The trade is Credit01 neutral and benefits from positive convexity and a positive carry of $27,000 per million notional. This seems to be an appropriate time to implement this trade, as the 3 to 6 percent appears expensive by historical standards (see Figure 6.11, which

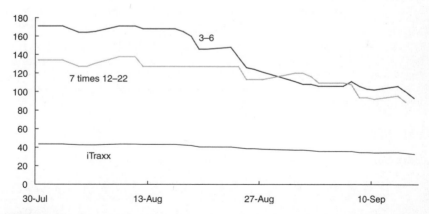

FIGURE 6.11 iTraxx Tranches—Spreads, August 1, 2004, to September 15, 2004 (in basis points)
Source: Citigroup.

shows its price change compared with changes in the iTraxx, as well as a delta-weighted amount of the 12 to 22 percent tranche).[11]

Comparing Delta-Hedged Equity and Mezzanines

We contrast the risk and return characteristics of the proposed hedged mezzanine trade with a hedged equity trade with a similar JTD risk. Table 6.19 shows the premiums, Credit01, and JTD numbers for the unhedged tranches and the average for underlying CDSs. It also reports the CDS hedges required to make a $1 million position Credit01-neutral.

Table 6.20 demonstrates the relative attractiveness of the mezzanine trade versus the equity trade. While the amount of carry per unit of notional is lower for the mezzanine than for the equity, the JTD risk is also markedly lower. This leads to a substantially better carry-to-JTD trade-off for the mezzanine trade. In Table 16.21, we compare the two trades for a given level of JTD risk.

Because investors are comfortable with default risk, they should compare the two routes based on equal default risk. The trade shown in Table 6.21 proposes that investors buy protection on $16.7 million of the 3 to 6 percent tranche and hedge by selling $181.5 million of CDS protection, giving equal default exposure to the delta-hedged $1 million 0 to 3 percent tranche.

Exposure to Single-Name Spread Movement

The positive macro-convexity of both trades enables investors to profit from marketwide increases in spreads. However, the widening of individual name spreads can adversely affect investors. Figures 6.12 and 6.13 show changes in the hedge ratio (ratio of a given name's micro-delta to the delta of the corresponding CDS), as spreads widen for a given counterparty. The hedge ratio of the equity tranche increases monotonically[12] as spreads widen, while the 3 to 6 percent hedge ratio is hump-shaped.

TABLE 6.19   Premium and Credit01 per $1 Million Exposure

	Premium (bp)	Credit01 ($000s)	JTD ($000s) (0% Recovery)	CDS Hedge ($MM)
3%–6%	335	5	96	10.9
0%–3%	1,808	10.5	441	22.8
CDS (Average)	55.2	0.46	10	

Source: Citigroup.

TABLE 6.20   Trade—Net Carry, Convexity, and JTD Risk for $1 Million Hedged Position

	Carry ($000s)	Gamma	JTD ($000s)	Carry/JTD
Hedged Mezzanine	27	17	13	2.09
Hedged Equity	55	163	213	0.26

Source: Citigroup.

TABLE 6.21 The Trade—Buy Hedged Protection on $16.7 Million Mezzanine

	Notional ($MM)	Carry ($000)	JTD ($000)	Gamma
Proposed Mezzanine Trade				
3%–6%	−16.7	−559	1,603	284
CDS	181.5	1,002	−1,815	
Net		443	−212	284
Traditional Equity Route				
0%–3%	1	181	−441	163
CDS	−22.8	−126	228	
Net		55	−213	163

Source: Citigroup.

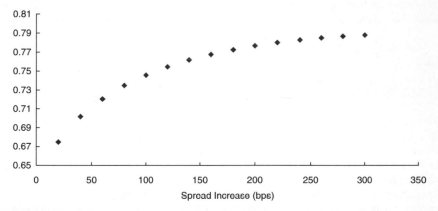

FIGURE 6.12 Hedge Ratio of 0 to 3 Percent Tranche as One Name Widens
Source: Citigroup.

What does this imply for a delta-hedged investor anxious to rehedge as spreads move out? Here, too, the mezzanine route offers a little leeway, particularly for tight spread names. Let's start with the bad news: Both trades suffer from negative microconvexity. As spreads blow out, the hedge ratio increases for the equity route (buy more protection at increasing cost), and decreases for the mezzanine route (also buy more protection, because the CDS hedge for this route is to go long CDSs). However, for a small spread widening, the mezzanine route shows positive microconvexity (the spread ratio increases and the investor needs to sell more CDS protection).

In addition, both strategies would be affected by movements in default correlation and changes in the correlation skew profile[13] across different levels of seniority within the capital structure. A global portfolio diversifies some of this risk: Default correlation within

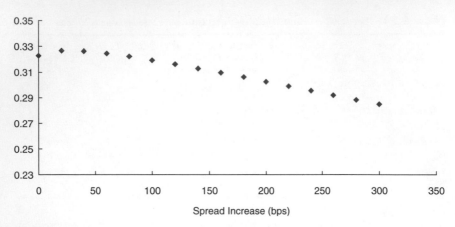

FIGURE 6.13 Hedge Ratio of 3 to 6 Percent Tranche as One Name Widens
Source: Citigroup.

the European iTraxx and U.S. CDX tranches, the visible indicators of default correlation and the basis for the pricing of bespoke tranches, have not been perfectly correlated.

Time-Decay Profile

Table 6.22 shows the changes in Credit01, JTD, and hedge ratios after one year, assuming that no prior rehedging has been performed and no default has occurred. It is clear from the table that investors in the mezzanine trade will need to buy back protection to reduce the size of their hedge. The loss incurred at the time of the rehedging, of course, will depend on realized CDS spreads in one year. If they are higher than current spreads, as implied by the forward curve, then the loss may be large. However, if realized spreads are close to current spreads, then the loss would be smaller. The same applies to

TABLE 6.22 Credit01 per $1 Million Exposure after One Year[a]

	Credit01 ($000s)	JTD ($000s) 0% Recovery	Previous/New Hedge Ratios
3%–6%	3.5	70	10.9/9.2
0%–3%	10.1	452	−22.8/−26.6
CDS (Average)	0.38	10	

[a]Assumes no default and unchanged spreads.
Source: Citigroup.

TABLE 6.23 Hedged Mezzanine and Hedged Equity Strategies—P&L

	Mezz PV ($000s) (55 bp Flat Curve)	Equity PV ($000s) (55 bp Flat (Curve)	Mezz PV ($000s) (Current Curve)	Equity PV ($000s) (Current) Curve)
0 Default	−269	45	144	−473
1 Default	−748	−69	−333	−590
2 Defaults	−952	−161	−534	−687
3 Defaults	−819	−218	−400	−745
5 Defaults	951	−175	1370	−702
10 Defaults	5,245	456	5,662	−68

Source: Citigroup.

investors in the equity trade who will need to increase their level of protection on individual names.

The cost of rehedging for both trades has to be balanced with the significant amount of carry earned by investors. In particular, as mentioned, the mezzanine trade currently offers a good carry/risk ratio.

In Table 6.23, we show the P&L of the mezzanine and equity trades, depending on prevailing spreads and the number of defaults in one year. In the first two columns, the P&L is reported assuming that the spread curve is flat and equal to 55 bp, while in the last two columns, the P&L is computed assuming that next year the curve is identical to the current curve.

Table 6.23 clearly shows the impact of defaults on our proposed trade. The first default leads to a large loss, and the second default also adds to the losses. The two defaults are absorbed by the equity tranche and, therefore, affect the mezzanine tranche less than its CDS hedge portfolio. Any additional defaults, however, contribute positively to the present value, as the subordination of the mezzanine tranche becomes progressively eroded and the loss on the tranche on which one has bought protection starts to exceed the loss on the CDS portfolio. The spread curve appears to be a very significant determinant of future trade performance. The lower the level of spreads next year, the better (or worse, respectively) the performance of the mezzanine (equity) trade.

Conclusion

Investors willing to take default risk can consider buying hedged protection on the 3 to 6 percent tranche of a global portfolio or an index. While exposed to JTD risk and correlation, the trade benefits from positive convexity and better carry per unit of JTD risk than the more traditional hedged equity trade. Custom mezzanine tranches can also be an interesting trade for tailoring specific risk/return profiles.

CHAPTER 7

Trading Credit Tranches: Taking Default Correlation out of the Black Box

Ratul Roy

For a tranched or single-tranche collateralized debt obligation (STCDO) investor, default correlation determines what share of the portfolio risk stays within a tranche, that is, the fair premium relative to the total portfolio spread. Until recently the Street quoted tranche-specific correlation for the various index tranches because no single correlation value with the Street-accepted Gaussian copula framework for portfolio risk could explain all the quoted prices. The method also had problems in relation to quoting bespoke tranche prices. This chapter describes an alternative framework that is now used Streetwide—a base correlation skew model that breaks a portfolio into a series of increasingly thick equity tranches and treats a mezzanine tranche as analogous to a spread of two equity tranches. We then highlight some relative value trading opportunities that may appear by looking at the base correlation skew across different markets (e.g., iTraxx and CDX) and conclude with a case study where we recommended investors put on a curve-flattener trade motivated by, among other reasons, a probable correction to the then Base Correlation Skew curve.

THE CREDIT TRANCHE MARKET

The past few years have witnessed tremendous growth both in credit derivatives, and in tranched credit products referencing pools of corporate credit risk. Usually the reference pools backing these tranched products are pure corporate default risk; more recently, mixed reference pools of

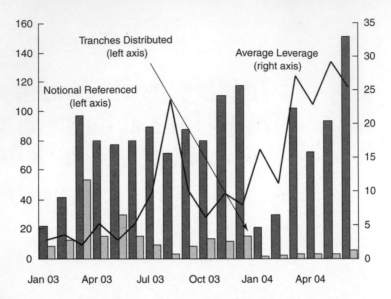

FIGURE 7.1 Global Issuance of Synthetic CDOs and Average Leverage

corporate and structured finance risk have become popular through synthetic asset-backed securities (ABS) CDO vehicles.

Tight corporate spreads have provided a further stimulus to investors' demand for tranched products. Investors have been more willing than ever to leverage up, shown by the line in Figure 7.1 that tracks this measure by taking the ratio of value of tranches distributed to the notional referenced in these structures.[1] This is partly due to more investors getting comfortable with taking equity risk in a low-default environment, and partly due to growth in structures leveraging mezzanine tranche risk—for example, CDO-squareds.

Despite the growth in the market, many investors remain on the sidelines, concerned by the black-box nature of the product. In particular, default correlation, which is an important parameter in pricing credit tranches, seems opaque to many investors. Index tranche trading and the prevalence of a common Street model for portfolio credit risk (Gaussian copula[2]) has helped to start taking default correlation out of the black box. By quoting prices on standardized tranches of standardized portfolios, participants can trade and hedge default correlation positions separately from their spread and default exposure. Further, as confidence and the number of participants in the product have increased, tranche bid/offer spreads have shrunk.

Importance of Default Correlation in Tranches

Why are we so concerned with default correlation? For a tranched investor, default correlation determines what share of the portfolio credit risk stays within a tranche. Using the industry-standard Gaussian copula model, we show in Figure 7.2 two excess loss distributions (i.e., the vertical axis shows probability of loss exceeding values on horizontal axis) for the same average default probability but for two different correlation assumptions (10 percent and 30 percent).[3] The importance of correlation can be illustrated by putting oneself in the shoes of a tranche holder who has 8 percent subordination (i.e., 8 percent equity below the investment). The second portfolio, with 30 percent correlation, would imply a much higher loss for this protection seller, and therefore require a higher premium to be paid in compensation. Higher correlations imply higher losses for senior tranches and lower losses for equity tranches.

Given the importance of this parameter, investors are justifiably concerned about how it should be quantified. Unfortunately, while the index tranche market has brought some welcome transparency, it has also evoked many important questions.

Problems with Traditional Correlation Measure

It is ironic and of concern that no single default correlation value explains all tranche prices. It is as if different tranche participants at different levels of risk attachment have their own views of the portfolio loss distribution. Table 7.1 shows the correlation variable for each tranche that matches the respective tranche premium using a Gaussian copula framework. Senior risk takers, for example, the 12 to 22 percent tranche, are asking for a higher premium, with correlations around 30 percent, than would be appropriate for more junior tranches. On the 3 to 6 percent tranche, meanwhile, correlations are far lower than on the other tranches, at only 4 percent.

We started the discussion with the leveraged position of tranche participants and the impact that default correlation has on the riskiness of any tranche. Yet, we find that the market standard model of calculating the implied tranche correlation is raising rather than answering questions. The inconsistencies shown earlier in correlation levels are, to say the least, nonintuitive. Supply and demand might cause small differences in traded correlation levels, but there is no reason to think that at different points in the capital structure correlation levels should be more than double the levels for another tranche. We would argue that these inconsistencies are not a problem with the market but, rather, evidence of a flaw in the traditional Gaussian copula model.

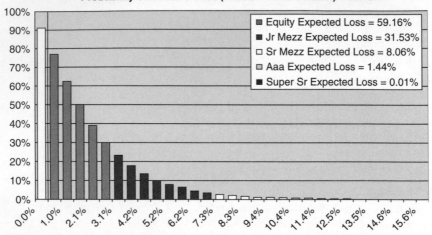

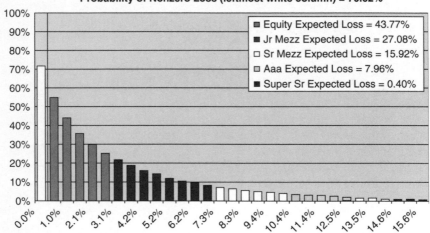

FIGURE 7.2 Impact of Correlation on Portfolio Loss Distribution
Source: Citigroup.

TABLE 7.1   Correlation Factor Fitting Tranche Prices

	5-Year, 20-Sep-09 (42.5 bp)		Correlation (%)	
	Bid (bp)	Ask (bp)	Bid (%)	Ask (%)
0%–3%	27[a]	28.5[a]	22.4	21.3
3%–6%	170	177	4.0	4.1
6%–9%	71	75	14.9	15.4
9%–12%	42	46	21.9	23.2
12%–22%	19.5	22.5	29.7	32.2

[a]Points up front + 500 bp running.
Source: Citigroup.

SKEW IN DEFAULT CORRELATION

Further Flaws in Tranche Correlation

The index tranche market, as we have seen, shows a different implied correlation number for each tranche when one fits the tranche expected loss implied by the traded tranche price as a share of the total overall portfolio loss. We have also seen that there is no simple pattern to this simple tranche correlation number. For example, 0 percent to 3 percent is trading at 22 percent, the next tranche up is at 4 percent, and then correlation rises again to 15 percent for the 6 percent to 9 percent tranche.

Nor is the inexplicable pattern of correlation the only problem with the traditional tranche correlation model. In many cases, this model fails to give a unique correlation value for a given spread level. Two correlation values fit the 3 percent to 6 percent tranche; that is, it is not clear whether one should use the higher or the lower number. Moreover, as Figure 7.3 shows, a premium much higher than 300 bp for the 3 percent to 6 percent tranche at the portfolio spread of 43 bp can never be explained by this approach.

If the tranche correlation pattern is really as skewed as Figure 7.3 shows, it is hard to know what correlation number should be used to price, say, a 4 percent to 7 percent tranche of the index, let alone a tranche from a bespoke portfolio. The pattern in tranche correlation does not offer any coherent insight into how investors view risk at different points in the capital structure, and so it is difficult to make comparisons between different portfolios, different maturities, and different risk attachment points within one portfolio. We believe an alternative framework is required.

Correlation Skew Is Like a Volatility Surface

Given the problems we have highlighted with tranche correlation, we propose a different way of looking at the market's risk appetite at various

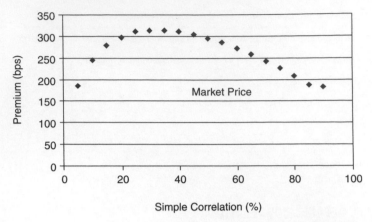

FIGURE 7.3 Premium of 3 Percent to 6 Percent Tranche as Function of Market-Standard Tranche Correlation for iTraxx = 43 bp
Source: Citigroup.

parts of the loss distribution. We would like to find a model that has an economic explanation and is able to explain the market data—for example, the relatively high risk premium that we have seen demanded by protection sellers at senior tranches. We take our cue from the equity or foreign exchange (FX) option markets, where two features are widely accepted:

No single implied volatility in the Black-Scholes framework explains different option prices at different strikes and maturities; however, the market accepts the framework as standard and extends it by using a "volatility surface."

Call/put spread options (options that have a payout between two different strike values) are priced as a difference between call/put options struck at the two strike points. The implied volatilities used at these strike points are given by the volatility surface seen in the market.

We therefore propose a "base correlation skew" model that does just this. It treats a mezzanine—for example, 3 percent to 6 percent—tranche as analogous to spread product, in this case as a spread of two equity (0 percent to 3 percent and 0 percent to 6 percent) tranches. Equity tranches are analogous to single strike options where the underlying payout to the protection buyer is the portfolio loss.

Quoted index tranche premiums provide information on the losses implied by the 0 to 3 percent and subsequent mezzanine tranches. As a result, by summing over the losses of mezzanine tranches, we can calculate the loss distribution curve for a series of equity tranches at increasing attachment points (0 to 3 percent, 0 to 6 percent, 0 to 9 percent, and so on).

Inputs: iTraxx = 43.5 bps; 0–3% = 28.5 points (up front) plus 500 bps running; 3–6% = 195 bps

Step 1: Calculate 0–3% correlation (equivalent for Skew and Tranche Correlation)

Correlation = 19.7%; Loss PV = 13.6 mil (1); Annuity01[a] = 101.1 mil (2)

Step 2: Calculate 0–6% correlation iteratively

Trial Correlation	Loss (3)	Annuity01 (4)	Premium 3-6% = [(3) − (1)]/[(4) − (2)]
25%	16.6 mil	233.9 mil	226 bp
31.25%	15.6 mil	236.2 mil	148 bp
27.6%	16.2 mil	234.8 mil	**195 bps**

FIGURE 7.4 Correlation Skew and Loss Are Interlinked: Correlation at 6 Percent Attachment Point
[a]Annuity01 is the change in present value of the premium leg due to a 1 bp change in swap spread. Breakeven premium for zero up-front tranches is equal to LossPV/Annuity01.
Source: Citigroup.

We can then iteratively[4] find a correlation that reprices each subsequent equity tranche while satisfying the constraint that the mezzanine tranche is priced and also holding the correlations calculated for each preceding equity tranche fixed. We illustrate the calculation for the 0 percent to 6 percent tranche in Figure 7.4: As the calculation shows a correlation value of 27.6 percent at the 6 percent attachment point, we can reprice the 3 percent to 6 percent tranche. Similarly, we would iteratively calculate the correlation skew at the 9 percent attachment point given the skew at the 3 percent and 6 percent points and the 6 percent to 9 percent tranche premium.

Rather than looking at the absolute correlation number at each attachment point, investors sometimes look at the correlation as a multiple or fraction of an underlying arbitrarily chosen "base correlation." For example, if we choose this number to be 25 percent, the default correlation at the 3 percent attachment point would be 79 percent of this number, and be 110 percent at the 6 percent attachment point. Note that the choice of the underlying number would not affect the slope or skew of the default correlation between the 6 percent and 3 percent attachment points.

Figure 7.5 shows an example of the skew calibration applied to iTraxx and contrasts this with the market-standard tranche correlation. Notice most importantly how different the levels are, especially at the 3 percent to 6 percent tranche. We have already highlighted the problem of tranche correlation for this risk level. Also note how for the tranche correlation approach the bid/offer lines cross: This is to do with the different sensitivities

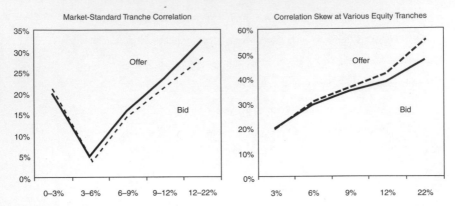

FIGURE 7.5   Market-Standard Tranche Correlation and Base Correlation Skew
Method for iTraxx Tranches
Source: Citigroup.

of the equity and mezzanine tranches to correlation when measured using
this approach. We will revisit this when discussing correlation risk.

Skew Is Market's Risk Preference

The correlation skew, we argue, expresses the market's risk preference for
losses at different attachment points. The loss distribution and the correlation curve are intimately linked: Our bootstrapping method in Figure 7.5
explicitly derives the correlation skew curve from the expected loss of the
tranche that is implied by its market spread. The method also allows us to
build up progressively a loss curve and a correlation skew curve for equity
tranches at all index attachment points (3, 6, 9, 12, and 22 percent for
iTraxx). We can then interpolate to price tranches at any attachment point
and thickness.

What do changes in the shape of the correlation skew curve mean for
participants? We represent this pictorially in Figure 7.6, which shows the
impact of a changing correlation skew curve (right diagram in Figure 7.5)
on the expected loss of each tranche. The circles represent the size of
the expected loss of three hypothetical tranches of different seniorities
(increasing from left to right), which start off with similar expected losses.
The vertical axis shows increasing correlation, and the gray bar shows the
correlation in the three tranches. A horizontal bar means that all attachment
points have a correlation equal to the base correlation, that is, there is
no skew. We show two types of changes: The top row depicts changes in
expected loss for a change in the absolute level of the base correlation across

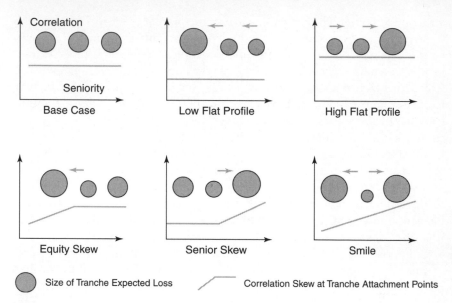

Base Case   Low Flat Profile   High Flat Profile

Equity Skew   Senior Skew   Smile

● Size of Tranche Expected Loss   ╱ Correlation Skew at Tranche Attachment Points

FIGURE 7.6   Correlation Skew as Loss Redistribution among Tranches
Source: Citigroup.

the capital structure while still remaining flat. The bottom row depicts changes in expected loss in situations where the correlation skew curve develops a positive slope for only part or the full height of the capital structure. A lowering of correlation at the junior tranches (through either a parallel shift downward or a steepening of the gray bar) tends to move out risk into those tranches; in contrast, an increase in correlation through a parallel or steepening move increases the expected loss of the senior tranche. When the skew curve is positively sloped throughout, as in the "smile" scenario, losses are pushed out from the mezzanine into the equity and senior tranches.

If there was no skew, it would be as if there was consensus on the true correlation among defaults of individual credits. As we know, this is not the case—in particular, today's skew, shown in the right diagram of Figure 7.5, resembles the "smile" scenario, and illustrates the relatively high risk aversion of senior—for example, 12 percent to 22 percent—tranche holders.

Supply and demand will change the profile of the skew and, therefore, the premiums for all tranches. Until recently, the market was dominated by substantial demand from ratings-driven institutional investors to sell protection to dealers on tranches typically between 3 percent and 9 percent attachment points. These tranches attract investment grade ratings and offer higher spreads than similarly rated corporates. This demand for one part of the capital structure puts pressure on tranche premiums and creates a "smile" scenario where mezzanine tranches are priced to lower expected loss. Other factors also influence the skew. Hedged tranche investors wishing to take default risk and positive carry through equity and junior mezzanine tranches but keen to hedge spread movement by buying protection on senior tranches also contribute to the smile (by bidding up the protection cost). Institutional investors wishing to hedge their cash portfolios, also by buying senior tranche protection, have a similar impact.

Similar to the apparent risk aversion at senior tranches (expressed through higher premium and therefore positively sloped skew curve), investors also seem to demand higher compensation at equity tranches. Investors view portfolios as carrying much more idiosyncratic risk and less systemic risk than senior tranche holders. Broker-dealers, too, can be part of this group—as a hedge against their long protection positions through transacting with investors, dealers have sometimes been keen to sell protection at these tranches to hedge their correlation risk. In skew terms equity tranches tend to be priced with lower correlation than would be true otherwise: This contributes to the "smile" effect.

To illustrate the impact of a change in skew on premiums, we take two skews—one based on iTraxx prices and the other hypothetical, which we call "Thin Tail." We call it so because even though the iTraxx is at the same level (42.5 bp in our example) the senior tranches of the Thin Tail pricing are at much lower premiums, implying that the probability of high losses is low relative to the risk of high losses implied by iTraxx tranche prices. Since the 0 to 3 percent in both are at the same level, this means that in the Thin Tail scenario, the expected losses of the senior tranche are now contained in the mezzanine tranche, which must therefore demand a higher premium. The pricing and correlation skew of the two scenarios are compared in Table 7.2. For completeness, in addition to our base correlation skew levels, we also include the traditional iTraxx tranche correlation. Note also that a 364 bp premium for the 3 percent to 6 percent tranche is possible in this theoretical scenario, unlike Figure 7.4.

We have already shown in Figure 7.5 that loss and skew are intimately linked (skew is derived from the losses implied by the tranche premiums). We should therefore expect that the two different skew curves (market and Thin Tail) in Table 7.2 show different loss distributions. We illustrate two measures of comparison in Figure 7.7—one, the cumulative losses at different attachment points (left diagram) and two, the probability of losses exceeding different attachment points (right diagram).

TABLE 7.2 Premium and Correlation for Equity Tranche at Different Attachment Points for Two Portfolios of Same Spread (42.5 bp) but Different Skews: One iTraxx Based, and the Other Hypothetical

Attachment Point	iTraxx Market Skew			Hypothetical Thin Tail Skew	
	Premium (bp)	Correlation (Tranche) (%)	Correlation (Skew) (%)	Premium (BP)	Correlation (Skew) (%)
3%	28.5[a]	19.8	20	28.5[a]	20
6	177	5.6	28	364	13
9	75	16.2	34	56	13
12	46	23.4	38	13	13
22	22.5	32.1	46	2	13

[a]Points up front + 500 bp running.
Source: Citigroup.

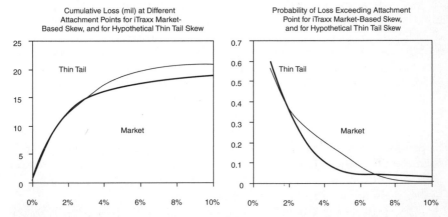

FIGURE 7.7 Cumulative Loss and Probability of Excess Loss for Two Different Skew Curves
Source: Citigroup.

Investor Risk Appetite May Scale Across Markets

If our premise of skew representing risk preference is true, then we should find some relationship among the few index tranche markets in the way investors view risk. Take for example the correlation skew seen in the 5-year and 10-year European iTraxx markets, and in the U.S. CDX markets. At first glance, the skew curves are divergent, as shown in Figure 7.8,

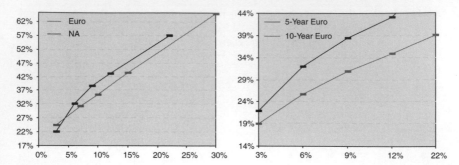

FIGURE 7.8 Correlation of 5-Year European iTraxx Skew with 5-Year U.S. CDX, and with 10-Year iTraxx, July 8, 2004
Source: Citigroup.

which compares the 5-year and 10-year European iTraxx indexes, and the 5-year iTraxx and U.S. CDX indexes. All three indexes show a positively sloped correlation skew curve, much like our smile scenario of Figure 7.6, but there are differences in the levels. For almost all attachment points, correlations on 5-year iTraxx are higher than those on 5-year U.S. CDX and 10-year iTraxx. This seems reasonable, because the same attachment point on 5 years represents a more senior point in terms of expected loss (since expected loss over 5 years is lower than over 10 years). Similarly, expected losses in the U.S. CDX are higher at each attachment point due to the higher spreads, implying more default risk. Hence, if risk aversion is greatest at the most senior attachment points (and therefore so is willingness to pay for protection for these low-probability default events) then it is fair that a senior tranche holder of the 5-year iTraxx is at a higher correlation position that one in the 10-year iTraxx (because higher correlation means higher premium for the senior tranches).

One way to test whether skew corresponds to risk aversion is to see if the differences in the correlation skew curves narrow if one somehow adjusts for the differences in default risk between the portfolios. We do this in two ways: first, by scaling the attachment point by the ratio of spread (as a proxy for default risk), and second, by the ratio of expected loss. The correlation seen at a specific attachment point for a high-risk portfolio must be compared with the correlation seen for a lower attachment point for a lower-risk portfolio. Only by doing this can we place the two positions at the same level of risk aversion along one common portfolio. For example, the 6 percent attachment point for a 10-year iTraxx should be compared with the 4.2 percent point for 5-year iTraxx if the 10-year spread is 35 percent more than the 5-year (the common portfolio being the 5-year iTraxx

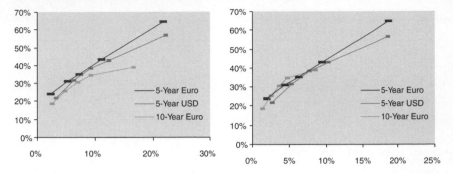

FIGURE 7.9   Correlation of 5-Year and 10-Year European iTraxx and 5-Year U.S. CDX, Rescaled to Spread (left) and Loss (right)
Source: Citigroup, July 8, 2004.

for this comparison). On doing this, we find some convergence, as shown in Figure 7.9.

The convergence that we have shown when scaling portfolios based on their risk is certainly very appealing and leads to credibility to our view that base correlation skew represents the market's risk preference at different risk attachment points. Historical data on index tranche trading is relatively short, however.

Greeks: Managing Correlation and Delta Risk

Now that we have established that the tranche correlation and base correlation skew methods are different ways of looking at the loss distribution of the mezzanine tranches (and we have argued for the more rational stance of the Skew approach), it will come as no surprise to see that risk measures from the two approaches show differences.

Skew Model Gives More Reliable Spread Sensitivities   The first dramatic result concerns spread sensitivity especially at the junior mezzanine 3 percent to 6 percent tranche. Even though both the skew and the tranche correlation models reprice to the same tranche price, the risk measures can be different. Tranche loss is a function of both portfolio spread and correlation. Moreover, the ratio of the tranche expected loss to that of the portfolio determines the at-the-money-ness of the tranche protection. For example, as the probability of portfolio losses recede because of tightening spreads, the mezzanine tranche starts to resemble the senior tranche. With increasing spreads, the behavior is more like equity. The 3 percent to 6 percent tranche sits at the crossroads of two very large jumps in tranche

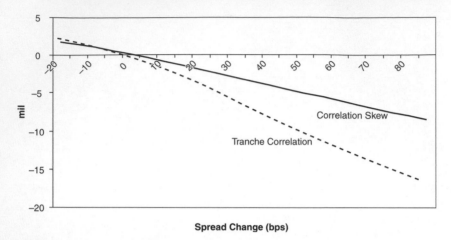

FIGURE 7.10   Issuance in Billions of USD and Leverage in Times
Source: CreditFlux, Citigroup.

correlation (see left diagram of Figure 7.5). When one uses the tranche correlation approach, a change in expected loss of the tranche can shift it into very different correlation territory. In contrast, the skew approach creates a smooth curve (right diagram of Figure 7.5) without these jumps. Figure 7.10 shows that the tranche correlation and skew methods give very different profiles of change in present value of the 3 percent to 6 percent tranche with respect changes in portfolio spread. Since Credit01 is the slope of the curve in Figure 7.10, one can see that the two approaches present different numbers. As a consequence, a risk taker who wants to position for convexity by doing a long tranche-short single-name Credit01-neutral trade is presented with two different hedge ratios.

We believe the sensitivity predicted by the correlation skew is more correct. The market, in fact, quotes Credit01s in relation to index tranche trading, which are closer to the theoretical values calculated by the skew framework. In Figure 7.11 we compare the spread sensitivity (Credit01) of the two methods by predicting the change in the daily 3 percent to 6 percent tranche premiums from the change in the iTraxx premiums, knowing the tranche duration.[5] A hedged investor would have performed better in general with the skew model. The divergence at the end, however, may indicate that model improvements can be made in our understanding of portfolio credit risk.

Skew Model Gives Unique Loss Exposure   As a tranche risk participant, one is anxious to know about the probability of loss exceeding various attachment

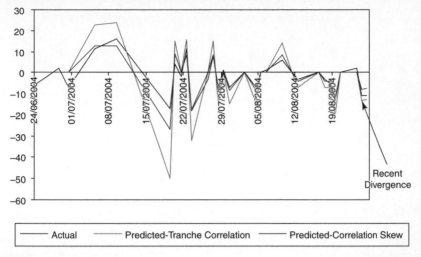

FIGURE 7.11 Actual versus Predicted 3%–6% Tranche Premium Change with Tranche Correlation and Skew
Source: Citigroup.

points—in particular, the lower attachment point of the tranche. Here, too, the two approaches provide different results. We note that the implied probability may be obtained by differentiating with respect to either the high or the low attachment point of each mezzanine tranche. However, we have two possible observations for each attachment point: the tranche below and the one above the point. For example, if we consider the 3 percent attachment point, we can obtain the probability of losses exceeding this level by either differentiating the 0 percent to 3 percent tranche or the 3 percent to 7 percent tranche. Since in the tranche correlation approach the two tranches are priced using very different correlations (see Figure 7.3 for example), we obtain two sets of different results for this and higher attachment points (see Figure 7.12). We also see quite different values than those we get based on using a base correlation skew approach of single correlation per equity tranche. Notice how the skew approach produces the widest probability of extreme losses by having the fattest tail for losses exceeding 30 percent.

Skew Model Allows Accurate Correlation Sensitivity Hedging   The Street is used to thinking of correlation sensitivity as change of tranche value by changing the simple tranche correlation by 1 percent. This is a relatively substantial change for the 3 percent to 6 percent tranche (which trades at a low tranche correlation) and much less for the others. In the base

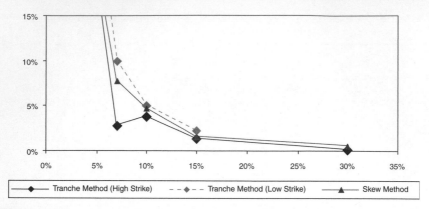

FIGURE 7.12   Implied Probability of Losses Exceeding Various Attachment Points
Source: Citigroup.

correlation skew framework, the correlation sensitivity of each mezzanine needs to be considered in terms of two or more buckets of equity tranches whose attachment points correspond to the upper and lower attachment points of the mezzanine. A seller of 6 percent to 9 percent mezzanine tranche protection is exposed to the short 0 percent to 6 percent and long 0 percent to 9 percent part of the correlation skew curve. If the skew curve moves in parallel, then the net sensitivity is just the sum of the two numbers.

Correlation bucketing is a powerful way of looking at correlation risk. It aggregates a portfolio of tranched products—index and bespoke portfolios—into various parts of the correlation skew curve and suggests suitable correlation hedges. Tranche correlation is not as robust because there is no underlying relationship to describe the correlation behavior of different tranches. For example, it would be unclear as to what hedges would be appropriate for a nonindex tranche—for example, 5 percent to 9 percent. In contrast, as shown in Table 7.3, which illustrates the sensitivities to the different buckets, this tranche has sensitivities to the 0 percent to 3 percent, 3 percent to 6 percent, and 6 percent to 9 percent tranche correlations.

Likewise, one can derive a term structure of correlation. Since indexes are increasingly quoted for several maturities, it is possible (and consistent) to imply a separate correlation skew for different maturities, thus ensuring that the pricing of a seven-year trade (for example) is consistent with both the skew at 5 years and the skew at 10 years. One can think of this as a line somewhere between the two curves in the right diagram of Figure 7.8.

Finally, remember that a skew approach is merely a framework for looking at mezzanine tranches as a payoff between two default strikes. It makes no assumptions about the copula model used (Gaussian or otherwise).

TABLE 7.3 Sensitivities to Correlation Using Two Approaches for Four iTraxx Tranches (each 30 million euros)

	Tranche Correlation	Skew (Parallel Move)	Correlation Skew Bucketed Risk			
			0–3%	0–6%	0–9%	0–12%
0%–3%	214,723	219,467	219,467			
3%–6%	(131,000[a])	(27,087)	(204,301)	177,214		
6%–9%	(73,952)	(4,137)		(172,678)	168,541	
9%–12%	(41,606)	(48,652)			(167,465)	118,813
5%–9%	NA	(17,014)	(63,025)	(125,957)	172,171	

[a]Average of 188,000 and (450,000).
Source: Citigroup.

We can also take a general correlation matrix, which may include different sectoral and subsectoral correlations, and apply the skew to the entire matrix: The most simple choice is to rescale all correlations by the same skew factor. In this way we can still calibrate the market skew while capturing more of the name-specific detail.

In Summary: Why Skew Is a Better Model

We think the base correlation skew model is a more robust way of looking at the well-established investor risk profile that the tranche correlation model shows. We have four main reasons. The first advantage is purely practical, and relates to the pricing of nonstandard tranche attachments. Given the jumps in tranche correlation, we have no insight into the value to be used for a tranche that spans, for example, part of two index attachment points. As we have illustrated, by being able to relate skews across a range of portfolios through their risk characteristics and maturities, one can price and hedge customized tranches of bespoke portfolios.

The second advantage is that the skew approach captures the market's risk preference—an example being the risk aversion at senior tranches manifested by relatively high premium for low risk probability. These risk preferences, commonly termed "fat tail" or "smile," can be represented, however, by other analytical approaches, for example, the Marshall-Olkin copula, which will exhibit different loss distributions from the Gaussian copula.

The third advantage is the uniqueness and range of correlation values, particularly for the 3 percent to 6 percent tranche. We have seen that at today's iTraxx index and tranche levels, the 3 percent to 6 percent tranche has two solutions for tranche correlation. Further, the maximum allowable premium for this tranche given today's index spread is limited irrespective of the tranche correlation used (see, for example, Figure 7.3, where the maximum allowed premium for the 3 percent to 6 percent tranche was a little over 300 bp). In contrast, the skew approach only has one solution and, as we have shown in Figure 7.8, can have solutions higher than this limit.

The last and most important benefit relates to risk measures. It has long been known that the spread sensitivity of the 3 percent to 6 percent tranche as predicted by the tranche correlation approach overpredicted risk. The market also quotes the spread sensitivity for this and other tranches in addition to premium—it does so by quoting the delta of the tranches as a multiple of the underlying iTraxx index. The quoted delta for the 3 percent to 6 percent tranche is usually close to what is predicted by the skew approach. Likewise, the correlation sensitivity for the tranche is better expressed by the skew approach for the reasons we have described.

That is not to say that the skew model is the final word on the subject. Part of the success, or otherwise, of the model is the level of detail in the assumptions that are used. Common instances where greater detail may be useful are the use of individual spreads for all credits instead of an average spread, and characterization of the default correlation between credits as due to several, and not just one (i.e., systemic) parameter. As presented in this chapter, we have not found it necessary to implement a multiparameter model for default correlation between credits, but this is one of several adjustments that can be accommodated within the skew framework. In many instances—for example, less diversified portfolios—we would recommend such additions. We have also just shown instances (for example, in spread sensitivity of the 3 percent to 6 percent iTraxx) where the skew model had good, but not perfect, predictive power. And, finally, as in any statistical model of portfolio loss, complete reliance on credit spreads and market-implied default correlation is not the best strategy if other information on individual credits—for example, bottom-up credit analysis—is available.

TRADING OPPORTUNITIES FOR INVESTORS

Tranche Correlation Can Still Provide Insight

Having spent most of the preceding section singing the praises of the correlation skew approach, it may come as some surprise to hear that we think tranche correlation can be useful in identifying relative value opportunities. Where there is little change in portfolio credit quality (for example, composition and spread), tranche correlation provides an attractive shorthand for changes in risk appetite across different attachment points. Thus, for

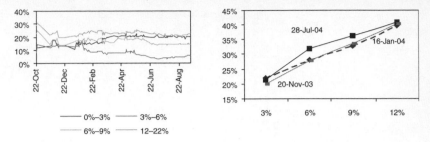

FIGURE 7.13 Evolution of Tranche Correlation and Base Correlation Skew
Source: Citigroup.

example, as shown in the left chart in Figure 7.13, tranche correlation moved out significantly on the 0 percent to 3 percent tranche from its low levels in late 2003 as greater participation from the hedge fund community was able to satisfy the natural desire of broker-dealers to buy protection at this tranche. Conversely, as market participants have started to view the senior (9 percent to 12 percent and 12 percent to 22 percent) tranches as an efficient and levered way to go short,[6] the tranche correlations for these tranches have also moved out. Deriving the same intuition from the correlation skew is less convenient; as the schematic representation Figure 7.5 shows, increasing risk aversion for the senior attachment points (i.e., higher premiums) is a function of both the level and steepness of the curve. The right chart in Figure 7.13 shows that this is the case by looking at three dates. Two features can be observed: first, the absolute correlation level at low attachment points was indeed the lowest late 2003, and second, the curve is indeed steeper in mid 2004, that is, risk has moved out currently from the mezzanine tranches to the equity and senior tranches (i.e., the sixth scenario in Figure 7.6). From a tranche correlation perspective, this would mean a lowering in implied correlation of the 3 to 6 percent tranche, which is what we see in the left diagram as well.

Often, though, the relationship between skew and tranche correlation is not that obvious. As a quick illustration, we show in Table 7.4 how a change in tranche premiums by the model Credit01 (for a 1 bp move in iTraxx, Scenario B versus A) has left the skew curve unchanged, but altered each of the tranche correlations. Likewise, a change in the premiums of a specific tranche—for example, the 3 percent to 6 percent without any change in iTraxx (comparing Scenario C with B)—will change only the tranche correlation of this specific tranche, but leave the others unchanged. In contrast, since the skew curve at each attachment point is bootstrapped from all the junior tranches below this point, such a change will affect the skew curve across all attachment points.

TABLE 7.4 Tranche and Skew Correlation

	Actual (A) (iTraxx = 36.5bp)			Full Delta Move (B) (iTraxx = 37.5 bp)			3–6% Offer Down (C) (iTraxx = 37.5 bp)		
	Premiums (bp)	Tranche (%)	Skew (%)	Premiums (bp)	Tranche (%)	Skew (%)	Premiums (bp)	Tranche (%)	Skew (%)
0%–3%	24[a]	18	18	25[a]	17.9	17.9	2.5[a]	17.9	17.9
3%–6%	115	5.4	28.3	122	5.2	28.3	117	4.8	28.9
6%–9%	52	16.4	34.5	56	16.5	34.5	56	16.5	35.1
9%–12%	33	24.1	38.7	34	23.8	38.7	34	23.8	39.4

[a]Points up front + 500 bp running.
Source: Citigroup.

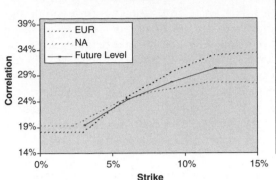

NA vs. Eur 10-Year Skew (scaled to expected loss)
27-July-04

	Current	Scenario	P&L
Eur			
3–6	460	476	16.1
6–9	216	240	**23.4**
NA			
3–7	662	649	13.8
7–10	327	297	**29.5**

FIGURE 7.14 Scenario for Skew Convergence to U.S.-Europe Average, and P&L for Trade, July 28, 2004
Source: Citigroup.

If investors share our view that the skew curve represents relative risk preference, then participants can put on trades that will profit from greater convergence between two markets. We made this case in an earlier publication[7] suggesting that investors position for convergence in correlation skew on the 10-year Europe iTraxx and U.S. CDX. This convergence had already happened in the 5-year Europe iTraxx and U.S. CDX, but had yet to be seen in the 10-year maturity. The recommended trade was to position for convergence in the most liquid tranches—in particular to buy protection on the 6 percent to 9 percent iTraxx versus selling protection on 7 percent to 10 percent CDX (the same idea could be expressed through other tranches—for example, 3 percent to 6 percent tranches of U.S. CDX and Europe iTraxx). Figure 7.14 shows one skew convergence scenario and the P&L impact on the trade. Clearly the most obvious downside for the trade would be if the European tranche became even more expensive relative to the U.S. tranche, causing the spread difference to widen. Since then, however, the skew did converge, resulting in a profit.

We think the base correlation skew framework will continue to be useful in identifying further such opportunities, as investors now have a common metric to compare various tranches and portfolios.

Pricing Off-Market Tranches

The way dealers price tranches of bespoke portfolios necessarily reflects observables in the tranched market, that is, 5-year and 10-year Europe iTraxx and U.S. CDX markets. This represents only two portfolios, five tranche attachment points, and two maturities (a total of 20 combinations). Broker-dealers have to use this data set to price tranches of a wide range of subordinations and thicknesses belonging to bespoke portfolios of all hues. Two common assumptions that are made are that default correlation between individual credits is uniform and independent of the specific sector, and that correlation skews between portfolios scale to the expected loss (as we have illustrated with some success in Figure 7.11). A third assumption is also sometimes made, often as part of the so-called homogeneous large pool model, which treats each credit at the average portfolio spread and ignores any barbelling in spreads. The set of steps that dealers often follow is:

1. Calculate portfolio expected loss using individual spreads, using the bid or offer side of the market, depending on whether protection is bought or sold.
2. Decide on a correlation skew proxy, using either the U.S. or European markets, based on the regional portfolio composition.
3. For trade maturities that do not correspond to the index, interpolate a skew based on the 5-year and 10-year points.
4. Scale up or down the index skew based on expected loss differences between the index and the transaction portfolios following the argument in Figure 7.11.
5. Calculate the tranche premiums and risk measures using a portfolio loss model.

Of course, some participants may continue to price using the simple tranche correlation model. Equally, some participants may choose to use average instead of individual spreads. What this means for the risk taker is that there may be some relative value arguments either for or against certain bespoke transactions. Take, as illustrated in Figure 7.15, differences in risk measures that emerge if one uses the individual credit spreads for a portfolio (the curved lines) versus modeling each credit at the same average spread (the horizontal lines). Depending on model choice, someone executing the trade on a delta (credit spread)-neutral basis will place somewhat different hedges.

Looking at the correlation skew in bespoke portfolios approach can lead to other trading opportunities, including exploiting any cheapness in default correlation. For example, if a participant is able to buy protection on a lumpy, low-diversity portfolio at levels that are cheap because the quoted spreads (and implied correlation) are more in line with the implied correlation observed for tranches of the higher-diversity CDX and iTraxx indexes, then there are relative value arguments to do the trade. The

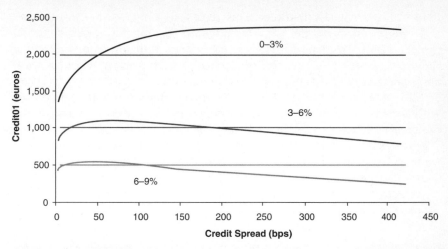

FIGURE 7.15 Credit01 for Tranches Using Actual 225-Name Portfolio Spreads versus Using Average Spread
Source: Citigroup.

participant can either hold the position outright or hedge the position against spread movements by selling protection on other tranches or single-name credit swaps. If the latter route is taken, the position would then be primarily on default correlation; any mark-to-market gain in future can be monetized by unwinding the trade.

CONCLUSION AND FUTURE AGENDA

The growing liquidity and emergence of indexes in the credit tranche market has opened up numerous trading opportunities for participants. Key among the new developments is a better understanding of one of the important factors driving tranche price and risk—default correlation. We believe the approach that we describe in this chapter—a base correlation skew approach similar to the pricing of currency and equity spread options—is better able to explain observable tranche prices and risk than the previous simple tranche correlation approach. The skew approach also has advantages in being able to make comparisons across markets.

We urge investors, however, to use both approaches as they seek to exploit trading opportunities in the market. Tranche correlation does have some benefits. It is simple. For commoditized index tranches, it provides a quick barometer of periodic price movements. But in our view, only the skew model gives a coherent framework for understanding market movements, and only the skew model provides a robust method for trading bespoke tranches. Unlike tranche correlation, it provides an unambiguous picture of the market's perception of a portfolio's loss distribution and gives investors an opportunity to trade default correlation.

While the approach discussed here, a combination of Gaussian copula with correlation skew, has enabled a better understanding of market's risk preference at various tranche attachment points, this is not the final word. We have shown instances—for example, in spread sensitivity of various tranches—where neither model has perfect predictive power. Alternative copula expressions for joint distributions of credit default, as well as introduction of additional risk parameters (for example, global catastrophic shock) are analytical variations that we are currently exploring.

CASE STUDY: CURVE TRADES IN TRANCHE MARKETS

The following case study describes a real-world example of trading credit tranches, specifically involving curve trades in the tranche markets. The case study presents a specific trade recommendation (a curve flattener) and analyzes the market factors driving the trade. This example helps to convey various aspects of formulating and analyzing a trade strategy in the tranche markets.

Curve Trades, Tranche Markets, and Technicals

Curve trades in the tranche market, where investors buy (or sell) protection on a tranche of a specific maturity and simultaneously sell (or buy) protection on a tranche of *another* maturity, provide new opportunities beyond the traditional curve trades.[8] We have seen increased interest and inquiries for curve steepeners and flatteners using liquid 5- and 10-year CDX/iTraxx tranches. These inquiries are mainly driven by the remarkable improvement in liquidity in the 10-year CDX/iTraxx tranche market over the past several months (the liquidity of 10-year tranches is becoming comparable to that in the more established 5-year CDX/iTraxx tranches). Here we present a curve-flattening trade and analyze the market factors driving the trade.

In the current environment of low spreads, CDO managers are under increased pressure to find higher-yielding collateral. When compared to similarly leveraged assets,[9] senior 10-year CDX tranches are providing higher yield for a given rating target. For that reason, senior CDX tranches with 10-year maturities are suitable collateral for CDO structures that combine structured finance and corporate risk, and there has been stronger demand for these tranches in the market. Thus, strong technicals in the 10-year CDX space are the main drivers that continue to flatten the 5-/10-year tranche curves. Based on the current credit environment, and generally scarce opportunities for CDO originators to source the collateral, we believe that the technical pressure on senior 10-year tranche market will persist and potentially push spreads on those tranches even lower. These conditions provide for an interesting curve-flattening trade between 5- and 10-year CDX tranches that are different from standard curve trades in the single-name or index space where the structured finance CDO managers are probably less active.

Trade Recommendation

Based on the current low-yielding environment in structured credit space and search for suitable collateral by CDO managers, we expect that the demand for senior 10-year CDX tranches will remain strong and spreads should stay stable or tighten further over the next several months. We recommend the following trade:

Sell protection on the 10-year 10 percent to 15 percent IG CDX March 2015 tranche and buy protection on the 5-year 7 percent to 10 percent CDX IG March 2010 tranche.

This trade can be structured as Credit01, Default01, or carry neutral. From these options, we recommend the carry-neutral combination. This trade recommendation has the following main characteristics:

Recommendation for this curve flattener is based on the view that senior 10-year tranches will continue to remain in demand, and spreads should stay firm or decrease further relative to the 5-year CDX tranches.

With this trade, investors are expressing the view that the implied correlation for senior 10-year CDX tranches would decrease.

The 5-year 7 percent to 10 percent March 2010 CDX tranche and the 10-year 10 percent to 15 percent March 2015 CDX tranche have similar risk sensitivities, almost matched deltas, and should achieve similar ratings (if rated).

A six-month holding period generates a positive P&L, which increases with a further drop in implied correlation for the 10 percent to 15 percent 10-year CDX March 2015 tranche. The trades have positive theta (time-decay) sensitivity over the first year.

In Table 7.5 we present the six-month P&L for each of the trade combinations relating to the change in implied correlation for the 10-year 10 percent to 15 percent CDX tranche. Note that the implied correlation is a measure of demand and supply for a specific tranche (everything else being equal). Within the context of implied correlation models, a drop in implied correlation of a senior tranche indicates that that tranche is trading richer relative to the index. Table 7.5 shows that as the implied correlation for the 10-year 10 percent to 15 percent CDX March 2015 tranche decreases (while the implied correlation for the 5-year tranche is held constant) the trade generates a positive P&L. It is not necessary for the implied correlation of the 10-year 10 percent to 15 percent CDX March 2015 tranche to decrease for the trade to be profitable. The trade already benefits if the implied correlation spread between two tranches widens. In the next subsection, we examine the drivers behind this trade.

Market Drivers for the Tranche Curve Trades

Role of Historical CDX Spreads   Current levels as compared to the variation of CDX historical spreads are some of the first indicators for a potential opportunity to position a curve trade. The most liquid indexes are on-the-run CDX IG indexes with maturities of

TABLE 7.5 Sell Protection on 10-Year 10 Percent to 15 Percent CDX IG March 2015 Tranche ($6.1 Million, $6.4 Million, $8.3 Million Notional, Respectively) and Buy Protection on 5-Year 7 Percent to 10 Percent CDX IG March 2010 Tranche ($10 Million Notional), Six-Month P&L ($000s) Relating to the Change in Implied Correlation for the 10 Percent to 15 Percent CDX March 2015 Tranche, October 13, 2004

	Six-Month P&L ($000s)				
	−2%	−1%	Unchanged	+1%	+2%
Credit01 neutral trade	48	18	(10)	(36)	(60)
Default01 neutral trade	57	25	(4)	(31)	(57)
Carry-neutral trade	107	67	29	(6)	(39)

Source: Citigroup.

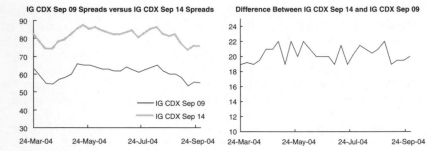

FIGURE 7.16 CDX IG September 2009 Spreads versus CDX IG September 2014, Spreads and Difference, March 24, 2004, to September 29, 2004
Source: Citigroup.

March 2010 and March 2015, respectively, but because the last roll occurred just recently[10] and we do not have a long time series of historical spread levels for the new on-the-run CDX indexes, we analyze the Series 2 CDX IG indexes with maturities of September 2009 and September 2014, respectively. Note that the new Series 3 CDX IG index and the off-the-run Series 2 CDX IG index follow each other relatively closely and are currently trading 0.25 bp (5-year CDX IG) and 0.5 bp (10-year CDX IG) apart (as of October 18, 2004). With recent spreads tightening and improvement of high-spread names in that index we observed that 5- and 10-year Series 2 CDX indexes tighten from their historical highs (see Figure 7.16, left panel).

More interestingly, the historical spread difference between the 10-year September 2014 and 5-year September 2009 CDX has been remarkably stable (see Figure 7.16, right panel), indicating that there might be no specific opportunity at the current levels to position a 5-/10-year curve trade with the CDX index. In contrast, tranches of the CDX indexes could perform differently due to variation of demand and supply of protection for a specific tranche in the market. Over the past several months, that has exactly been the case: Certain CDX tranches (especially the senior part of the capital structure) performed differently than other

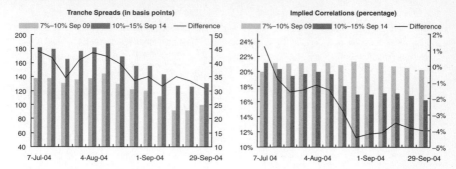

FIGURE 7.17 Comparison of Tranche Spreads and Implied Correlations, July 7, 2004, to September 29, 2004

tranches and underlying CDX indexes. As discussed in the next subsection, this driver is reflected in variation of implied correlation (and change in the slope of the base correlation) for CDX tranches.

Tranche Spreads and Implied Correlations   There has been a significant tightening of protection premium for standard senior CDX tranches with 5- and 10-year maturities over the past several months (see Figure 7.17). We have compared the 5-year 7 percent to 10 percent CDX tranche with the 10-year 10 percent to 15 percent CDX tranche, as these two tranches have similar sensitivities to the spread changes in the underlying indexes. Also they have similar sensitivity to historical default losses and should achieve similar rating from the rating agencies (if they are rated). In Figure 7.17, left panel, we can observe that the tranche spreads have been narrowing and the spread difference between the 10-year 10 percent to 15 percent September 2014 CDX tranche and 5-year 7 percent to 10 percent September 2009 CDX tranche has narrowed approximately 15 bp over the three-month period.

It is true that this tightening trend in tranche spreads could be just a leveraged reflection of tightening in the reference indexes over the past three months, but the change in spread difference becomes clearer when we compare the historical levels of implied correlation for each tranche (see Figure 7.17, right panel). Over the past three months, implied correlation for the 10-year 10 percent to 15 percent CDX tranche has decreased dramatically as compared to the implied correlation for the 5-year 7 percent to 10 percent CDX tranche (which stayed almost unchanged). From the perspective of implied correlation—which is an indicator of the demand and supply for tranche protection—the premium for the 10-year 10 percent to 15 percent September 2014 CDX tranche has been decreasing on a relative basis to the 10-year CDX index, and therefore this tranche is trading richer than the index.

Base Correlation Analysis and Market Technicals

As the implied correlation for tranches is one of the main indicators of demand and supply for the tranche protection that reflects relative cheapness and richness of the tranche as compared to the reference index, base correlation skews are becoming a standard tool for

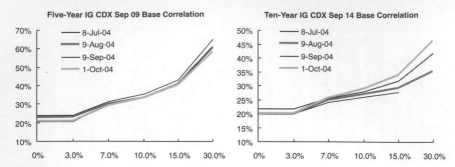

FIGURE 7.18 Five-Year CDX IG September 2009 Base Correlation versus 10-Year CDX IG September 2014 Base Correlation, Midlevels
Source: Citigroup.

the relative value analysis for tranches.[11] By analyzing historical trends in the steepness of base correlation skews of each specific tranche we can observe relative value across the capital structure and between different reference portfolios. In general, if the correlation skew steepened, that change indicates that the tranche on that part of the skew curve is outperforming and the protection premium is decreasing relative to other tranches.

This trend has been exactly the case when we compare the 5-year CDX September 2009 tranches with the 10-year September 2014 CDX tranches. Base correlation skew has been relatively stable over the past three months for the 5-year CDX tranches (see Figure 7.18, left panel), but has steepened significantly for the 10-year CDX tranches, especially on the senior part of the capital structure (see Figure 7.18, right panel). Therefore, senior 10-year CDX tranches are trading richer relative to the index and the relative value trend has been steadily directed toward an increasingly steep skew curve.

Technicals Driving the Flattening of Tranche Curves

We have already mentioned that strong technicals are the primary driver for the recommended tranche curve trade. We can observe from the change in base correlation skew for the 10-year CDX tranche that the senior tranches have been trading richer relative to the index over the past several months. The correlation skew for 5-year tranches has been stable. In our opinion, this variation has been driven by a strong bid for senior 10-year tranches from the structured finance CDO originators. With the current low-spread environment and scarce asset collateral with suitable yield, CDO managers are looking for alternatives. Anecdotal evidence suggests that the 10-year CDX tranches, attached at approximately a 10 percent subordination level, provide the highest yield for given historical default estimates as compared with similar tranches linked to other traded indexes. If that is the case, and given that we do not expect any major increase in supply of relevant collateral for structured finance CDOs, it is natural to expect that the bid for these tranches will continue and the spreads on 10-year CDX tranches could narrow further.

Analysis of Investment Strategy

Tranche Curve Flatteners   Although the tranche curve trades can be constructed at various degrees of leverage—actually, we observed a stronger interest for junior, higher-leveraged tranche curve trades in the tranche market—we focus on a curve trade with two senior tranches in the 5- and 10-year sector. We choose a combination of the 5-year 7 percent to 10 percent CDX IG March 2010 tranche versus the 10-year 10 percent to 15 percent CDX IG March 2015 tranche. Although not rated, these two tranches (in a swap format) would likely achieve the same AAA rating if they were rated. As the 10-year tranche provides a higher spread than the 5-year tranche, CDO managers are making the trade-off between higher yield and shorter maturity. For that reason 10-year tranches should be suitable assets for CDO managers that are ramping high-rated structured finance and corporate collateral. Over the past several months, we observed stronger demand for 10-year tranches, indicating that the CDO originators are willing to extend the maturity of the structures to reach the targeted spreads.

In Table 7.6 we present mark-to-market analysis and risk sensitivities of the 5-year 7 percent to 10 percent CDX IG March 2010 tranche and the 10-year 10 percent to 15 percent CDX IG March 2015 tranche as a function of changes in spreads, number of defaults, changes in implied correlation, and passage of time.

We recommend the following trade:

Sell protection on the 10-year 10 percent to 15 percent CDX IGMarch 2015 tranche and buy protection on the 5-year 7 percent to 10 percent CDX March 2010 tranche.

This trade can be structured in various ways:

Credit01 neutral. Sell protection on the $6.1 million 10 percent to 15 percent March 2015 CDX tranche and buy protection on the $10 million 7 percent to 10 percent March 2010 CDX tranche.

Default01 neutral. Sell protection on the $6.4 million 10 percent to 15 percent March 2015 CDX tranche and buy protection on the $10 million 7 percent to 10 percent March 2010 CDX tranche.

Carry neutral. Sell protection on the $8.3 million 10 percent to 15 percent March 2015 CDX tranche and buy protection on the $10 million 7 percent to 10 percent March 2010 CDX tranche.

Correlation01 neutral. Sell protection on the $5.8 million 10 percent to 15 percent March 2015 CDX tranche and buy protection on the $10 million 7 percent to 10 percent March 2010 CDX tranche.

Theta six-month neutral. Sell protection on the $5.7 million 10 percent to 15 percent March 2015 CDX tranche and buy protection on the $10 million 7 percent to 10 percent March 2010 CDX tranche.

In Table 7.7 we present mark-to-market analysis and risk sensitivities for each of these trades. Based on the performance relating to different risks, we suggest that investors consider the carry-neutral trade option. That trade has the highest P&L profile if spreads tighten, if correlation differences decrease, and as time passes.

TABLE 7.6 Five-Year 7 Percent to 10 Percent CDX IG March 2010 Tranche and 10-Year 10 Percent to 15 Percent CDX IG March 2015 Tranche, $10 Million Notional, Mark-to-Market Analysis ($000s), October 13, 2004

	No-tional ($M)	Annual Carry ($000s)	Spread Change ($000s)					Default ($000s)		Correlation Change ($000s)					Theta ($000s)	
			−10 bp	−5 bp	Unchanged	+5 bp	+10 bp	One Default	Two Defaults	−2%	−1%	Unchanged	+1%	+2%	6-Month	12-Month
7%–10% March 2010 CDX	10.0	101.5	207.8	108.0	—	(115.4)	(237.2)	(84.6)	(184.1)	50.5	24.7	—	(23.7)	(46.4)	67.4	125.5
10%–15% March 2015 CDX	10.0	122.5	345.1	178.3	—	(188.4)	(385.0)	(131.5)	(277.1)	93.5	44.8	—	(41.7)	(80.2)	116.1	227.6

Note: Mark-to-market analysis is based on mark-to-market change in value of tranches if selected parameters change. Bid/ask spreads affect the profitability of these trades. Spread scenarios assume no defaults and constant implied correlation. Spread changes are simultaneous changes to all underlying names. The recovery rate is 40%. Correlation changes indicate the change in implied correlation for each tranche. The theta calculation indicates the time-value change in the mark-to-market value of tranches.
Source: Citigroup.

TABLE 7.7 Tranche Curve Flatteners, Sell Protection on 10-Year 10 Percent to 15 Percent CDX IG March 2015 Tranche and Buy Protection on Five-Year 7 Percent to 10 Percent CDX IG March 2010 Tranche, Mark-to-Market Analysis ($000s), October 13, 2004

	Notional ($M)		Annual Carry ($000s)	Spread Change ($000s)					Default ($000s)		Correlation Change ($000s)					Theta ($000s)	
	7%–10% March 2010 CDX	10%–15% March 2015 CDX		−10 bp	−5 bp	Unchanged	+5 bp	+10 bp	One	Two	−2%	−1%	Unchanged	+1%	+2%	6-Month	12-Month
Credit01 neutral	(10.0)	6.1	(27)	3	1	—	0	2	4	15	7	3	—	(2)	(3)	4	14
Default01 neutral	(10.0)	6.4	(23)	14	7	—	(6)	(10)	—	6	10	4	—	(3)	(5)	7	21
Carry Neutral	(10.0)	8.3	—	78	40	—	(41)	(82)	(24)	(45)	27	12	—	(11)	(20)	29	63
Theta 6M Neutral	(10.0)	5.8	(30)	(8)	(5)	—	6	14	8	23	4	1	—	(0)	(0)	—	7
Correlation01 Neutral	(10.0)	5.7	(32)	(11)	(6)	—	8	18	10	26	3	1	—	(0)	1	(1)	4

Note: Mark-to-market analysis is based on mark-to-market change in value of tranches if selected parameters change. Bid-ask spreads affect the profitability of these trades. Spread scenarios assume no defaults and constant implied correlation. Spread changes are simultaneous changes to all underlying names. The recovery rate is 40%. Correlation changes indicate change in implied correlation for each tranche. The theta calculation indicates time-value change in the mark-to-market value of tranches.

Source: Citigroup.

CHAPTER 8

Understanding CDO-Squareds

Ratul Roy

Matt King

S ynthetic CDO-squareds (CDO^2s) have evolved as a result of the market's search for higher yields than synthetic CDOs can provide. By now, single-tranche synthetic CDOs are not a new product, being on the investment portfolio of an ever-increasing list of real-money and leveraged buyers.

CreditFlux compiles a database of synthetic CDOs or portfolio credit swaps. Although they do not have a separate category for CDO^2s, they estimated that between 10 percent and 20 percent of the $61.3 billion of tranches that referenced corporate or sovereign names in 2004 were structured as CDO^2s.

Synthetic CDO^2s work by securitizing a portfolio of mezzanine tranches of synthetic CDOs typically referencing corporate credits (i.e., an outer CDO of a portfolio of inner CDOs, hence the "squared"). Figure 8.1 illustrates the basic format of a CDO^2. N reference credits are distributed among five inner CDO portfolios of $1 billion each. The inner CDO tranches being securitized are all 6 percent thick, that is, have $60 million notional, and all have 4 percent (or $40 million) subordination below them. The CDO^2 (or outer CDO) portfolio is the sum of these five inner tranches and has a notional of $300 million; this is then tranched as shown on the right-hand side of Figure 8.1.

We will show that this "squaring" process transforms mezzanine CDO risk, simply speaking, by leveraging it (similar to the leveraging of credit default swaps into various CDO tranches) and thereby boosting potential returns to note holders. We will also show that the additional leverage works differently from, say, going from a mezzanine to an equity tranche of the same CDO, and that all three (that is, mezzanine, equity, and CDO^2) have different mark-to-market and default risk characteristics. Some investors

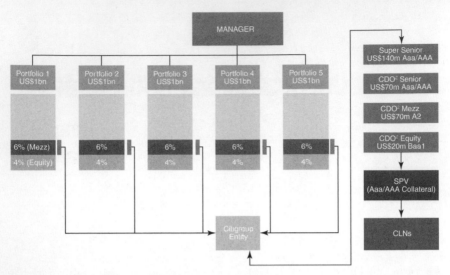

FIGURE 8.1 Payoff Structure of a Managed CDO^2
Source: Citigroup.

may find that the risk/return profile of CDO^2s suit them better than any combination of straightforward mezzanine and equity tranches.

This chapter is divided into three parts. First, we explain how CDO^2 work and what determines their value. Second, we analyze the different types of CDO^2s and show which ones are appropriate for which investors. Finally, we assess the value of management, and argue that it is potentially much greater in the case of CDO^2s than in the case of ordinary CDOs.

CDOs VERSUS CDO^2

How should we qualitatively compare an investment in a CDO (e.g., any of the 6 percent inner CDO tranches in Figure 8.1) with one in a CDO^2 (e.g., the CDO^2 mezzanine)? Let us begin with the similarities. Both are tranched investments, that is, they are leveraged, and also, in this example, have subordination below them (4 percent for the inner CDOs and the CDO^2 equity below the CDO^2 mezzanine, respectively, see Figure 8.1). They are leveraged because once the subordination is eroded, both these products take the first loss from their respective reference portfolios (for the inner CDOs, these are the credit default swap portfolios, and for the CDO^2 mezzanine, this is the $300 million portfolio of five inner CDOs, i.e., 5 times 6 percent of $1 billion). Even before the subordinations are completely eroded, any partial reduction in subordination or deterioration in the credit quality of the reference portfolios will adversely impact the quality (and hence mark-to-market) of the two investment alternatives.

Now let us focus on the differences between CDOs and CDO^2s. The first one for the CDO^2 mezzanine is the double subordination. Successive credit events have to have eroded any of the inner CDO subordination (4 percent in Figure 8.1) and eaten into the inner CDO tranche, and in an amount sufficient to have also eroded the CDO^2 equity, before the CDO^2 mezzanine is affected. This feature gives greater initial protection to CDO^2 holders from idiosyncratic risk.

The second is the double leverage. If we look at notional leverage, we can illustrate this by the following example. Assume that, following the complete erosion of the 4 percent subordination (that is, \$40 million in the first inner CDO), we have a \$10 million subsequent credit loss, which erodes the first inner (6 percent) tranche. This loss represents only 1/100th of the original reference notional of the inner CDO portfolio but a larger 1/6th (\$60 million is the size of the inner tranches in Figure 8.1) of the inner tranche (reflecting the levered position of the latter). This loss represents an even larger 50 percent (10/20) of the CDO^2 equity, since any loss in the inner CDOs will immediately impact the CDO^2 equity. This higher ratio is the second level of leverage.[1] Notice, however, that despite the higher leverage, the CDO^2 equity was affected at the same time as the inner CDO tranche, that is, after \$40 million of losses. For the higher leverage (and greater sensitivity to broad market movements) but similar protection from idiosyncratic defaults, the CDO^2 premium is also higher, making it attractive to many investors. Such investors need to accept the market volatility that leverage brings. We will deal with this point in detail later.

The third important point is path dependence of credit events. Path dependence is irrelevant in any of the individual inner CDOs, as each subsequent default progressively reduces the subordination below the inner tranche. This is not so with the CDO^2. If, in Figure 8.1, the first \$60 million of losses had been equally split among three inner CDO portfolios and not just been present in one portfolio, the CDO^2 equity would not have been affected, as each of the inner tranches had \$40 million subordination below them. In a CDO^2, the distribution of any credit events among the inner CDOs is almost as important as the number of those credit events.

Finally, we have the issue of credit overlap. A single CDO has many individual credits, each of which occur only once. A typical CDO^2 portfolio, however, will often have credits featuring in several of the inner portfolios. Overlap introduces perfect correlation in the way two inner CDO tranches are affected by the common credit, thereby exacerbating the impact of single-name defaults.

VALUE OF CDO²s DERIVES BROADLY
FROM INNER CDOs

To answer the question whether CDO^2s represent an attractive proposition, we need to understand the source of the value of the product. We can then compare it with other similar opportunities, in particular, synthetic CDOs.

The value of the protection sold by the risk taker is compensated by premium paid. In this, the CDO^2 is no different from a plain-vanilla CDO. For a CDO, the value of the protection is given by the subordination below the tranche, the thickness of the tranche, and the portfolio loss distribution (characterized by the individual name risk and default correlation among names). Individual name risk for mark-to-market participants depends on spread levels. Observations of default correlation can be taken from trading in the iTraxx or CDX indexes.[2]

For a CDO^2 tranche, the first two parameters are the same, that is, the subordination below the tranche and the thickness of the tranche. However, here the portfolio loss distribution is more complicated. We must now consider the joint distribution of losses across the inner CDOs, which is a new dimension that we have not had to consider in CDO pricing. To value a CDO^2 tranche, it is not enough to know the distribution of loss on each inner CDO portfolio. One must also consider the correlation of defaults taking place across the various inner CDO portfolios. The most visible (but not the only) driver of this is the overlap of names among the different inner portfolios. If we were to take the limiting case where all the underlying CDOs were defined on identical portfolios, we would find that the losses on each underlying portfolio were 100 percent correlated, while if we go the other extreme and assume no overlap, we would find that they were less than perfectly correlated. However, in the benchmark Gaussian copula model, even with no overlap among portfolios, there is still a significant correlation between the losses on each portfolio. This is because even if each of the inner CDO portfolios is highly diversified, they are all impacted by the same source of broad market risk, which leads to correlation among the portfolio losses.

To illustrate the point that the value of the CDO^2 is driven by the inner CDOs, we show three scenarios in Figure 8.2. In all of the scenarios, the inner CDO portfolios and the risk of the shaded CDO^2 tranche are the same. The difference lies in the thickness and subordination of the inner and outer tranches. Let us compare the leftmost and rightmost, being the two extreme cases. In both cases, the inner tranches have the same thickness (i.e., notional) but very different subordinations. The left inner tranches are clearly much riskier, being junior in the capital structure. The CDO^2

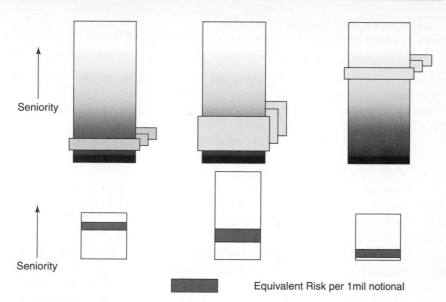

Seniority

Seniority

Equivalent Risk per 1mil notional

FIGURE 8.2 Value is Determined by Total Risk Transfer; All Three CDO^2
Tranches have the Same Risk per Million of Investment
Source: Citigroup.

portfolio has the same notional in either case, being the sum of the inner
CDO notionals. However, the left portfolio has a higher total amount of
risk (expected loss). Therefore, for two tranches in the two CDO^2 portfolios
to have the same expected loss, the one in the left portfolio must have a
much higher subordination than the one in the right. Figure 8.2 shows this.

Now compare the left and middle scenarios. Both tranches have the
same subordination below them, but the ones from the middle are thicker;
that is, they have a larger notional. Since the two underlying CDO portfolios
are the same, the thicker tranches have less risk per notional amount: They
start at the same attachment point, but detach at a more senior point within
the CDO capital structure. Since they have a higher notional, the middle
inner CDOs sum up to a larger CDO^2 portfolio than the ones on the left.
However, since they have less expected loss per notional, the middle CDO^2
tranche that is equivalent to the one on the left has less subordination
below it.

We have chosen to ignore the fourth combination, that is, a thick tranche
with a high subordination similar to the right scenario. This combination
would not be commercial: The value of the expected loss per notional of
the inner CDOs would not justify attractive premiums to risk takers.

CDO^2 VERSUS INNER CDO

Is investing in any of the inner mezzanine CDO tranches a very different choice to one in the CDO^2? After all, we have argued that the CDO^2 is a leveraged position on the mezzanine tranche, which suggests that an alternative could be to invest in a more junior tranche of the CDO (say, the equity).

We believe that investors who want high premiums, yet wish to minimize the chance of principal loss, but who also can put up with higher market sensitivity, should be looking at the CDO^2 product.

To show this, we use a hypothetical CDO^2 trade and compare risk numbers for a CDO^2 tranche with those of the inner CDO tranches forming the CDO^2 portfolio. Our five-year CDO^2 trade, shown in Table 8.1, consists of five tranches from five inner CDO portfolios of 80 BBB credits, each 10 mil notional and 36 bp spread, and with no overlap of credits among the portfolios. Thus, each CDO has a total notional of 800 mil and the total universe of credits is 5 times 80, or 400 credits. The inner CDO tranches are 6 to 8 percent, that is, tranche size of 16 mil and subordination of 48 mil. Given the BBB reference pool, the tranche has an expected rating of roughly AA. Given our assumption of a 36 bp portfolio, models show that the tranche has a spread sensitivity (Credit01) of 14,000 per 10 mil. Note that

TABLE 8.1 Risks of Various Investment Alternatives: Five-Year CDO^2 Structure Based on Five Inner CDO Portfolios of 80 Nonoverlapping BBB Credits, Each of Notional 10 mil and Spread 36 bp

	Rating	Premium (BP)	Credit01 ('000) per 10 mil	Spread Leverage	JTD ('000) per 10 mil	Credit01/ JTD	Convexity per 10 mil
Inner CDO, 6–8% of BBB portfolio	AA	36	14	3.1x	178	8%	(645)
CDO^2, 10–20% of 5 inner CDOs	AA	78	29	6.5x	84	35%	(1,330)
Junior inner CDO, 4.5–6.5% of BBB portfolio		83	29	6.5x	454	6.5%	(922)

Source: Citigroup.

an unlevered 10 mil pool of this spread has a Credit01 of approximately 4,500 per 10 mil, so this 6 to 8 percent tranche has a spread leverage of 3 times the portfolio (second row in Table 8.1). Combining the same 6 to 8 percent tranche (16 mil) from all five portfolios, we could create a CDO^2 portfolio with a total notional of 80 mil. Given rating agency stresses in 2004, the 10 to 20 percent tranche of this portfolio would also have a rating of roughly AA. However, the Credit01 of this tranche is higher, that is, 29,000 per 10 mil, double that of any of the underlying inner tranches and 6.5 times the Credit01 of an investment in the underlying portfolios (third row of Table 8.1). To find a tranche within any of the single CDOs with a comparable spread sensitivity, we would have to take a more junior 4.5 to 6.5 percent tranche (last row in Table 8.1). This tranche, unlike the 6 to 8 percent, would not, however, achieve a AA rating, being more junior in the capital structure.

From a default perspective, CDO^2s have low default risk for the same amount of spread sensitivity. Tranches allow spread and default risk to be separated, and this is also true for CDO^2s. A 10 mil investment in an 80-name underlying portfolio would lose—that is, have a jump-to-default (JTD) risk of—125,000 as a result of the first default (assuming zero recovery). Since the Credit01 of the portfolio for a 10 mil notional is 4,500, the ratio of spread to default risk is 3.6 percent. For the AA inner CDO tranche, that ratio increases to 8 percent, and for the CDO^2 the ratio is 35 percent. Even comparing the 10 to 20 percent of the CDO^2 with the 4.5 to 6.5 percent inner CDO tranche (both of which have the same Credit01), the CDO^2 has a higher Credit01-to-JTD ratio[3].

The high spread-to-default risk makes the product attractive to any investor willing to accept greater mark-to-market volatility, but wanting to minimize the chance of principal loss because of default. Another difference from a junior tranche in an ordinary CDO is convexity. CDO^2s are often negatively convex, which also contributes to market loss when spreads start to widen.

LIKE MEZZANINE, BUT WITH TAILS

CDO^2s behave like mezzanine tranches, but have fatter tails. To understand the fatter tails, we need to consider the effect of leverage. Levering a pool of mezzanine inner CDOs means that when sufficient defaults have occurred in the universe of credits to lead to losses in one of the mezzanine tranches, it does not take a great deal more to wipe out the entire pool. This is why, as shown in Figure 8.3, CDO^2s have a more barbelled loss distribution than CDO tranches of the same spread sensitivity. Here we are

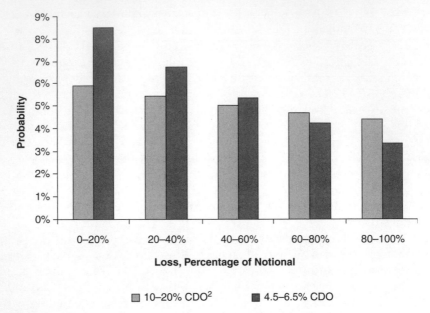

FIGURE 8.3 CDO² has More Barbelled Distribution Compared with Junior Mezzanine
Source: Citigroup.

comparing the 10 to 20 percent CDO² tranche with the 4.5 to 6.5 percent inner CDO tranche (third and fourth rows of Table 8.1). Compared with ordinary mezzanine, both ordinary equity and CDO² mezzanine have a higher chance of not receiving their final principal back by dint of their greater leverage. But because of the higher subordination, the CDO² itself has a higher probability of having zero losses compared with the equity. The flip side is that, should losses strike, the leveraged position of the CDO² means that extreme losses are more probable.

CDO² investors rely on lower exposure to event risk, highlighted in the preceding section, to be unaffected by the high severity of losses given default.

In summary, the premium and risks of CDO²s, compared with ordinary mezzanine and equity CDO tranches, can be seen in Table 8.2.

CDO² VERSUS MASTER CDO

Finally, the CDO² skeptic is bound to suggest that a highly diversified CDO comprising all the credits of the CDO² (a "master" CDO) is able to provide

TABLE 8.2 Our Risk Rankings of CDO²s Compared with Mezzanine and Equity CDO Tranches

	Premium	Default Risk	Spread Risk	Negative Convexity	Default Pattern	Overlap	Tail Risk
CDO²	Moderate	Moderate	High	High	Yes	Yes	Moderate
CDO mezzanine	Low	Low	Moderate	Moderate	N/A	N/A	Low
CDO equity	High	High	Low	None	N/A	N/A	Low

Source: Citigroup.

all the diversification benefits of the CDO² within a more traditional structured credit product. The idea is that, by making the tranche thin enough, one could even obtain the leverage that a CDO² structure provides. We broadly agree with this premise.

That said, there are a couple of points on which this analogy might fail. The first is that, even though the market sensitivity and premium paid might be the same, the ratings might not be.

The second is the fact that while the average loss of both competing products might be the same (and hence the premium paid), many of the high-loss scenarios in the CDO² would arise because of defaults being concentrated in a few CDOs. Conversely, there would be many low-loss scenarios in the CDO² because of the same number of defaults being spread across all the inner CDOs. In the latter case, the double subordination helps CDO² holders. While it is true that the premium is paid on the average loss, which takes into account all these different outcomes, based on the risk-neutral (credit swap implied) default probabilities and correlations, a portfolio manager may be able to avert the high-loss scenarios through substitution of credits among the inner CDOs. The less the CDO² performance depends on the specific pattern of defaults across all the inner portfolios, for example through minimizing the amount of overlap, the closer is the resemblance between a CDO² and a highly diversified CDO.

Figure 8.4 provides a graphical comparison of CDO and CDO² performance. We go back to our example in Table 8.1 of five tranches from five portfolios of 80 BBB credits, each 10 mil notional and 36 bp spread, and with no overlap (i.e., a total universe of 400 credits). Now, though, imagine that the inner tranches are different—they are 4 to 11 percent tranches. The 4 to 5.4 percent of the 400-name portfolio is similar to the 0 to 20 percent of the CDO² as they will have the same notional (56 mil) and same total subordination (160 mil). However, the CDO² will have a higher loss

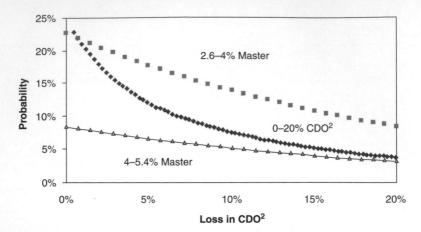

FIGURE 8.4 The Performance Band of a Hypothetical CDO^2
Source: Citigroup.

probability, since fewer than 160 mil of total losses can affect it if all the defaults happen to occur in only one or two of the inner CDOs. Hence, for different numbers of defaults, the 4 to 5.4 percent therefore corresponds to the minimum loss the CDO^2 might experience, and is shown as a lower band in Figure 8.4. However, a more junior 2.6 to 4 percent master CDO tranche has the same probability of first loss as the 0 to 20 percent CDO^2, but would exaggerate more senior losses (because of the double subordination in the CDO^2 and the fact that a part of the default outcomes would be spread across most of the inner CDOs, thus avoiding losses in the CDO^2). This tranche therefore represents the upper band in Figure 8.4.

Except for its very junior (equity) tranche, the CDO^2 therefore performs like a thin tranche of a highly diversified CDO.

ECONOMIC VALUE VERSUS RATING QUALITY

Investors often ask about the difference in premiums between tranches of CDO^2s and single-tranche CDOs that have the same rating. The difference comes from the value of the protection sold by the investor. CDO mezzanine investors sell a call on the loss of the reference portfolio. The expected loss of this leveraged position, as measured by historical agency default data, is the same as an unlevered investment in the reference portfolio (hence achieving the same rating). The distribution of those losses, though, will typically have fatter tails. These fatter tails result in a higher spread (if you like, the option carries a higher premium).

The double leverage of CDO^2s enhances this option position, as CDO^2 tranche holders are now selling an option on the loss of the tranches. Based on rating agency stresses of historical default rates and assumed correlations, the CDO^2 and CDO tranches have the same expected risk. However, as with CDO tranches, the fatter tails now lead to higher spreads. Just as we saw in Figure 8.4, although average losses are the same, the CDO^2 has a higher probability of high losses, but also a higher probability of experiencing no loss at all.

USES OF CDO^2: LONG, SHORT, AND CORRELATION!

Our discussion so far has been in the framework of a long-only investor who looks at the CDO^2 tranche as an alternative to CDO investing. There are at least two other applications of the product. The first one is as a spread-hedge which has a higher ratio of spread sensitivity (Credit-01) to carry either than a comparably rated CDO tranche, or even than a CDO tranche that has the same absolute level of spread sensitivity (i.e., compare the third row with the second and fourth rows of Figure 8.3, respectively).

The second use is a hedge against implied default correlation movements in the traded tranche market. CDO^2s are created out of mezzanine tranches whose value depends partly on the implied default correlation in that part of the capital structure. Therefore, a long CDO^2/short portfolio of inner CDOs trade has both legs in the same part of the correlation skew curve.[4] There is a basis risk, however. As we previously outlined, the valuation of a CDO^2 tranche is significantly affected by the correlation between losses on the underlying CDOs. For this CDO-CDO correlation, there is no transparent index market that makes this parameter visible. This is unlike the index tranche market, where default correlation is a very visible parameter. Moreover, depending on the pattern of successive defaults, the performance of a specific CDO^2 trade could be different from the underlying CDOs.

In the next section, we extend our discussion to the several variations on this generic CDO^2 theme. The aim is to understand differences in risk and return profiles as a result of the structural variations.

STRUCTURES: GOOD, BAD, AND UGLY

A number of different shades of CDO^2 have either been executed. The most highly rated (say, AAA) tranche of two CDO^2s could be constructed very differently. Even though they satisfy the same rating agency stresses, they could have quite different value and risk characteristics. The key features that distinguish one CDO^2 from another are:

- Subordination of inner CDO tranches.
- Thinness of inner CDO tranches.
- Subordination below outer CDO tranche.
- Average, as well as distribution of, credit quality within inner CDOs.
- Overlap of credits among portfolios.
- Presence of external CDO^2 manager.

Except for the last, all aspects relate to the structure of the trade, and are set at trade closing. The good news for investors is that rating agencies also look at these parameters in their rating assessment. Therefore, the question for investors to consider is the value of the trade versus the rating-implied premium expectation. Next we look at the important differentiating factors.

Inner CDO Tranche Seniority and Thinness

The two most important factors to consider are tranche seniority and thinness. When it comes to seniority, CDO^2s tend to resemble the type of mezzanine tranche from which they originated. For example, the more junior the inner CDO tranche, the more idiosyncratic (default) risk it carries. In absolute terms, junior tranches also carry more spread risk per notional amount than senior tranches, but, relatively speaking, they carry more default risk than spread risk. For senior tranches, the relationship is reversed. We also showed in Figure 8.2 that for two CDO^2 tranches to have the same level of risk, one based on a portfolio of junior tranches and the other on senior tranches, the subordination required for the first would be much greater.

The same thing applies to convexity. Where (as is normal for high-grade portfolios) junior mezzanine tranches are more negatively convex than senior tranches, CDO^2s made from the former will be more negatively convex than those made from the latter. Table 8.3 shows one such example.

When it comes to thinness, for the same subordination thinner tranches bring more risk, a point we schematically showed in Figure 8.2. Thin tranches do two things: They carry more expected loss per notional (for which CDO^2 investors get paid), and they create a more barbelled distribution of returns (i.e., a high probability of getting the promised returns, with some chance of having the entire investment wiped out because of event risk). Figure 8.5 compares the loss distribution for a 5 percent inner CDO

TABLE 8.3 CDO^2 Tranche Based on Junior and Senior Inner CDO Tranches: Five-Year CDO^2 Structure Based on Five Inner CDO Portfolios of 80 Nonoverlapping BBB Credits, Each of Notional 10 mil and Spread 36 bp

	CDO Tranche	CDO^2 Tranche	CDO^2 Credit01	CDO^2 JTD	CDO^2 Convexity	Premium
Junior	4–11%	12–24%	35,000	85,000	(6,000)	93
Senior	6–8%	10–20%	29,400	84,000	(1,330)	78

Source: Citigroup.

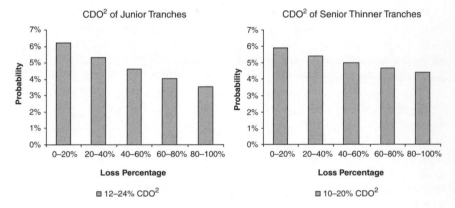

FIGURE 8.5 Impact of Tranche Thinness on CDO^2 Loss Size and Distribution
Source: Citigroup.

thickness and a 2 percent inner CDO thickness. In both cases, the subordination below the tranche is the same. As the figure shows, however, the CDO^2 of senior, thinner tranches has a higher probability of both extreme losses and low losses.

Even though expected loss and premium are based on simulations over a large number of outcomes based on risk-neutral default probabilities, investors need to satisfy themselves about a simple "smell" test—how many defaults does it take before my tranche is blown away? Many structures based on very thin tranches do not stand up well in this light. Often it is only one to two individual defaults that mark the difference between an AAA tranche and another rated much lower. This is particularly true for structures based around senior inner CDOs where, as we have said before, the low probability of losses is compensated for by high severity of losses in case of default.

Overlap of Credits

The third feature which distinguishes one CDO^2 from another is overlap. Overlap both reduces diversification and reinforces the way path dependence affects CDO^2 returns. Intuitively, overlap is like perfect correlation, so increasing overlap should be good for CDO^2 equity holders at the expense of senior note holders. Similarly, rating agencies, in rating senior notes, prefer diversification. As a result, portfolio credit quality and sector diversification being equal, they require lower subordination for portfolios with no overlap. This is shown in the right diagram of Figure 8.6, which shows the subordination required to achieve a triple-A and single-A rating in a CDO^2 portfolio for the case of 400 credits distributed among five inner CDOs of 80 credits each (i.e., with no overlap) versus a total universe of only 240 credits (i.e., with some overlap). Since more idiosyncratic risk is contained in the unrated junior tranches of the 400-name CDO^2 (because of its greater number of credits), it takes less subordination to achieve a rating for a more senior tranche.

What does this mean for the investor who is faced with two CDO^2 deals, one with and one without any overlap? We have already suggested that the agencies factor in the greater idiosyncratic risk of no overlap. However, most CDO^2 investors prefer to participate in the senior and mezzanine tranches whose risk increases as overlap increases (in contrast to the equity), as shown in the left diagram of Figure 8.6. This is especially true for those ratings that address only the probability of getting affected, but not the severity of losses given default.

All else (e.g., subordination below the inner CDO tranches) being equal, investors afraid of event risk should seek to minimize overlap. Our view,

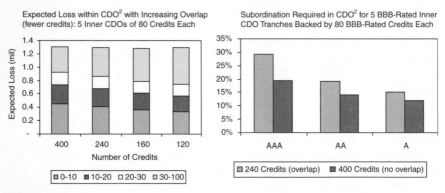

FIGURE 8.6 Impact of Increasing Overlap on Risk and Rating
Source: Citigroup.

however, is that having overlap among fewer well-chosen credits may be preferable to buying the market universe. This logic is especially true for the junior tranche holders of managed deals who may have an incentive to capture the upside from a manager-selected portfolio of credits that are trading cheap for their default risk. Under these circumstances, a large pool of credits would simply dilute the effects of the manager's credit selection.

Overlap is less of an issue where thin senior tranches are selected as the inner tranches, since they have higher subordination. However, since senior inner CDO tranches are thin to ensure there is still some spread, and since such deals typically have no manager, overlap should still in general be minimized.

Nonuniformity of Portfolios

A greater challenge for investors is the distribution of risk on either side of its average value. Just as astute CDO equity investors, being first in line for losses, concern themselves with the riskiest segments of credit portfolios as much as the average portfolio risk, CDO^2 investors who also are participating in leveraged positions (often of junior mezzanine inner tranches) should similarly understand their idiosyncratic risk.

Nonuniformity comes in two ways. First, the presence of high-yield buckets within the reference portfolios of otherwise investment-grade credits creates a nonuniform return distribution. The higher premium on such credits may well make their inclusion worthwhile within the portfolio. This is especially true in structures where portfolios are selected with the assistance of credit analysts. The distortion of risk is obviously smaller when credits are in crossover space, rather than distressed.

Very similarly, major differences in risk among the inner CDO tranches are also highly important. This may be because some tranches are more junior than the others (for similar reference portfolios), or because the tranches have similar characteristics but there are large differences in the reference portfolios. Again, part of this barbelling will impact the CDO^2 rating (to the extent that riskier names have higher spreads and worse ratings) and serve to increase the CDO^2 tranche premium. Figure 8.7 shows the effect on expected loss of making the inner portfolios less uniform (in this case for the portfolio of Table 8.1). The first bar shows the loss distribution across the CDO^2 when all the five inner portfolios have a spread of 36 bp. In the second bar, the average across the five portfolios is still 36 bp, but three of the portfolios have a spread of 30 bp and two have a higher implied default probability as a result of a higher 45 bp spread. The right bar is the most barbelled case—four portfolios have an average spread of 30 bp and the last has a 60 bp average spread. Not only does the total CDO^2 portfolio

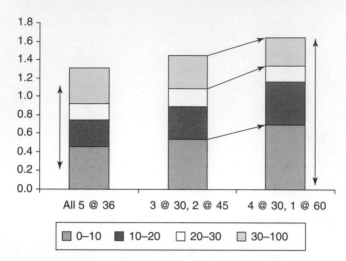

FIGURE 8.7 Potential Impact of Collateral Nonuniformity on Expected Loss Junior CDO^2 Tranches
Source: Citigroup.

get riskier, but the risk also moves into the more junior (0 to 10 percent and 10 to 20 percent) tranches from the supersenior (30 to 100 percent) tranche.

Again, in the hands of an astute manager or where the inner tranches are senior enough to withstand the first few defaults, barbelling may be a way of extracting value from the CDO^2 structure.

Fungible and Tradable Subordination

A fungible CDO^2 structure is one in which the subordination below all of the inner tranches must be exhausted before any of the inner tranches (and hence the CDO^2) is affected. This is very similar to replacing the series of inner CDO mezzanine tranches by a series of equity tranches (comprising the mezzanine tranches and the subordination below them). We show this by comparing the fungible mezzanine case (structure 1 in Figure 8.8) with the equivalent equity structure (structure 2 in Figure 8.8). In structure 1, there will be no loss on the CDO^2 portfolio unless there is a loss exceeding 5 percent of the combined underlying portfolios, that is, $100 million. If there are more than 5 percent losses on one individual portfolio but less than 5 percent on the other, the seller of protection would be expected to move subordination between the two to avoid a payout. Upon reaching 5% of the combined portfolios, the CDO^2 portfolio's subordination would begin to

Structure 1: CDO² Fungible Structure   Structure 2: Equivalent Equity Tranches

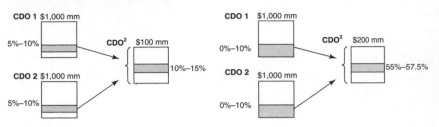

FIGURE 8.8   Fungible Subordination
Source: Citigroup.

be eroded. A further $10 million of defaults (a total of $110 million) would fully erode the subordination. Protection would then be based on the next 5% of $100 million—that is, $5 million.

In structure 2, every default would erode the subordination in the CDO² portfolio. However, there would be no loss to our tranche until 55 percent of the CDO² portfolio had defaulted—that is, $110 million. Protection would then be based on the next 2.5 percent of $200 million—that is, $5 million.

The disadvantage of the fungible structure occurs with very high losses, especially if concentrated in a few CDOs. Assume a $150 million loss in structure 1: All of the subordination of the two CDOs, the two respective inner tranches, the subordination below the CDO² tranche, and finally the CDO² tranche will have been eroded. In structure 2, however, since subordination is not fungible, CDO 1 can lose only $100 million; additional losses are not passed through to the CDO², thus protecting the CDO² tranche from losses.

Note how when the subordination is made fungible, a thick mezzanine tranche now appears like a thinner senior tranche (i.e., a 55 to 57 percent tranche of a master pool as opposed to a 10 to 15 percent tranche). By making cross-subordination automatically fungible, the structure immunizes the CDO² tranche holders from a low level of idiosyncratic defaults. Therefore, it makes the most sense in structures with higher idiosyncratic risk—for example, many credits with low overlap—or where the inner CDO tranches are very junior. There is no free lunch, however; to restore value to the protection that is given up by making the CDO² tranches senior, we often find that fungible CDO²'s have very little subordination in the master CDO as well as consisting of thinner inner CDO tranches. In particular, in managed structures where investment advisers are paid to take cheap idiosyncratic risk, this option may not be optimal.

As an alternative to the automatic use of fungible subordination, we would instead recommend the opportunistic use of unused subordination. This can consist of trading subordination, that is, purchasing subordination from an inner tranche whose reference portfolio is performing well, to benefit another tranche with a credit-impaired reference portfolio and eroded subordination. Alternatively, on a case-by-case basis, structures can exchange subordination for cash (or vice versa) through movement into and out of a trading account during the life of the trade.

Faced with a range of opportunities, investors understandably ask what is the best product for them. The answer depends on the investors' view of future default versus systemic risk, and their risk appetite to lever up either. What CDO^2s do is to take a levered exposure to systemic risk, rather than increasing idiosyncratic risk, to maintain the same return. Among specific structures, however, the relative importance of the two risk types varies.

In our view, investors prepared to take a very levered position on systemic shocks should look for thin, highly senior inner tranches (or equivalently CDO^2s with fungible subordination) to earn as much carry as possible. We caution that such investors should be prepared for a large tranche loss in the tail event that large losses occur in the portfolio. They may not find it necessary to buy managed deals because of the nature of the risk they are taking. They should, however, be wary of overlap, since this could exacerbate the erosion of subordination. To minimize idiosyncratic risk, such investors should avoid non-investment-grade names. Finally, this group of investors should be comfortable with the high spread volatility and negative convexity of their investment. They may even use the product to go short the market.

In contrast, investors who are either not prepared to risk the house on senior risk or are eager to capture the return from a portfolio of cheap credits using the leverage of a CDO^2 structure should, in our view, consider thick, junior tranches of reference portfolios of credits trading cheap for their default risk, even if they are high-yield names. They should also actively consider using a third party manager. As we will show in the chapter's concluding section, managers can help investors not only in credit selection, but also in controlling the adverse path dependence that we showed is a feature of a CDO^2.

HOW MANAGERS CAN ADD VALUE

Not Just Credit Selection

The obvious risk to CDO^2 tranches is the possibility of credit losses on any of the reference portfolios backing the inner mezzanine CDO tranches. Like any CDO manager, CDO² managers are expected to pick cheap credits and avoid default risk. The job is easier in an ordinary CDO, where the manager is typically faced with the task of selecting 100 or so credits from a pool of 800 or so moderately liquid credits. It becomes less easy as the number of reference credits in the CDO² pool increases.

The less obvious challenge is managing the pattern of successive credit losses. A given number of defaults spread uniformly across all the reference pools, and leaving all the inner mezzanine CDO tranches unaffected, would have very different results from the case where the defaults were concentrated in only a few CDOs. The zero losses in the unaffected portfolios would not help to decrease the losses in the CDO² portfolio at all. Figure 8.9 is an improbable but illustrative example of what can go wrong in a CDO² portfolio—in this case comprising three inner CDOs. At closing, the inner tranches have 3 percent subordination each, but it so happens that the first two credit events affect CDO². The third credit event also strikes CDO² and leads to all subordination below the tranche being eroded. Since the CDO² consists of the three inner tranches, any further loss in the second of the inner tranches means that the CDO² portfolio would suffer principal loss.

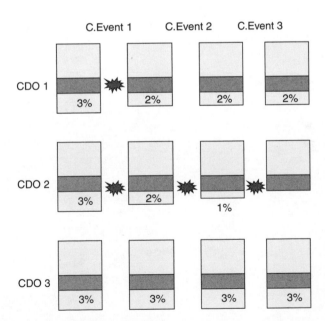

FIGURE 8.9 Path Dependency in CDO²
Source: Citigroup.

Manage to the Structure

An astute manager should also manage to the structure. In Figure 8.10, we show two ways this can be done. In the left part of the diagram, the first two credit events have had the effect of reducing the subordination of CDO 2 to 1 percent and CDO 1 to 2 percent from their initial 3 percent levels. CDO 3 is untouched. If the manager recognizes that the third impaired credit is in CDO 2, he can take it completely out of the universe and replace it with a safer one (which would imply a cost), or exchange the risky credit from CDO 2 with a safer one from CDO 3. There would still likely be a cost, but the net costs should be lower than a complete replacement. When the third credit does eventually default, it has an impact on the third CDO, but the CDO^2 tranche is unaffected. This is the scenario shown in the top right of Figure 8.10.

The second alternative, shown in the bottom right, would be to extract the value of unutilized subordination. In the example shown, the manager has purchased subordination for CDO 2 from CDO 3, which it partly or wholly financed by selling subordination from CDO 3. Any deficit or excess can also be settled by movement into and out of a trading account during the life of the trade.

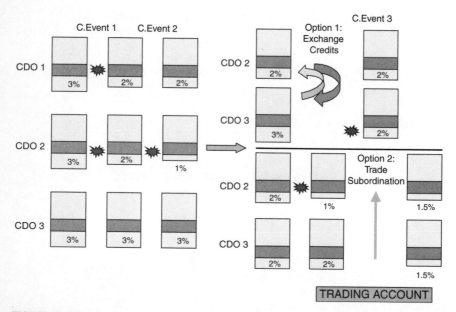

FIGURE 8.10 How a Manager Uses the CDO^2 Structure to Add Value
Source: Citigroup.

Managers can thus enhance the performance of CDO 2. Their impact is likely to be highest in structures with relatively high idiosyncratic risk. They are likely to work with a universe of a few attractively priced credits, leading to overlap of credits among portfolios and thus increasing the risk of defaults being concentrated in a few CDOs. Structures that provide greater flexibility (for example, through monetizing subordination) allow greater input from managers. For their part, managers need to understand not just credit, but the challenges of managing an interlinked, leveraged pool of credits.

CONCLUSION

CDO^2s offer investors a higher premium for taking more systemic credit risk and yet still restrict exposure to idiosyncratic default risk. As such, they are an alternative to investing in mezzanine or equity CDO tranches. More levered on credit spreads than on mezzanine CDO tranches, CDO^2s have similarities and differences with mezzanine and equity tranches. In particular, CDO^2s benefit from double subordination (at the inner CDO tranche level and any secondary subordination within the master CDO portfolio). Because of the large number of names among the inner CDO portfolios, the impact, too, of any one credit event is initially low. Unlike ordinary CDOs, the performance of CDO^2s also depends on the pattern of defaults among the inner portfolios: The concentration of a moderate number of defaults in a few of the portfolios is a markedly worse outcome than a broader distribution.

Many structural and collateral features of CDO^2s affect the product's market and default risk. Other than the subordination below the inner CDO and CDO^2 tranches, these include the thinness of the tranches, the overlap of credits among the inner CDO portfolios, and any nonuniformity or barbelling of risks, both within and among the inner CDO portfolios. Rating agency stresses today broadly address these structural parameters; for investors looking at alternative structures, the question, therefore, is comfort with the specific combination of exposures. Finally, managers can add value by sourcing credits that are trading cheap for their default risk, and by managing the pattern of successive credit losses among the inner portfolios. For the best impact, managers need to understand not just credit, but the challenges of managing an interlinked, leveraged pool of credits.

CASE STUDY: TERM SHEET

Our case study of CDO^2s is of a managed deal that is similar to one closed in 2005. In particular, study the capital structure, spreads, and structure overview.

CDO-Squared

Preliminary Capital Structure

	Target Rating (S&P)	Size ( )	Size (%)	Subordination	Indicative Spread	7-Year Expected Maturity
Super Senior	On request					
Class A	[AAA]	[11.2]	5.00%	15.25%	[80]	June 2012
Class B	[AA]	[11.5]	5.90%	9.35%	[130]	June 2012
Class C	[A]	[11.2]	5.00%	4.35%	[230]	June 2012
Income Notes	NR		4.35%			

Capital structure and terms may change from those presented above.
Investors should read the final transaction documents in their entirety prior to making a decision to invest.

Structuring Alternatives

- **Currencies:** EUR, USD, GBP, JPY, AUD, SGD
- **Tenor:** 5- and 7-year maturities
- **Coupon Structure:** Fixed, floating, inflation-linked or floating spread (CMCDS) coupon
- Junior Super-Senior available on request

They can be offered in:
- Funded or unfunded form
- Straight tranches or combination notes such as principal-protected equity-linked coupon

Transaction Overview and Highlights

- Transaction is a 7 year-managed synthetic CDO-squared transaction referencing 5 mezzanine tranches of investment grade credits, managed by an external manager.

- Each of the 5 Inner CDOs reference 75 credits with equal notional amounts. The 200 individual reference entities are diversified across industries, ratings, and countries.

- There will be a Trading Account that will enable the manager (subject to Rating Agency criteria) to monetize excess Inner CDO subordination. Similarly, money from the Trading Account (e.g., derived from net trading gains) may be transferred to the Inner CDOs to stabilize structural performance.

- Noteholders benefit from:
  - Two levels of subordination both at the Inner CDO and Master CDO levels
  - Subordination cushion built into the structure at both Master CDO and each Inner CDO tranche levels in excess of the minimum subordination requirement of S&P
  - Active management between Inner CDOs to rebalance risk and defensively manage credits in/out of the Transaction

- Alignment of Interest:
  - A portion of the manager's fees is paid quarterly as a junior fee. As the equity tranches of the underlying CDOs are impacted from losses, the amount of junior fee payable will be reduced.
  - Value in the Trading Account will be shared at maturity 80:20 to Noteholders:Manager.

Structure Overview

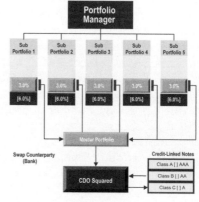

- The Transaction ramps up upon closing
- Standard documentation based on the 2003 ISDA Credit Derivatives Definitions
- Citigroup acts as counterparty under the Swap to make interest payments to the Issuer

Initial Target Reference Portfolio Characteristics

- Each Inner CDO tranche is [3%] of the Inner CDO with [6.0%] subordination
- Average rating: [A-/BBB+]
- Inner CDO obligor concentration: [1.33%]
- Aggregate portfolio obligor concentration: [0.80%]
- Aggregate portfolio percentage of sub-IG names: [0.53%]
- Maximum overlap: [40%]

Trading Guidelines

- **Discretionary Trading** – There is an annual 20% bucket for discretionary trading. Such portfolio adjustments must satisfy the S&P ratings test.

- **Credit Impaired/Credit Improved** – Credit impaired/credit improved entities are determined by the manager. Substitutions involving credit impaired entities cannot worsen the rating on the notes.

Credit Structuring

FIGURE 8.11 Term Sheet of a Hypothetical Synthetic CDO-Squared
Source: Citigroup.

CDO-Squared

Rating Distribution on a Portfolio Aggregate Basis

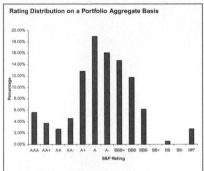

Percentages are given on a portfolio aggregate basis. NR* – Not Rated by S&P although rated IG by at least one other Rating Agency. Portfolio is subject to change.

Regional Distribution on a Portfolio Aggregate Basis

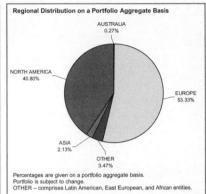

Percentages are given on a portfolio aggregate basis. Portfolio is subject to change.
OTHER – comprises Latin American, East European, and African entities.

Industry Distribution on a Portfolio Aggregate Basis

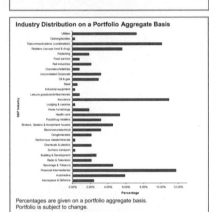

Percentages are given on a portfolio aggregate basis. Portfolio is subject to change.

Overlap Between Each CDO Sub-portfolio*

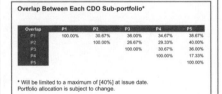

Overlap	P1	P2	P3	P4	P5
P1	100.00%	30.67%	36.00%	34.67%	38.67%
P2		100.00%	26.67%	29.33%	40.00%
P3			100.00%	30.67%	36.00%
P4				100.00%	17.33%
P5					100.00%

* Will be limited to a maximum of [40%] at issue date.
Portfolio allocation is subject to change.

Stress Scenario – Default and Downgrade Analysis

The figures reflect the stability of the structure to downgrades and defaults.

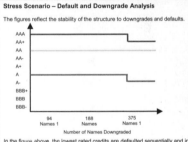

In the figure above, the lowest rated credits are defaulted sequentially and in such a manner that the defaults are spread out evenly across the different Inner CDOs.
In the figure below, downgrades are made evenly across the different rating categories according to the following scenarios: 25% downgrade - 94 credits, 50% downgrade - 188 credits, 100% downgrade - 375 credits based on a 375 aggregate name portfolio*.

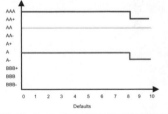

* Defaults and downgrades are assumed to occur on the second anniversary of the transaction and are equally weighted across the inner CDOs. Defaulted names have an assumed recovery rate of 40%.

Credit Structuring

FIGURE 8.11 *(continued)*
Source: Citigroup.

CHAPTER 9

CPPI: Leveraging and Deleveraging Credit

Olivier Renault

C onstant proportion portfolio insurance (CPPI) products are leveraged principal-protected investments whose return depends on the performance of an underlying trading strategy. Credit CPPIs are relatively new to credit space: They combine principal protection with a credit-linked investment that leverages up or leverages down depending on the performance of a credit trading strategy.

This structure means CPPIs have dynamic leverage, compared with other levered strategies with principal protection. Investors in CPPI products can see the size of their exposure to the trading strategy increase when the profit/loss (P&L) is positive, and can benefit from more leverage and more return if the strategy keeps performing well. By contrast, should the trading strategy underperform, the CPPI could return sub-LIBOR performance or, in extreme situations, pay back only the principal at maturity.

These products have been very popular with retail funds for many years and have usually referenced equity indexes. Now, the tradability of credit indexes (iTraxx and CDX) and the liquidity of many credit default swap (CDS)-based products allow this methodology to be applied to credit. Many long-term credit strategies can be applied to a CPPI setting, and can generate excess return over LIBOR through the leveraging of credit indexes.

PRODUCT MECHANICS

CPPI products offer principal protection and a target return over LIBOR by investing the present value of the interest in levered strategies. These products usually have a relatively long maturity (7 to 10 years). In order to protect $100 of principal at maturity, the present value of the principal, say $70, is invested in a high-quality zero-coupon bond. The remaining $30 is then invested in a credit strategy according to a rule that increases the leverage when the underlying investment is performing well and deleverages when the investment return is negative.

Although the capital is protected by the arranger of the structure, the remainder (value of interest payments) is at risk. Should the performance of the trading strategy be very poor, the trade could be unwound and the investor would get only the principal back at maturity. The implicit cost is therefore the value of interest lost as well as the opportunity cost of investing in a higher-yielding asset. For moderate leverage, unwinding is an unlikely event. However, even if the trade is not unwound, it can return sub-LIBOR performance.

Before explaining the mechanics of the structure, we need to clarify some jargon:

The *reserve* (R) is the difference between the value of the note and the value of the principal protection. Initially, it is simply the difference ($30 in the example) between the notional value of the investment and the value of the principal protection. As time goes by, the value of the note will reflect the P&L of the trading strategy and the value of the reserve will fluctuate up or down accordingly.

The *target leverage* (TL) is set at the inception of the CPPI note. It measures how many times the reserve amount is invested in the risky strategy. For example, a TL of 20 would lead to an initial notional investment of $600 in our example.

The *portfolio notional* (PN) is defined as the market value of the levered strategy while the *target notional (TN)* is the target leverage times the value of the reserve ($600).

The *rebalancing multiplier* (RM) determines how frequently changes in leverage will occur. A high RM implies less frequent changes in leverage; a low RM implies more frequent changes.

Figure 9.1 describes the general dynamics of the CPPI structure. The trade's P&L determines the leverage of the strategy. If the trade is performing well (positive P&L) and to such an extent that the portfolio notional deviates substantially from the target notional, the leverage is increased. To be more precise, no rebalancing takes place if the portfolio notional is within $(RM \times R)$ of the target notional. If $PN > TN + RM \times R$, then the trade is levered up, while if $PN < TN - RM \times R$, the leverage is lowered. At the leverage reset, the new portfolio notional is set to $PN = TM \times R$. As mentioned previously, it is clear that the higher the RM, the less frequent would be the changes in leverage.

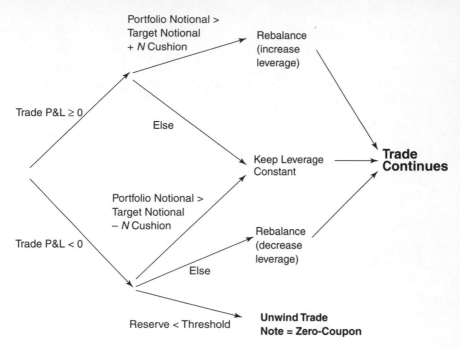

FIGURE 9.1 Basic CPPI Dynamics
Source: Citigroup.

If the P&L becomes sufficiently negative to reach the unwind threshold (e.g., 5 percent of the initial reserve), then the trade is unwound and the note is replaced with a zero-coupon bond. In order to give a numerical example, let us use the values suggested before. Assume we start with a notional investment of $100, of which $70 corresponds to the principal protection. The initial reserve is $30, which leads to a portfolio notional of $600 being invested in the trading strategy. Assume further that the rebalancing multiplier is equal to 3. Over a certain period of time, the P&L of the trade is a gain of $10. The portfolio notional therefore becomes $610, and assuming that the value of the principal protection has increased to $72, the reserve increases to $38(= 30 + 10 − 72 + 70). The target notional thus jumps to $38 × 20 = $760, which is higher than 610 + 3 × 38 = 724. The investment in the trading strategy is thus increased such that the portfolio notional is $760.

In Figure 9.2, we consider two possible paths for the performance of the trading strategy. On path A, the trade performs consistently well and is levered up on four occasions. At maturity, the trade generates a substantial

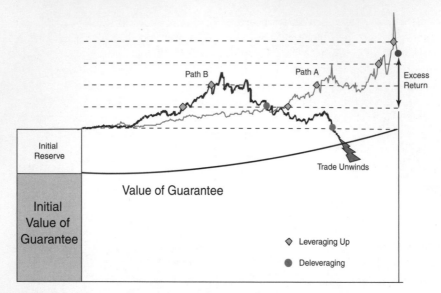

FIGURE 9.2 Examples of CPPI Performance on Two Possible Strategy Paths
Source: Citigroup.

return over the LIBOR rate. By contrast, on path B, the trade at first performs strongly and is levered up, but then loses money, is delevered twice and finally unwound.

Note how the performance becomes more volatile on both paths when the strategy is levered up (symbolically when it crosses leverage barriers).

MANAGED CPPIs

CPPIs are long-term investments, and few static trading strategies can generate consistently high returns for 7 to 10 years. A manager can improve the returns on a CPPI strategy by:

- Selecting portfolios that go long credit with high spreads for their risk or go short expensive credits. This can be done using fundamental credit analysis or models such as Citigroup's hybrid probability default (HPD) model.
- Spotting distressed credits early to avoid credit events (downgrades or defaults).
- Positioning for credit curve steepening or flattening by selecting different maturities for credits in long/short trades.

If allowed by the CPPI structure, a manager could switch from one strategy to another during the life of the trade if he believes that it is in the interest of investors. For example, in a credit/equity trade, it may make sense to go long credit and short equities when companies are deleveraging and use most of their cash flow to reduce their debt, but then to reverse that strategy when companies start increasing dividends and carry out share buybacks. Having a manager has a cost, and each structure will be different. Investors should assess whether the benefits listed earlier outweigh the cost of the manager.

When Is CPPI Suitable?

Thanks to the greater liquidity of the CDS market, CPPI products are now offered to credit investors. While these trades can be attractive due to their principal protection and high target returns, investors should be conscious that their choice of trading strategy, leverage level and mechanism, and the maturity of the trade are all key factors determining the performance of their investment. By selecting portfolios, avoiding defaults, and potentially changing the trading strategy during the life of the note, a manager can add value. Its actual benefit should be assessed by comparing the added value to the cost of the manager. Overall, we think simple trading strategies are most appropriate for a CPPI setup as they suffer from lower transaction costs, are less likely to be affected by a liquidity crunch, and are easier to structure in large sizes.

Choice of Trading Strategies

There are a number of trading strategies that can be employed in CPPI. Simple long strategies can appeal to investors who are bullish on credit risk or who believe that spreads compensate them adequately for bearing default risk. Some examples of strategies might include:

1. A 5-year long-only credit trade.
2. A 10-year long-only credit trade.
3. A 5-year constant maturity CDS (CMCDS) versus CDS trade.
4. A 10-year versus 5-year long/short trade.
5. A long stock versus short 5-year credit trade.

The following case study compares the five different strategies in an unlevered setup, outside of the CPPI structure, in order to examine its impact on the performance. Our results from the case study show that a simple structure, either a simple long or a long 10-year/short 5-year, exhibit better overall performance. Those strategies have several key advantages. First, they are straightforward and do not add an already complex strategy to the sophistication brought by the dynamic leverage structure. Second, they can be done in relatively big sizes because the CDS market is liquid, in particular for index names (iTraxx and CDX). This liquidity, in turn, minimizes transaction costs, which are a concern for CPPI strategies due to the frequent rebalancing of the trade.

CASE STUDY: PERFORMANCE COMPARISON OF STRATEGIES

Baseline: Unlevered Strategies

Before assessing the performance of various CPPI strategies, it is useful to analyze how the same trading strategies would have fared in an unlevered setup outside the CPPI structure. This lets us see what part of the return is due to the intrinsic performance of the trade and what part is due to the CPPI leverage. The five strategies we consider are:

1. A 5-year long-only credit trade.
2. A 10-year long-only credit trade.
3. A 5-year CMCDS versus CDS trade.
4. A 10-year versus 5-year long/short trade.
5. A long stock versus short 5-year credit trade.

Simple long strategies can appeal to investors who are bullish on credit risk or who believe that spreads compensate them adequately for bearing default risk. The long 10-year versus short 5-year strategy is immune from default risk and should therefore offer lower volatility than simple longs. It also has positive albeit lower carry. CMCDS/CDS combinations also eliminate or reduce default risk (depending on the ratio of long to short). Taking a long position on CMCDS versus an equivalent short position in CDS reflects a bearish view on spreads. It is initially a negative carry trade but would benefit from spread widening or curve steepening. The last strategy may appeal to investors who believe the future will be associated with more shareholder-friendly activity such as share buybacks or large dividend payouts at the expense of debt holders.

Simulations

Using levels from April 2005 together with realized spread changes over the past 10 years, we can construct a back-tested scenario. By contrast, in order to take a more forward-looking view and assess the distribution of potential returns, we rely on Monte Carlo simulations to indicate what returns on these trades could be over the next 10 years. We note that past performance is no guarantee of future performance, and thus feel more comfortable with a broader analysis of performance.

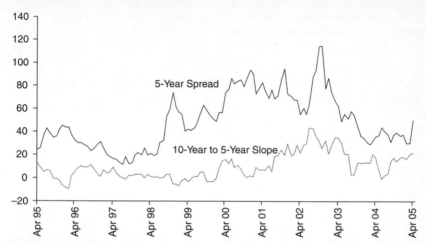

FIGURE 9.3 U.S. Spread Levels and Slopes (basis points)
Source: Citigroup.

To simulate spread and default scenarios, we estimated three mean-reverting processes: one for the 5-year spread, one for the 10-year minus 5-year slope, and one for the S&P 500 index (total return). Because liquid CDS indexes (iTraxx, CDX) have been trading for only a few years, we back-populated the CDX series using Citigroup's 5-year and 10-year U.S. investment-grade indexes since 1995. The reconstructed spread series, as well as the 10-year minus 5-year slope are plotted in Figure 9.3. We then simulated 500 monthly paths for the aforementioned variables over the next 10 years[1] and calculated the returns (carry plus marked-to-market gains or losses) on these strategies for each path. All strategies were assumed to roll every six months; please note that none of the calculations factor in fees and transaction costs.

A key determinant of most trades' performance is the assumption about default rates. For each trade, we considered three possible default rates: In the "low" scenario, we use the average annual default rate on investment-grade credits as reported by S&P (0.13 percent). The "high" scenario assumes an annual default rate of 1 percent per annum, which is roughly the spread-implied default rate. The "medium" scenario takes the average default rate of the high and low scenarios (0.56 percent). We believe that the medium scenario is quite realistic as it takes into account the historical default experience (rating agency average) and also adds a further layer of losses, which could be interpreted as marked-to-market losses at the index rolls.[2]

Results

Table 9.1 reports our results for the long and long/short trades. "Expected return," "min-imum," and "maximum" are annualized (excess) return figures over the 10-year holding

TABLE 9.1 Simulated Performance[a] of Long and Long/Short Strategies
(basis points except information ratio)

Default Scenario	Strategy						Long 10-Year vs. Short 5-Year
	Long 5-Year			Long 10-Year			
	Low	Medium	High	Low	Medium	High	All
Expected return	42	16	−10	59	33	7	18
Minimum	3	−28	−61	17	−20	−57	−10
Maximum	79	50	38	107	79	70	40
Standard deviation	40	45	51	53	59	66	31
Information ratio	1.04	0.35	−0.2	1.12	0.57	0.11	0.57

[a]Excluding transaction costs.
Source: Citigroup.

period across our 500 scenarios. The standard deviation is the annualized standard deviation of returns, and the information ratio is the ratio of expected return to standard deviation. The table clearly shows how important the default assumption is to the performance of the long-only trades. If the low default scenario is verified, the 5-year trade returns a healthy average excess return of 42 basis points per annum but loses money on average in a high default scenario. Our preferred medium default scenario yields a moderate excess return. Similar—albeit slightly higher—values are obtained for the 10-year trade. The long 10-year versus short 5-year trade benefits from being default neutral and, therefore, results are not sensitive to our default rate assumption. Considering the medium scenario, the best information ratio is achieved by the 10-year and the long/short trade, the latter being both less profitable and less volatile than the former.

Table 9.2 shows the results for the long CMCDS versus short CDS strategies either equally weighted (1/1) to be default neutral, or with a weight of 3.26 to 1 to create a position neutral to parallel spread widening (ZeroCredit01). Both strategies return extremely poor results. Going long CMCDS and short CDS is a negative carry trade initially (due to the participation rate below one[3]) and expects to become positive carry in the long term as spreads widen. By rolling frequently, the investor almost always suffers from negative carry (as the participation rate and reference rate are reset at each roll) but benefits only from possible marked-to-market gains implied by spread widening or curve steepening over a six-month period.

Note that CMCDS trades would face higher roll costs than plain-vanilla index trades. The Credit01-neutral trade is long default risk and would generate only positive expected returns in a low-default environment.

TABLE 9.2 Simulated Performance[a] of CMCDS versus CDS Strategies[b] (basis points except information ratio)

Default Scenario	CMCDS vs. CDS (1/1)	CMCDS vs. CDS (3.26/1)		
	All	Low	Medium	High
Expected return	−17	39	−20	−79
Minimum	−35	−26	−94	−176
Maximum	−3	108	58	17
Standard deviation	13	70	86	101
Information ratio	−1.31	0.56	−0.23	−0.78

(header spanning "CMCDS vs. CDS (1/1)" and "CMCDS vs. CDS (3.26/1)" under "Strategy")

[a]Excluding transaction costs.
[b]Long one unit of CMCDS versus short one unit of CDS (1/1), or long 3.26 units of CMCDS versus short one unit of CDS (3.26/1).
Source: Citigroup.

TABLE 9.3 Simulated Performance[a] of Stocks Versus Five-Year Credit[b] (basis points except information ratio)

Default Scenario	Long Stocks vs. Short 5-Year Credit (1/12)		
	Low	Medium	High
Expected return	412	698	989
Minimum	−1,138	−862	−537
Maximum	1,796	2,025	2,316
Standard deviation	1,643	1,657	1,662
Information ratio	0.25	0.42	0.60

[a]Excluding transaction costs.
[b]Long one unit of stock versus short 12 units of 5-year credit.
Source: Citigroup.

Finally, Table 9.3 shows the returns on a long S&P 500/short five-year credit index. The ratio we chose was 1:12, so that the equity volatility is matched by the credit volatility. The short credit position implies that the trade benefits from defaults and, in our medium scenario, the expected return is nearly 700 basis points. However, this comes at the cost of very high volatility and downside risk. Overall, the 0.42 information ratio is lower than that of the 10-year long-only trade and of the long 10-year/short 5-year.

To summarize our findings, Table 9.4 gathers the results of all the trades under the medium default scenario. From this preliminary analysis, the 10-year long-only and the long/short trade appear to be the most efficient (highest information ratio). Table 9.5 shows the historical performance of the strategies over the past 10 years. Spread changes used for these calculations were observed spread changes between April 1995 and April 2005, and defaults were assumed to be scattered evenly though time. The two rows of the tables show the importance of the carry for the performance of the trades. When starting from 1995 spread levels, the results are quite disappointing for most of the credit trading strategies. Starting from 2005 levels (wider spreads) strongly benefits the long credit trades as they add between 25 and 30 basis points of carry per annum. All the results on historical data are consistent with the simulation results in Table 9.4 as they are within one standard deviation of the expected return.

TABLE 9.4 Simulated Performance[a] of Competing Strategies under Medium Default Scenario (basis points except information ratio)

Strategy	Long 5-Year	Long 10-Year	CMCDS vs. CDS (1/1)	CMCDS vs. CDS (3.26/1)	10-Year vs. 5-Year	Equity vs. 5-Year
Expected return	61	33	−17	−20	18	698
Minimum	−28	−20	−35	94	−10	−862
Maximum	50	79	−3	58	40	2,025
Standard deviation	45	59	13	85	31	1,657
Information ratio	0.35	0.57	−1.31	−0.24	0.57	0.42

[a]Excluding transaction costs.
Source: Citigroup.

TABLE 9.5 Simulated Return[a] of Strategies under Medium Default Scenario and Realized Spreads (basis points)

Strategy	Long 5-Year	Long 10-Year	CMCDS vs. CDS (1/1)	CMCDS vs. CDS (3.26/1)	10-Year vs. 5-Year	Equity vs. 5-Year
Starting from 1995 spreads	6	−1	−12	−24	−7	769
Starting from 2005 spreads	31	33	−24	−9	2	468

[a]Excluding transaction costs.
Source: Citigroup.

Performance Comparison in CPPI Setup

Now that we have seen how different hypothetical unlevered strategies can have different expected returns and volatilities, we can consider their performance when levered in the context of CPPI. When building a CPPI note, structurers have to make several choices, which drive the performance and the risk of the trade. Naturally, the choice of the investment strategy and the maturity are the main factors. The choice of maturity will determine what fraction of the notional can be invested in the risky strategy: the longer the tenor, the more exposure to the risky strategy. Two other degrees of freedom that are available to structurers are the level of target leverage (TL) and the rebalancing multiplier (RM).

As explained earlier, the rebalancing multiplier determines the frequency of changes in leverage. While a relatively low number is necessary to obtain a dynamic leverage structure,[4] it should not be too low, in order to avoid unnecessary transaction costs. As a rule of thumb, we have chosen $RM = TL/5$, such that, for a target leverage of 25, the leverage would be adjusted if the portfolio notional deviates from the target notional by an amount greater than 5 times the reserve. Structures with lower leverage would have lower RMs in order to mitigate the impact of the lower volatility. This prevents the frequency of rebalancing from falling too dramatically.

Increasing the target leverage has mixed effects on the strategy (see Figure 9.4). Increased leverage raises the likelihood of very high returns but also the probability of the trade being unwound. For most trading strategies, the shape of the relationship between TL and expected excess spread is concave, which enables the identification of an optimal leverage level.

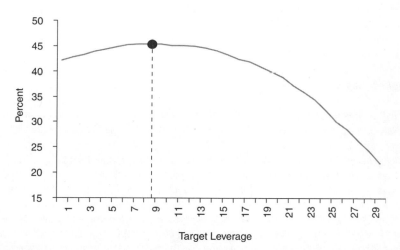

FIGURE 9.4 Five-year Credit Strategy Expected Total Return for Different Target Leverages[a] (percent)
[a]These returns include LIBOR. Transaction costs are excluded.
Source: Citigroup.

TABLE 9.6   Simulated Performance[a] of CPPI Under Medium Default Scenario (basis points except times for leverage)

Strategy	Long 5-Year	Long 10-Year	CMCDS vs. CDS (1/1)	CMCDS vs. CDS (3.26/1)	10-Year vs. 5-Year	Equity vs. 5-Year
Expected return	39	78	−6	−7	61	514
Minimum	−116	−131	−13	−13	−91	−241
Maximum	182	336	−1	−1	215	2750
Leverage	9	9	1	1	12	1
Historical performance	120	61	−9	−9	14	56

[a]Excluding transaction costs.
Source: Citigroup.

Table 9.6 shows the performance of these same trading strategies when levered and in CPPI format. All returns here should be understood as annual excess return over LIBOR for the entire CPPI note—not for the risky strategy only. Not surprisingly, the pattern of results for the CPPI structures follows those of the same strategies when unlevered. The best two performers in terms of information ratio are the long 10-year and the long/short. The equity versus credit trade and the long 5-year also produce excess returns but suffer from higher volatility. The CMCDS trades return sub-LIBOR performance, as expected. The last two rows of the table show the optimal target leverage for each strategy and the performance using historical spread changes over the past 10 years, assuming 2005 starting levels. Using these historical and simulated numbers, the long strategies fare best and all the other strategies have disappointing results.

Other Strategies

The list of strategies we have reviewed in this study is by no means exhaustive. Among the others we could have considered are tranche-based strategies and managed strategies.

Tranche-Based Strategies Must Consider Spreads, Defaults, and Correlation   The difficulty we see with tranche-based strategies is that one needs not only to assess the possible changes in spreads and the number of defaults during the life of the trade, but also to consider future changes in correlations. Correlation changes can lead to significant marked-to-market swings even when spread changes in the underlying credits remain moderate. Figure 9.5 shows how, at the beginning of May 2005, a fall in correlations led to strong underperformance of the equity tranche and the outperformance of the mezzanine 6 to 9 percent tranche, which rallied despite a sell-off in the index. A CPPI referencing a long equity versus short mezzanine strategy on iTraxx or CDX would have suffered significant marked-to-market losses and, depending on its leverage, could even have been unwound (see Figure 9.5 for a graph illustrating changes in correlations and resulting changes in

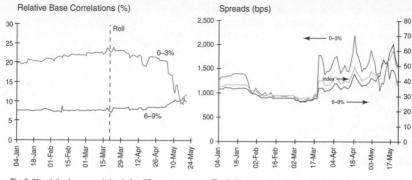

The 6–9% relative base correlation is the difference between the base correlation of the 0–6% tranche and of the 0–3% tranche.

The 0–3% tranche is not quoted in terms of all-running premium. The figures have been converted from points up front to running premium.

FIGURE 9.5 Five-Year iTraxx Relative Base Correlations and Spreads
Source: Citigroup.

tranche spreads). Tranche strategies (as well as CMCDS strategies) would also suffer from higher transaction costs than would straightforward long or long/short CDS strategies.

Further Levels of Sophistication Can Involve Noncredit Markets More sophisticated strategies combining credit and foreign exchange or credit and interest rates, possibly with an inflation hedge component, can also be devised. As in the case of managed trades, investors should carefully consider whether the added cost and lower liquidity of such sophisticated trades are adequately compensated for by either enhanced expected returns or lower risk.

Keeping It Simple Looks Best to Us By analyzing five different strategies over many default and spread scenarios, we have shown that simple strategies (long or long/short) tend to perform best across our forward-looking simulations. Had we included transaction costs, which tend to be higher with more complex strategies, we expect we would have found that the results favored the simpler strategies even more.

We highlight the crucial importance of the choice of strategy and of the target leverage for the performance of the CPPI structure. While sophisticated strategies including tranches or CMCDSs may be grabbing the headlines, we think simple strategies are actually more appropriate for a CPPI setup.

APPENDIX: OUR METHODOLOGY

Our Estimations and Simulations

From our spread data set, we estimated mean-reverting processes for 5-year spreads and the 5-year/10-year slope.

Processes were assumed to follow:

$$\Delta S_t \equiv S_{t+\Delta t} - S_t$$
$$= \alpha + \beta S_t + \varepsilon_t,$$

where Δt is one month and $\beta < 0$, which implies mean reversion. The residuals ε_t are assumed to be normally distributed. The correlation between residuals of the 5-year spread process and the slope is also estimated from the data. A similar process was used for the total return (capital returns plus 2 percent dividend yield) on the S&P 500.

In our simulation experiments, we generated 500 paths of length 120 months, all starting from 49 bp for 5-year and 70 bp for 10-year spreads. This was done simply by drawing correlated normal random variables (ε_t) and moving forward by iterations using the preceding equation. The 5-year spread was floored at 3 bp, and the 5-year/10-year slope was constrained to remain in the range [−20bp; 50bp]. Both constraints were very rarely binding due to the mean reversion in the processes.

For each time step, defaults were simulated using a Poisson distribution with mean calibrated on the assumed default probability. The actual numbers of defaults were obtained by drawing uniform random variables and inverting the cumulative Poisson distribution. In our simulations, the number of defaults and spread levels are correlated such that more defaults are expected when spreads are wide.

For the CMCDS trade, we used Citigroup's pricing model to determine the present value of the position under the various scenarios. The participation rate was recalculated at each semiannual roll.

Collateralized Debt Obligations

Collateralized Loan Obligations

Glen McDermott
William E. Deitrick
Alexei Kroujiline
Robert Mandery

The impressive growth that the leveraged loan market has displayed over the past decade has been accompanied by greatly improved liquidity and transparency. The benefits of this asset class, which include stable prices and high recovery and prepayments rates, can be accessed efficiently by collateralized loan obligations (CLOs). During the previous credit cycle (2000–2003), CLOs on average demonstrated more stable performance than both high-yield bond CDOs and straight corporate debt. This stability has fueled CLO growth: as of 2005, CLOs accounted for over one-third of the primary CDO market.

The leveraged loan market has exhibited significant growth over the past decade, with $295 billion of new issuance in 2004, triple the new-issue high-yield bond market. The liquidity and transparency of the loan market continue to improve, with the number of investors increasing from 18 to over 425 in the past 10 years.

Investors have been drawn into market by the advantageous charac-teristics of leveraged loans, which include floating interest rates, discount pricing, high prepayment rates, and greater control over the borrower in times of stress. The long-term, historical track record is strong: Analysis shows that loans have performed solidly under various economic conditions, revealing a history of stable prices and robust recovery rates.

The stability of loans and inefficiencies of the loan market make leveraged loans particularly attractive to CLO investors, who rely on the asset-backed structuring technologies to gain leveraged exposure to this market. CLOs represent a subcategory of the collateralized debt obligation (CDO) market, which has grown by more than 1,000 percent since 1995 to reach $166 billion of new issuance in 2005.

The primary reason for CLO market growth has been the strong performance of this asset class through the last credit cycle: Loans lend themselves to leverage in the CLO context. From 1997 to 2005, on average, CLOs have exhibited higher ratings stability relative to both high-yield bond CDOs and straight corporate debt. Drivers of this stability include high recovery and prepayment rates, price stability, and CLO manager expertise.

Despite these obvious benefits, challenges remain. The recent surge in demand for institutional loans by structured vehicles has resulted in a significant tightening of the loan spreads, with some CLOs containing an unacceptably high level of loans purchased at a premium. In addition, investors should be aware that a CLO portfolio built solely with broadly syndicated institutional loan tranches may contain significant name overlap. Recognizing this risk, CLO market participants are now looking to other sectors of the leveraged loan market in search of alternative collateral assets. Revolving credit obligations, middle-market loans (MMLs), and European leveraged loans provide promising opportunities for further diversification, offering comparable yield and credit stability.

LEVERAGED LOAN MARKET OVERVIEW

Strong Primary Market Growth

Syndicated loans can be segmented into two market categories, leveraged (or high-yield) and investment grade. The former is comparable to the high-yield bond market from a ratings and issuer leverage perspective. In most instances, a loan will be classified as a leveraged loan if it generally meets one of the following criteria: (1) debt ratings of below Baa3/BBB–from Moody's Investors Service and S&P, respectively, or (2) debt/EBITDA ratio of 3.0 times or greater.

Leveraged loans constitute a significant part of the syndicated loan market: New issuance was $254 billion in 2004, up from $166 billion in 2003 and greater than the 2004 high-yield bond market issuance of $150 billion. This loan issuance was composed of $154 billion institutional term loans and $100 billion pro rata loans (see Figure 10.1).

During the past decade, institutional investors have driven leveraged loan market growth and have made the fully drawn term loan (or "institutional" term loan) the most widely used structure in the leveraged loan market. New issue volume for the institutional term loan tranche set a

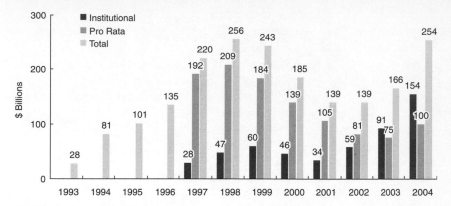

FIGURE 10.1   Annual Leveraged Loan New Issue Volume, 1993 to 2004
($ billions)
Source: Standard & Poor's.

record of $154 billion in 2004, or 61 percent of the total leveraged loan market. This level was up considerably from the $91 billion issued in 2003 and the $59 billion issued in 2002.

With respect to the overall market, the total amount of institutional leveraged loans outstanding is estimated at $193 billion, up $45 billion from 2003 (see Figures 10.2 and 10.3).[1] As Figure 10.3 illustrates, this large market is diversified across many different industries.

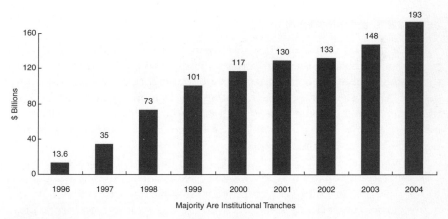

FIGURE 10.2   Par Amount of Outstanding Institutional Leveraged Loans, 1996 to 2004 ($ billions)
Source: Standard & Poor's.

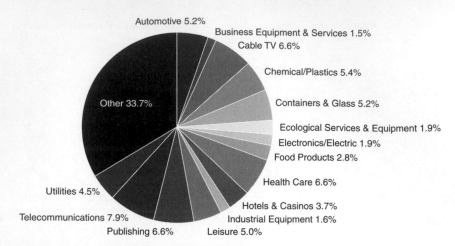

FIGURE 10.3 Par Amount of Outstanding Leveraged Loans by Industry, 2004
Source: Standard & Poor's.

The growth in the institutional market has had many implications. For example, issuers and arranging banks structure deals to be more attractive to institutional investors, especially the larger issues. Furthermore, rating agencies, whose fortunes are tied to the needs of institutional investors, have dramatically increased the number of loans that they rate in the past few years. These positive trends, among others, should help overcome some of the obstacles that previously inhibited the growth in the market.

Broadening Investor Base

Until the mid-1990s, the universe of loan investors included only banks and prime funds.[2] Because these investors generally took positions in loans with the intention of holding until maturity, there was little need for a secondary market. Over the past few years, however, as more institutions realized that loan products could deliver high risk-adjusted returns, new types of investors, such as high-yield bond funds, hedge funds, insurance companies, and CDOs began to enter the market.

Figure 10.4 illustrates the dramatic rise in the loan market share of CDO investors, in particular, during the past decade from only 4.2 percent to 63.6 percent in 2004. The current investor base has diverse needs, and many participants actively look for arbitrage opportunities and trade ideas in the secondary loan market. This impulse has helped fuel the secondary market and the dominance of the institutional loan tranche structure. We discuss the dynamic secondary loan market in the next section.

Distribution of Investors in 1994   **Distribution of Investors in 2002**

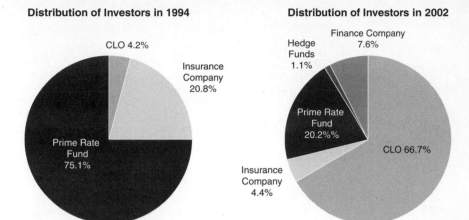

FIGURE 10.4 Primary Market for Institutional Loans by Investor Type, 1994 versus 2004
Source: Standard & Poor's.

Increasing Secondary Market Liquidity

As mentioned, the number of institutional investors in the leveraged loan market has grown dramatically over the past decade. The rise in the number of participants (with varying investment vehicles and agendas) has had a positive impact on liquidity. As shown in Figure 10.5, from 1993 to 2004, the number of active institutional investment vehicles in leveraged

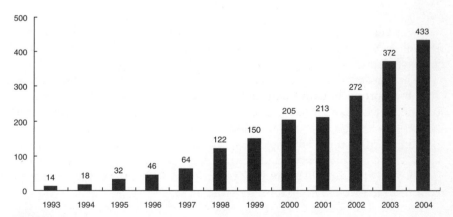

FIGURE 10.5 Total Active Institutional Loan Investors, 1993 to 2003
Source: Standard & Poor's.

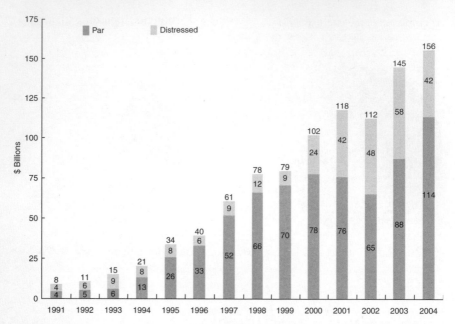

FIGURE 10.6 Annual Secondary Trading Volume, 1991 to 2004 ($ billions)
Source: Standard & Poor's.

loans increased from 14 to 433, and the annual volume of leveraged loans traded followed suit, climbing from approximately $15 billion to about $156 billion. Higher secondary trading volumes (see Figure 10.6) and smaller average trade sizes are direct indicators of the increasing vibrancy and liquidity of the secondary loan market. Ten years ago, the average trade size was $10 million. In 2003, the average trade size was approximately $1 million as loans traded readily among a variety of different types of counterparties.

The industry's trade association, the Loan Sales and Trading Association (LSTA) has contributed significantly to improved liquidity in the secondary loan market by standardizing documents, trade settlement time frames, and industry practices. The organization was founded by a group of banks including Citigroup in 1995 and has expanded to 143 members since then. The LSTA is open to participants in the loan market on both the buy side and the sell side. In 2003, the LSTA continued to implement a number of reforms to the secondary loan market including the following:

■ New primary market standardized documents including credit agreements, bank books, amendments, and tax shelters.

- New secondary market standardized documents including distressed purchase and sale agreements, netting agreements, and trade criteria.
- Introduction of the Committee on Uniform Securities Identification Procedures (CUSIPs) to the loan market for use as unique identifiers by agent banks, loan participants, and rating agencies. Use of CUSIPs is the critical first step in moving the loan market to an eventual straight-through processing platform.

Continuing Challenges to Loan Market Liquidity

Despite dramatic improvements, liquidity in the loan market remains constrained for a few reasons, including minimum purchase sizes. A decade ago, $10 million was the industry standard trade size. This minimum requirement served as an impediment to secondary investors in the loan market. Although there is no official minimum amount that can be assigned, credit agreements can still have provisions that require this amount to exceed $5 million, or in some deals, even $10 million. However, the trend is positive: Assignment minimums and trade sizes have been declining as a result of investor pressure. Investors are very sensitive to the relative weights of loan exposures in their portfolios, so they look to the secondary market as a way to balance this exposure. As shown in Figure 10.7, average assignment minimums dropped to $1.12 million in 2004.

In addition to minimum purchase sizes, high transfer fees have limited liquidity. The lead administrative agent bank charges a fee for each trade as compensation for keeping track of holders for documentation purposes.

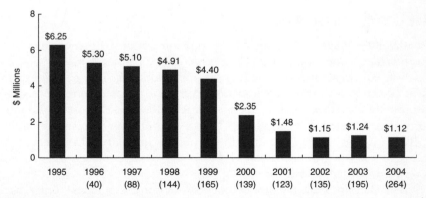

FIGURE 10.7 Average Institutional Assignment Minimum for Loans of $100 million or More
Source: Standard & Poor's.

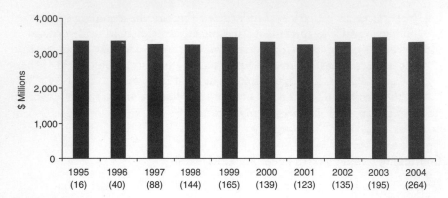

FIGURE 10.8   Average Institutional Assignment Fee for Loans of $100 million or More, 1995 to 2004
Source: Standard & Poor's.

Although certain banks in the industry are trying to lower the cost of these fees to promote greater liquidity in the market, others are not, and as Figure 10.8 illustrates, average fees have remained in the range of $3,000–$3,500 per assignment since the mid-1990s.

Although loan market liquidity clearly remains a challenge for investors, it has improved enormously from only a few years ago. As loan investors continue to increase the pressure, liquidity will rise. We expect secondary loan market liquidity to approach that of the high-yield bond market as documentation and trade procedures standardize, transaction fees are eliminated, and minimum assignments are reduced.

Key Loan Characteristics

Floating-Rate Coupon   Leveraged loans pay interest on a floating-rate basis, so interest payments on loans increase as market interest rates rise. This floating-rate structure is created by setting the interest rate of a leveraged loan at a spread above a benchmark market floating interest rate. The most commonly used benchmark in the leveraged loan market is the London Interbank Offered Rate (LIBOR). So a loan paying 3.0 percent above LIBOR (or L + 300 bp) would yield 4.2 percent annually if LIBOR were at 1.2 percent for a given period. As LIBOR moves, the interest payments of a leveraged loan will move with it.

This floating-rate coupon is one of the most significant differences between leveraged loans and high-yield bonds. Because high-yield bonds pay a fixed interest rate using a U.S. Treasury bond benchmark, investors are exposed to movements in interest rates. If market interest rates rise, the fixed-rate high-yield bond will continue to pay the same lower interest rate. While derivatives can be used to hedge away this risk, this can only be done at a cost that cuts into expected returns. By contrast, the floating-rate interest payments of loans move with the market.

Maturity Term loans generally mature in five to eight years from the time of issue, a considerably shorter period than the ten-year average high yield bond maturity. In 2004, term loans had average maturities of approximately 6.0 years, as shown in Figure 10.9.

Callability Loans are generally callable at par without penalty, meaning that issuers can repay their loans partially or in total at any time. This structure differs from that of high-yield bonds, which are usually structured with a noncall period of three to five years. Occasionally, loans will have noncall periods or call protection that requires the issuer to pay a penalty premium for prepaying loans. These features are usually added to loans in the primary market only when investor demand is weak and a loan needs additional incentives to attract sufficient buyers. Figure 10.10 shows the 12-month rolling prepayment rate for loans at approximately 14 percent in 2004.

Covenants Loan facilities are structured with covenant tests that limit a borrower's ability to increase credit risk beyond certain specific parameters. Covenants are outlined in the legal credit agreement of a loan facility that is executed at the time that a loan is issued. Typically, covenants are tested every quarter, and results are sent to all of the members of the bank group.

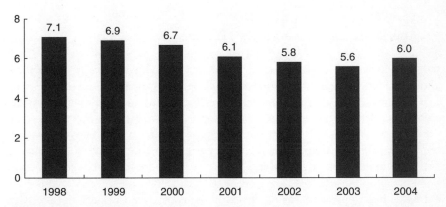

FIGURE 10.9 Average Weighted Term of Institutional Loans, 1998 to 2004 (years)
Source: Standard & Poor's.

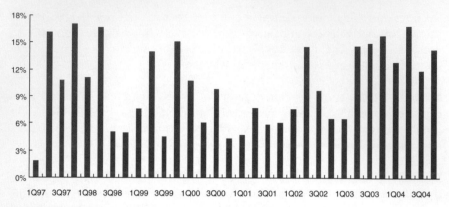

FIGURE 10.10 Repayment Rates, 1Q 97–4Q 03
Source: Standard & Poor's.

Covenant tests provide lenders with a more detailed view of the credit health of a borrower and allow lenders to take action in the event that a borrower gets into credit trouble. A credit agreement for a leveraged loan may generally have between two and six covenants, depending on the credit risk of the borrower and market conditions. Some commonly used covenants include:

- Minimum earnings before interest, taxes, depreciation, and amortization (EBITDA).
- Total leverage debt/EBITDA.
- Senior leverage senior debt/EBITDA.
- Minimum net worth.
- Maximum capital expenditures.
- Minimum interest coverage EBITDA/interest.

Covenants on leveraged loan facilities improve recovery because they allow lenders to limit credit risks such as, but not limited to, capital expenditures, leverage, and acquisitions. Covenants also allow lenders to have an early look at an issuer's credit problems, often before the rest of the market, as an issuer must amend or repay its loans when covenants are breached. This amendment process allows lenders to improve their control and security interest in a troubled issuer, raising potential recovery values.

Ratings In response to strong investor demand over the past decade, the major debt rating agencies have dramatically increased the number of leveraged loan issuers that they rate. Moody's, S&P, and Fitch Ratings all actively rate and monitor loan deals. The number of rated loans has soared to the point where now 70 percent of all new issues receive a rating from at least one agency.

Although methodologies used to determine the ratings differ somewhat from agency to agency, significant progress in refining the methodology has occurred across all agencies, meaning that investors are receiving more accurate information on a wider number of loans, and this should allow for more reliable pricing. Such information is especially important given the material rise in secondary trading and the corresponding entry into the market of a large number of investors who have to carry out regular mark-to-market portfolio pricing. This phenomenon has transformed the leveraged loan market so that a rating change by any one of the agencies can cause a significant change in the value of a loan. When this type of price swing occurs, these mark-to-market investors have to rearrange their portfolios, creating arbitrage opportunities for investors who can act quickly to take advantage of these opportunities.

The ratings given to loans are primarily based on two factors:

1. Probability of default.
2. Expected recovery rate.

The probability of default for a bank loan is approximately equal to that of a bond. Despite this fact, a loan is frequently given a higher rating than a bond of similar size and duration. The reason for this disparity lies in the fact that default rates do not capture a critical, value-adding component of a loan—its higher status in the capital structure of a firm relative to a bond. Because a bank loan is generally a senior secured debt obligation, the average recovery rate for loans is significantly higher than that for bonds, which, at best, tend to be senior unsecured debt obligations.

The widespread rating of loans is a relatively recent phenomenon that did not take off until the mid-1990s. In the past, when loans were not rated, market participants generally estimated that the loan should be one notch up from the most senior unsecured bond. While this rule is fairly accurate on average, it has some serious shortcomings when used to evaluate pricing for individual credits. In fact, according to a 1998 study carried out by Moody's, only 37 percent of loans were actually rated exactly one notch higher than the senior unsecured bond. This means that an investor exclusively using this one-notch rule to price the premium paid on a loan's higher recovery rate would have mispriced the loan more than 60 percent of the time.

This is not to say that the one-notch rule does not have practical uses. It is still useful as a benchmark from which to start one's credit analysis. As a tool to price loans, however, it is clearly inadequate. Instead, investors need to follow the lead of the rating agencies and look very carefully at the credit's attributes to determine how such factors as industry, corporate structure, legal subordination, underlying collateral quality, and a host of other factors will affect recovery rates in cases of default, because these factors can cause the recovery rates of seemingly similar loans to differ significantly.

Security Leveraged loans are generally structured with a lien against the assets of the borrower. These asset claims are also known as the security of the loan. Secured loans have a number of advantages over unsecured parts of a company's capital structure. In the event of a default, the lenders can take possession of the borrower's assets to which they have a claim and sell them or operate them for cash. The position of a debt instrument in the firm's capital structure and the degree to which the debt is backed by liquid assets are important indicators of expected recovery rates.

Recovery rates on defaulted loans are consistently higher than recoveries on unsecured parts of the capital structure. As we discussed, the higher recovery rates are primarily due to the senior position of leveraged loans in an issuer's capital structure and the security interest that loan holders have in an issuer's assets.

Fees The fees for leveraged loans generally comprise up-front fees and commitment fees that vary with market conditions. Figure 10.11 shows historical fee levels for the past 10 years.

Up-Front Fees In the leveraged loan market, issuers pay one-time up-front fees at closing to attract banks and institutional investors to invest in their

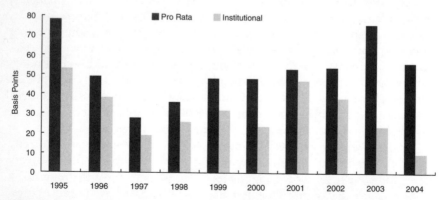

FIGURE 10.11 Average Total Fee, 1995 to 2004 (in Basis Points)
Source: Standard & Poor's.

of the TLA, the universe of lenders tends to be restricted to traditional corporate lending banks.

Pro Rata Market   At $75 billion in 2003, new issuance in the pro rata loan market was essentially flat with the $81 billion issued in 2002. The pro rata loan market is comparable in size to the high-yield bond market, which produced $137 billion in new issue in 2003 and $65 billion in 2002. The large size of the pro rata loan market means that investors have opportunities to invest across a wide spectrum of industries and credits and to benefit from the relative value relationships between pro rata loans and other asset classes.

Pro Rata CLOs   Higher recoveries and discount pricing, along with the overall depth of the market, make pro rata loans an attractive option for CLO collateral. The major challenge for the CLO market was to create an appropriate structure to handle the funding risk of the revolving part of the loan. In 2003, Citigroup created the very first CLO transaction backed by pro rata loans. In that transaction, Citigroup introduced a new synthetic structure to separate the funding and credit risks of the revolvers, capitalizing on the high ratings of the bank. The funding risk stayed with the bank, whereas the credit risk was sold into the CLO structure. This was the first transaction that provided CLO investors with wide access to the broad pro rata loan market.

Key Characteristics

Discount   Pro rata loans generally trade at a discount to par. The discount is due to the combination of a lower coupon for the pro rata loan relative to institutional term loans, certain impediments to liquidity, and the selling pressure caused by banks seeking to rationalize their balance sheets and credit exposures. Pro rata loans are attractive for buyers, including structured vehicles, that may benefit from purchasing discounted instruments.

Security   Pro rata loans, like institutional term loans, are senior secured and have maintenance financial covenants. Covenants give investors an early seat at the table in the event that the issuer's credit deteriorates, and lenders often use them to improve their position in terms of security, collateral, coupon, or fees.

Prepayment Rate   Because of amortization, prepayments, refinancings, and corporate events such as assets sales and mergers or acquisitions, pro rata loans tend to be repaid prior to their scheduled maturity. Increases in the prepayment rate garner yield windfalls because of quicker-than-expected recovery of purchase price discounts. Prepayment benefits holders of pro rata loans more than holders of institutional term loans because pro rata loans are generally bought at deeper discounts to par.

Superior Recovery   Losses in the event of default are generally lower for pro rata asset classes than for institutional term loans, because the revolving credit portions of pro rata loans, on average, are not fully drawn at default. The obligation to fund the undrawn portion of a revolving credit facility ceases upon default, and thus creates an effective windfall (i.e., tantamount to a repayment of that portion of the pro rata loan at par).

Barriers to Entry   Pro rata loans represent a robust yield/value opportunity. The potential price arbitrage versus institutional term loans will likely be maintained because of credit agreements that restrict ownership to banks or other holders the issuer finds acceptable. The requirement for borrowers to consent to transfers of pro rata loans means that the pool of acceptable counterparties is likely to grow slowly. An agent bank can facilitate this approval process but may require cash collateral to do so. Similarly, lenders/investors must be capable of properly managing the variable funding requirements of revolver borrowing. This restricts the number of investors who can buy pro rata loans.

Investment Opportunities

Revolvers and TLAs are attractive from a relative value perspective as they can trade at a discount to par depending on the market, while institutional term loans generally trade at or above par. Because the majority of corporate leveraged loans can be repaid at par (100 cents on the dollar) at any time without a penalty, investors who buy below par collect the difference as a gain upon refinancing. A number of market forces have driven this relationship, including short new issue supply in the loan market, relatively fewer pro rata lenders, the rise in the number of institutional loan investors, and a strong demand for product that has focused on term loan Bs (TLBs).

The fact that few investors are able or willing to participate in the prorata loan market creates additional investment opportunities. The majority of pro rata loan holders are relationship banks that buy the loans during original syndication. Banks continually readjust their balance sheet strategies to diversify credit risk and free up capital for new deals, creating ongoing opportunities to buy pro rata loans in the secondary market at a discount. As the number of pro rata lending banks decreases, we expect this market dynamic to persist for the foreseeable future.

MIDDLE-MARKET LOANS

Overview

The middle-market segment of the leveraged loan market generally comprises smaller companies that satisfy the following criteria: (1) less than $500 million in revenues and $50 million in EBITDA; and (2) a loan facility smaller than $150 million in total size. Within those criteria, large middle-market loans have deal sizes of $100 million to 150 million and issuers with EBITDA of $25 million to 50 million, while standard middle-market loans are smaller. In 2004, 257 middle-market loans were issued with a total size of $25.9 billion, up considerably from $12.5 billion in 2003. Middle-market loan lenders vary across different industrial sectors, with the health care, services/retail, industrial, and media sectors accounting for 51 percent of the total market volume in 2004 (see Figure 10.12).

Key Characteristics

Liquidity Middle-market loans are generally less liquid than leveraged loans because of their smaller size and lower visibility among the institutional investor community. This tighter liquidity makes middle-market loans more suitable for buy-and-hold investors who want to collect the higher yield and tend not to trade as actively. Many CLO structures could benefit from holding discounted middle-market loans and collecting the higher associated yields, because they do not require the liquidity to trade the loans actively.

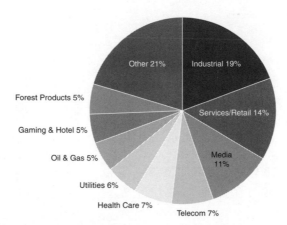

FIGURE 10.12 Loan Volume by Broad Industry Classification for Deals with $50 million or Less of EBITDA, 2004
Source: Standard & Poor's.

FIGURE 10.13 Average Weighted Institutional Spreads: BB/BB–Leveraged Loans versus Middle-Market Loans, 1Q 99–4Q 04
Source: Standard & Poor's.

Middle-market institutional loans pay a coupon of approximately L + 400bp, nearly 150 bp more than the coupon on a comparable BB/BB–rated institutional leveraged loan (see Figure 10.13).

Leverage   Leverage on middle-market loans can be slightly higher than that for comparable leveraged loans, but is currently very similar at an average of about 4.1 times debt/EBITDA compared with the 4.2 times average for the overall leveraged loan market. Figure 10.14 illustrates historical middle-market loan leverage, and Figure 10.15 shows the same for the overall loan

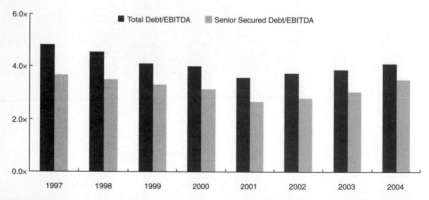

FIGURE 10.14 Rolling Three-Month Debt/EBITDA and Senior Debt/EBITDA Ratios for Issuers with EBITDA of $50 Million or Less, 1997 to 2004
Source: Standard & Poor's.

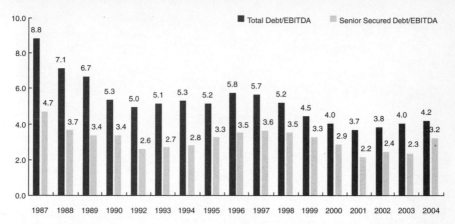

FIGURE 10.15 Average Debt Multiples of Highly Leveraged Loans, 1987 to 2004
Source: Standard & Poor's.

market. In general, middle-market loans tend to include more secured bank debt, so senior secured leverage is often higher than in the leveraged loan market, as evidenced by senior leverage of 3.5 times for middle-market loans versus 3.2 times for the overall loan market.

Ratings   Middle-market loans are frequently not rated by the major debt rating agencies like Moody's and S&P. In 2004, only 17 percent of middle-market loans issued had debt ratings (see Figure 10.16). The primary reasons for the lower number of ratings are weaker investor demand and rating

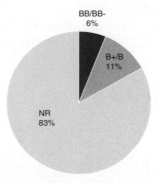

FIGURE 10.16   Loan Volume by Rating for Deals by Issuers with EBITDA of $50 Million or Less (Total New-Issue Volume: $25.9 billion), 2004
NR: not rated.
Source: Standard & Poor's.

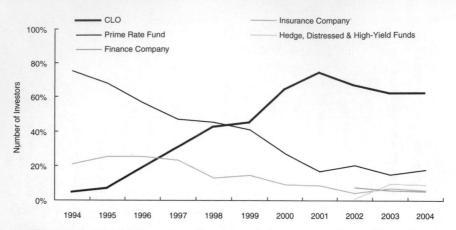

FIGURE 10.17 Primary Markets for Highly Leveraged Loans for Issuers with EBITDA of $50 Million or Less, 1994 to 2004
Source: Standard & Poor's.

fees. Investors tend to focus on larger, widely syndicated leveraged loan deals with debt ratings that allow them to match loan investments to the requirements of their investment vehicles. In addition, the smaller size of a middle-market deal makes it more difficult to justify paying the fees (which can amount hundreds of thousands of dollars) required to obtain a debt rating. As a result, the primary lenders/investors in the middle market are commercial banks and finance companies that do not require debt ratings for their lending process (see Figure 10.17). Moreover, these institutions tend to view their middle-market loan activity as a part of a larger overall business relationship with the issuing company. Institutional investors have just begun to increase exposure to middle-market loans recently because of a lack of standard leveraged loan paper, but they remain a small portion of today's overall market.

Investment Opportunities

Middle-market loans offer investors credit exposure to a pool of issuers beyond those found in the broadly syndicated leveraged loan and high-yield bond markets. Middle-market loans can provide higher yields and attractive price discounts for investors who are willing, in some cases, to take on additional credit risk. The potential for higher yield versus institutional term loans will likely persist because of significant structural differences between the two classes that result in a limited lending group for middle-market issuers. Besides potentially higher yields, middle-market loans, like institutional term loans, are senior secured and have maintenance financial covenants. We think that it is reasonable to expect that middle-market loan recoveries should be roughly comparable to institutional term loans because both asset classes have a senior secured claim on the assets of the issuer.

EUROPEAN LEVERAGED LOANS

Overview

The European leveraged loan market provides additional opportunities for investors within the senior secured loan asset category. Annual issuance for this market reached a record €78.5 billion in 2001. Issuance then declined to €40.0 billion in 2002 and climbed to €64.8 billion in 2004 (see Figure 10.18).

The new issuance was diversified across industries and countries. In 2003, four countries (the United Kingdom, France, Italy, and Germany) accounted for 71 percent of the total new issuance, with the U.K. constituting a little more than one-third. Lending was well balanced across a number of different industrial sectors, with the cable sector leading with 13 percent of market share (see Figure 10.19).

European banks have traditionally dominated the primary issue leveraged loan market, with almost two-thirds of the total market volume (see Figure 10.20). Institutional investors (mostly CLOs) accounted for only 21 percent of the total size of the European leveraged loan market. These findings are in sharp contrast with the United States where institutional investors dominate the primary loan market.

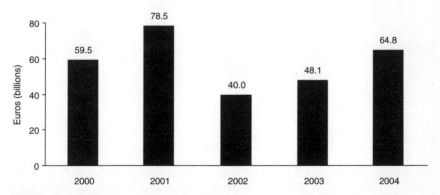

FIGURE 10.18 European Leveraged Loan Volume, 2000 to 2004 (euros in billions)
Source: Standard & Poor's.

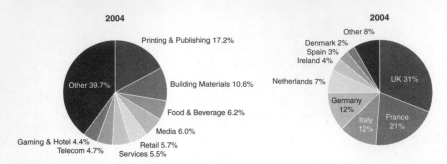

FIGURE 10.19 European Leveraged Loan Volume by Industry and Country
Source: Standard & Poor's.

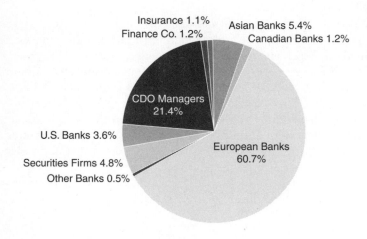

ªExcludes U.S. dollar tranches.

FIGURE 10.20 Primary Market for European Leveraged Loans by Investor Type,[a]
Latest 12 Months as of December 31, 2004
[a]Excludes U.S. dollar tranches.
Source: Standard & Poor's.

EUROPEAN MEZZANINE BANK LOANS

A growing part of the European loan market is the European mezzanine market (see Figure 10.21 for the historical growth of the market), which has now become the primary source of funding for European leveraged buyouts. A European mezzanine loan is generally a subordinated second secured debt obligation.

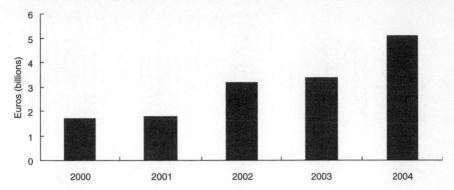

FIGURE 10.21 European Mezzanine Market Evolution
Source: Standard and Poor's.

TABLE 10.1 A Comparison of Typical European Funding Structure Characteristics

	Senior Debt	Mezzanine	High Yield	Equity
Security	Yes—first ranking	Yes—second ranking	Usually none	None
Ranking	Senior	Contractually subordinated	Structurally subordinated	Junior
Covenants	Generally comprehensive	Often track senior debt covenants	Less restrictive; mostly financial	None
Term	5–9 Years	6–10 Years	7–10 Years	Open ended
Income	Cash pay—floating	Cash pay—floating	Cash pay—fixed	Dividends—uncertain, usually cash pay

Source: Fitch.

European mezzanine bank debt is a floating-rate instrument, and its coupon usually includes cash and a pay-in-kind (PIK) component. Table 10.1 shows a typical mezzanine structure and compares it with other debt instruments. Investors are attracted by the higher spread relative to senior secured loans and greater protection than offered by high-yield bonds, achieved through covenants and security. However, European mezzanines still largely constitute a privately rated asset class, and only limited performance data are available.

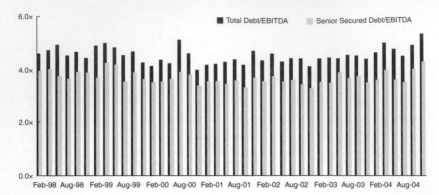

FIGURE 10.22 Average European Leverage Statistics—Rolling Three-Month Debt Multipliers, February 1998–November 2004
Source: Standard & Poor's.

Key Characteristics

Leverage European leveraged loans exhibit debt multipliers similar to those of U.S. leveraged loans. Figure 10.22 shows debt-to-EBITDA ratios for the European loan market.

Recoveries Recovery data for European loans is limited, given the private nature of the loan market. In 2000, the Fitch rating agency conducted research on an unnamed basis that showed an average recovery rate of 76.5 percent, which is slightly lower than the correspondent recovery rate for U.S. loans. However, these findings were hampered by the small size of the data sample used in the analysis. In addition to the limited data availability, differences exist in insolvency regimes across Europe. Because of these differences, recovery rates are expected to vary across European countries depending on the jurisdiction.

Primary Spreads Figure 10.23 provides comparison of the historical spreads on institutional BB/BB–rated new issues in the United States and Europe. The historical data show that European spreads were generally lower than U.S. spreads between 1999 and 2002. However, by 2004, U.S. spreads were rallying significantly, and European spreads ended up almost 75 bp wider than their U.S. counterparts.

Investment Opportunities

Investing in European leveraged loans can provide additional geographic and issuer diversification opportunities beyond the U.S. obligors. Although

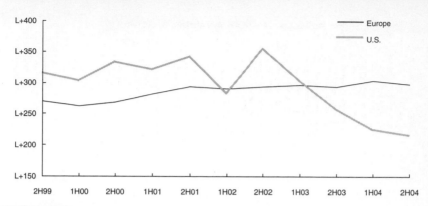

FIGURE 10.23 Weighted-Average New Issue Spread of European and U.S. BB/BB–Institutional Issuers, 2H 99–2H 04
Source: Standard & Poor's.

recovery data are limited, a European leveraged loan represents the senior secured debt of an issuer, and therefore it is expected to have significant recoveries in case of default.

COLLATERALIZED LOAN OBLIGATIONS

Efficient Access to Loan Market Investment Opportunities—Introducing CLOs

As we have discussed in this chapter, leveraged loans represent a broadly diversified, rapidly growing market. The unique characteristics of loans, such as high recoveries and stable prices, appeal to many investor types (including CLOs), especially during events such as the most recent bear credit market.

Despite its unprecedented growth, the loan market investor base has yet to reach the scale of the high-yield bond market. Participation in CLOs allows investors to capitalize on existing price inefficiencies in the loan market, diversify their exposure to the bank loans, and utilize professional management expertise and resources. Various types of investors, ranging from banks to high net worth individuals, have used CLOs to gain leveraged exposure to bank loans (see Figure 10.24).

Basic CLO Structure

CLOs are created by applying asset-backed structuring technology to a pool of bank loans. The formation of a CLO begins with the establishment

Senior/Subordinate (AAA/AA/A/BBB) Securities
Banks
Insurance Companies
Conduits
Fund Managers

Mezzanine (BBB/BB) Securities
Insurance Companies
Banks (Specialized Funds)
Hedge Funds
Fund Managers

Income Notes (CDO Equity)
Insurance Companies
Banks
High Net Worth Individuals
Alternative Investment Group/Special Investment Groups

FIGURE 10.24 CLO Investor Profile
Source: Citigroup.

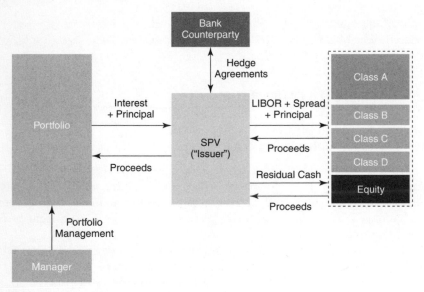

FIGURE 10.25 A Typical CLO Structure
Source: Citigroup.

of a special purpose vehicle (SPV) to acquire a pool of bank loans
(see Figure 10.25). The average collateral pool size is usually between
$300 million and $500 million par value, with the total exposure diversified
across 100 to 200 distinct obligors in 20 to 30 industries.

To fund the acquisition of the debt obligations, the SPV issues rated
and unrated liabilities (tranches). The expected average lives of these CDO

liabilities range from 6 to 12 years, depending on the tranche's seniority. Because the majority of these liabilities are highly rated, the CLO can raise most of its capital cheaply in the investment-grade market and invest it more profitably in the leveraged loan market.

A typical CLO consists of five to seven rated tranches with the ratings ranging from AAA to BB and unrated income notes (also known as the *equity tranche*). The desired tranche ratings are achieved through obligor and sector diversification and leverage, and by employing the payment distribution waterfall designed to protect the more senior note holders of the deal's liability structure.

The waterfall directs proceeds from the underlying collateral pool to the liability note holders, ensuring higher asset coverage for the senior tranches (see Figure 10.26). Principal and interest cash flow is paid sequentially from the highest-rated class to the lowest. However, if the cash flow is insufficient to meet rated note costs or certain asset coverage tests are not met, most or all cash flow is diverted from the equity tranche and paid to the most senior tranche. The asset coverage tests are divided into two groups: overcollateralization (OC) and interest coverage (IC) tests. The

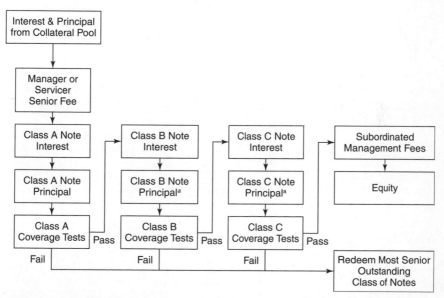

FIGURE 10.26 A Simplified Waterfall
[a]Subject to delevering of the more senior tranches.
Source: Citigroup.

former measures the amount of debt/asset coverage for a tranche, while the latter evaluates available interest proceeds to make coupon payments on the liability tranches.

A CLO investor can achieve a targeted return/risk profile by choosing a particular tranche in which to invest. The coupon margin reflects the relative riskiness of the tranche, and it increases with the lower ratings of the notes. Figure 10.27 shows a sample CLO capital structure. The income notes represent the riskiest investment, and therefore, they offer the highest potential return to compensate for this exposure. These notes receive the residual interest cash flow remaining after payment of fees, rated note holder coupons, and the satisfaction of any asset coverage tests. Depending on their risk/return objectives, investors can position themselves across the capital structure of a CLO.

CLO Asset Manager[3]

Once a CLO is issued, the collateral manager manages the portfolio according to the investment guidelines set forth in the bond indenture and within parameters necessary to satisfy the rating agencies. Within these guidelines, the manager sells and buys assets and, during the reinvestment period, reinvests collateral principal cash flows into new loans. The investment guidelines typically require that the CLO manager maintain a minimum average rating and portfolio diversity with the goal of muting any adverse effects that trading activity may have on note holders. The primary responsibility of the CLO collateral manager is to manage the portfolio in a way that minimizes losses to the note holders stemming from defaults and discounted sales. To this end, all note holders rely on the manager's ability to identify and retain creditworthy investments. In particular, income note

Assets					
Average S&P Rating of the Collateral Loans	B+				
Principal Amount (mm)	$325.0				
Liabilities	**Class A**	**Class B**	**Class C**	**Class D**	**Equity**
S&P Rating	AAA	A-	BBB	BB	NR
Moody's Rating	Aaa	A3	Baa2	Ba2	NR
Principal (mm)	$245.0	$33.0	$13.0	$14.8	$25.5
Percentage of Capital Structure	74.0%	10.0%	3.9%	4.5%	7.7%
Stated Final Maturity (years)	12.0	12.0	12.0	12.0	12.0
Average Life (years)	6.3	8.5	9.1	9.6	—

NR = not rated.

FIGURE 10.27   Sample CLO—Capital Structure
Source: Citigroup.

holders are substantially dependent on a manager's performance; the initial asset selection and trading activity throughout the reinvestment period are critical to achieving high returns.

Because note holder returns hinge upon good collateral manager performance, the choice of a CLO manager is a crucial decision for the investors. When choosing the collateral manager, the following key attributes should be examined in depth:

- The track record managing loan portfolios.
- Experience managing within the CLO framework.
- Level of institutional support.
- Investment and trading philosophy.
- Expertise in each asset class that the manager is permitted to invest in.
- Importance of CLO product to overall organization.
- Manager's access to loans.

A manager with a deep understanding of the underlying credit fundamentals of the various loan markets can make informed credit-based trading decisions, not trading decisions based on price movements.

CLO Market Today

The CLO market is a subsector of the broader CDO market. The latter has grown dramatically since the mid-1990s, reaching $110 billion in new issuance in 2004, eclipsing its record of $78 billion set in 2001 (see Figure 10.28).

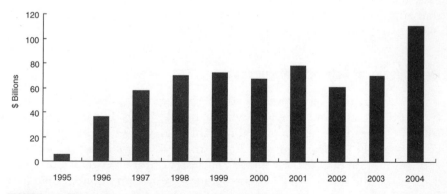

FIGURE 10.28 Global CDO Growth, 1995 to 2004
Source: Bloomberg, Creditflux, IFR Markets, MCM, Fitch, Moody's, and Standard & Poor's.

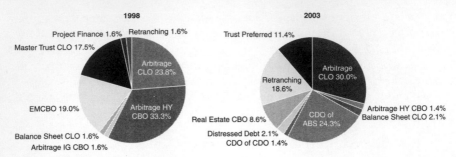

FIGURE 10.29 CDO Collateral—Distribution of U.S. Cash Flow CDOs, 1998 versus 2003
Source: Standard & Poor's.

As the overall CDO market has grown, so has the CLO portion of that market. As Figure 10.29 illustrates, CLOs accounted for 30 percent of all U.S. transactions rated by S&P in 2003, up by 6.2 percent since 1998. By contrast, high-yield bond transaction (high-yield CBO) issuance data show a sharp decline from approximately 33 percent in 1998 to just above 1 percent in 2003.

The credit market blowups and soaring default rates of 2000 to 2002 confirmed the resilience of leveraged loan collateral, steering more investors toward CLOs and away from traditional high-yield CBOs. In 2003, S&P rated only two new high-yield CBOs as opposed to 42 new CLO transactions. Many CDO investors have moved from CBOs into CLOs, attracted by the higher stability and strong returns associated with CLOs. This has caused a surge in the overall demand for primary loan issues. S&P estimates that approximately 67 percent of all issues in the primary institutional loan market were placed into various CLO vehicles in 2002.[4]

Key Drivers of CLO Outperformance

Rating agency data have revealed striking differences in the historical performance of CLOs and compared with high-yield CBOs. In particular, CLO tranche ratings have been much more stable than CBO tranche ratings and corporate debt ratings. Figure 10.30 illustrates Moody's Investors Service's rating transition rates in these three asset classes.[5] Moreover, as evident from Table 10.2, the severity of CLO downgrades was less pronounced than that for CBOs. The historical performance of CLOs indicates far fewer and less pronounced rating downgrades than for high-yield CBOs and corporate debt.

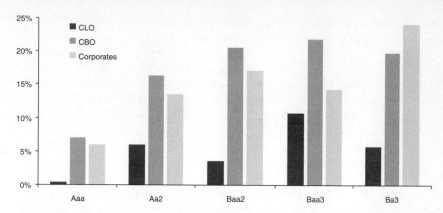

FIGURE 10.30 Moody's Historical CLO and CBO Rating Downgrades,
1996 to 2002
Source: Moody's Investors Service.

TABLE 10.2 Maximum One-Year
Historical Downgrades

Rating	Lowest One-Year Rating Transition	
	CBO	CLO
Aaa	Ba3	Aa2
Aa2	Caa1	A1
A3	Caa3	Baa3
Baa2	Ca/C	Ba2
Baa3	Ca/C	B2
Ba3	Ca/C	Ca/C

Source: Moody's Investors Service.

In addition to the slower pace and scale of downgrades, most CLO downgrades were localized: According to a Moody's 2003 study, the majority of CLO downgrades have been limited to a handful of CLO managers. In fact, 56 percent of all CLOs downgraded by the agency in 2002 were associated with just three collateral managers. The same study indicated that all downgrades in earlier years were associated with the same three managers.

Why are CLO ratings so stable? The answer can be found in two main areas: superior performance of loan collateral and CLO-specific collateral manager expertise. Broad obligor and sector diversification, floating-rate collateral, and high recovery and prepayment rates all augur well for CLOs.

In addition, as we discuss later, the typical bank loan manager mentality is well suited to managing loan portfolios in the CLO context.

Recovery Rates Because they occupy the most senior part of an issuer's capital structure and are secured by its assets, defaulted bank loans often have substantially higher recovery rates than the more subordinated debt obligations of an issuer (see Figure 10.31). Over the 1988 to 2003 period, senior secured bank loans had an average recovery of 77.5 percent of par value, while senior unsecured debt recovered 41.5 percent of par value and junior subordinated bonds recovered only 22 percent. Even in times of credit duress, such as the 1998 to 2002 period, loans realized an average recovery rate of 74.1%, while senior unsecured debt recovered less than half that amount (36.8 percent). High recovery rates make it less likely that the collateral backing the CLO will deteriorate sharply. The CLO manager receives significant principal proceeds from the defaulted assets and has the opportunity to reinvest the cash flow into new collateral.

Prepayment Rates Most corporate bonds have covenants that govern an issuer's prepayment/call rights. High-yield bond prepayments are typically restricted for the first three to five years. By contrast, the vast majority of bank loans can be prepaid at par at any time without penalty. In fact, the average leveraged loan prepayment rate during the recent low interest rate environment was approximately 20 to 25 percent, easily topping the average 5 to 8 percent call rate in the high-yield corporate market. For this reason,

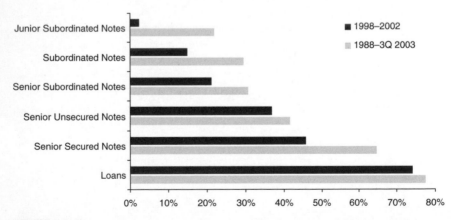

FIGURE 10.31 Historical Recovery Rates, 1988 to 2003 versus 1998 to 2002
Source: Standard & Poor's.

the CLO collateral manager usually has significant principal cash flows to reinvest in additional collateral assets or to de-lever the liabilities. This is particularly useful in a stressed economic environment with the downward credit pressure in the underlying portfolio.

Floating Interest Rates   Because most CDO liabilities bear floating-rate coupons (i.e., a spread over LIBOR), floating-rate leveraged loan collateral effectively eliminates the interest rate mismatch between the assets and liabilities of a CLO. By contrast, CDOs that are backed predominately by fixed-rate high-yield bonds must enter into an interest rate hedge agreement with a third party to hedge against interest rate risk. Typically, a high-yield CBO periodically pays the counterparty a predetermined fixed interest rate on a fixed notional amount and in turn it receives floating-rate payments (usually determined by the value of LIBOR on the preceding payment date). The hedge balance is typically structured to decrease over time to mimic the expected amortization schedule of the notes and, hence, reduce the risk of the transaction's being overhedged. Hedge payments are more senior than liability payments in a payment waterfall structure and, thus, may have a pronounced effect on the overall performance of a high-yield CBO.

Although the outstanding balance of the hedge amortizes with the time, the amortization schedule is determined at inception and may differ significantly from the realized amortization of CDO liabilities. In particular, in a highly stressed credit environment (e.g., 2000 to 2002), the most senior tranche of a CDO may experience rapid prepayment caused by the failure of the asset coverage tests. Consequently, the hedge balance grows significantly larger than the reduced balance of the liabilities, and the transaction becomes overhedged. Under stressed economic conditions, which are typically coupled with decreasing interest rates, a CDO can suffer from both an asset/liability balance mismatch and an increase in the periodic payments to the hedge counterparty. This phenomenon has plagued high-yield CBOs over the past few years.

Floating-rate bank loans eliminate the asset/liability mismatch and greatly reduce the interest rate risk in the transaction. Therefore, CLOs are unlikely to suffer from the double blow of being overhedged in a decreasing interest rate environment under stressful credit conditions.

Price Stability   High expected recoveries and a surging demand for loans (especially from CLO issuers) are two of the primary reasons why loan prices have remained very stable over the past few years. Although CDOs are not net asset value (NAV)-based vehicles, price stability is very important for

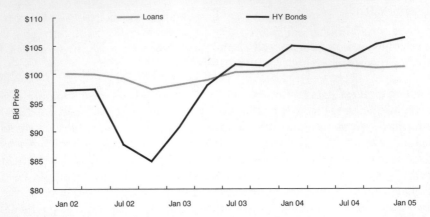

FIGURE 10.32 High-Yield Bonds and BB-Rated Institutional Loans—Average Bid Prices, January 2002–January 2005
Source: Standard & Poor's.

two reasons: credit risk sales and reinvestment into new assets. Regarding the former, if a CLO manager sees signs of credit deterioration at a company, he or she may decide to sell the loan. The ability to sell this asset into a market that has very solid price stability can be a powerful mitigant to loss of par in the CDO. By contrast, as Figure 10.32 illustrates, if the CDO manager sold high-yield bonds of the same issuer, the loss of par could be much more pronounced.

Reinvestment of principal proceeds is the flip side of this issue. Because the loan market (unlike the high-yield bond market) typically does not trade much above par, when a CLO manager has to redeploy principal proceeds into new assets he or she typically will not pay above par for an asset, or if a premium is paid it will be slight as compared with the high-yield bond market.

CLO Collateral Manager The final driver of CLO outperformance is the least tangible, but perhaps one of the most important: *t*he mind-set of the bank loan manager. As we have discussed in the previous section, bank loans are prepayable at par without penalty, and as a result they do not trade much above par. Loan managers recognize this, and the good ones focus zealously on credit risk, because they realize that every point of par lost as the result of trading and/or default is exceedingly difficult to counterbalance through the sale of loans trading at a premium. Not all total return high-yield managers have had the same mind-set, and some high-yield CBOs have suffered as a result.

CONCLUSION

The impressive growth that the leveraged loan market has displayed over the past decade has been accompanied by greatly improved liquidity and transparency. The benefits of this asset class, which include stable prices and high recovery and prepayment rates, can be accessed efficiently by CLOs. During the previous credit cycle, CLOs on average have demonstrated more stable performance than both high-yield bond CDOs and straight corporate debt. This stability has fueled CLO growth: CLOs now account for almost one-third of the primary CDO market.

The growth has not come without challenges. The recent surge in demand for institutional loans by structured vehicles has resulted in a significant tightening of the loan spreads and increased obligor concentrations among some institutional loan CLOs. CLO market participants have acknowledged this and are now searching for ways to complement their institutional loan CLO portfolios. Alternative loan categories, such as revolving credit obligations, middle-market loans, and European leveraged loans, provide new chances for diversification, yield, and credit stability.

MIDDLE-MARKET CLO HANDBOOK

Middle-market collateralized loan obligations (CLOs) offer investors the ability to diversify away from issuers found in the standard leveraged loan and high-yield bond markets. With a single investment, investors can obtain broad, professionally managed exposure to middle-market loans at a risk level of their choosing.

Strong middle-market loan performance has resulted in strong middle-market CLO performance. Of the 39 middle-market CLOs issued through September 30, 2004, none were downgraded by Moody's or Standard & Poor's.[6]

Middle-market CLOs issued for balance-sheet purposes often contain structural features not commonly found in traditional CLOs. These middle-market CLOs often have zero-tolerance loss tests that trap cash immediately upon credit delinquency or default.

Middle-market loans are similar to leveraged loans, but they are issued by medium-size companies and often are not syndicated. Middle-market loan issuers generally have less than $500 million in revenues and less than $50 million in EBITDA. As a result, loan facilities are typically less than $150 million in total size.

We expect loans to continue to deliver superior recovery rates relative to other debt given their advantages in security, seniority, and covenant protection. In the period from 1988 to 2003, senior secured bank loans had an average recovery of 77.5 percent of par value, while senior unsecured debt recovered only 41.5 percent of par value and junior subordinated bonds recovered only 22 percent.

Middle-Market Size and Definition

Middle-market loans are similar in structure to leveraged loans but they are issued by medium-size companies and often are not syndicated. For the first nine months of 2004, $17.1 billion of middle-market loans were issued, which was nearly double the $9.0 billion issued during the same period of 2003 (see Figure 10.33). Middle-market loan issuance stalled for the three years prior to 2004, as lenders had a much lower appetite for risk owing to rising defaults and volatility in the equity and bond markets.

Middle-market loan issuers generally have less than $500 million in revenues and less than $50 million in EBITDA. As a result, loan facilities are typically less than $150 million in total size. Within these criteria, middle-market loans of $150 million or more are considered large and are normally issued by companies with EBITDA of $25 million to $50 million. Standard middle-market loans are smaller ($50 million to 150 million in size) and small middle-market loans constitute the balance (see Table 10.3). Specialized lenders cater to the middle market given the small loan size and specific needs of these companies. Middle market lending is generally relationship driven, and deals tend to have fewer participants than leveraged loans that are broadly syndicated.

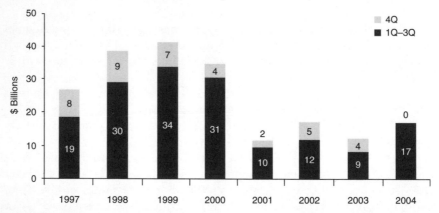

FIGURE 10.33 Total Middle-Market Volume by Year, December 1997–December 2004
Source: Standard & Poor's/Leveraged Commentary and Data.

TABLE 10.3 Middle-Market Segments (all values in $millions)

Loan Size	Revenues	EBITDA	Deal Size	Lender Type
Large	$250–$500	>$50	>$150	Syndicate group
Standard	$100–$250	$25–$50	$50–$150	Regional banks and finance Companies
Small	<$100	<$25	<$50	Finance companies and special lenders

Source: Citigroup.

Middle-market lending increased in the third quarter of 2004 with strong investor appetite and a low default environment fueling the primary market. Increased merger and acquisition (M&A) and leveraged buyout (LBO) activity drove new issuance in 2004, making up over 56 percent of deals done during the third quarter and driving issuance up 42 percent over the same period the prior year. The new deal pipeline is strong, with institutional money chasing yield downmarket and abundant M&A and LBO transactions pending.

Growing Investor Demand

As yields tightened considerably in the traditional leveraged loan and high-yield bond markets during 2004, investors increasingly looked for opportunities to earn higher yields, and some invested in middle-market loans. Institutional investors make up nearly 70 percent of primary investors in the middle market, and CLO structures comprise nearly 70 percent of institutional money (see Figure 10.34).

Dominance of Institutional Term-Loan Debt

In 2004, 62 percent of new-issue middle-market loans were institutional tranches, compared with only 37 percent the prior year (see Figure 10.35). Institutional debt set all-time records for middle-market loans in 2004, outpacing even 1999, which was a record year for new issues but had a smaller proportion of institutional tranches. Institutional tranches, which are fully funded term loans, are much easier for investors to hold because of stable funding requirements and more predictable maturities. These characteristics also make them more attractive for CLO structures.

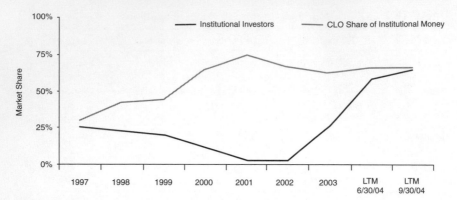

FIGURE 10.34 Institutional Investors' Share of the Primary Market for Highly Leveraged Loans for Issuers with EBITDA of $50 million or Less versus CLOs' Share of the Institutional Market
Source: Standard & Poor's/Leveraged Commentary and Data.

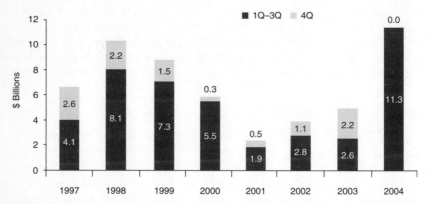

FIGURE 10.35 Total Middle-Market Institutional Volume by Year, December 1997–September 2004
Source: Standard & Poor's/Leveraged Commentary and Data.

Second-Lien Loans Emerge

Second-lien middle-market loans emerged as a significant part of the new-issue market in 2004 as well, with nearly $2.0 billion issues year to date, or 12 percent of the total market (see Figure 10.36). Traditional loan investors and hedge funds are attracted by the high yields paid on the second-lien tranches. Demand is settling, however, as average second-lien middle-market loans had a spread of LIBOR + 750 bp in the third quarter

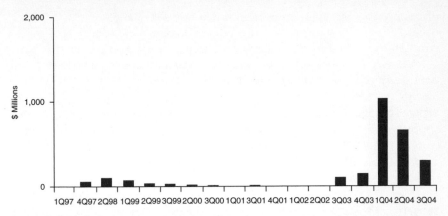

FIGURE 10.36 Volume of Second-Lien Loans for Middle-Market Issuers, March 1997–September 2004
Source: Standard & Poor's/Leveraged Commentary and Data.

of 2004, wider from the tights of LIBOR + 623 bp in the first quarter of 2004 when new investors flooded the market. While second lien loans provide attractive yields and can provide a significant boost to portfolio performance, investors should consider that a secondary claim on the assets of the borrower could have a negative impact on recovery rates for these securities if the obligor defaults.

Investment Considerations for Middle-Market Investors

Middle-market loans[7] can provide higher yields and attractive price discounts for investors who are willing to take higher risk. Because of lower market liquidity, many middle-market loans trade at a discount to par and price points considerably lower than comparable leveraged loans. Investors should consider the following issues when considering whether to buy middle-market loans.

Discount Middle-market loans generally trade at a discount from par and often trade at price points considerably lower than similarly rated leveraged loans. The discount is caused by certain impediments to liquidity (e.g., small deal sizes, few market makers, small lending groups, private information) and the selling pressure caused by banks seeking to rationalize their balance sheets and credit exposures. Middle-market loans are attractive for institutional loan investors, including structured vehicles that benefit from purchasing discounted instruments with higher coupons. Discounted prices become especially important when loans refinance, which generally occurs at par. Investors who have bought loans at a discount will reap a windfall from the difference between purchase price and par at that time. Conversely, investors who buy loans at a premium above par stand to lose the difference in a potential refinancing.

Higher Coupons   Middle-market institutional loans currently pay an average coupon of approximately LIBOR + 361 bp, nearly 140 bp more than a comparable BB/BB–rated institutional leveraged loan, and 80 bp more than a comparable B/B–rated institutional leveraged loan (see Figure 10.37 for this comparison).

Security   Middle-market loans, like institutional term loans, are often senior secured, and have maintenance financial covenants. Covenants give investors the ability to restrict the debt capacity and cash flow use of a borrower and provide an early seat at the table in the event of credit deterioration of an issuer, which lenders often use to improve their position in terms of security, collateral, coupon, or fees.

Diversification   Middle-market loans offer investors credit exposure to issuers outside of the standard leveraged loan and high-yield bond markets. Limited overlap between middle-market obligors and broadly syndicated obligors or high-yield bond issuers enhances the diversity of a portfolio of leveraged investments. Issuers of middle-market loans come from a varied group of industries, as seen in Figure 10.38. Additionally, middle-market

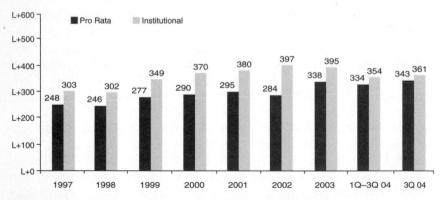

FIGURE 10.37   Average Coupon of Middle-Market Transactions, 1997–September 2004
Source: Standard & Poor's/Leveraged Commentary and Data.

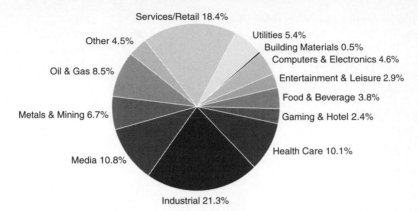

FIGURE 10.38 Total Middle-Market New-Issue Volume by Broad Industry, September 2004
Source: Standard & Poor's/Leveraged Commentary and Data.

loans are not typically available or sought out by the broad market, leading to reduced correlation in a portfolio of loan investments.

Prepayment Rate   Because of amortization, prepayments, refinancings, and corporate events such as asset sales and M&As, middle-market loans, like traditional leveraged loans, tend to be repaid prior to scheduled maturity. Increases in the prepayment rate lead to yield windfalls owing to quicker-than-expected recovery in the event of purchase price discounts. Prepayment generally benefits holders of middle-market loans more than holders of institutional term loans because middle-market loans are usually bought at a discount from par, while the average leveraged loan traded at a price of approximately 101 in 2004.

Default Performance and Recovery Rates   Leveraged loan default rates were as high as 7.0 percent in the first quarter of 2002, but dropped below 1.0 percent in 2004 (see Figure 10.39). This shows that when the credit cycle turns, default rates can go quite high and put many companies into jeopardy. It is during these times of high default that the value of security in leveraged loans shows its greatest worth in consistently higher recovery rates.

Senior secured bank loans have produced higher recovery rates compared to other asset classes in recent history and over multiple credit cycles (see Table 10.4). The higher recovery rates are primarily due to the senior position in an issuer's capital structure and the security interest that loan holders have in an issuer's assets.[8] Similar to leveraged loans, covenants

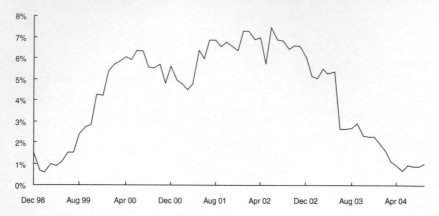

FIGURE 10.39   Rolling 12-month Default Rate
Source: Standard & Poor's/Leveraged Commentary and Data.

TABLE 10.4   Recovery Rates by Strength of Collateralization

	Average Recovery Rate	
	1988–3Q 2003 (%)	1998–2002 (%)
Loans	77.5	74.1
Senior secured notes	64.7	45.8
Senior unsecured notes	41.5	36.8
Senior subordinated notes	30.7	21.3
Subordinated notes	29.5	15.0
Junior subordinated notes	22.0	2.5

Note that 256 defaulted loans and bond issues defaulted between 1987 to 2003; 746 defaulted loans and bond issues defaulted between 1998 and 2002. Recoveries are discounted at each instrument's predefault interest rate.
Source: S&P/PMD LossStats™ Database.

on middle-market loan facilities improve recovery since they allow lenders to limit credit risks such as capital expenditure, leverage, and acquisitions. Covenants also allow lenders to have an early look at an issuer's credit problems, often before the rest of the market, as an issuer must amend or repay its loans when covenants are breached. This amendment process allows lenders to improve their control and security interest in a troubled issuer, further positioning loans for a higher recovery.

Average recovery rates on defaulted debt tend to be in the 30 to 40 percent range, but senior secured loan recoveries are consistently significantly higher. Table 10.4 shows recoveries over two time periods. In the period from 1988 to 2003, senior secured bank loans had an average recovery of 77.5 percent of par value, while senior unsecured debt recovered only 41.5 percent of par value and junior subordinated bonds recovered only 22 percent. Even in times of duress like the period from 1998 to 2002, when default rates increased sharply, loans continued to recover an impressive 74.1 percent on defaulted debt while senior unsecured debt recovered only 36.8%.

Lower Liquidity   Trading liquidity for middle-market loans is significantly lower than the comparable leveraged loan market for a number of reasons. Middle-market deals are inherently smaller owing to smaller issuer sizes, so there is less loan paper to trade. Lenders in the middle market generally have business relationships with the issuing companies, which would make them reluctant to trade the bank debt. Middle-market deals are generally not rated by the major debt rating agencies, so many investors cannot buy them due to the rating requirements built into their fund structures.

Higher Senior Leverage   Leverage on middle-market loans can be slightly higher than comparable leveraged loans, but is currently similar at an average under 4.0 times debt/EBITDA compared to the 4.2 times average for the overall leveraged loan market. See Figure 10.40 for a historical graph of middle-market loan credit statistics. In general, middle-market loans tend to have more secured bank debt, so senior secured leverage is often higher than the leveraged loan market, as evidenced by senior secured leverage of

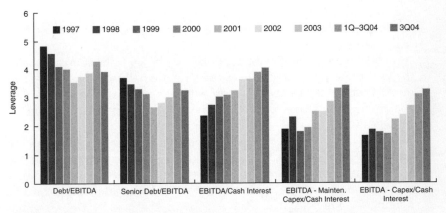

FIGURE 10.40 Average Pro Forma Credit Statistics for Middle-Market Transactions, 1997–September 2004
Source: Standard & Poor's/Leveraged Commentary and Data.

3.7 times for middle-market loans versus 2.9 times for the overall leveraged loan market.

Legal Considerations

As one might expect, middle-market loans are highly individualized trans-actions. Thus, some middle-market loans lend themselves to securitization while others do not. For example, middle-market loans, like larger loans, are more favorable for CLOs if they are fully assignable without consent from the obligor. In addition, there should be no right of set-off between the obligor and the lender—anything else could compromise the CLOs' ability to collect from the obligor upon default of the original lender/servicer. Finally, if multiple facilities exist, cross collateralization and cross default language should ensure that the lenders' rights are preserved if a payment is missed on a different obligation.

Middle-Market CLOs

Middle-market loans lend themselves well to CLO technology[9] and an investment in middle-market loans through a CLO structure offers the following five advantages:

1. Middle-market loan CLOs are backed by a large and diverse number of loans, which permit investors to buy broad exposure to the middle-market loan asset class in a single investment.
2. Middle-market loan CLOs are often professionally managed. Therefore, investors who are looking to diversify into this asset class do not need to create the infrastructure necessary to invest and trade in middle-market loans directly.
3. A middle-market CLO investment may be chosen to be consistent with the investor's risk appetite. Investors who are bullish on the sector can invest lower in the capital structure whereas more cautious (or ratings constrained) investors will likely prefer to invest in a more senior tranche of the CLO.
4. Although middle-market loans are not liquid themselves (obligors are often privately owned companies that are not required to disclose financials), a growing secondary market in CDOs affords investors a reasonable assurance that they may sell their middle-market CLO holding at a fair price.[10]
5. Middle-market loans often have attractive yields relative to comparably secured larger, syndicated loans (see the subsection entitled "Higher Coupons" earlier in this chapter). The incremental cash flow improves

the expected return of CLO equity and provides a powerful source of subordination for CLO debt holders.

Middle-Market CLO Variations   Middle-market CLO structures vary depending on the specific blend of middle-market loan and traditional leveraged loan collateral. For CLOs that are backed by large middle-market loans, and especially for those pools that consist of a blend of traditional leveraged loans and middle-market loans, a traditional CLO structure is often applied, complete with overcollateralization tests and collateral quality tests. In fact, based on structure alone, many investors would be hard-pressed to distinguish these arbitrage transactions from many traditional leveraged loan CLOs. At the other end of the spectrum, transactions backed purely by small middle-market loans often have unique structural features that are not common to traditional CLOs (see the discussion entitled "Unique Structural Features" later in this chapter). These transactions provide issuers with a crucial form of funding (see Figure 10.41).

Completed Middle-Market CLO Transactions   By our estimates, 39 middle-market CLO transactions representing $20 billion of rated debt have been issued from 1999 through 2004 (see Table 10.5). Roughly a third of these transactions were issued for balance-sheet (or funding) purposes and are backed purely by middle-market loan collateral. The remaining two-thirds are backed by a blend of middle-market collateral and larger, more broadly syndicated loans and were predominately issued for arbitrage purposes.

Middle-market CLO growth has tracked the growth of the CLO market as a whole, representing about 20 percent of issuance (by deal count) for the past five years (see Figure 10.42). However, we expect this trend to change as

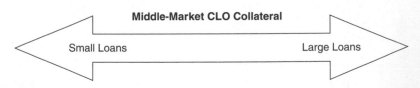

Middle-Market CLO Collateral

Small Loans   Large Loans

Balance Sheet MMCLOs
\ Transactions are often executed for balance sheet or funding purposes.
\ Collateral is often composed of club loans or single-lender loans.
\ Structural features include zero loss tolerance tests, substitution rights.

Arbitrage MMCLOs
\ Collateral is composed of a mix of middle-market loans and large, syndicated loans.
\ Transactions are generally executed for arbitrage purposes.
\ Structurally, these transactions look very much like traditional CLOs.

FIGURE 10.41   Variations of Middle-Market CLOs
Source: Citigroup.

TABLE 10.5 Middle-Market CLO Issuance through October 2004

Closing Date	CLO	Servicer/Manager	Deal Size ($M)	Rated Par Amount ($M)	Percentage MMLs[a]
Feb. 10, 1999	Ableco Finance LLC	Ableco Finance LLC	1,644	1,205	Mix
Aug. 27, 1999	First Source Financial (Cayman), L.P.	First Source Financial Inc.	2,181	1,820	Mix
Dec. 14, 1999	Antares Funding LP	Antares Capital Corporation	560	517	Mix
Oct. 11, 2000	First Source Loan Obligations Trust	First Source Financial LLP	717	640	Mix
Nov. 1, 2000	Fleet Commercial Loan Master LLC 2000-1	Fleet National Bank	2,073	2,039	Mix
Dec. 20, 2000	ACAS Business Loan Trust 2000-1	American Capital Strategies, Ltd.	154	115	100%
Dec. 29, 2000	Ark CLO 2000-1 Ltd.	Patriarch Partners	1,200	1,001	Mix
Mar. 7, 2001	First Source Loan Obligations Insured Trust	First Source Financial LLP	462	265	Mix
Oct. 23, 2001	Endeavor LLC	PPM America Inc.	470	435	Mix
Oct. 26, 2001	Ark II CLO 2001-1 Ltd.	Patriarch Partners II LLC	675	566	Mix
Oct. 30, 2001	Denali Capital CLO I, Ltd.	U.S. Funding Funding Partners, LLC	400	368	Mix
Dec. 27, 2001	MCG Commercial Loan Trust 2001-1	MCG Capital Corporation	354	265	100%

(continued)

TABLE 10.5 (*continued*)

Closing Date	CLO	Servicer/Manager	Deal Size ($M)	Rated Par Amount ($M)	Percentage MMLs[a]
Mar. 15, 2002	ACAS Business Loan Trust 2002-1	American Capital Strategies, Ltd.	196	147	100%
May 15, 2002	CapitalSource Commercial Loan Trust 2002-1	CapitalSource Finance LLC	275	248	100%
Jul. 11, 2002	Mariner CDO 2002 Ltd	Antares Capital Corporation	411	378	Mix
Jul. 30, 2002	Denali Capital CLO II, Ltd.	U.S. Funding Funding Partners, LLC	400	341	Mix
Aug. 7, 2002	ACAS Business Loan Trust 2002-2	American Capital Strategies, Ltd.	211	158	100%
Aug. 20, 2002	Fleet Commercial Loan Master LLC 2002-1	Fleet National Bank	1,000	347	Mix
Aug. 29, 2002	GSC Partners Gemini Fund Ltd	GSC Partners	523	497	Mix
Oct. 30, 2002	CapitalSource Commercial Loan Trust 2002-2	CapitalSource Finance LLC	326	293	100%
Apr. 17, 2003	CapitalSource Commercial Loan Trust 2003-1	CapitalSource Finance LLC	450	405	100%
May 21, 2003	ACAS Business Loan Trust 2003-1	American Capital Strategies, Ltd.	308	239	100%
Jul. 16, 2003	Denali Capital CLO III, Ltd	U.S. Funding Funding Partners, LLC	434	403	Mix

(*continued*)

TABLE 10.5 (*continued*)

Closing Date	CLO	Servicer/Manager	Deal Size ($M)	Rated Par Amount ($M)	Percentage MMLs[a]
Nov. 20, 2003	A3 Funding LP	Cerberus Capital Mgmt (Ableco)	600	420	Mix
Nov. 20, 2003	A4 Funding LP	Cerberus Capital Mgmt (Ableco)	1,000	700	Mix
Nov. 25, 2003	CapitalSource Commercial Loan Trust 2003-2	CapitalSource Finance LLC	500	430	100%
Dec. 17, 2003	Foxe Basin CLO 2003	RBC Capital Partners	416	384	Mix
Dec. 19, 2003	ACAS Business Loan trust 2003-2	American Capital Strategies, Ltd.	397	318	100%
Dec. 19, 2003	Navigator CDO 2003	Antares Capital Corporation	460	424	Mix
Dec. 22, 2003	Special Situations Opportunity Fund I, LLC	LaSalle Bank N.A.	572	300	Mix
Apr. 1, 2004	Bernard National Loan Investors Ltd.	LaSalle Bank N.A.	200	157	Mix
Apr. 1, 2004	Bernard Leveraged Loan Investors, Ltd.	LaSalle Bank N.A.	103	68	Mix
Jun. 22, 2004	CapitalSource Commercial Loan Trust 2004-1	CapitalSource Finance LLC	875	766	100%
Jul. 14, 2004	CoLTS Trust 2004-1	Wachovia Securities	263	247	Mix
Jul. 30, 2004	Fortress Credit Op I & II	LaSalle Bank N.A.	1,500	1,000	Mix
Aug. 25, 2004	Denali Capital CLO IV, Ltd	U.S. Funding Funding Partners, LLC	400	368	Mix

(*continued*)

TABLE 10.5 (*continued*)

Closing Date	CLO	Servicer/Manager	Deal Size ($M)	Rated Par Amount ($M)	Percentage MMLs[a]
Sep. 30, 2004	MCG Commercial Loan Trust 2004-1	MCG Capital Corporation	398	341	Mix
Oct. 14, 2004	Navigator CDO 2004	Antares Capital Corporation	511	471	Mix
Oct. 28, 2004	CapitalSource Commercial Loan Trust 2004-2	CapitalSource Finance LLC	1,108	1,000	100%
Total			24,724	20,084	

[a]If the exact collateral composition is unknown, the transaction is assumed to be a mix of leveraged loans and middle market loans.
Source: Fitch, Moody's, Standard & Poor's, and Citigroup.

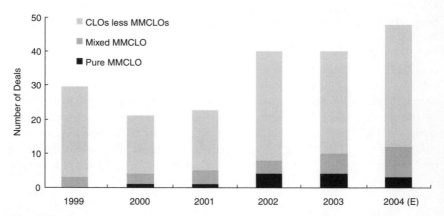

FIGURE 10.42 Growth of the Middle-Market CLO Sector by Deal Count
Source: Citigroup.

tight spreads in the broadly syndicated market push traditional bank lenders back into the middle-market space, and as specialty finance companies expand operations. In addition, several new business development funds have been created to specifically focus on the middle-market loan space. Several of these new funds likely have designs on CLO issuance as well.

Middle-Market CLO Performance Middle-market CLOs performed well
through the difficult credit environment of 2001 to 2002. In this subsection,
we look specifically at two subclasses of the middle-market CLO market: (1) CLOs backed purely by middle-market loans; and (2) those backed
by a mixture of middle-market loans and broadly syndicated loans. The
first group was issued exclusively for balance sheet, or funding, purposes,
while the second, mixed collateral group was primarily issued for arbitrage
purposes (although a few balance-sheet type deals are also included).

CLO Performance Backed Exclusively by Middle-Market Collateral A study by
Fitch Ratings in March of 2004 indicated that pure middle-market CLOs
have performed well.[11] Of the six 100 *percent* middle-market loan CLOs
rated by Fitch with at least one year since issuance, none have experienced
a downgrade and four have experienced upgrades. The remaining two were
affirmed. By tranche count, seven of 15 tranches were upgraded, six were
affirmed, and two have been paid in full (see Table 10.6).

Fitch attributes the strong performance of the middle-market loan
CLOs to three things. First, middle-market loan prepayment rates have
been high and, since pure middle-market CLOs are static in nature, those
unexpected dollars have been used to pay down senior CLO notes quickly.
Of the six transactions with a year of maturity, the weighted average
prepayment rate was 28.3 percent on an annualized basis. Second, middle-
market loan quality has remained relatively firm. After an extensive rerating
process, Fitch concluded that some collateral quality deterioration has
occurred on average, but the six collateral pools stayed within a single
rating subcategory of the original pool rating on average. The resilient
nature of middle-market loans is a testament to the underwriting standards
of the middle-market specialty finance companies that sponsored these
transactions (e.g., American Capital Strategies, CapitalSource Finance, and
MCG Capital). Third, Fitch credits strong structural features contained in
pure middle-market loan CLOs that deflect excess cash flows whenever a

TABLE 10.6 Performance of CLOs Backed Exclusively by
Middle-Market Collateral

	Deals	Tranches Rated	Upgraded	Affirmed	Downgraded	Paid in Full
By number	6	15	7	6	0	2
By volume ($M)	1,515	1,227	277	782	0	167

Source: Middle-Market CLO Performance Update: 2003, Fitch.

loan becomes 60 days delinquent. Excess cash in an amount equal to the balance of the delinquent loan is directed to a reserve account and released to senior note holders in the event that the troubled obligor defaults. Effectively, this amounts to a zero-loss policy that is designed to keep the outstanding amount of CLO liabilities and the outstanding amount of assets at an even one-to-one ratio.

CLO Performance Backed by Mix of Middle-Market and Syndicated Collateral

We conducted a Fitch-like study of mixed collateral CLOs using S&P and Moody's rating changes (Fitch has not rated many of the arbitrage middle-market CLOs). These transactions have also performed well on the whole. Of the 14 mixed-loan CLOs rated by S&P or Moody's with at least one year since issuance, none have experienced a downgrade and two have experienced upgrades. Four more deals have paid in full. By tranche count (see Table 10.7), two of 43 tranches were upgraded and 10 have been paid in full. No tranches have been downgraded by either agency.[12]

We attribute the strong performance of the mixed-loan CLOs to the same drivers that have led to solid performance in the general CLO market. First, leveraged loan prepayment rates have been high and, since many mixed middle-market CLOs are static in nature, those dollars have been used to pay down CDO debt. Second, when loans do default, recoveries have been robust even through the credit downturn (see the earlier discussion entitled "Default Performance and Recovery Rates"). Finally, the mind-set of CLO managers, including middle-market CLO managers, is often one that emphasizes loss avoidance rather than maximization of total portfolio return. Unlike bonds that can, and often do, trade at a significant discount or premium to par, loans generally trade relatively close to par. For example, a loan might trade from 99 to 101, but this potential gain is small when compared with the losses that could be incurred should the credit default. In contrast, a bond manager might buy a credit at 80 with the hope of selling it at par or higher if the credit improves. The lure of large gains gives bond

TABLE 10.7 Performance of CLOs Backed by Middle-Market Loan and Leveraged Loan Collateral

	Deals	Tranches Rated	Upgraded	Affirmed	Downgraded	Paid in Full
By number	14	43	2	NA	0	10
By volume ($M)	12,625	10,323	NA	NA	0	3,160

Source: Moody's, S&P, and Citigroup.

managers more incentive to take chances and, in a bad credit environment, that could be a disastrous strategy. The incentive to trade for gains is not as strong for loan managers and, as a consequence, we believe loan managers are more likely to maintain a sound portfolio.

CLO Investment Considerations

A convenient way for investors to diversify into the middle-market loan asset class is through a middle-market CLO. However, some unique investment considerations are introduced when a CLO structure is imposed onto a middle-market loan pool. In this section, we draw your attention to the considerations that we believe to be the most important and then discuss them in greater detail:

- The reliability and quality of the CLO sponsor (sometimes acting as the collateral originator and servicer).
- The push for diversity.
- Rating agency assumptions regarding collateral quality and middle-market loan recovery rates.
- Middle-market loan and middle-market CLO liquidity.
- Unique middle-market CLO structural features.

Sponsor/Servicer/Originator   Depending on the specific middle-market loan transaction, several CLO administrative and credit activities may be conducted by the same individuals. The sponsors of balance-sheet middle-market CLOs also often serve as loan originators and loan servicers for the CLO transaction. Therefore, special consideration should be given to these sponsors, which we discuss here. Arbitrage middle-market CLOs, however, generally have a more traditional partition of responsibilities, with independent portfolio managers and trustees.

As the loan originator, balance-sheet middle-market CLO sponsors are the primary gatekeeper with respect to the quality of collateral that will enter the CLO pool. Therefore, sound credit analysis is supremely important. Further, as servicer, the sponsor also plays an integral part of the day-to-day function of the CLO: tracking loan covenants and payments, and facilitating (with the trustee) the distribution of cash to CLO debt holders. Therefore, it is imperative that the sponsor has the proper systems in place to track loan performance, obligor financial health, collateral cash flows receipts, and CLO cash distributions.

In addition, as the loan servicer, the sponsor is an important driver of recovery upon default. The servicer has the ability to identify troubled credits more quickly because of the close relationship between the originator and obligor and, in the situation of a bilateral loan or small club loan, to maximize recovery value. Several options are available to the originator, such as modification of the loan covenants, limitation of capital expenditures, facilitation of additional equity investments, taking operational control, partial asset sales, replacement of management, or, ultimately, the sale or liquidation of the company. For middle-market CLOs where the loans are primarily sourced from a single lender, extra consideration should be given to ensure consistent monitoring of the loans.

Because the role of the servicer is so significant and central to the successful execution of a balance-sheet middle-market CLO, a backup servicer is sometimes required—another institution that can service the loans and complete the tasks necessary for the smooth operation of the CLO if needed. We encourage investors to consider only middle-market loan CLO sponsors who have established systems and procedures for monitoring these loans and the transactions that they support.

Collateral Diversification   Earlier, we highlighted the diversity advantages of middle-market loans. The diversity of collateral within the CLO is also an issue, and we take up that topic here.

It is generally accepted that diverse collateral pools are less risky than concentrated ones, all else held constant. Traditional CLO managers and arbitrage middle-market CLO managers often strive for and aggregate a diverse collateral pool. However, investors and rating agencies should avoid pushing middle-market CLO sponsors into industries that are not part of their core expertise. Indeed, part of the strength of the middle-market loan CLO transaction is the deep relationship (and understanding) of the lender with the borrower. Therefore, some middle-market loan CLOs may contain higher concentration limits at the obligor level and at the industry level than a traditional CLO. Investors should also consider the geographic concentration of loans, particularly for balance-sheet middle-market CLOs sponsored by specialty finance companies. Some lenders, while diversified across industries, could be relatively concentrated geographically.

Collateral Quality   Most middle-market loans are not publicly rated (as shown in Figure 10.43), often because public information on the obligor is scarce, the size of the loan is small, and the cost of rating prohibitively high. Furthermore, many middle-market lenders do not require public obligor ratings. Therefore, when rating CLOs backed by middle-market loans, traditional measures of credit quality (ratings, for example) are not available and alternative methods of collateral quality estimation are needed. In these cases, the participating rating agencies inspect the collateral pool

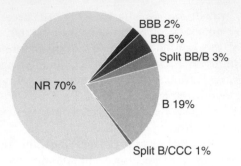

FIGURE 10.43   Total Middle-Market New-Issue by Rating, September 2004
NR: not rated.
Source: Standard & Poor's/Leveraged Commentary and Data.

and assign "shadow ratings" to each loan. This can be accomplished in one of two ways.

For those loan originators (primarily banks) with established internal rating systems, unrated loans (from the perspective of the agencies) can be assigned a rating through a rating mapping process in which a sample of middle-market loans are independently assessed by the rating agency and the bank, and the two rating scales are statistically mapped to one another. Provided enough loans are reviewed, a well-defined link can be established between the rating system of the loan originator and of the rating agency. This mapping is then used to determine the equivalent public rating (shadow rating) for each loan based on the bank's internal credit scoring system. In this way, the overall quality of the CLO collateral pool can be estimated.

CLO sponsors rarely pursue this approach today because the rating mapping process can be unusually harsh in its rating estimation if a large data sample is not available to establish the rating link, or map, because confidence intervals become quite wide. Hence, even quality credits can be given low shadow ratings. Though this method is no longer frequently used, Moody's and Standard & Poor's will consider this approach if asked.

More frequently, and as a general rule for arbitrage middle-market loan CLOs, the rating agencies review the financials of each obligor and assign a private rating to each. Often, this is done through proprietary risk models (e.g., Moody's RiskCalc, and S&P's CreditModel) in conjunction with a deliberate review of several loan files. The risk models are driven by the obligor's financial ratios and typically return a credit estimate that is within two notches of a public rating. For example, Fitch estimates that its CRS model yields a credit estimate that is within two notches of the true rating over 80 percent of the time for nonpublicly traded companies.[13]

Financial obligors and utilities are singled out for a more elaborate analysis. In addition, loans that are estimated to be unusually high or low in quality are also set aside for further analysis. Finally, as part of the review, recovery rates are estimated depending on the specific collateral, the seniority of the loan, and the servicer's track record. Each loan's rating and recovery rate are updated on a periodic basis.

We believe that the models used by the rating agencies for estimating the credit quality of the middle-market loan pools is fair to conservative. Ratings from the credit model often depend on the size of the company and, since middle-market obligors tend to be small, their financial ratios must be commensurately better to achieve the same rating as a larger obligor who issues a broadly syndicated loan. Although one can debate whether this is fair to smaller companies, it does present a significant difference between similarly rated middle-market loans and broadly syndicated loans that we feel is important when evaluating recovery rates.

Liquidity   As discussed previously, middle-market loans themselves can be notoriously illiquid, especially if they are small bilateral or club loans. In part, this is because many middle-market obligors are not publicly rated, let alone publicly traded, so timely information can be hard to come by. Furthermore, they often require a long, hands-on workout process should the borrower default. Therefore, frequent valuation of middle-market loans can be difficult.

In contrast, liquidity in the CDO market is vastly improved relative to a few years ago. Clean, AAA/Aaa-rated CDO paper usually trades within a bid/ask spread of a quarter point and often within an even narrower range. Troubled senior CDO debt and junior CDO debt can trade at a much wider spread, but usually not wider than a few points, and often much narrower. Middle-market CLOs do not trade frequently, but we would expect similar trading friction (or the lack thereof). Every transaction is different, however, and investors should not expect these benchmarks to apply to all transactions. In addition, there is no guarantee that the secondary market for middle-market CLOs or CDOs in general will remain at these bid/ask spreads.

Unique Structural Features   Arbitrage middle-market CLOs have structures that are often similar to traditional CLO structures backed by broadly syndicated loans. These CLOs tend to track the structural advances being made in the traditional CLO market (pro rata pay-down, longer revolving periods, and senior revolving tranches,for example). However, balance-sheet middle-market CLOs that are sponsored by small specialty finance companies often have unique structural features that are not found in traditional leveraged loan CLOs. Here are the three most significant structural differences between balance-sheet middle-market loan CLOs and traditional CLOs.

Substitution   Most balance-sheet middle-market CLOs permit the substitution of credit-impaired loans with loans of higher quality, subject to limits and other criteria.[14] Servicers often find it beneficial to support their transaction in this way to ensure future access to the capital markets. CLOs represent a significant form of funding for these lenders; therefore, even one troubled CLO could jeopardize future working capital. We believe that this is a powerful incentive for sponsors to manage their transactions in a fashion that protects debt holders.

Cash Trapping   Several balance-sheet middle-market loan transactions have zero-tolerance overcollateralization tests that delever the CLO through the accelerated pay-down of senior tranche notes after any collateral loss. As a result, the CLO assets and liabilities remain equal. In addition, while traditional CLOs have recently moved toward look-ahead tests that trap cash when the collateral pool begins to deteriorate, balance-sheet middle-market loan CLOs generally have cash trapping mechanisms that take effect soon after a loan becomes delinquent (generally 60 days), even if an actual default has not yet occurred. Excess cash is trapped until the offending loan balance is fully protected.

Servicer Advances   In certain transactions, a provision is made that permits the servicer to advance cash to the transaction in an amount equal to a missing payment from a delinquent obligor. A servicer may support a CLO transaction in this fashion for quite some time. However, *this* does not prevent the loan from being deemed delinquent or defaulted. Hence, cash-trapping tests will be triggered regardless. Servicers may do this when *either* removal of the credit from the pool is not possible (no suitable substitutes) or it is expected that the loan will become current soon. The servicer may be repaid from a senior position in the waterfall on a future distribution date.

CONCLUSION

Tight credit spreads and a desire to diversify away from broadly syndicated loan obligors have contributed to a renaissance in the middle-market loan sector. Issuance has rebounded and continued growth seems likely. The renewed attention to this asset class, combined with the general strength of the credit markets, has reduced spreads over the past two years for middle-market loans. Still, these loans often yield more than larger, broadly syndicated loans and we contend that relative value remains. Data from Standard & Poor's/LCD indicate that middle-market loans have higher yields for comparable ratings (see Figure 10.37) and, should the obligor run into trouble, strong recoveries as well (see Table 10.4).

Investors who are looking to diversify their holdings and investors who seek relative value should consider a middle-market loan CLO as an alternative to a direct investment into middle-market loans. This alleviates the need to create specialized systems and expertise in this asset class. Middle-market CLOs are often professionally managed and, owing to the growing liquidity in the CDO market, middle-market CLOs are becoming a convenient avenue to obtain access to the middle-market loan market at the risk tolerance of one's choosing.

APPENDIX A: MIDDLE-MARKET LOAN CHARACTERISTICS

Floating-Rate Coupon

Middle-market loans pay interest on a floating-rate basis, like other corporate loans, so interest payments on loans increase as market interest rates rise. This floating-rate structure is accomplished by setting the interest rate of a middle-market loan at a spread above a benchmark market floating interest rate. The most commonly used benchmark in the leveraged loan market is the London Interbank Offered Rate (LIBOR). So a loan paying 3.0 percent above LIBOR, or LIBOR + 300 bp, would temporarily yield 5.2 percent annually if LIBOR was at 2.2 percent. As LIBOR moves, the interest payments of a leveraged loan will move with it.

When comparing middle-market loans to high-yield bonds, one of the most significant differences is the interest rate. High-yield bonds pay a fixed interest rate using a U.S. Treasury bond benchmark that leaves investors exposed to movements in interest rates, the risk being that if market interest rates rise, the fixed-rate high-yield bond will continue to pay the same lower interest rate. While derivatives can be used to hedge away this risk, this can only be done at a cost that cuts into expected returns. Loans, by contrast, have floating-rate interest payments that move with the market.

Maturity

Term loans generally mature in five to eight years from the time of issue, which is less than the 10-year average high-yield bond maturity. In 2003, term loans had average maturities of approximately 5.6 years.

Callability

Loans are generally callable at par, meaning that the issuer can repay its loans partially or in total at any time. This differs from comparable high-yield bonds, which are usually structured with a noncall period of three to five years. Occasionally, loans will have noncall periods or call protection that requires the issuer to pay a penalty premium for prepaying loans. These features are usually only added to loans in the primary market when investor demand requires additional incentives to attract sufficient buyers. The 12-month rolling prepayment rate for loans was approximately 15 percent during 2003, but spiked as high as 57 percent in 2004. Additionally, 31 percent of loans repriced at lower coupons during the 12-month period ended September 30, 2004.

Covenants

Loan facilities are structured with covenant tests that limit a borrower's ability to increase credit risk beyond certain specific parameters. Covenants are outlined in the legal credit agreement of a loan facility that is executed at the time that a loan is issued. Generally, covenants are tested every quarter and results are sent to all of the members of the bank group. Covenant tests provide lenders with a more detailed view of the credit health of a borrower and allow lenders to take action in the event a borrower gets into credit trouble. When a borrower breaches a covenant, the loan is required to be repaid unless the lenders agree to amend the covenants to keep the borrower in compliance with the credit agreement. A credit agreement for a middle-market loan may generally have between two and six covenants, depending on the credit risk of the borrower and market conditions. Some commonly used covenants include:

- Minimum EBITDA.
- Total leverage debt/EBITDA.
- Senior leverage senior debt/EBITDA.
- Minimum net worth.
- Maximum capital expenditures.
- Minimum interest coverage EBITDA/interest.

Structure of a Middle-Market Loan

Middle-market loan facilities are typically made up of three to four types of loans:

1. Revolving loans provide liquidity and are structured to be drawn and repaid at the borrower's discretion.

2. Term loan A tranches are fully drawn and structured to amortize over the life of the loan.
3. Term loan B tranches are fully drawn and structured with a bullet amortization payment similar to bonds.
4. Second-lien loans are term loans with a claim on the assets of the borrower that falls in priority behind the first-lien loan facilities.

Revolvers and Term Loan As   The pro rata portion of a corporate bank debt facility is the traditional loan structure, historically syndicated and held almost entirely by banks. It is usually composed of two structures, a revolving credit facility and a term loan (called term loan A) tranche. This segment of the loan is called the pro rata segment, because banks that take part in the syndication must commit to an equivalent proportion of both the revolving credit facility and the term loan A. Coupons (shown as LIBOR plus a spread) on pro rata tranches are often lower than comparable coupons on institutional tranches because of higher up-front fees and the accelerated payments associated with pro rata tranches. Pro rata loans are generally committed to by traditional corporate lending banks owing to the funding requirements of the revolver and the accelerated amortization of the term loan A, which are difficult for investors to service.

Term Loan Bs   Term loan tranches are structured to perform like a bond in that they are fully funded and generally have a bullet maturity. This structure makes them easier for institutional investors to hold owing to the less onerous documentation and funding requirements. Term loans also favor institutional investors as a result of more predictable funding requirements, maturities, and interest income streams. In fact, these loans are often referred to in the loan market as "institutional term loans."

Second-Lien Term Loans   As the name implies, second-lien term loans have a secured claim to the borrowers' assets behind the first-lien debt of the borrower. In general, second-lien term loans are put in place when an issuer has borrowing requirements that extend beyond the willingness of the first-lien lenders to extend credit. As a result, the second-lien term loan usually has a significantly higher coupon and is sold to funds with a greater appetite for risk and yield. This structure is infrequently used, but has been growing in importance in the middle-market space.

APPENDIX B: THE BASIC CLO STRUCTURE[15]

Collateralized loan obligations (CLOs) distribute cash flow from a pool of loans to investors such that some investors take a greater risk of payment

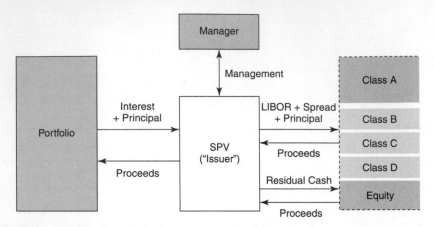

FIGURE 10.44 Basic CLO Structure
Source: Citigroup.

and others take less. The formation of a CLO begins with the establishment of a special purpose vehicle (SPV). The SPV acquires the pool of loans, called the collateral, and issues rated and unrated liabilities (CLO debt and equity) to fund the acquisition of the collateral (see Figure 10.44). Because the majority of the CLO liabilities are highly rated, the CLO can raise most of its capital cheaply in the investment-grade market and invest it more profitably in the collateral.

Coupon payments from the loans are passed to the various debt and equity holders (tranches) according to the rules set forth in the waterfall, which works as follows: The waterfall first assigns proceeds from the collateral to the senior CDO debt holders, resulting in higher asset coverage for those investors (see Figure 10.45), and then to the junior CDO debt holders and equity holders.

If the collateral deteriorates such that doubts arise over the sufficiency of future collateral cash flows to meet obligations (as measured by certain tests), the waterfall can be changed to divert cash flow from the equity tranche (or other junior tranches) to the most senior tranche. The tests are divided into two groups: overcollateralization (OC) and interest coverage (IC) tests. The former measures the amount of collateral coverage for a tranche,[16] while the latter evaluates the sufficiency of available interest proceeds to make coupon payments on the CLO liabilities. Some middle-market CLOs have no OC or IC tests. Instead, these transactions divert cash to senior debt holders immediately upon any collateral loss. A typical CLO consists of five to seven rated tranches, with the ratings ranging from AAA to BB and preferred shares.

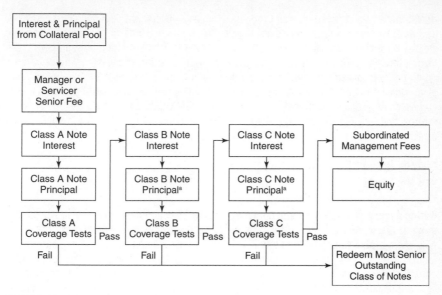

FIGURE 10.45 Basic CLO Waterfall
Source: Citigroup.

The unique combination of CLO tranches, waterfall, and cash diversion tests constitute the structure of the CLO. By analyzing the structure, a CLO investor can achieve a desired return/risk profile by choosing the appropriate tranche in which to invest. The coupon reflects the relative riskiness of the tranche, and this riskiness increases with the lower ratings (and lower seniority) of the notes. The preferred shares represent the riskiest investment and therefore offer the highest potential return.

CASE STUDY: CDO COMBINATION SECURITIES—TAILORING RISK/RETURN PROFILES

CLOs provide investors with a variety of investment options. Given the targeted risk/return profile, investors can choose different tranches. However, during the tight credit conditions in March 2004, investors were further exploring structured credit products looking for higher yields in rated instruments. The case study, written at that time, recommends a CDO combination security that can provide substantial yield pickup as compared to a similarly rated plain-vanilla CDO tranche.

Introduction

At various points in a cycle, credit market conditions may pose a challenge for investors as credit fundamentals continue to improve, but yields remain low. During these times, investors often turn toward structured credit products, such as collateralized debt obligations (CDOs), as a way to increase returns. As we discussed a few weeks ago, one way to pick up additional yield is through an investment in a CDO equity fund.[17] This structure, although attractive from a targeted return perspective, would not be suitable for an investor who requires a rating on their investments. However, some investors are not excited by traditional, rated plain-vanilla CDO tranches because of their limited upside. A CDO combination security addresses this dilemma: It can be rated investment-grade as well as deliver targeted returns that are higher than those provided by a comparably rated, plain-vanilla CDO tranche.

Equally Rated CDO Combination Securities Are Not Equal

Rating Agency and Deterministic Analyses The CDO combination security can be loosely thought of as the cash flow CDO alternative to the synthetic single-tranche CDO—its risk/return profile can be tailored to an investor's rating, coupon, yield, and capital requirements, just as the credit and return profile of the single-tranche CDO can be carefully constructed. The return on a CDO combination security is derived from the cash flows of two or more underlying CDO tranches.[18] Various parts of the underlying CDO capital structure can be blended together to create a variety of similarly rated combination securities.

An important consideration is that two CDO securities can have the same Moody's rating (and hence, the same Moody's expected loss) but substantially different return profiles. For example, Figure 10.46 compares the return characteristics of a plain vanilla Baa3-rated CLO tranche for various annual constant default rates (CDRs) with those of a Baa3-rated combination security issued from the same CLO. An A1-rated tranche (50 percent) and

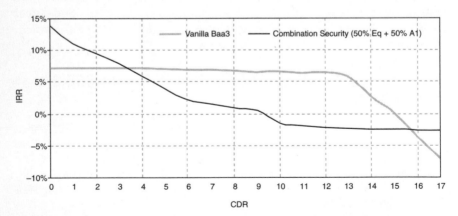

FIGURE 10.46 Plain-Vanilla Baa3 CLO Tranche versus Baa3 Combination Security (50 Percent Equity + 50 Percent A1, Flat LIBOR Coupon)—Stress Analysis of Annualized IRRs
Source: Citigroup.

equity (50 percent) from the underlying CLO back the combination security, and the Moody's rating reflects the LIBOR flat coupon of the security.

In Figure 10.46, the plain-vanilla tranche can withstand about a 13 percent CDR without losing its timely interest or ultimate principal payments, resulting in a stable internal rate of return (IRR) in the range of 6 to 7 percent.[19] This default rate is high relative to the average credit quality of the portfolio supporting this tranche—the average credit quality of the portfolio implies an average CDR of around 3.4 percent. The combination security has a steeper return profile. Under low to moderate default stresses (0 to 3.5 percent CDR), the CDO equity portion of the combination security contributes to a targeted return (between 14 percent and 7 percent) that exceeds the plain-vanilla tranche return. For higher CDRs, the combination security underperforms until CDRs exceed 15.5 percent, at which point the A1-rated component of the CDO combination security allows it to once again outperform the plain-vanilla tranche. In this example, an investor would buy the combination security only if he or she thought that the realized portfolio default rate (over the life of the CDO) would be lower than that implied by the average credit rating.

Monte Carlo and Gaussian Copula Analyses   Constant default rate analysis is a simple and quick way (albeit limited) to characterize the quality of a CDO. That is, defaults do not occur uniformly but, instead, fluctuate over time and the resulting volatility of returns cannot be captured by CDR analytics. Thus, we use a Monte Carlo method to simulate defaults and a Gaussian copula technique to establish time-to-default relationships among the assets in a portfolio.[20] Figure 10.47 illustrates the application of these techniques using the combination security shown in Figure 10.46 as an example.[21]

The frequency distributions of returns from the combination security that appears in Figure 10.47 results are consistent with a well-documented fact: Return distributions from fixed-income portfolios are not normal. In this example, the distribution is skewed toward the high IRRs and has a fat, bumpy right tail. Consequently, use of traditional performance measures, such as mean and standard deviation, can be misleading, and it is customary to

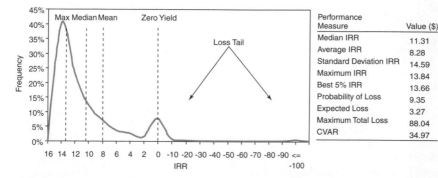

FIGURE 10.47   Baa3 Combination Security (50% Equity + 50% A1, Flat LIBOR Coupon)—Frequency Distribution of Annualized IRRs
Source: Citigroup.

augment these measures with median returns, percentile breaks, and conditional value at risk (CVAR) measures.

In our example, the median return value of 11.31 percent is about 300 bp greater than the average return of 8.28 percent, reflecting the distribution's skewness toward positive outcomes. The CVAR provides a measure of the fatness of the distribution's loss tail (i.e., it estimates an average level of losses in the tail).[22] In particular, the CVAR in Figure 10.47 indicates that if the combination security were to incur any loss, the expected loss would be approximately 35 percent.[23]

Value in Baa3-Rated CLO Combination Securities

We analyze three hypothetical combination securities from a hypothetical CLO and we conclude that there is substantial value in Baa3-rated CLO combination securities as compared with Baa3-rated plain-vanilla CLO notes whose frequency distributions of returns appear in Figure 10.48.[24] We chose a collateralized loan obligation because this CDO asset class performed very well throughout the last credit cycle.[25] The return distributions of all CLO combination securities in Figure 10.48 are shifted to the left relative to the plain-vanilla

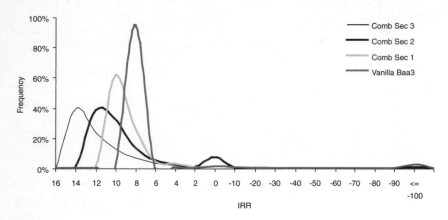

	Equity (%)	Baa3 Tranche (%)	A1 Tranche (%)
Combination Security 1	10	90	0
Combination Security 2	30	20	50
Combination Security 3	50	0	50

FIGURE 10.48 Baa3 Combination Securities (Flat LIBOR Coupon)—Frequency Distribution of Annualized IRRs
Source: Citigroup.

TABLE 10.8 Baa3 Combination Securities (Flat LIBOR Coupon)—Frequency Distribution of Annualized IRRs

Performance Measure	Vanilla Tranche Baa3	CCS1 10% Eq + 90% Baa3	CCS2 30% Eq + 20% Baa3 + 50% A1	CCS3 50% Eq + 50% A1
Median IRR	7.1%	8.3%	9.4%	11.3%
Average IRR	1.4	2.5	7.0	8.3
Standard deviation IRR	34.1	32.3	15.0	14.6
Maximum IRR	7.1	9.0	11.2	13.8
Best 5% IRR	7.1	8.9	11.1	13.7
Probability of loss	4.4	4.7	8.4	9.3
Expected loss	3.1	3.2	2.0	3.3
Maximum total loss	95.6	93.5	90.9	88.0
CVAR	69.1	66.6	23.9	35.0

Source: Citigroup.

tranche, illustrating the greater potential upside that CLO equity provides to these securities. The potential upside and downside become more pronounced as the equity percentage within these combination securities increases.

Table 10.8 provides further detail on the performance characteristics of these securities. We believe that the most balanced security is CLO Combination Security 2 (CCS 2). The median and average returns for CCS 2 (9.4 percent and 7.0 percent, respectively) exceed those of both the plain-vanilla tranche and CCS 1, although they are lower than the median and average returns for CCS 3 (11.3 percent and 8.3 percent). The main attraction of CCS 2, however, is that its returns substantially exceed the plain-vanilla tranche returns *and* it provides substantially more protection than CCS 3 in terms of downside protection. In fact, although the probability of loss for CCS 2 is almost twice that for the plain-vanilla tranche (8.4 percent versus 4.4 percent), the level of losses is lower, as measured by expected loss (2.0 percent versus 3.1 percent) and CVAR (23.9 percent versus 69.1 percent).[26]

For those investors who are less concerned with downside risk at this point in the credit cycle, CCS 3 provides an attractive alternative. Its median return is over 400 bp higher than that of the plain-vanilla tranche.

Conclusion

A CDO combination security can be customized to meet an investor's rating, coupon, yield, and risk/return preferences. Because return profiles from similarly rated combination securities are not equal, we recommend that investors use stochastic and correlated default techniques to better understand the benefits and risks of a given CDO combination security. Given the historically strong performance of CLOs and the analysis of the combination securities described in this case study, we recommend a Baa3-rated combination security that is backed by CLO mezzanine and equity tranches for investors who seek pickup in yield using a leveraged credit investment.

ABS CDOs

Ratul Roy
Glen McDermott

OVERVIEW OF THE STRUCTURED FINANCE MARKET

S tructured finance securities (SFSs), commonly referred to as asset-backed securities (ABSs),[1] are the product of securitization technology, first applied to pools of mortgage loans in the 1970s, and have rapidly developed into the biggest component of the global fixed-income markets. Securitization technology relies on the financing of a diversified portfolio of assets by the issuance of structured finance securities collateralized by the cash flow from the pool. Securitization is based on the true sale of assets: No creditors of the seller or the originator have any claims on the assets, and the assets should not be treated as part of the estate of the originator if the originator files for bankruptcy.

Basic Structure

Figure 11.1 illustrates the basic structure. The multiple tranches of SFSs have differing levels of seniority, with the most senior tranches usually rated AAA and the first-loss, residual, or equity piece being unrated. Losses arising due to default on the pool are generally applied in inverse order of priority (i.e., they are allocated first to the residual piece and last to the seniormost tranches). The cash flows from the assets are used to pay the interest and principal amounts of the rated tranches in a specified priority or waterfall; residual cash is passed through to the first-loss tranche. SFS ratings are a function of the structure and credit quality of the asset pool backing the securitization, not of the seller that is the source of the assets.

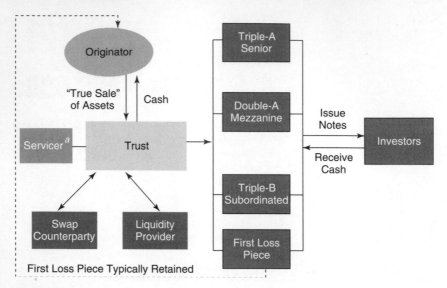

FIGURE 11.1 Creation of Tranched SFS from a Portfolio of Assets
[a]May also be originator.
Source: Citigroup.

Roles of Multiple Parties in a Securitization

While sale of the assets is the first step, there are a number of parties involved in a transaction, summarized in Table 11.1. The seller or originator usually retains interest in the transaction by taking a share of the residual piece, and it may also service the collateral.

ABS Market Fundamentals

Asset-backed securities' many advantages have spurred investor demand for this asset class. In parallel, supply has been growing as issuers have used securitization technology to embrace a wider variety of collateral from a broader range of countries. Growth has been in three dimensions—the type of collateral, the type of risk offered (in particular the amount of subordinated risk), and the overall total volume in the United States and Europe.

Collateral Class Growth   There is a wide variety of collateral backing SFSs. The three biggest categories are residential mortgage-backed securities (RMBS), commercial mortgage-backed securities (CMBS), and asset-backed securities (ABSs), whose collateral most commonly comprise consumer

TABLE 11.1 Key Securitization Parties

Party	Role
Originator	Sells assets to trust. Motivated by requiring funding and/or lowering regulatory and economic capital. Usually retains whole or part of first-loss piece, thus retaining interest in performance of transaction.
Servicer	Collects and distributes cash from asset pool and deals with defaulted assets. Usually same as originator. Effectiveness of servicer has strong bearing on deal performance.
Issuer	Issues SFS and is usually a bankruptcy-remote trust.
Liquidity provider	Advances cash when required to rectify timing mismatch between asset and SFS cash flows.
Swap counterparty	Provides hedges typically to exchange fixed and floating rate–linked cash flows.
Rating agencies	Credit enhancement for SFS, sized to meet rating agency criteria in order to achieve target ratings.
External credit enhancer	Provides guarantee to SFS if required.

Source: Citigroup.

receivables (e.g., credit cards). There are other types of ABSs that are collateralized by more esoteric assets, for example, mutual fund fees. Other types of SFSs comprise collateralized debt obligations (CDOs) backed by bonds; loans and credit derivatives (as well as other structured finance securities); aircraft leases; and securitizations of whole businesses (e.g., retail chains). A brief description of the various asset classes within the three main categories is shown in Tables 11.2 and 11.3.

Subordinated Tranche Market Growth   While the overall SFS market has grown tremendously over the past few years (we will explore this in the next subsection on the U.S. and European markets), the strong growth in the subordinated tranche market is just as impressive. This is a powerful indication of investor confidence in the SFS market. Buying centers of these more junior tranches have increased, in particular the structured product vehicles such as collateralized debt obligations (CDOs) of ABS. These investors are attracted by the yield pickup in and relative stability of the asset class. The relative lack of liquidity of the mezzanine tranches is not a concern for such buy-and-hold investors, who are attracted by the additional yield. Note in Figure 11.2 the decline in percentage of initial ABS ratings that are AAA and AA and the rise in percentage of initial ABS ratings that are A and below.

TABLE 11.2   Major Structured Finance Asset Types

Residential mortgage-backed securities (RMBSs)	These are securities that are backed by residential mortgages. The performance of these transactions is affected by the characteristics and quality of the underlying pool of mortgages, and the abilities of the seller/servicer. In addition, prepayment characteristics of the pool influence the expected maturity and price of the bonds. This is a very large component of the SFS market, and there are several types of RMBSs depending on the type of mortgages backing the security.
Agency mortgages	A large proportion of U.S. mortgages are securitized by government-sponsored enterprises (GSEs)—that is, Ginnie Mae, Fannie Mae, and Freddie Mac. These securities are typically rated AAA, have very low spreads, and are not covered by the paper.
Residential A mortgages	Residential A mortgage securities are similarly backed by a diversified pool of first-lien mortgages underwritten to Fannie Mae and Freddie Mac standards.
Home equity loans (HELs); residential B/C mortgages	HELs comprise the major segment of securitizations of mortgages that do not conform to the GSE criteria. The principal reasons a loan would be pooled in an HEL include larger loan size and/or weaker credit than permissible by the GSEs. Sometimes the first-lien mortgages are referred to as residential B/C mortgages, while HEL refers only to the second lien.
Commercial mortgage-backed securities (CMBSs)	CMBSs are securities backed by one or more mortgage loan(s) secured on commercial properties. Properties may include office buildings, shopping centers, multifamily housing complexes, industrial buildings, warehouses, and hotels. Three subsectors are usually seen: (1) conduit securities, which are backed by a diversified pool of commercial mortgage loans; (2) credit tenant lease securities, which are backed by a pool of commercial mortgage loans on properties leased to corporate tenants; and (3) large loan securities, which are backed by a pool of commercial mortgage loans in which the five largest loans in the pool typically comprise more than 20% of the total pool. In the European market, credit tenant leases are often to a single tenant, thus combining credit (single tenant) and property risk.

TABLE 11.2 (*continued*)

Real estate investment trusts (REITs)	REITs are corporate debt, as they are trusts of a company that purchases and manages real estate or real estate loans using money from shareholders. They are viewed similarly to CMBSs.
Asset-backed securities (ABSs)	Asset-backed securities are collateralized by the cash flows of a variety of financial assets, typically receivables or loans that are originated by banks and other credit providers. These pooled assets can include auto loans, credit card receivables, consumer loans or personal loans, and trade receivables. Credit cards and auto loans are the most liquid segment of the ABS market.
Franchise loans	These are usually considered as ABSs, but there are strong similarities to CMBSs. Franchise loans are secured by the going-concern value, inclusive of real estate, of each unit within the lender's pool. Industries included under franchise include quick-service restaurants, car washes, auto dealerships and aftermarket units, and gasoline stations.
Credit-card ABSs	These are ABSs backed by the receivables of credit cards and constitute the largest share of the ABS market. They are normally not encountered in the CDO market because of relatively tight spreads reflecting the large diversity of the pools and liquidity in the credit card market.
Auto-loan backed ABSs	These are backed by a diversified pool of installment sale loans made to finance the acquisition of, or from leases of, automobiles; again, because of low spreads this collateral class is not part of most CDO portfolios.

Source: Citigroup.

U.S. and European Market Growth U.S. volume of issuance has increased sharply, as illustrated in Figure 11.3. Also apparent is the increasing share of nontraditional ABS types. Recent credit card ABS issuance, for instance, represents a much lower share of total issuance than in previous years. Sectors described as "Other" had little presence in the ABS market even five years ago—these nontraditional ABS sectors (such as student loans, 12b-1 fees, equipment leases, and franchise loans) are a more important market segment.

TABLE 11.3 Niche Structured Finance Asset Types

Manufactured housing	Loans are given to U.S. buyers of manufactured homes, which are dwellings constructed at a factory and transported in one or more sections to a land site for attachment. Units are financed as personal property when sold without land, or as real estate when land is included. Manufactured housing is a significant form of home ownership in parts of the United States.
12b-1 fee, mutual fund fee securitizations	Mutual fund distributors sell the agreed revenue stream from a shareholder in the fund. The stream comprises a separate distribution fee (referred to as a 12b-1 fee) and a contingent deferred sales charge to compensate the distributor for lost fees in case of early redemption.
Student loans	Loans to students in the United States are of two main types: Federally insured student loans with principal insurance of 98% or 100% of the principal amount, ultimately guaranteed by the U.S. Department of Education; and privately insured student loans that only have protection against default via the guaranty of private companies or from reserves pledged to the securitization.
Small business loans (SBLs)	These are backed by the cash flow from general-purpose corporate loans made to "small business concerns" (generally within the meaning given to businesses by the United States Small Business Administration).
Stranded costs	As a result of introduction of competition into electric utility industry, the older utility companies were straddled with unrecoverable and sunk costs as a result of previous investments (e.g., nuclear and fossil plants). U.S. statutes enabled recovery of these costs through a tariff that is collectable from the utility's customers; these tariffs are securitized.
Equipment leases, aircraft securities/Enhanced Equipment Trust Certificates (EETCs)	Through leases, users of equipment (lessees) pay owners (lessors) regular payments for use. Collateral types can be relatively small (e.g., copiers, PCs, fax machines) with many borrowers or much bigger (for example, aircraft, farming and medical equipment) with fewer borrowers.
Recreational vehicle (RVs)	These are loans that are secured by new and used recreational vehicles, automobiles, and light-duty trucks. Lenders are traditional commercial banks and finance companies, as well as some RV manufacturers. RVs are classed as second homes, and loans are tax-deductible.

TABLE 11.3 *(continued)*

Government-sponsored ABSs	European governments have sponsored ABSs where the underlying assets are owned by the government. For example, the Italian government is an active user of securitization to manage its balance sheet with receivables backed by the national lottery scheme or overdue state pension receivables from employers.
Whole business securitizations	The securitization ring-fences a specialized, typically asset-intensive whole business with strong credit characteristics. What investors rely on are isolated cash flows for repayment. Examples include telecom service providers, health care providers, infrastructure-based groups (such as the water utility sector), transport groups, and leisure operators.
Other ABSs	In addition there are other niche sectors—for example, securitizations from receivables as diverse as timber, tobacco, and time share sales. These are a small part of the ABS market.

Source: Citigroup.

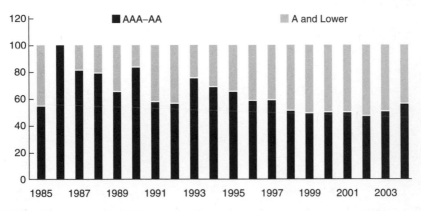

FIGURE 11.2 Annual ABS Ratings at Issuance by Standard & Poor's, 1985 to 2004
Source: Standard & Poor's.

In contrast to the U.S. market (Figure 11.3), the European market is not quite as deep. This is evident by comparing the total volume of European ABS issuance in Figure 11.4 with the U.S. issuance shown in Figure 11.3.[2]

Because the European SFS market is more modest in size than the U.S. market, it is a greater challenge for investors who wish to get exposure

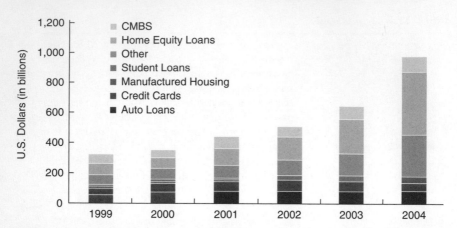

FIGURE 11.3   Annual U.S. ABS and MBS Issuance by Collateral Type, 1999 to 2004 ($ billions)
Source: Citigroup.

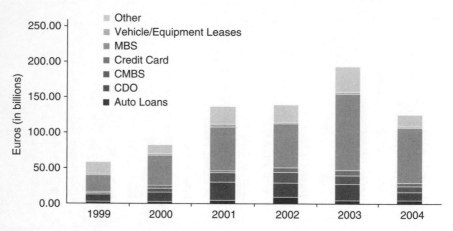

FIGURE 11.4   Annual European ABS Issuance, 1999 to 2004 (euros in billions)
Source: MCM Structured Finance Watch and Citigroup.

to a diversified portfolio of European SFSs. Access to collateral directly or having an external collateral adviser with access are necessary for success. And because only part of the European issuance is in euros (see Figure 11.5), appropriate currency hedges are required for an investor who wishes to make a euro-denominated investment in a diversified portfolio.

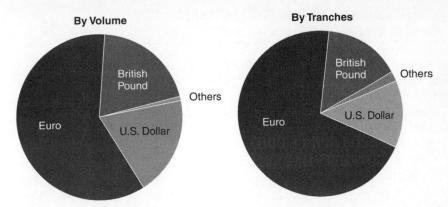

FIGURE 11.5 Currency of Issuance for European SFS, 2004
Source: MCM Structured Finance Watch and Citigroup.

For an investor focused on the higher-yielding mezzanine classes of European SFSs, building diversification is constrained by the large share of CDOs and RMBSs. Figure 11.6 shows the breakdown of SFSs rated single-A and below that were issued. Most of the supply side of this market consists of RMBSs and CDOs. This issue can be overcome by some CDO structures, described later, that are able to use multicurrency, multiregion portfolios without passing currency risk on to investors.

In the next section we explore the features of the SFS asset class, their attractiveness to investors, and some of the challenges to further growth.

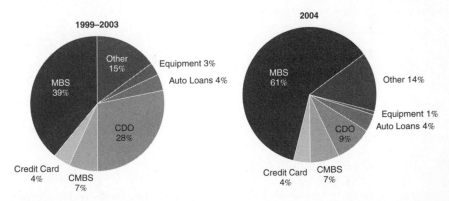

FIGURE 11.6 European SFS Issuance in Single-A and Below Rating Classes, 1993 to 2004
Source: MCM Structured Finance Watch and Citigroup.

MAJOR CHARACTERISTICS OF STRUCTURED FINANCE SECURITIES

The attractions of investing in structured finance securities stem from (1) relative value as compared to other classes of fixed-income securities, (2) structural protections inherent in these securities, and (3) diverse stable asset pools. An investment in an SFS can also provide diversification away from sectors in which an investor has existing exposure (e.g., corporate bonds and loans).

In addition to these strong features, we also need to be aware of some of the challenges to growth in this asset class. We address each of these issues in turn.

Relative Value

Structured finance securities often offer considerable spread pickup as compared to comparably rated corporate debt, and it is this spread difference that structured finance CDOs try to capitalize on. This spread differential is primarily due to two key factors: The perceived lower liquidity in the SFS market and the structural complexity of some structured finance securities. Table 11.4 illustrates triple-A spreads for different SFS categories, all of which carry higher spreads than similarly rated supranationals and corporates.

Figure 11.7 shows the spread differential between CMBSs and corporate bonds of similar issuers.

Figure 11.8 shows the spreads for home equity loans and compares them with corporates. The case for relative value is even stronger in the current market of tight corporate spreads.

TABLE 11.4 Spreads in SFS Market for Triple-A Ratings, as of January 30, 2004

CMBS	64
Retail auto[a]	5
Credit card	14
Stranded assets	17
Home equity	115
Manufactured housing	165
CDO (leveraged loan)	65

[a]Maturity for all asset types seven to 10 years, except for retail autos, whose maturity is three years.
Source: Citigroup.

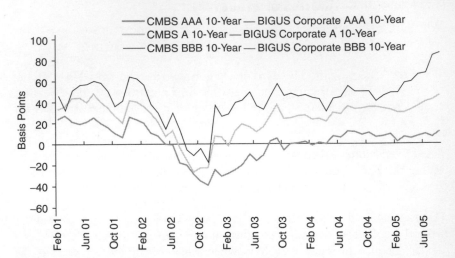

FIGURE 11.7 Spread Against U.S. Dollar LIBOR of AAA-Rated Corporates and Mortgage-Backed Securities (in basis points)
Source: Citigroup.

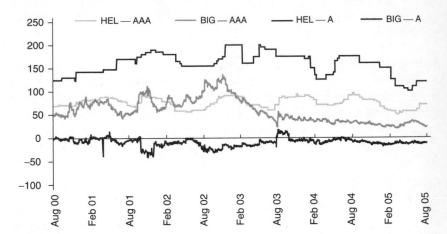

FIGURE 11.8 Spread of Home Equity Loans (HELs) and Similarly Rated Corporates, as Measured by the BIG Index, over Swaps, August 13, 2000, to August 30, 2005
Source: Citigroup.

Structural Protection

When analyzing structured finance securities, it is important to consider the following five features that provide protection to noteholders.

True Sale   Securitization is based on the concept of a true sale: No creditors of the seller or the originator have any claims on the assets, and the assets should not be considered part of the estate of the originator if it files for bankruptcy.

Asset Overcollateralization   The asset coverage cushion is calculated by taking the par amount of the tranche in question, plus par amounts of all tranches senior to it, subtracted from the aggregate par amount of assets.

Excess Cash Flow   Positive excess cash flow is generated when cash flows from the collateral assets exceed the amount required to service the rated debt. This also provides a cushion when collateral underperforms, as the cash may be trapped either to pay down liabilities or to be deposited in a reserve account to protect against further losses.

External Credit Enhancement   In addition to intrinsic sources of credit protection described earlier, some transactions rely on a letter of credit from a bank or a monoline insurance guarantee. These are used less frequently today as investors have become comfortable with structured finance technology.

Collateral Servicer   When analyzing SFS, investors and rating agencies also consider the quality and experience of the collateral servicer. The servicer is particularly important for not just cash collection from the portfolio but also for minimizing losses by dealing appropriately with impaired credits (e.g., defaulting borrowers on residential mortgages). The originator is often the same entity as the servicer and retains a share of the residual piece.

Collateral Stability

SFSs have shown lower ratings volatility, on average, than corporates, and we believe this is due to the portfolio diversification and the structural protections that SFSs contain.

Diverse Asset Pools   The collateral backing many structured finance securities is comprised of a diversified pool of obligors. For example, a pool backing an RMBS transaction may consist of up to several thousand mortgages. This low borrower concentration protects the structure from idiosyncratic or event risk.

TABLE 11.5 Standard & Poor's One-Year Rating Transition Activity within Investment-Grade Categories

	ABS One-Year Rating Changes 1978–2004					Corporate One-Year Rating Changes 1981–2004				
	To					To				
	AAA	AA	A	BBB	Sub-IG	AAA	AA	A	BBB	Sub-IG
From AAA	99.20	0.60	0.10	0.10	0.04	92.64	6.69	0.54	0.04	0.10
AA	6.20	91.50	1.70	0.40	0.22	0.62	90.52	7.91	0.69	0.26
A	1.80	3.80	90.80	2.80	0.90	0.06	2.21	91.19	5.73	0.81
BBB	0.60	2.10	3.20	89.70	4.39	0.03	0.24	4.42	89.17	6.13

Source: Standard & Poor's and Citigroup.

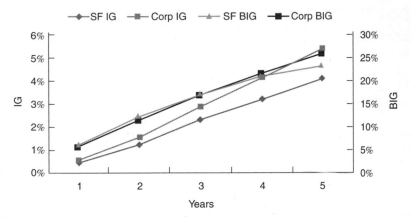

FIGURE 11.9 Average Cumulative Ratings Transitions to Caa and Below, 1983 to 2003
Source: Moody's.

Rating Stability The relative stability of SFSs as compared with corporates is shown in Table 11.5, which summarizes average transition rates. More detailed data is shown in the appendix at the end of this chapter.

Moody's findings,[3] illustrated in Figure 11.9, show, however, that while below-investment-grade (BIG) corporates have had much higher cumulative transition rates to serious credit impairment (rating of Caa and below) than ABSs, the evidence for higher-quality credits contradicts this over longer time periods.

Low Average Default Rates Structured finance security defaults have been rare. From 1978 to 2004, Standard & Poor's rated over 19,500 structured finance tranches (RMBS, CMBS, and ABS) and during this period only 409 tranches migrated to a D rating, with 87 of these defaults occurring in 2004.[4] Moody's, in their structured finance default study of 34,451 tranches rated from 1993 to 2004, identified 1,051 tranches (3.1 percent) that had become impaired. Investors should interpret these studies in the context of the following two observations and caveats.[5] First, these default studies (as well as the rating transition studies that we discussed in the previous section) report average behavior of a limited data set. There are, in fact, a few niche SFS sectors that have much higher default and transition rates than the average and have had, as a result, a disproportionately negative effect on the studies.[6] Second, a typical CDO of ABS is not backed by thousands of obligors, so investors should be careful when using average, actuarial methods to analyze a limited pool of obligors. Single names matter in collateralized debt obligations.

Limited Recovery Data   The relatively rare incidence of default in the structured finance market precludes robust recovery rate analysis. The initial results, however, are interesting. Standard & Poor's tracked the following defaults over the life of its study (as described in the previous section): RMBS (143), CMBS (70), and ABS (135). Based on this data, current recovery rate estimates range from 42 percent (B-rated tranches) to 98 percent (AAA-rated tranches) for RMBS; 43 percent (B) to 99 percent (AAA) for CMBS; and 22 percent (B) to 78 percent (AAA) for ABS. In the end, the data set is too short to make a strong prediction about future recovery values in SFS, but it provides a rough guide as to what can be expected.

Challenges

While these benefits provide substantial comfort, there are several challenges that the asset class is facing. Key among these are the underperformance within some niche subsectors and the contagion risk of accelerated downgrades within the lower-rated tranches. Other challenges for investors new to the asset class are the long legal maturities, lower liquidity of the mezzanine tranches, and complexity of understanding the large variety of collateral.

Niche Sector Performance Undermines Strong Average Performance   Performance of the SFS sector was mixed in 2004, with some subsectors performing better than others.[7] On the positive side, the RMBS and CMBS sectors on average had higher upgrade rates than downgrade rates, with stability tending to be higher at the higher rating categories (see Figure 11.10).

Other sectors, such as manufactured housing, aircraft, and small business loans, fared poorly historically. A large portion of downgrades

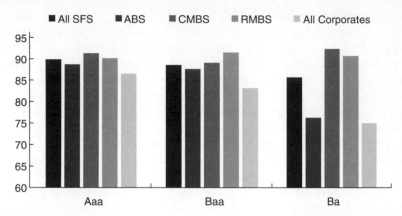

FIGURE 11.10   Annual Percentage of Tranches with Rating Category Unchanged or Higher, 1983 to 2003
Source: Moody's Investors Service.

emanated from the manufactured housing subsector. These sectors are not currently observed in asset-backed CDOs. As we will discuss later, CDO of ABS investors must be cognizant of this performance divergence by sector and pay careful attention which asset classes a CDO is permitted to invest in.

Maturity Considerations   Structured finance securities have legal final maturities that can span 30 years or more. The legal final maturity is the last date that any asset in the trust may contractually mature, and this is the period over which agencies stress the transaction to ensure that the rating is valid. Investors normally focus on the expected maturity, which is the date the bond is expected to be fully retired—through amortization, a cleanup call, a scheduled bullet, or an expected refinancing.

The expected life is based on a base-case or expected scenario of collateral prepayments and defaults. This will include collateral prepayment and default. To the extent that these factors behave differently from the initial assumptions, the average life might shorten or lengthen, creating some uncertainty for investors. For example, under expected collateral pool performance (i.e., in the absence of large credit losses), mezzanine tranches have lower volatility in average life since the senior tranches are first to receive principal pay-downs.

Liquidity Considerations   Secondary-market liquidity in the structured finance market varies depending on the SFS subsector, tranche rating, and size of issuance. In some sectors (e.g., U.S. CMBSs) several hundred million dollars' worth of AAA-rated certificates can be bought and sold in minutes at bid/ask spreads of 1 to 2 basis points. The liquidity in this portion of the SFS market is similar to that of agency debentures and less like that of many other structured credit products.

In other parts of the secondary market for senior SFS tranches, liquidity is less deep, and it declines further in the market for mezzanine and subordinated tranches. Liquidity in the secondary market is less evident when transaction sizes are small, esoteric asset classes are securitized, or in the case of some derivatives-based transactions, where a small slice of risk is sold into the capital markets and the rest is retained by the sponsor. Despite these challenges, liquidity continues to grow in many areas of the subordinate tranche market, including liquidity in CMBSs and CDOs.

Why is secondary market liquidity important to investors in CDOs of ABS? If the transaction is managed, good secondary market liquidity allows the manager to exit a credit when it starts to deteriorate instead of waiting for it to potentially decline further.

Having examined the strengths of SFSs along with some of the challenges, we now turn our attention to the arguments for using CDO technology to unlock the value of this asset class.

CDOs OF STRUCTURED FINANCE SECURITIES

Investor Motivation

CDOs of SFSs combine the benefits of structured finance securities with a CDO's customized structural advantages. As we have explained previously in this chapter, structured finance securities have good rating stability and low default characteristics on average. These securities have the potential to add diversity and additional yield to any fixed-income portfolio. CDOs are an efficient way to unlock the economic benefits of owning a pool of SFSs, and the form of ownership can be tailored to meet an investor's requirements. Through tranching, the benefits are transferred to a variety of investor classes with different risk/return thresholds.

A Customized Investment

The tranching of portfolio credit risk allows investors to participate in an asset class at a risk/reward level that is consistent with their objectives. Each tranche has a different leverage ratio, amount of subordination, coupon, and rating. As Figure 11.11 illustrates, after payment of fees, all cash flow is paid in order of priority, from the AAA-rated senior down to the unrated equity. Portfolio losses are applied in inverse order of priority, first to the equity.

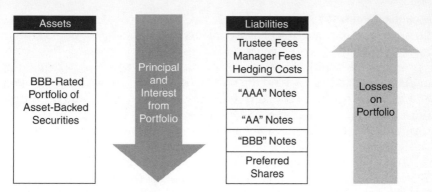

FIGURE 11.11 CDO as Investment Vehicle Allows Risk Participation at Various Levels
Source: Citigroup.

For equity investors the ability to obtain non-recourse leverage on a stable asset class is attractive. Although it is the equity tranche that stands to gain most from a strong credit performance by virtue of its leverage, other noteholders also share in the excess spread. First, mezzanine and senior tranches of the CDO have an attractive spread pickup from corporates and many types of SFSs (e.g., credit-card-backed ABS). Second, the mezzanine tranches are not only protected by the par subordination from the collateral, but are also able to benefit from diversion of excess spread away from the equity to the rated notes in case of portfolio deterioration.

Relative Value

Real estate–related SFS collateral offers a practical example of why investors like the advantages of a CDO structure. Many of the same investors who buy real estate SFSs—for example, commercial mortgage-backed securities (CMBS) and real estate investment trusts (REITs)—for their portfolios buy the junior tranches of CDOs of real estate collateral. They are attracted by the combination of collateral, the nonrecourse leverage provided by the collateral, and the spread pickup for the same rating.

Major Considerations in CDO Investing

Like the underlying SFS, the performance of any specific tranche of the CDO of SFS will depend on the performance of the underlying portfolio, the structural protection given to it, and the performance of the collateral servicer, in this case the CDO manager. In addition, during the life of the CDO there are investment guidelines that must be met.

Structural Protections CDOs contain two broad types of investment guidelines; one group relates to collateral quality and the second group relates to asset versus liability coverage (coverage tests).

Collateral quality tests relate to specific tests that govern average rating quality, diversification within the portfolio, and sizes of individual obligors and sectors. Breaching these guidelines beyond trigger levels leads to restrictions on future trading. These CDO investment guidelines are intended to maintain the portfolio at the minimum standards to which it was rated at closing.

In addition, most arbitrage CDOs contain two types of coverage tests: a principal coverage test and a liquidity coverage test. If these tests are violated, cash is diverted from the normal priority of payments. The first course of action is diversion of excess spread from the equity tranches to the most senior note. Reinvestment of principal ceases, and principal and interest collections are used to accelerate the redemption of the senior notes until these tests are brought back into compliance.[8] These triggers function as structural mitigants to credit risk. Because violation of these coverage tests can result in the payment of all cash flow to the senior note holders (and consequently none to the equity holders), equity and rated note holders should have a firm understanding of how they function.

Diversified CDOs versus Sector-Focused CDOs CDOs of SFSs have referenced a variety of asset types, of which two classes have formed the majority of new issues:

1. **Multisector CDOs.** These structures aim to build a diversified pool of various SFS collateral types including RMBSs, ABSs, operating company securitizations, and other CDOs. These pools often contain a large amount of obligor and sector diversity that allows the rating agencies to rate the transaction with less required enhancement, all other things being equal (i.e., the structure may issue less equity, resulting in more leveraged returns to the equity). In addition, this diversity partially insulates senior note holders in these CDOs from idiosyncratic risk.
2. **Real estate CDOs.** The assets consist mainly of real estate collateral, including RMBSs, home equity loans, REITs, and CMBSs. Real estate market investors typically favor these deals because they afford a leveraged exposure on an asset class that they are familiar with. These pools have less diversity than the multisector CDOs and they may carry more correlated systemic risk that in stressed credit environments may be more adverse to note holders, especially senior note holders.

As we have discussed previously, certain niche sectors of the SFS market have performed poorly in the past few years, and this has caused many CDO

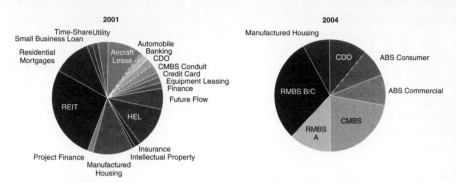

FIGURE 11.12 Typical 2001 Vintage SF CDO Portfolio versus Typical 2004 Vintage SF CDO Portfolio
Source: Citigroup.

investors to exclude these sectors in newly created multisector CDOs. Recent transactions place greater emphasis on the well-tested RMBS, CMBS, and well-established ABS sectors. Figure 11.12 starkly illustrates the sharp shift in the portfolio composition of CDOs of ABSs from 2001 to 2004. While this restriction in portfolio composition may enhance stability in the future performance of structured finance (SF) CDOs, it may also ironically prevent a manager from finding relative value in certain out-of-fashion sectors. In today's markets, an astute investor may find attractively priced assets in these out-of-fashion niche sectors (e.g., aircraft lease) that enhance portfolio yield and add diversification to the portfolio.

Static Versus Managed Deal The decision on whether to hire a CDO manager or invest in a static CDO hinges upon the type of collateral in general, and in particular, the investor's view of each of the names designated for inclusion in the pool. There are two main areas where one could reasonably invest in a static deal. One is a high-quality portfolio (with a low double-A average rating) where investors rely on low statistical probabilities of default. In this case, investors need to be mindful of the more volatile SFS subsectors, as well as funding and interest rate risk management, given the leverage in these vehicles. A second strategy is more focused: Astute investors can use the CDO vehicle to obtain leveraged exposures to an asset class that they understand and within which they can pick credits with confidence (e.g., real estate).

Portfolio managers, through the process of initial asset selection and managing the portfolio over time, can also add value to certain SF CDOs, especially CDOs of mezzanine SFS tranches. Although SFSs show considerable merit as an asset class from both stability and spread perspective, contagion risk, which is more pronounced in mezzanine ABSs, can threaten a transaction. A diligent manager is able to identify to spot and deal with impaired credits, either by working them out or by trading them (liquidity permitting). The manager may also be able to rotate the portfolio among various SFS subsectors in light of changing economic fundamentals and market liquidity. This manager can be a traditional portfolio adviser or, in some cases, a focused service provider (e.g., a real estate management company). This expertise, however, comes at a cost: management fees that reduce the excess spread within the structure.

Leveraging Stability—Performance of SF CDOs

How have CDOs of SFSs performed? For the most part, the stability of the underlying structured finance market has translated to good performance in the SF CDO market, save for the transactions that were disproportionately weighted in the niche underperforming SFS sectors such as manufactured housing, franchise loans, and 12b-1 fees.

The data in Table 11.6 are derived from Moody's published data on CDO transition rates and show the one-year weighted average percentage of tranches that have remained at the same rating or have been upgraded.[9] One important caveat: CDOs have a relatively short track record as compared to corporate debt and SFSs, and within the CDO category of SF CDOs have even less history (they were created in 2000).[10] It is important to note that this recent history has coincided with a benevolent, low-interest-rate environment.[11]

CDOs of SFSs Take Many Forms

Because of the sheer diversity of SFS collateral, numerous structures have evolved for the repackaging of SFSs into CDOs. The development of the

TABLE 11.6 One-Year Weighted Average Percentage of Unchanged or Upgraded Ratings

	CDO of SFS	CLO	Balance Sheet U.S. Cash	Balance Sheet Non-U.S. Cash	EM	CBO	Balance Sheet U.S. Synth	Syn Arb Non-U.S.	Syn Arb U.S.
Aaa	96.1	99.8	98.0	99.0	100.0	93.4	90.9	86.3	91.0
Aa	91.4	96.6	100.0	98.4	86.6	82.2	86.4	72.9	82.0
A	93.7	97.5	95.4	96.9	88.9	80.5	83.4	77.5	78.9
Baa	87.4	97.2	95.7	94.4	94.8	76.6	72.8	72.7	79.2
Ba	86.2	95.0	95.2	100.0	94.4	67.0	67.7	64.7	73.7

Source: Moody's Investors Service (adjusted for withdrawn ratings).

structures has also been influenced by the requirement of investors and the availability of any arbitrage opportunities. Fully funded cash flow structures with term-funded notes are best geared to higher-yielding collateral. Synthetic structures, on the other hand, are especially appropriate to handle very high-quality, low-yielding assets.

Mezzanine SF CDOs   Because of the requirement to place the entire capital structure in the form of term notes, cash flow CDOs require higher-yielding, lower-rated SFS collateral. Typically, the average rating of the collateral is BBB. Also, since the assets are physically held by the issuer, any hedging (e.g., currency hedging) must be done explicitly within the special purpose vehicle (SPV). As a result of the search for yield especially under current market conditions, these structures have significant buckets in the higher-yielding SFS collateral types (e.g., CDOs, subprime RMBSs and HELs, whole business securitizations, and nonperforming loans). Mezzanine SF CDOs can be structured as multisector or sector specific, and an example of each is shown in Figure 11.13.

The collateral for the real estate CDO contains, as expected, fewer types of SFSs. As a consequence of the lower diversification, the real estate CDO requires a greater proportion of subordinated notes as part of the capital structure. Similarly, the proportion of AAA-rated liabilities is higher for the diversified multisector structure.

Higher-Quality SF CDO (AAA Through A Rating)   Some arrangers have been able to create funding efficiency within the framework of a cash flow CDO by having the most senior part of the capital structure placed in the commercial paper (CP) market, as shown in Figure 11.14. In one type of transaction, more than 50 percent of the assets would be rated AAA with the majority

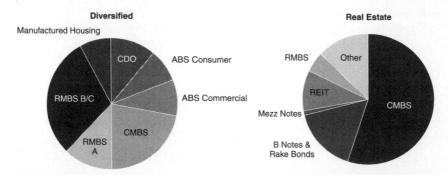

FIGURE 11.13   Collateral Mix in Diversified Multisector versus Real Estate CDO
Source: Citigroup.

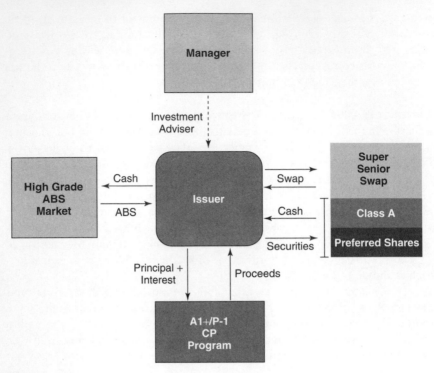

FIGURE 11.14   How CDOs Funded by Commercial Paper Achieve
Funding Efficiency
Source: Citigroup.

of the remainder rated AA. More than 85 percent of the portfolio would be
funded by the issuance of CP and the remainder would be funded by rated
term notes and unrated term subordinated notes.

The immediate impact of this is to lower the weighted average liability
cost and therefore the minimum average required spread of the collateral
to create an attractive equity arbitrage opportunity. Because of the high
quality of collateral, the subordinated note tranche may be only 1 percent
of the capital structure and consequently highly levered. In the structure
shown, the funded notes are exposed to the junior risk of the high-grade
ABS portfolio, while the senior risk is transferred on an unfunded basis
to a credit swap counterparty. The CP structure is popular in the U.S.
market where there is an appetite for U.S. dollar–denominated CP. The
CP structure would be more difficult to execute outside the United States
because currency hedging is expensive and would have to be done within
the CDO.

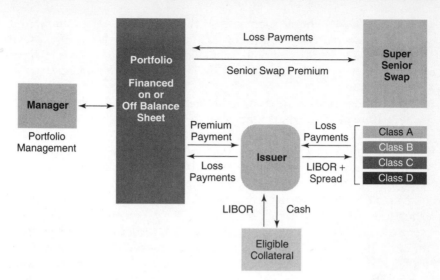

FIGURE 11.15 Hybrid Structure Using Cash High-Quality Assets but Synthetic Credit Transfer to Note Holders
Source: Citigroup.

An alternative to the CP route (not shown) is to fund the underlying collateral in the short-term repo market supported by a backstop liquidity facility. Similar to the CP route, the mezzanine and equity risk are transferred through term notes.

The final way of creating funding efficiency is to use the balance sheet of a counterparty to buy the collateral. This is illustrated in Figure 11.15. A portfolio of higher-quality (rated A and above) SFSs is funded on the balance sheet. The portfolio, in this case, is managed by an external portfolio adviser. Mezzanine and senior note holders (class A through D notes) sell loss protection on the SFS collateral and are paid a spread for the risk. Loss is crystallized through definitions of credit event and loss valuation, discussed in detail later.

The structure also allows the separation of default risk of the portfolio from any market or currency risk (e.g., the portfolio may be denominated in several currencies but senior and mezzanine note holders may take default risk only on the collateral with the amount of any loss being pegged to currency exchange rates at the time of transaction closing). The market risks (e.g., currency risks) may be transferred to only the equity holder, retained by the arranger, or hedged outside the CDO structure. The structure is particularly appealing for investors who are looking for a globally diversified pool of senior mezzanine SFSs motivated by insufficient diversification in their own currency.

Synthetic SF CDOs   The development of the credit derivatives market referencing residential and commercial SFS collateral has led to the growth of synthetic or hybrid (cash and synthetic collateral) SF CDOs. Growth of this market has also been helped by the increasing standardization of documentation.

The standard corporate credit event definitions do not fully capture the specific nature of SFSs. First, events need to be declared with reference to the tranche and not the whole transaction. Second, standard credit event definitions like "failure to pay" need to be modified. This definition would not cover materially impaired coupon-deferrable tranches since these tranches, by definition, can miss coupon. Industry participants have therefore been comfortable with two main definitions—a modified "failure to pay" and a "loss event," both of which try to capture the commercial reality of an impaired transaction. Importantly, events can be declared, and investors can incur loss, before a security is declared defaulted. This is because agencies have obtained comfort that there is very high correlation between the threshold ratings at which these events can be declared (typically double-C) and subsequent defaults on the SFS.

CONCLUSION

The multitrillion-dollar global structured finance market is characterized by significant sector diversity, rating stability, and low average default rates. Credit-impaired assets have been predominately confined to a few niche sectors, while the bulk of RMBS, CMBS, and mainline ABS tranches have performed very well through the end of the last credit cycle. Despite this broad, impressive array of choices, investors should remain wary of contagion, the adverse selection of portfolios, and the underperformance of some sectors.

The relative stability of most structured finance asset classes lends itself well to leverage in the CDO context. Numerous CDO structures have been created to extract the value inherent in the structured finance market. The three main categories are (1) CDOs of mezzanine SFSs, (2) cash flow CDOs of high-grade SFSs, and (3) synthetic CDOs of high-grade SFSs. Within each of these categories there are a number of different structures that investors can use, depending on their risk tolerance, yield targets, and desired sectors.

CASE STUDY: RELATIVE VALUE IN HIGH-GRADE STRUCTURED FINANCE CDOs

As discussed in the chapter, high-grade structured finance CDOs are funded primarily by the issuance of short-term liabilities and have highly levered subordinated tranches. The following case study, written in April 2004, discusses how the mezzanine tranche of a high-grade SF CDO can withstand severe credit stress scenarios and still deliver attractive returns in spite of the tight spread levels prevalent at the time.

In response to a persistent trend in spread tightening for a given rating across most collateral classes, high-grade SF CDOs have become popular. The vast majority of these vehicles' liabilities (about 85 percent) are funded in the short-term market (e.g., money market and commercial paper markets), which enables it to fund a high-quality structured finance portfolio (average rating of double A) that has the potential to deliver attractive CDO equity and mezzanine returns.[12] In this article, we discuss why we think the mezzanine notes issued by these structures offer value (with certain important caveats).

Transaction Overview

Collateral Characteristics The average credit quality of the portfolios that we have analyzed is around double-A, with a majority of the collateral in the triple-A (50 percent) and double-A (40 percent) categories, and with some securities rated down to (but not below) single A (10 percent). Average obligor concentrations are around 1 percent, although positions can reach 2 to 2.5 percent in the case of AAA-rated securities. The minimum weighted average asset spread is typically at least LIBOR + 70 bp.

As for sector concentrations, the CDO collateral pool is generally allocated across four main collateral types (RMBSs, CDOs, ABSs, and CMBSs), although the percentage allocations among the four sectors have shifted materially over the past year.[13] For example, the 2003 vintage high-grade SF CDOs revolved around CMBS and RMBS collateral, but since then, high-grade CMBS spreads have rallied by more than 60 bp, making CMBS less attractive as raw material for these deals. Consequently, many current transactions have swapped much of the CMBS portfolio allocation with the CDO allocation (see right panel of Figure 11.16). High-grade SF CDOs typically limit their CDO exposure by restricting

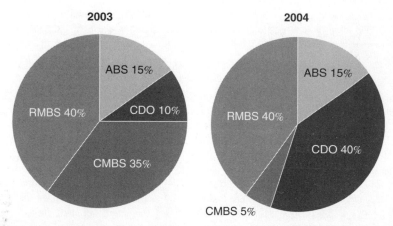

FIGURE 11.16 High-Grade SF CDO Collateral Distribution by Sector, 2003 versus 2004
Source: Citigroup.

investment to senior and second-priority CDO tranches issued by CLOs and CDOs of ABSs. These two CDO classes demonstrated stable performance throughout the 2000–2003 cycle of high default and low recovery rates.[14]

Structural Characteristics   The key distinctive characteristics of the high-grade SF CDO capital structure are: (1) short-term funding of the senior notes; (2) the resulting lower subordination levels; and (3) the combination of a pro rata and sequential mezzanine note amortization schedules.

Senior Notes Funding   The senior notes of a high-grade SF CDO are funded in the short-term market. Because these notes represent the largest part of the capital structure (85 to 90 percent), the weighted average cost of funds for this structure is much lower than for traditional SF CDOs, allowing the vehicle to purchase a very high-credit-quality pool. If the vehicle is unable to roll the notes at maturity, the notes are put to the liquidity provider, which then owns term CDO notes at a stepped-up coupon. From a mezzanine note holder's perspective, the uncertainty in the coupon rate of the senior notes introduces an additional risk that we analyze in this case study.[15]

Leverage and Subordination Levels   Because of the high quality of the underlying portfolio, the subordination level for a typical A3/A–rated mezzanine tranche is generally around 2 percent, which is 5 to 8 percent lower than subordination levels from the traditional SF CDOs backed by triple-B average portfolios. Although subordination is low in these structures, it is still many multiples greater than the Aa2-implied cumulative default rate (0.2 percent). That said, risk in these portfolios cannot be fully understood by comparing subordination levels with the average cumulative default rate implied by historical rating agency studies. The chief risk in these portfolios (albeit very remote) is a significant number of large, highly rated structured finance securities making a transition precipitously to default. For example, assuming an average obligor size of 1 percent and a 55 percent recovery rate, five obligors would have to default to reach the attachment point of the mezzanine tranche.

Pro Rata Pay   Some high-grade SF CDOs combine pro rata and sequential amortization schedules in their payment waterfall provisions. In these transactions, all rated tranches are designed to amortize pro rata until the collateral balance has decreased by half, at which point the amortization schedule switches back to the traditional sequential order.

    The pro rata amortization is subject to all coverage test compliance and is not applicable in case of any test failure. Figure 11.17 illustrates the effect of the pro rata amortization on the A3/A–rated mezzanine tranche in the hypothetical high-grade SF CDO under various default scenarios. In the CDO structure that we analyze, the pro rata pay allows for almost 46 percent principal paydown on the notes under a 0.6 percent constant annual default rate.[16] We estimate that the pro rata amortization feature can shorten the weighted average life of the A3/A–rated mezzanine tranche by almost two years and therefore helps to mitigate credit risks associated with possible back-loaded credit events in the underlying portfolio.

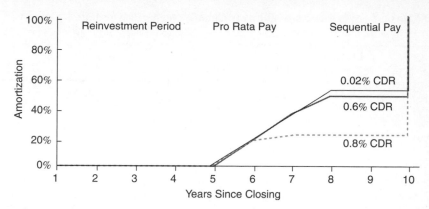

FIGURE 11.17 A3/A–Rated Mezzanine Tranche of a Hypothetical High-Grade SF CDO under Various Stress Scenarios—Amortization Profile
Source: Citigroup.

High-Grade SF Securities: A Strong Track Record

Default and Recovery Experience The high-grade ratings and seniority of the collateral assets imply a very low loss-given-default rate and limited downward rating migration rate in these portfolios. An average Aa2 portfolio rating corresponds to 10-year cumulative default rate of approximately 0.20 percent.[17] This is an average idealized default rate derived from a corporate default study that can differ significantly from realized default rates. What has historical experience in the high-grade structured finance market shown us? As Table 11.7 illustrates, across the 10 years of the Moody's study, the cumulative impairment rate for high-grade structured finance securities (as a whole) was low, even though some segments of the market have experienced much higher rates.

Finally, regarding loss given default, while the relatively rare incidence of default in the structured finance market precludes robust recovery rate analysis, an interesting phenomenon is starting to emerge: Analogous to the corporate market, the higher the security in the capital structure of the underlying company, the higher the recovery rate. For instance, a Standard & Poor's study found that, similar to the corporate universe, SF recovery rates are correlated with the seniority level of the defaulted security (see Table 11.8). The estimated ultimate recovery rate varied from 40 percent on A- rated ABS securities to up to 98 percent on AAA- rated senior tranches of RMBS securities. This bodes well for the future performance of high-grade SF CDOs.

Rating Migration Table 11.9 compares the average annual rating migration for high-grade SF securities with the migration rate for high-grade corporate securities. SF securities exhibit a lower downgrade risk than corporate debt across the Aaa, Aa, and A ratings categories. For instance, an average Aaa-rated SF security has a historical average annual downgrade risk of 1 percent per annum, which is approximately 7.3 percent lower than the corresponding rate for corporates (8.3 percent). In addition, the high-grade SF security historical upgrade percentage is significant (e.g., 5.7 percent for Aa ratings).

TABLE 11.7   SF Securities—Multiyear Cumulative Impairment Rates, 1993 to 2004

SF Type	Original Rating	1-Year	2-Year	3-Year	4-Year	5-Year
RMBS	Aaa	0.01	0.09	0.26	0.48	0.59
	Aa	0.02	0.10	0.28	0.48	0.53
	A	0.29	0.84	1.12	1.19	1.28
ABS	Aaa	0.04	0.12	0.30	0.45	0.65
	Aa	0.82	2.20	4.50	7.28	9.82
	A	0.36	1.66	3.16	4.55	5.75
CMBS	Aaa	0.00	0.00	0.00	0.00	0.00
	Aa	0.00	0.00	0.00	0.00	0.00
	A	0.05	0.28	0.62	0.62	0.62
All	Aaa	0.02	0.08	0.21	0.36	0.48
	Aa	0.28	0.76	1.63	2.67	3.51
	A	0.31	1.25	2.29	3.20	3.88

Source: Moody's Investors Service.

TABLE 11.8   Historical Repayment and Realized Loss Characteristics by Original Rating, 1988 to 2004

	U.S. RMBS (%)			U.S. ABS (%)		
	AAA	AA	A	AAA	AA	A
Average cumulative principal repayment	97.62	73.72	14.4	63.59	0	7.36
Average cumulative realized principal loss	0.41	21.44	16.84	9.06	28.16	18.26
Average current principal at risk	1.98	4.84	68.76	27.36	71.84	74.39
Estimated ultimate recovery rates	98	72	60	78	52	40

Source: Standard & Poor's (2005).

Caveats   Although the data presented are promising, investors should exercise caution when interpreting the numbers. First, the data that support the default, recovery, and rating transition studies are relatively limited. The averages drawn from this data set may change materially as additional data are collected and incorporated into the studies. Also, a small number of sectors within the ABS market have performed substantially worse than the averages dictate. These sectors have been excluded from most present-day SF CDOs, but investors should carefully review CDO investment guidelines for the list of

TABLE 11.9 SF Securities versus Corporates—Historical Average Rating Transition Matrix, 1983 to 2004

	ABSs, 1983–2004				Corporates, 1983–2004			
From/To	Aaa	Aa	A	Below A	Aaa	Aa	A	Below A
Aaa	98.97	0.69	0.20	0.15	91.68	7.53	0.76	0.02
Aa	5.70	91.01	2.12	1.18	0.92	90.61	8.03	0.44
A	1.12	2.85	92.83	3.20	0.04	2.50	91.09	6.36

Source: Moody's Investors Services.

TABLE 11.10 Hypothetical High-Grade SF CDO: A3/A–Rated Mezzanine Tranche—Discount Margin (in basis points)

	CDR								
Scenario	0%	0.02%	0.25%	0.50%	0.75%	0.90%	1.00%	1.25%	1.50%
Put	180	180	180	180	180	180	166	67	−42
No-put	180	180	180	180	180	180	180	156	77

Source: Citigroup.

eligible investments.[18] Finally, average default rate analysis in all CDOs, especially in highly leveraged vehicles such as high-grade CDOs, given the low number of actual events cannot fully capture the risks in any CDO.

Cash Flow Analysis

CDR Analysis Table 11.10 shows results of cash flow analysis of the A3/A–rated, L+180bp coupon tranche under various annual constant default rate (CDR) assumptions.[19] The CDR of 0.02 percent corresponds roughly to the CDR implied by the Moody's idealized default rate for an Aa2-quality portfolio. As for more stressful scenarios, the tranche can withstand up to 1.0 percent CDR under the no-put scenario and 0.9 percent CDR under the put scenario without compromising its timely interest and ultimate principal payments. In addition, we estimate that the tranche can withstand up to 2.1 percent CDR under the put scenario (2.3 percent under no-put) before its total yield moves to the negative territory.

Monte Carlo Simulations We ran a Monte Carlo analysis[20] as a complement to the CDR analysis, and we measured the probability of a missed timely interest payment or ultimate principal payment on a mezzanine tranche of a hypothetical high-grade SF CDO (Probability 1) and the probability of losing this initial amount invested, ignoring time value of money (Probability 2) (see Table 11.11).[21]

As Table 11.11 illustrates, the mezzanine note holders received timely coupon (LIBOR + 180 bp) and ultimate principal payments under the vast majority of the 20,000 simulations. The calculated probabilities of nonpayment were 0.05 percent (put scenario) and 0.03 percent

TABLE 11.11 Hypothetical High-Grade SF CDO: Mezzanine Tranche—Loss Probabilities

	Scenario	
	Put	No-Put
Probability 1 (%)	0.05	0.03
Probability 2 (%)	0.01	0.005

Source: Citigroup.

(no-put scenario). These numbers are much lower than the idealized default rates for A3-rated credits—according to Moody's, the A3 implied 10-year cumulative default rate is 1.8 percent.

Finally, with regard to the realized amortization schedule of the mezzanine tranche, we estimated that the tranche received close to half of its total principal payments under the pro rata schedule in 97 percent of the no-put scenario simulations and 88 percent of the put scenario simulations. Thus, in a large majority of the simulations, the prorata amortization schedule reduced the tranche's average life to eight years from the 10-year average life under the traditional sequential payment schedule.

Conclusion

The high-grade SF CDO is an increasingly popular structure in light of the continued credit-spread tightening over the past year. Although SF CDO's performance track record is limited, the performance data on the underlying structured finance markets are supportive. These data suggest that a high-grade SF portfolio, with significant obligor diversification and intelligent sector allocations, can provide the basis for a successful, stable CDO investment. In particular, a mezzanine investment in this type of vehicle can withstand significant credit stress and still deliver a good risk-adjusted return.

CASE STUDY: UNTANGLING MEZZANINE AND HIGH-GRADE STRUCTURED FINANCE CDOs

As the CDOs of ABS were gaining more and more popularity at the beginning of 2005, investors were taking a closer look at the options of investing in high-grade structured finance CDOs and mezzanine structured finance CDOs. The following case study addressed the queries on the similarities and differences between the two CDO submarkets.

Some investors have asked whether investing in a mezzanine structured finance CDO (mezzanine SF CDO) versus a high-grade structured finance CDO (high-grade SF CDO) means one is taking markedly different views of the ABS market, and, if so, what those views might be. After all, the portfolios that support these two CDO subsectors often appear similar if one ignores the obvious difference of average collateral rating. Further, one may ask

TABLE 11.12 Mezzanine and High-Grade CDO Collateral Composition

Mezz. ABS CDO				HG ABS CDO		
Lower Bound (%)	Upper Bound (%)	Typical (%)	Collateral	Typical (%)	Upper Bound (%)	Lower Bound (%)
10	20	14	Resi A	13	25	10
45	56	52	Resi B/C	44	50	40
0	10	3	HEL	8	11	4
5	15	10	CMBS	5	8	2
1	26	17	CDO	25	29	9
3	18	3	Other	5	10	1

Source: Citigroup.

whether systematic differences between the two CDO submarkets might lead investors to favor one sector versus the other. In this case study, we address these important questions while highlighting the similarities and differences between mezzanine SF CDO investments and high-grade SF CDO investments. We explore collateral composition (on a par-weighted basis and a risk-weighted basis), expected loss, correlation views, and other factors that investors should consider.

Collateral Composition

Depending on the specific instance, the collateral pool that supports a mezzanine SF CDO and the collateral pool that supports a high-grade SF CDO can be either very similar (aside from ratings) or distinctly different. However, on average, the collateral pools of mezzanine SF CDOs and high-grade SF CDOs seem surprisingly similar (see Table 11.12). For example, both are largely backed by residential A/B/C paper, which accounts for nearly two-thirds of the collateral pool for each. Allocations to CMBSs (approximately 10 percent and 5 percent of the collateral pools, respectively) and CDOs (approximately 15 percent and 25 percent of the collateral pools, respectively) also seem to be in line. One could even argue that total consumer versus corporate exposure is often similar: average total consumer exposure (through residential A/B/C, HEL, and other paper) and corporate exposure (CMBS and CDO) in mezzanine SF CDOs are typically 72 percent and 28 percent, respectively. For high-grade SF CDOs, the corresponding numbers are 70 percent and 30 percent of the collateral pools—again, surprisingly similar.

Still, the collateral composition of any two individual SF CDOs may vary greatly. For example, one high-grade SF CDO transaction may have a bias toward CDOs (as much as 30 percent of the collateral pool), while a mezzanine SF CDO largely avoids them (as low as 1 percent of the collateral pool). Clearly, similar swings in other collateral categories must balance out the shortfall/excess in the CDO category. As a result, investors must consider the distinct collateral characteristics of any SF CDO relative to their views on the individual asset classes being securitized.

TABLE 11.13 Risk-Weighted and Par-Weighted Collateral Composition of Two
Structured Finance CDOs

Mezz. ABS CDO			HG ABS CDO	
% of Risk[a]	% of Collateral	Collateral	% of Collateral	% of Risk[a]
8	13	Resi A	19	10
57	56	Resi B/C	49	73
6	7	HEL	5	11
14	13	CMBS	4	1
10	8	CDO	16	5
4	3	Other	7	0

[a]Measured as (1) the sum/product of the par amount and the Moody's rating factor
for each item in the category divided by (2) the sum/product of the par amount and
the Moody's rating factor for all collateral items.
Source: Citigroup.

Collateral Risk

Investors must also consider the primary sources of risk in the collateral, which may or
may not be consistent with a cursory review of the collateral composition on a par-weighted
basis. In other words, one particular segment of the collateral, though small in terms of
dollars allocated, may represent a much larger percentage of the risk in the collateral pool.
Consider the mezzanine SF CDO and high-grade SF CDO transactions in Table 11.13, both of
which were completed in 2004. While the composition of the collateral in the mezzanine SF
CDO is a relatively good guide for the primary sources of risk, collateral composition is not a
good guide for source of risk in the high-grade ABS CDO. For example, in the high-grade ABS
CDO, HEL paper constitutes only 5 percent of the collateral pool but represents 11 percent
of the total risk. Conversely (perhaps surprisingly for some), CDOs represent 16 percent of
the collateral pool but only 5 percent of the risk. Thus, while a cursory review of two SF
CDO transactions may indicate similar collateral composition, a risk-weighted analysis may
indicate that the two portfolios are very different.

Expected Loss

However, if we set aside differences in collateral support and assume that two generalized
CDOs—one mezzanine and the other high-grade—have the same collateral exposure on a
composition and risk-weighted basis (though the absolute risk levels are different in each
collateral pool), what can we say about the two investments? Should investors be indifferent
between these two investments assuming, for example, that they have the opportunity to
invest at the single A level for each? We can explore this idea if we consider two SF CDOs
that are both backed by the same set of ABS transactions, except that one CDO invests in
the AA-rated tranches and the other invests in the BBB-rated tranches (see Figure 11.18).
    One thing is clear: Both CDO investors are long the underlying ABS market, and
both have a vested interest in the good performance of consumer and corporate debt that

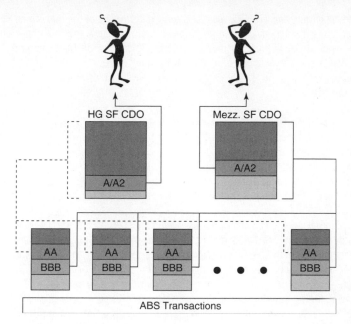

FIGURE 11.18 Structured Finance CDO Quandary—Mezzanine or High-Grade?
Source: Citigroup.

supports the ABS securities. One may even be tempted to say that the A-rated high-grade SF CDO investor's position is more conservative relative to the A-rated mezzanine SF CDO investor's position because each underlying ABS tranche has more subordination. Surely, the BBB-rated tranches will default and even disappear before the AA-rated tranches lose even a dollar, or so the argument goes. This conclusion would be a mistake, however. Implicit in this argument is the assumption that all ABS collateral pools behave identically; that is, the amount of loss is equivalent at all times for all ABS transactions. This argument does not consider the possibility that a loss could occur in an AA-rated tranche while the BBB-rated tranches of the other ABS transaction perform well. In other words, it does not consider idiosyncratic performance in the ABS collateral pools, and therefore it does not consider the idiosyncratic behavior in the default/loss of the individual ABS tranches. Thus, another important factor is the amount of subordination below each of the A-rated SF CDO positions, which is much less in the case of the high-grade SF CDO.

Still, the reality is that the probability of default for an AA-rated ABS security is far less than the probability of default for a BBB-rated ABS security. Therefore, the probability of a loss in the high-grade SF CDO portfolio is also lower than that of the mezzanine SF CDO collateral pool. However, if a default occurs in each pool, the impact on the high-grade SF CDO position will be much greater because of the low level of subordination in the high-grade ABS CDO. Fortunately, the rating agencies consider both of these factors when assigning ratings and, provided they have performed their tasks well, one should have a very difficult time discerning whether losses should be greater or smaller for the A-rated tranche of the high-grade SF CDO than for the A-rated tranche of the mezzanine SF CDO. In fact, based on rating agency assumptions, one should conclude that the expected loss for the A-rated high-grade SF CDO position and the expected loss for the A-rated mezzanine SF CDO position are nearly identical, or at least indistinguishable.

Correlation Views

So, is the A-rated high-grade SF CDO investment really identical to the A-rated mezzanine SF CDO investment? No, because we have not considered the effects of collateral default correlation. Until now, we have considered only average, or expected, default rates for both the collateral that supports the ABS transactions as well as for the ABS tranches themselves. However, the likelihood that defaults might cluster (indicative of high correlation) has a large impact on the risk (and thus price) of an ABS tranche and, by extension, the SF CDO tranches as well.

For example, if default correlation between the obligors in a collateral pool is higher than assumed by the market (or higher than assumed by the rating agencies when formulating subordination levels), then senior noteholders are exposed to more risk than originally thought. For this reason, we often say that senior note holders of ABSs or CDOs are short correlation—that is, they benefit if realized correlation is low (a constant but near-average number of defaults). Conversely, equity holders of ABS or CDO transactions are long correlation—that is, they benefit if realized correlation is high. We tend to think of mezzanine noteholders as correlation neutral.[22] Therefore, because an SF CDO is a structure within a structure, it is possible to construct a rather nuanced view of correlation: one view at the corporate or consumer loan level and another view at the ABS level.

Applying these concepts to our example in Figure 11.18, we would thus say that the A-rated high-grade SF CDO investor is short consumer and corporate default correlation (as a result of an indirect investment in the senior part of the ABS transactions) and is neutral ABS tranche default correlation (by virtue of the mezzanine SF CDO investment). The A-rated mezzanine SF CDO position is similar, but instead of a short view of underlying consumer and corporate default correlation, the view is neutral. Simply semantics? Perhaps, but we do not think so.

Other Differences

There are several additional risks that investors should consider when contemplating mezzanine and high-grade SF CDOs.

First, while it is very rare that senior ABS securities default, senior (i.e., AAA-rated or AA-rated) ABS defaults are not impossible and can occur as a result of such things as corporate fraud. In fact, an argument could be made that the largest risk in a high-grade SF CDO collateral pool is the potential for loss due to servicer fraud and not the potential for outsized loss in the underlying ABS collateral pools. Hence, while this type of risk is very hard to quantify or hedge, close inspection of the ABS servicers is warranted. That said, investors should find comfort in the fact that historical loss rates for senior defaulted RMBS and HEL paper, for example, are less than 10 percent.

Second, for high-grade SF CDO equity investors, expected returns are often tied to the ability of the CDO transaction to roll the most senior CDO debt in the money markets.

Commercial paper (CP) issued from CDOs often yields only slightly more than LIBOR, and most CDO equity return projections are based on this assumption. However, should there be difficulty in reselling the CP, the spread can balloon to LIBOR + 40bp or more, significantly reducing the expected returns to equity. Hence, while high-grade SF CDO equity investors are much more removed from the performance of the consumer and corporate obligors, CP roll risk, although remote, becomes much more important.

Conclusion

The similarities and differences between similarly rated investments in a mezzanine SF CDO and a high-grade SF CDO are not readily apparent. True, one might anticipate that the expected loss or probability of default of the two identically rated investments would be the same, or at least indistinguishable. But beyond this there are distinct views that one is likely taking by investing in one versus the other. First, and most obviously, there are likely collateral composition differences between any two SF CDO investments, which must be measured and considered relative to the investor's sector views. Second, by investing in a high-grade SF CDO as opposed to a mezzanine SF CDO, the investor is taking a nuance view of default correlation. Third, new risks such as fraud and transaction execution risk become important to high-grade SF CDO investors as risks associated with the performance of the consumer and corporate obligors become more removed.

APPENDIX: RATING TRANSITION MATRICES OF COMMON STRUCTURED FINANCE COLLATERAL

As Table 11.14 illustrates, depending on the class, significant differences in rating stability exist.

TABLE 11.14 Transition Probabilities

	AAA	AA	A	BBB	BB	B	CCC	CC	C	D
CMBS[a]										
AAA	99.5	0.4	0	0	0	0	0	0	0	0
AA	7.7	91	0.9	0.3	0	0.1	0	0	0	0
A	1.8	4.5	91	2.2	0.3	0.1	0.1	0	0	0
BBB	0.5	2	3.7	90.6	2.3	0.7	0.1	0	0	0.2
BB	0	0.2	0.6	2.9	91.8	2.7	0.8	0.1	0.3	0.5
B	0	0	0	0.3	2	91.2	4.4	0	0	2
RMBS[b]										
AAA	99.9	0.1	0.007	0.007	0	0	0	0	0	0
AA	8	90.6	1.2	0.1	0.05	0.04	0.03	0	0	0
A	3.2	6.8	88.8	0.9	0.16	0.05	0.16	0	0	0.01

(*continued*)

TABLE 11.14 (*continued*)

	AAA	AA	A	BBB	BB	B	CCC	CC	C	D
BBB	0.7	3.9	4.7	88.9	0.6	0.9	0.2	0.03	0	0.2
BB	0.2	0.5	4.2	8.1	84.2	0.9	0.9	0.3	0	0.7
B	0.1	0.2	0.1	2.2	4.9	88	2.2	0.3	0	2
Other ABS[c]										
AAA	99.2	0.4	0.2	0.1	0	0	0	0	0	0
AA	1.8	93.2	2.8	1.3	0.5	0.3	0	0	0	0
A	0.8	1.3	91.7	5	0.4	0.4	0.2	0	0	0.2
BBB	1	0.7	1.1	88.9	2.5	3.5	1.5	0.2	0	0.7
BB	0.3	0.8	0.6	1.4	76.6	6.8	8.8	0.5	0	4.2
B	1.2	0	0	0	0.4	46.5	25.4	3.9	0	22.7
CDO[d]										
AAA	97.9	1.2	0.4	0.3	0	0	0	0	0	0
AA	2.5	92.3	3	1.4	0.6	0.1	0.1	0	0	0
A	0.4	2.3	90.7	3.8	1.7	0.4	0.5	0	0	0
BBB	0.3	0.3	1.4	90.4	3.8	2.1	1.7	0	0	0
BB	0.1	0	0.1	1.9	88.8	3.2	4.5	1.1	0	0.3
B	0.4	0	0	0	1.8	78.7	13.5	5	0	0.7

Corp[e]	AAA	AA	A	BBB	BB	B	CCC/C	D
AAA	87.44	7.37	0.46	0.09	0.06	0	0	0
AA	0.6	86.65	7.78	0.58	0.06	0.11	0.02	0.01
A	0.05	2.05	86.96	5.5	0.43	0.16	0.03	0.04
BBB	0.02	0.21	3.85	84.13	4.39	0.77	0.19	0.29
BB	0.04	0.08	0.33	5.27	75.73	7.36	0.94	1.2
B	0	0.07	0.2	0.28	5.21	72.95	4.23	5.71

[a]*Source:* "Rating Transitions 2004: U.S. CMBS Upgrades Overwhelms Downgrades Amid Improved RE Fundamentals," S&P, 2005.
[b]*Source:* "Rating Transitions 2004: U.S. RMBS Stellar Performance Continues to Set Records," S&P, 2005.
[c]*Source:* "Rating Transitions 2004: U.S. ABS Stability Improves Despite Adverse Behavior of Manufactured Housing Securities," S&P, 2005.
[d]*Source:* "Rating Transitions 2004: Global CDO Rating Trends Show Improved Stability," S&P, 2005. See Appendix C.
[e]*Source:* "Annual Global Corporate Default Study: Corporate Defaults Poised to Rise in 2005," S&P, 2005.

CHAPTER 12

CDO Equity

Glen McDermott
Alexei Kroujiline

Collateralized debt obligations (CDOs) are formed when asset-backed structuring technology is applied to a pool of corporate credit exposures. Total rated issuance of CDOs has boomed in recent years (see Figure 12.1). CDO structures can be segmented into three categories:

1. Cash flow.
2. Market value.
3. Credit derivative.

Cash flow CDOs, which currently are the most prevalent CDO structures, rely on the cash flow generated from the pool of assets to service the issued debt. This chapter focuses on cash flow CDO income notes.

A CDO is created when a special purpose vehicle (SPV) is established to acquire a pool of high-yield corporate bonds, bank loans, or other debt obligations (see Figure 12.2). In order to fund the acquisition of the debt obligations, the SPV issues rated and unrated liabilities. Since the majority of these liabilities are highly rated, the CDO can raise most of its capital cheaply in the investment-grade market and invest it more profitably in other markets including the bank loan and asset-backed security (ABS) markets.

In a typical cash flow CDO, the rated liabilities are tranched into multiple classes, with the most senior class receiving a triple-A or double-A rating and the most subordinated class above the income note receiving a double-B or single-B rating. The ratings on the classes are a function of subordination and how cash flow and defaults are allocated among them. Principal and interest cash flow are paid sequentially from the highest-rated

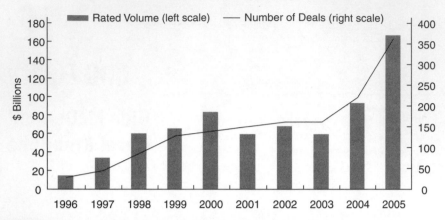

FIGURE 12.1 Moody's Rated Volume, 1996 to 2005
Source: Moody's Investors Service.

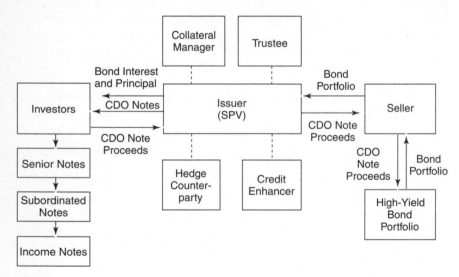

Seller:	Sells the bond portfolio to the issuer.
Issuer:	Issues CDO notes and uses note proceeds to buy bond portfolio.
Investors:	Purchase CDO Notes.
Collateral Manager:	Manages bond portfolio.
Trustee:	Fiduciary duty to protect investors' security interest in bond portfolio.
Hedge Counterparty:	Provides interest swap to hedge fixed/floating rate mismatch.
Credit Enhancer:	Guarantees payment of principal and interest to note holders. Optional.

FIGURE 12.2 Typical CDO Structure
Source: Citigroup.

class to the lowest, but if the cash flow is insufficient to meet senior costs or certain asset maintenance tests are not met, most or all cash flow is paid to the most senior class.

CASH FLOW CDO INCOME NOTES

CDO income notes are typically unrated and represent the most subordinated part of the CDO capital structure. These notes will receive the residual interest cash flow remaining after payment of fees, rated note holder coupon, and the satisfaction of any asset maintenance tests. Factors that will impact the residual interest cash flow include the level and timing of defaults, the level and timing of recoveries, and the movement of interest rates. Income notes returns are generated by capturing the spread differential between the yield on the pool of fixed-income assets (the majority of which are high-yield bonds and bank loans) and the lower borrowing cost of the investment-grade and the noninvestment-grade debt issued by the SPV. This positive spread relationship can produce risk-adjusted returns to income note holders in the range of 12 to 17 percent.

Once a cash flow CDO is issued, the collateral manager will manage the portfolio according to the investment guidelines set forth in the bond indenture and within parameters necessary to satisfy the rating agencies. Pursuant to these guidelines, the manager will sell and buy assets and, during the reinvestment period, will reinvest collateral principal cash flows into new bonds. The investment guidelines typically require that the CDO manager maintain a minimum average rating and portfolio diversity such that any trading will have a minimal impact on the senior CDO bondholders.

The primary responsibility of the cash flow CDO collateral manager is to manage the portfolio in a way that minimizes losses to note holders resulting from defaults and discounted sales. To this end, all note holders rely on the manager's ability to identify and retain creditworthy investments. A manager's trading decisions can have a substantial impact on the returns paid to income note holders; the initial asset selection and its trading activity throughout the reinvestment period are critical to achieving high returns. A manager with a deep understanding of the underlying credit fundamentals of each of its investments can make informed, credit-based trading decisions, not trading decisions based on price movements.

Cash flow CDO income notes have many favorable characteristics. Among them are:

Healthy returns. The risk-adjusted internal rate of return (IRR) to income note holders can range from 12 to 17 percent. This return rate compares favorably with that of other investment opportunities (see Table 12.1). We explore the volatility of this return in the "Return Analysis" section of this chapter.

Lack of correlation with other asset classes. CDO equity, depending on the underlying referenced assets, can add diversification to a portfolio.[1]

Top-tier fund managers. An income note investment allows an investor to gain exposure to an experienced CDO manager and the healthy

TABLE 12.1 Historical Returns—Various Asset Classes, 1995 to 2005

Index	10-Year Average (%)	Standard Deviation	Sharpe Ratio	5-Year Average (%)	Standard Deviation	Sharpe Ratio
Fixed Income						
Emerging Market Sovereign Bond Index	10.37	42.03	0.13	3.61	26.30	−0.05
SSB HY Market Index	11.48	94.20	0.07	6.36	97.74	0.02
Corporate Bond Index	7.16	53.24	0.04	3.96	34.27	−0.03
Intermediate Term Treasury Index	6.96	53.24	0.04	3.57	90.62	−0.01
Mortgage Bond Index	6.54	155.51	0.01	3.11	78.75	−0.02
SSB Broad Investment-Grade (BIG) Index	7.09	173.27	0.01	3.92	111.29	−0.01
AAA-Rated Corporate Bond Index	6.93	160.64	0.01	3.71	95.58	−0.01
Equities						
NASDAQ Composite	8.06	788.92	0.00	−10.87	529.44	−0.03
S&P 500	8.12	240.37	0.01	−3.78	149.58	−0.06
DJIA	8.42	1,814.65	0.00	−0.82	876.12	−0.01

Source: Citigroup.

returns it can generate, with a smaller initial investment than might otherwise be required.

Access to esoteric assets. An income note investment can be an efficient way for an investor to gain exposure to a variety of esoteric asset classes. Certain asset types, such as leveraged loans, mezzanine loans, and project finance loans, are asset classes to which relatively few investors have access.

Cash flow-based returns. Returns on cash flow CDO income notes are driven by the cash flow generated from the assets, not the market value or the price of those assets. This characteristic enables the investor to mitigate market risk and allows the manager to focus on the underlying credit fundamentals of the high-yield collateral. The investment is especially attractive when there is a dislocation in the high-yield market due to technical, not credit, factors (e.g., in fourth quarter 1998). This stands in stark contrast to high-yield mutual fund returns, which are sensitive to market value fluctuations.

Diversification. A relatively small investment in a cash flow CDO income note can confer substantial diversification benefits. An investor can gain exposure to 50 to 120 obligors across 15 to 25 industry sectors.

Structural protections. Income note holders benefit from a variety of structural features present in cash flow CDOs. Chief among them is the ability to remove the portfolio manager and the right to call the deal after the end of the noncall period.

Front-loaded cash flows. Unlike other alternative investments (e.g., private equity), an investment in cash flow CDO income notes will typically generate cash flow within six months of the initial investment.

Transparency. Income note investments are more transparent than many alternative investments. Every month, the trustee reports, among other things, trading activity, obligor names and exposure amounts, industry concentrations, and compliance or noncompliance with liquidity and asset maintenance tests.

Imbedded interest rate hedges. Many CDOs are floating-rate obligations backed by pools of fixed-rate bonds. In order to hedge the mismatch between the fixed-rate assets and the LIBOR-indexed liabilities, most CDOs purchase a combination of interest rate swaps and/or caps. Although these hedges are bought for the benefit of the rated note holders, they also benefit the income notes as the residual interest beneficiary.

Although CDO equity has many favorable characteristics, prospective note holders should consider the risks associated with ownership. Some risks include:

Subordination of the income notes. The income notes are the most subordinated notes in the CDO capital structure. They receive interest cash flow only after fees and rated coupon interest are paid, and asset and cash flow coverage tests are satisfied. No payment of principal of the income notes is paid until all other notes are retired and, to the extent that any losses are suffered by note holders, such losses are borne first by the income note holders.

Since the income notes are subordinated, prospective investors should consider and assess for themselves, given the manager's track record, the likely level and timing of defaults, recoveries, and interest rate movements. The following section, "Return Analysis," provides numerous examples that will help investors understand how these variables impact income note returns.

Limited liquidity and restrictions on transfer. Currently, potential income note buyers should not rely on a secondary market for CDO income notes. The investment trades on a "best efforts" basis, and in a typical transaction the income notes will be owned by a relatively small number of investors. Also, before selling an income note in the secondary market, the seller must comply with various regulations that restrict the transferability of certain types of securities.

Mandatory principal repayment of senior notes. If the aggregate asset balance is insufficient to meet the minimum overcollateralization test or the aggregate asset yield is insufficient to meet the minimum interest coverage test, cash flow that would have been distributed to the income notes will be diverted to amortize the most senior notes. If this occurs, the capital structure will delever until the test(s) is/are brought back into compliance. A delevering structure will have a negative impact on income note returns.

Reinvestment risk. During the reinvestment period the collateral manager will reinvest principal collections in additional bonds and loans. Depending on market conditions and the CDO's investment guidelines, the manager may purchase loans and bonds with a lower yield than the initial collateral (i.e., spread compression), resulting in less cash flow for all note holders.

One way to mitigate some of these risks is to bundle the income note with a zero coupon Treasury STRIP (or other security free of credit

Price (Treasury Zero) + Price (Income Notes) = Par (Treasury Zero)

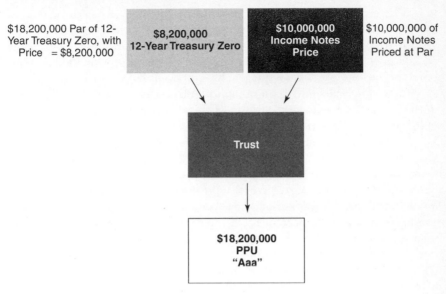

$18,200,000 Par of 12-Year Treasury Zero, with Price = $8,200,000

$8,200,000 12-Year Treasury Zero

$10,000,000 Income Notes Price

$10,000,000 of Income Notes Priced at Par

Trust

$18,200,000 PPU "Aaa"

FIGURE 12.3 Principal-Protected Units
Source: Citigroup.

risk) and create a principal-protected structured note or principal-protected unit (PPU) (see Figure 12.3). These units are designed to protect income note holders from the loss of their initial investment while still providing the potential of some yield upside. Moody's can rate PPUs Aaa, thereby allowing insurance company investors to gain NAIC1 capital treatment.

RETURN ANALYSIS

An internal rate of return (IRR) of 12 to 17 percent is often bandied about in the marketplace, but how robust and predictable is this return? What assumptions underlie such forecasted returns? The answers to these questions depend on the confluence of a number of factors, including:

- Magnitude and timing of defaults and sales at a discount to par.
- Magnitude and timing of recoveries.
- Interest rate movements.
- Calls and tenders.

Defaults

It is also important to note that although in general the performance of the CDO sector is correlated with the underlying collateral sectors, they are far from perfectly correlated. A CDO, after all, does not own all the credits in a given collateral universe. It owns a carefully selected, diverse portion. Top-tier portfolio managers have proven that they can consistently experience lower defaults than the marketplace as a whole. As is discussed in the "Collateral Manager" section of this chapter, asset selection and the manager's long-term track record are key.

As Figure 12.4 shows, collateral default rates are dependent on a security's rating and can vary widely over time. Default rates on leveraged loans surged from 2.17 to 6.41 percent and then fell back down to 1.31 percent over a period of five years. On the structured finance side, annual impairment rates hover around .01 percent for Aaa-rated tranches and average around 5 to 8 percent for B-rated issues. The upshot: The prudent investor will take a view on future default behavior and test an income note under varying default assumptions before investing.

In the following pages, we describe the main parameters CDO equity investors should look at while analyzing performance. We have used high-yield bond CBOs as our CDO example even though this asset class is not currently popular among CDO buyers. Nonetheless, the same broad principles apply across all CDO asset types. Unless otherwise stated in a particular figure, the base assumptions listed in Table 12.2 apply in all figures. Figures 12.5 and 12.6 illustrate the impact of various default scenarios on equity returns.

Figure 12.5 is representative of the equity pricing paradigm of applying a smooth default number over the life of the cash flow scenario. If a CDO's collateral defaults at 3 percent annually, the equity IRR would equal 14.8 percent, the principal-protected unit (PPR) IRR would equal 10.1 percent, and an unleveraged investment in the pool would return 9.3 percent. As Figure 12.5 illustrates, the annual default rate must exceed 4 percent over the life of the CDO in order to make the unleveraged investment in the collateral pool a better value relative to the leveraged equity investment. Interestingly, if annual defaults stay at a 3 percent rate, the PPU investment returns a paltry 0.8 percent above the collateral yield (10.1 percent versus 9.3 percent).

Figure 12.6 illustrates the impact of default rate spikes on the equity IRR. Since relatively small pools of collateral may have no predictable loss curve, default rate spike scenarios are key to understanding potential returns. If default rates remain in the 4 percent range (i.e., 33 percent above

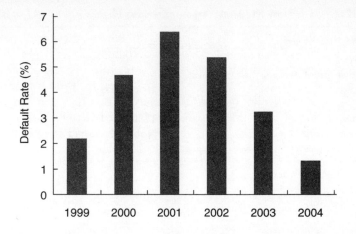

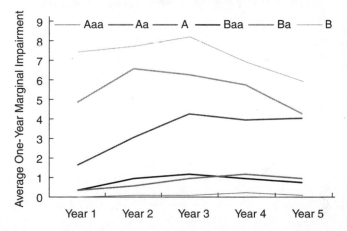

FIGURE 12.4   Historical Default Rate, Loan Market, 1999 to 2004 (top); ABS
Average One-Year Marginal Impairment Rates, 1993 to 2004 (bottom)
Sources: Moody's Investors Service and Citigroup.

the historical average) for the next two years and then revert to 2 percent per
annum, Figure 12.6 shows an IRR of about 15 percent (14.6 percent). If,
over the next two years, default rates rise 50 percent above today's average
default rate (4.0% × 1.5 = 6.0%) and then revert to 2 percent per annum,
the equity IRR in Figure 12.6 will equal approximately 11.1 percent.

   As Figure 12.6 illustrates, loss avoidance in the early years is key.

TABLE 12.2 Cash Flow Modeling Assumptions for High-Yield Bond Deals

Base-Line Default Rate	2%
Recovery rate	50–70%
Liability weighted average cost of funds	10-year UST + 2.25%
Asset yield[a]	10-year UST + 5.20%
Fees	0.55%
Reinvestment rate	11%
Interest rate hedge	Notional amount equal to 90% of initial asset base

[a]Net of management fees.
Note: High-yield bond deals are not popular currently.
Source: Citigroup.

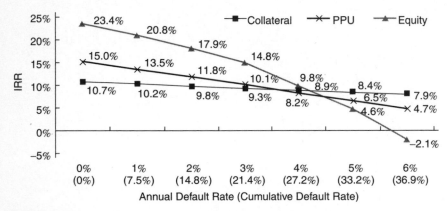

FIGURE 12.5 CDO Income Note Returns for a High-Yield Bond
CBO—Sensitivity to Annual Default Rates
Note: High-yield bond CBOs are not prevalent in today's market.
Source: Citigroup.

Recoveries

As default rates rose in the early 2000s, recovery rates dropped. The credit
environment has improved in recent years, and recovery rates have risen
again. In general, market conventions assign a recovery rate of 70 percent to
leveraged loans and 50 percent to asset-backed securities for the purposes
of forward-looking simulations (see Figure 12.7).

   As seen in Table 12.3, beside absolute recovery levels, all recovery studies show a tiering in recovery rates based on the defaulted instrument's level
of seniority and security.[2] Among corporate debt issues, senior secured bank

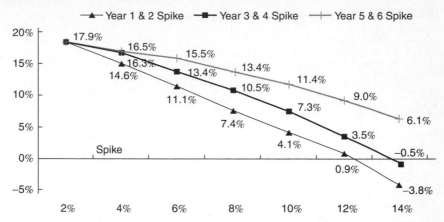

FIGURE 12.6 CDO Income Note Returns for a High-Yield Bond
CBO—Sensitivity to Default Rate Spikes
Note: High-yield bond CBOs are not currently popular.
Source: Citigroup.

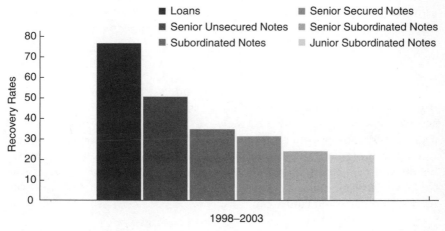

FIGURE 12.7 Historical Recovery Rates of Corporate Debt, 1998 to 2003
Sources: Standard & Poor's and Citigroup.

loans have shown the best recovery potential, followed in descending order
by senior unsecured bank loans, senior secured bonds, senior unsecured
bonds, and subordinated bonds. An investor should determine the potential
asset mix of a CDO and the assets that are most likely to default before
taking a view on the average recovery rate that the CDO may experience,

TABLE 12.3 Repayment and Realized Loss Characteristics by Original Rating, 1988 to 2004

	ABS Repayment	ABS Realized Loss	CMBS Repayment	CMBS Realized Loss	RMBS Repayment	RMBS Realized Loss
AAA	63.59	9.06	0	0	97.62	0.41
AA	0	28.16	85.18	11.3	73.72	21.44
A	7.36	18.26	60.42	5.09	14.4	16.84
BBB	0.63	32.78	21.72	5.78	24.59	19.03
BB	0	58.33	6.25	6.51	31.72	36.33
B	0	66.93	1.91	14.63	36.98	48.21
CCC	0	0	0	12.38	99.8	0.2

Source: Standard & Poor's.

depending on the mix and the time period in question—for instance, recovery rates on leveraged loans went from 74.1 percent in 1998 to 2003 to 95.4 percent in 2004.

Among asset-backed securities, recovery rates are more difficult to estimate given the dearth of recovery data and the relatively complex nature of ABS defaults. When an ABS defaults, it may continue to repay its principal for years after the actual default event. Thus, the recovery statistics available at any given time for these securities are expressed in terms of "realized loss" (the percentage of principal that will not be paid back), "repayment" (the percentage of principal that has been paid back), and "principal at risk" (the percentage of principal that could be lost or paid back). As Figure 12.8 shows, these numbers can vary widely depending on the rating and type of a given ABS. So, as with leveraged loans, the generally accepted recovery rate assumption (in this case, 50 percent) may vary in its accuracy. For best results, it is advisable to adjust this rate to meet the collateral characteristics of the CDO in question. Figures 12.8 to 12.9 illustrate the impact of various recovery scenarios on equity returns.

Interest Rate Risk

Many CDOs are floating-rate obligations backed by pools of fixed-rate bonds, and, in order to hedge potential interest rate mismatch, most CDOs purchase a combination of interest rate swaps and caps. Hedging is one of the least standardized features of a cash flow CDO and, as a result, it must be analyzed on a deal-by-deal basis.

Most CDOs are not perfectly hedged because such a hedge would be prohibitively expensive. Incremental hedging costs are funded by the

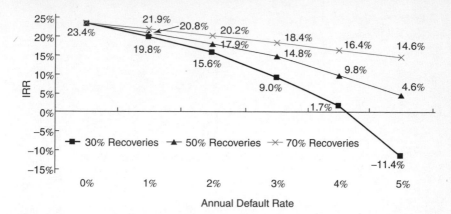

FIGURE 12.8   CDO Income Note Returns for a High-Yield Bond
CBO—Sensitivity to Recovery Rates and Annual Default Rates
Note: High-Yield Bond CBOs are Not Currently Popular.
Source: Citigroup.

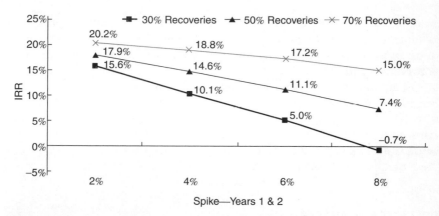

FIGURE 12.9   CDO Income Note Returns for a High-Yield Bond
CBO—Sensitivity to Recovery Rates and Default Rate Spikes
Note: High-yield bond CBOs are not currently popular.
Source: Citigroup.

issuance of additional income notes, thereby diluting equity returns. Historically, as a result, most equity investors have been willing to accept some interest rate risk in exchange for returns that have not been dampened by excessive hedging costs.

   In a typical CDO, the trust pays a fixed rate of interest to the counterparty and the counterparty pays LIBOR to the trust. The swap notional

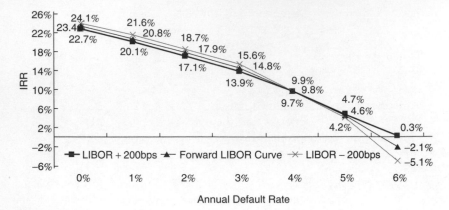

FIGURE 12.10 CDO Income Note Returns for a High-Yield Bond CBO—Sensitivity to LIBOR Movements
Note: High-yield bond CBOs are not currently popular.
Source: Citigroup.

amount amortizes pursuant to a schedule set at closing. Figure 12.10 assumes that the notional amount of a hedge is equal to 90 percent of the CDO capital structure and that the CDO liabilities are floating rate notes indexed to LIBOR.

In addition to the numerous quantitative considerations explained earlier, there are a number of key qualitative factors that will determine relative value among income note investment opportunities. These factors fall into three main categories: (1) collateral manager, (2) asset characteristics, and (3) structural features. The remainder of this chapter explores these qualitative factors in depth.

COLLATERAL MANAGER

Collateral Manager Review

An arbitrage CDO is a hybrid-structured finance/corporate instrument whose performance is linked not only to the credit quality of the collateral and the nature of the structure but also to the portfolio manager's trading decisions. The collateral manager's initial asset selection and trading decisions throughout the reinvestment period are crucial.

The key attributes of a manager that investors should examine in depth are:

- Track record.
- Experience managing within the CDO framework.
- Level of institutional support.
- Investment and trading philosophy.
- Expertise in each asset class that the manager is permitted to invest in.
- Importance of CDO product to overall organization.
- Manager's access to assets.

An asset manager review is the best way for an income note investor to get a firm grasp of a manager's strengths, weaknesses, and historical performance. Some key discussion points and portfolio performance information requirements are listed in Figures 12.11 and 12.12.

Asset Selection

A CDO manager can outperform the market depending on which names and industries it chooses initially and the trading decisions it makes during the reinvestment period.

Investors should be aware, however, that the time period during which the collateral manager purchases its collateral ("cohort" or "time stamp") can have as much effect on the performance of a CDO as the skill of the manager. For example, as a general matter, CDOs that ramped up during the spring of 1998 have not performed as well as other CDOs. During early 1998 asset spreads were tight and managers had to venture down the credit curve and invest in marginal credits in order to generate sufficient returns to CDO equity investors. One way CDO equity investors can mitigate the potential risk associated with the cohort is to identify a list of approved, blue-chip CDO managers and invest serially in CDOs issued by those managers.

Time stamp aside, we agree with the thesis that the high-yield market is not as efficient as other markets and, as a result, there are opportunities for CDO managers who are well versed in fundamental credit analysis and have access to timely information to outperform their competitors.[3] The high-yield market does not price every asset accurately. An experienced manager knows which assets are cheap relative to default probability and which are priced properly. Those CDO managers with strong research teams, good industry contacts, robust deal flow, and sophisticated systems have a good chance of outperforming the market.

Company Overview
Financial strength of the company
Experience in corporate lending and managing portfolios of high-yield bonds and bank loans
How does managing a CDO fulfill the company's strategic objectives?
Importance of CDO to overall organization
Prior history managing CDOs
Is entire CDO managed by a couple of key decision makers ("key person" risk)?
Number of high-yield funds under management
Performance results relative to peer group and index benchmarks
Compensation arrangements for the collateral managers
Will the company purchase part of the CDO income note?

Research
Research methodology
Industries covered
Number of analysts and credits per analyst
Depth of analyst contacts with industry participants
Ability to expand research to cover additional industries required in a diversified CDO
Sample research reports

Underwriting and Investment Strategy
Credit and approval policy
Investment style
Facility with and understanding of bond indentures and loan convenants
Decision-making process for buy and sell decisions
Pricing sources and polices regarding securities valuation

Credit Monitoring
Procedures to service the CDO and to ensure compliance with the CDO transaction documents
Does the manager have in-house cash flow modeling capabilities or does it rely solely on the trustee and/or underwriter?
Frequency of credit reviews
Technological tools used to monitor the portfolio
Procedures for managing credit-risk and defaulted assets

FIGURE 12.11   Collateral Manager Review Checklist
Sources: Standard & Poor's, Fitch IBCA, and Citigroup.

Prudent asset selection is crucial because the asset pool supporting a typical arbitrage CDO is granular. Although the trend is toward larger pools and smaller obligor concentrations, a given CDO may have as few as 70 to 120 names. With obligor concentrations ranging from 1 percent to 3 percent, a handful of poor investment choices may substantially reduce returns to income note holders.

CDO Investment Guidelines

A good total return leveraged loan or ABS manager does not necessarily equate to a good CDO manager. Two major differences exist. Total return arbitrage CDOs are typically leveraged 8 to 12 times, and this leverage greatly magnifies returns and losses to the CDO income notes. Also, managing within a CDO's arcane and cumbersome investment guidelines (which

Defaults and Credit-Risk Sales
Default history
Credit-risk sales below 80
Asset-specific rationale for each credit-risk sale
Where has each credit-risk asset traded after sale? Did it ultimately default?
Length of time between an asset purchase and its sale as a credit-risk asset

Recoveries
Recovery history
Method of disposition: sale after default or buy-and-hold
Recovery timing

Trading
Annual turnover rate for the profile
Frequency of credit-improved sales
Credit-improved sales: average premium to purchase price

Returns
Compare annual returns to peer group and index benchmarks
Volatility of annual returns

FIGURE 12.12 Portfolio Performance
Source: Citigroup.

have been crafted to garner investment-grade ratings on the senior notes from the rating agencies) can be challenging.

In a typical CDO, a manager must satisfy some 20 investment guidelines before making a trade. No trade is easy. Figure 12.13 illustrates guidelines that must be satisfied before a manager can make a purchase.

Given the complexity of these investment guidelines, a manager who currently manages one or more CDOs will have a distinct advantage over a first-time CDO manager, all other factors being equal. Although a new CDO manager may have a conceptual understanding of each of these guidelines in isolation, until a manager operates within them and understands the interrelationship among all guidelines, they are difficult to master.

If a CDO collateral manager has mastered the investment guidelines within a CDO, in what ways may this benefit the income note holders? One way involves industry diversification. All rating agencies encourage industry diversification for the benefit of the rated note holders. A manager must seek the optimal amount of industry diversification: diversification that maximizes the rating agency credit to rated note holders, minimizes forays into unknown industries, and generates a fair risk-adjusted return to income note holders.

Another way that an experienced CDO manager can benefit income note holders is by taking a balanced view of a CDO's asset eligibility parameters. Many modern CDOs allow a manager considerable flexibility to invest in various nontraditional assets, such as emerging market debt and structured

---

Minimum average asset debt rating
Minimum percentage of assets rated B3 or better
Minimum percentage of assets in U.S.
Maximum percentage of assets outside U.S., Canada, and U.K.
Maximum percentage of synthetic securities
Minimum diversity score
Maximum single issuer exposure
Maximum percentage in any S&P industry group
Maximum percentage in any Moody's industry group
Maximum percentage of zero coupon bonds
Maximum percentage of loan participations
Maximum percentage of floating rate securities
Weighted average life test
Class A, B, and C minimum QC tests
Class A, B, and C minimum IC tests
Minimum weighted average recovery test
Maximum percentage of securities maturing after a certain date
Minimum average asset margin test
Minimum average asset coupon test
Maximum annual discretionary trading bucket

FIGURE 12.13 Typical CDO Investment Guidelines
Source: Citigroup.

finance obligations. These asset types may generate significantly more yield than comparably rated high-yield bonds. They present an enticing way for a manager to juice up returns to income note holders. But, as with the perils of industry diversification, a manager who is too aggressive in searching for additional yield in nontraditional products may invest in asset types that it does not understand. Enhanced returns to the income note holder may not provide adequate compensation for the additional risk. A prudent CDO manager will resist this urge and instead stick to asset classes that it understands, even if that means forgoing some yield opportunities. In the long run, this should ensure a more stable risk-adjusted return to the income notes.

CDO Manager Types

CDO managers run the gamut from giant, highly rated banks and insurance companies to small, specialized bank loan portfolio managers. The size of the CDO manager does not, on its own, determine whether a particular income note is a good investment opportunity. For example, a CDO business that is a tiny part of a large insurance company or bank may not receive the same level of attention as a CDO business that is managed by a bank loan boutique. In the latter case, the success of the CDO business is crucial to the success of the business as a whole. However, if an insurance company–sponsored CDO falters or a key portfolio manager departs, the insurance company will have greater financial wherewithal to support the CDO business and hire a capable replacement.

An income note buyer should also understand how the portfolio manager makes its investment decisions. An institution that centralizes its investment decisions with one or two key people runs the risk that those key people might leave the institution for other opportunities. For this reason, income note investors should try to ascertain whether the sponsoring institution espouses an investment philosophy and whether this philosophy is shared by a broad cross section of the CDO management team. These team members should participate actively in all trading decisions.

Another key indication of support is whether an institution has issued multiple CDOs. If so, this indicates an institutional commitment to the CDO business. That commitment is further strengthened if the institution is an income note investor in each of its CDOs.

Investment and Trading Philosophy

A CDO manager's investment philosophy and trading style will have a significant impact on returns to the income notes. A key indication of this style is how the manager strikes a balance between the rated notes and the income notes. Although rated note holders and income note holders share many of the same concerns, their interests diverge in some important ways. Their viewpoints often differ as to the optimal investment and trading philosophy for a CDO manager.

Rated note holders occupy the majority of the capital structure of the CDO, and their primary concern is the preservation of principal and a coupon entitlement that is attractive relative to other similarly rated fixed-income instruments. These note holders are concerned with initial asset selection before closing and during the ramp-up period. Once a transaction is ramped up, triple-A note holders are averse to a CDO collateral manager that actively trades the portfolio because they rely on asset cash flow, not trading gains, to service their debt. As long as assets do not default, they will produce the necessary cash flow to service the rated debt. The market value of the underlying asset pool may be of interest as a leading indicator of credit quality, but it is not of primary importance to rated note holders.

Income note holders do not think in terms of preservation of principal and a fixed coupon payment. They think in terms of cash flow and a return on their initial investment. As we have explained, this return is driven by, among other things, defaults, recoveries, interest rates, premiums, and trading gains and losses. Like rated note holders, income note holders focus on a manager's initial asset selection, because prudent asset selection can minimize losses and benefit all note holders. Unlike rated note holders, however, income note holders are concerned with the market value of the assets in the CDO and the manager's trading decisions, if any, regarding assets that are trading at premiums or discounts.

There are three categories of trades that a manager can make: credit-risk, credit-improved, and discretionary sales. Rated note holders and income note holders often have differing views as to the advisability of a particular trade. If a manager has a CDO or CDOs outstanding, a potential income note investor can analyze the manager's past trades and infer whether the manager has worked to preserve principal for all note holders or has concentrated on enhancing returns to the income note holders.

1. **Credit-risk sales.** A credit-risk sale is a sale of an asset that has declined in credit quality and that the manager reasonably believes will default with the passage of time. A credit-risk asset is sold at a discount to par and this sale, in isolation, results in the reduction of the asset base supporting the notes. This loss of principal will move the actual overcollateralization (OC) closer to the minimum OC trigger. If the minimum OC trigger is tripped, collections will be used to pay down the senior notes.

   Rated note holders will view credit-risk sales favorably only if: (1) the asset ultimately defaults and (2) the sale price is greater than ultimate recovery on the defaulted asset. If an asset is sold as credit risk and does not default before the CDO is retired, the CDO has taken a loss (i.e., sale at discount to par) that it could have avoided if the asset had been held to maturity.

   Income note holders may have differing views concerning credit-risk sales. Some may prefer managers to hold onto credit-risk assets because any discounted sale would push actual OC closer to the minimum OC trigger and increase the risk of delevering. Other income note investors may prefer early aggressive sales of credit-risk assets at slight discounts rather than waiting for an asset to trade at a steep discount.

2. **Credit-improved sales.** Credit-improved sales can benefit both rated and income note holders. The issue hinges upon how the premium is treated in the structure. The premium generated from a credit-improved sale may be treated as interest collections and used to enhance returns to the income note holder, or it can be used to grow OC through the purchase of additional assets. Clearly, the latter method benefits all note holders. When a manager sells an asset that has improved in credit quality, the rated note holders lose the benefit of upward credit migration; but if the sale proceeds (including premium) are reinvested in additional assets, the manager may be able to maintain or increase OC.

3. **Discretionary sales.** Depending on the structure, a CDO manager also has the discretion to trade 10 to 20 percent of the portfolio annually. Not surprisingly, rated note holders have a bearish view of unfettered discretionary trading: They prefer managers with strong credit fundamentals to execute a long-term investment strategy. Any problem credits can be traded under the credit-risk trading rules. In contrast, income note holders favor discretionary trading provisions, because these allow the manager to continually search for assets with the best risk-adjusted returns.

In the final analysis, trading is a two-edged sword. Trading can expose cash flow CDO note holders to market value risk, but it also can be used to improve the credit profile of the pool of assets and could ultimately be a very positive force in mitigating credit risk.

ASSET CHARACTERISTICS

Collateral Mix

In addition to high-yield bonds and bank loans, arbitrage CDOs increasingly include nontraditional investments (see Figure 12.14).

Most CDOs have certain limitations or buckets for these types of assets, but the limitations are different for each CDO. Such assets are often included in arbitrage CDOs because their generous yields enhance arbitrage opportunities for the collateral managers and, ultimately, the income notes. Although these nontraditional assets offer enticing yield pickup, the income note holders must be certain that the collateral manager has sufficient investment experience in the particular asset class. If not, enhanced short-term income note returns may be outweighed by significant long-term credit risk.

Loan participations
Emerging markets sovereign debt
Emerging markets corporate debt
Distressed debt
Convertible bonds
Mezzanine loans with warrants
Project finance loans and bonds

FIGURE 12.14 Nontraditional Assets
Source: Citigroup.

The inclusion of nontraditional assets also raises a credit question. The credit risk inherent in all cash flow CDOs is analyzed using various corporate default studies. Since these are studies of corporate instruments, they are not directly applicable to assets like structured finance obligations and project finance loans. Some have argued, however, that applying corporate default studies to structured finance instruments is overly conservative, given that there have been far fewer structured finance defaults than corporate defaults over the past 10 years.

Some nontraditional investments can be categorized as bivariate-risk assets. These include loan participations, emerging market corporate debt, and credit derivatives. With respect to each of these assets, the CDO is exposed to the nonperformance risk of more than one counterparty. For example, if a collateral manager invests in a credit derivative, the CDO will not receive payment if either the underlying referenced obligation or the credit derivative counterparty fails to perform. Most CDOs allow a manager to invest up to 20 percent of a CDO's assets in bivariate-risk assets, but many managers do not avail themselves of this opportunity. If the collateral manager plans to utilize the 20 percent bivariate risk bucket or has used it in past transactions, the income note holders should determine whether they are being compensated for this additional risk.

Finally, the inclusion of nontraditional asset types may have an impact on assumed recovery values. Over the past few years, several large recovery studies have been completed, but each revolves around defaulted U.S. corporate bonds and loans. If a manager aggressively invests in sovereign debt or structured finance obligations, the applicability of these studies becomes questionable.

Time Stamp or Cohort

The period of time during which a CDO is ramped up can have a significant impact on its long-term performance. Depending on market conditions, the collateral manager will purchase assets from both the primary and the secondary market. Historically, a large percentage of the assets (10 to 50+ percent) are sourced from the new-issue calendar, and during the average ramp-up period (three to six months), that calendar contains a finite number of names. Consequently, arbitrage CDOs that are ramped up during the same period may share a large percentage of the same names. Accordingly, if an investor purchases multiple income notes from CDOs that have concurrent ramp-up periods, there is the risk that the performance of these income notes may be correlated. This risk will decline after the end of the ramp-up period as the manager starts trading the portfolio and the risk may not be as pronounced if one CDO manager is purchasing loans and the other is purchasing high-yield bonds.

The prices of asset-backed securities and bank loans during the ramp-up period can also have a big impact on the performance of a CDO. As we mentioned earlier in the chapter, during the fall of 1998 prices for high-yield bonds dropped and spreads widened considerably for technical reasons, although underlying credit fundamentals were relatively stable. CDO managers that purchased collateral during that time frame were able to buy good credit quality collateral at discounted prices. Discounted prices allowed managers to purchase much more collateral than they had projected without going down the credit spectrum. Many of these deals, consequently, have asset buffers that are significantly above their minimum overcollateralization tests. These managers did not time the market: It was fortuitous that they came to the market during that period.

For these reasons, if an investor is going to build a portfolio of income note investments, we recommend the purchase of income notes that are issued during different time periods or cohorts. Investors can execute this strategy in two ways. They can review the new-issuance calendar for the next quarter or two and select income notes from various CDO issuers. This would give them maximum exposure to different credits and CDO manager investment styles. Alternatively, since the performance of CDO income notes is tied so closely to the skill of the manager, an investor may approve certain blue-chip managers and buy income notes from each of their deals over time. An investor who chooses the second strategy will likely be exposed to some of the same credits across all CDOs that a manager issues. Managers tend to buy additional exposure to names they like.

Diversification

The rating agency methodologies encourage obligor and industry diversity. The theory is simple: Since CDO asset pools are lumpy to begin with, the more names in the pool, the less any one obligor default can hurt note holders. Similarly with industries, if one industry is experiencing higher than average defaults, note holders' exposure to that industry is limited. Rated note holders favor broad diversification because they are interested in preservation of principal and the payment of a fixed coupon. Income note holders are less sanguine about zealous diversification because diversification, while limiting credit risk, also limits upside opportunities. Some income note holders want the manager to make a few right picks that can have a disproportionately beneficial impact on income note returns.

How does the manager strike a balance between the interests of the rated note holders and the interests of income note holders? At some point, too much diversity can work against all note holders. No note holder benefits if overly restrictive CDO investment guidelines force a manager to invest in obligors and industries that it does not fully understand. Credit risk increases and income note returns decline.

STRUCTURE

Unlike certain structured finance products (e.g., credit card ABS), CDO structures are far from commoditized. Every CDO underwriter uses a different base structure, and even CDOs underwritten by the same banker can contain significant structural variations that can affect the income note holder. Income note investors who study these features in each CDO before deciding to invest may be able to deduce how the manager intends to strike a balance between the interests of the rated note holders and the interests of the income note holders.

The structure of a CDO is an important consideration for the income note holder because the income notes are structurally subordinated to the other notes issued by the CDO. From a cash flow perspective, the income note holder is not entitled to cash flow until payment of: (1) all fees and expenses (capped and uncapped); (2) interest and principal to more senior notes; and (3) all hedging costs (including termination payments). If these obligations have been paid and the minimum interest coverage (IC) and overcollateralization (OC) tests are in compliance, the income notes are eligible for distribution.

Trigger Levels

All arbitrage CDOs contain two types of coverage tests: An asset coverage test (minimum OC test) and a liquidity coverage test (minimum IC test). If these tests are violated, reinvestment of principal ceases and principal and interest collections are used to accelerate the redemption of the senior notes until these tests are brought back into compliance. These triggers function as structural mitigants to credit risk. Because violation of these coverage tests can result in the payment of all cash flow to the senior note holders (and consequently none to the income note holders), income note holders should have a firm understanding of how they function.

One of the key ways to gauge the robustness of a projected IRR is to compare the actual OC and IC in the transaction to the minimum IC and IC triggers set by the collateral manager and deal underwriter. If the difference between actual and minimum is small, the triggers have been structured tightly by the collateral manager and the deal underwriter in an effort to give the CDO issuer a higher degree of leverage (i.e., enhance the projected IRR to the income note). If the relationship between actual and minimum is larger, the triggers have been structured more loosely. Although it may allow an underwriter to present a higher IRR to potential income note investors, a tight trigger is easier to violate and thus makes the IRR potentially more volatile.

An income note investor should also explore the relationship between the actual levels of OC and IC and the trigger points in the context of the overall credit quality of the portfolio. A portfolio with an average credit quality of single-B should, all other factors being equal, have a larger income note and less leverage (as a percentage of the deal) than a portfolio with an average credit quality of double-B. Also, the CDO supported by the single-B portfolio should have a larger buffer between the actual OC level and the minimum OC trigger, since single-B default rates are more volatile than double-B default rates.

Finally, in most CDO structures, each class has its own minimum OC and IC test and the tests associated with the most subordinated rated class should trigger first. Nevertheless, the income note investor should analyze cash flow runs to understand under a variety of stress scenarios which tests trigger the pay-down of the deal.

Senior Costs, Swaps, and Caps

Portfolio management fees and the coupon payable to the rated note holders are two costs that can affect the cash flow payable to the income notes. An income note holder should examine the manager's fee in each CDO and compare it to fees payable in other arbitrage CDOs. A typical fee structure will pay the manager 0.25 percent prior to payment of interest on the rated notes and at least 0.25 percent after payment of fees and rated note interest and the satisfaction of the IC and OC tests.

More importantly, as we have described in the "Return Analysis" section of this chapter, in many arbitrage CDOs the assets are primarily fixed-rate bonds and the liabilities are issued as LIBOR floaters. These deals typically use a combination of swaps or caps to hedge interest rate risk. The swaps and caps usually have notional amounts that amortize on a predetermined basis. This presents the risk that the transaction may be underhedged or overhedged at any point in time (see Figure 12.10). If the deal is underhedged, for example, more of the asset cash flow will be used to meet rated note debt coverage and less will be available for the income notes. Moreover, these hedges can terminate, and if the SPV owes a termination payment to the counterparty the payment will be made senior to payment of any residual cash flow to the income notes. Since termination payments can be large, investors should analyze the swap documents for each deal and understand which events can cause the termination of the swap.

Manager Fees and Equity Ownership

There are a few ways that a structure can more closely align a portfolio manager's economic interests with those of the income note holders. One way is through the payment of the portfolio manager's fee. In some older transactions, the manager's fee is paid before payment of rated note holder interest. This senior position is beneficial if the CDO needs to attract a replacement manager but it does not align the interests of the manager and the income notes. Even if the CDO is performing very poorly, the manager still gets paid the full fee. For this reason, most deals pay part of the fee at the top of the waterfall (base management fee) and part of the fee after payments of other fees, rated note holder interest, and the satisfaction of the IC and OC tests (performance management fee). By subordinating a portion of the manager's fee, these structures encourage the manager to generate enough cash flow to service the rated debt in a fashion that preserves the asset base and does not violate the IC and OC tests. Some structures pay the manager an additional fee if the actual IRR paid to the income note holder hits a certain target.

Another way managers can align their economic interests with those of the income note holders is by purchasing a portion of the income note. This is the case in most CDOs. The theory: Since the manager owns part of the income notes, it will manage the portfolio so as to produce reasonable returns to the income notes while protecting them from unreasonable credit risk. Although many deals do not explicitly prohibit managers from selling their portion of the income notes, as a practical matter the market for income notes is limited. In all likelihood, if a manager purchases income notes, it will retain them.

Credit-Improved Sales — Treatment of Premium

CDO investment rules allow a portfolio manager to sell an asset that has improved in credit quality and is now trading at a premium (credit-improved sale). What is a credit-improved sale, and how are sale proceeds distributed? Definitions vary. Some structures define a credit-improved sale as a sale of an asset that has improved in credit quality and can be sold at a premium to purchase price. Other CDO structures describe a credit-improved sale as a sale of an asset that has improved in credit quality and can be sold at a premium to par.

CDO structures treat gains differently. Some treat premiums as principal proceeds that will be reinvested in new collateral. Rated note holders favor this treatment because premium sale proceeds are used to buy more collateral and enhance overcollateralization in the structure. Some income note holders may favor this treatment for the same reason. Other structures treat premium sale proceeds as interest proceeds that can be distributed to the income note holders if fees and rated coupon have been paid and the IC and OC tests have been satisfied. Rated note holders do not favor this version, because it allows a manager to skim all the credit upside off the pool of assets and stream it to the income note holder in the form of an enhanced IRR. Still other structures give the manager the option of designating premium proceeds as either interest or principal. Finally, another variation weighs the cumulative losses against the cumulative gains that a manager has incurred over the life of the CDO. If cumulative losses exceed cumulative gains, the proceeds of any credit-improved sale are deemed principal proceeds.

CONCLUSION

During the past few years, demand for CDO equity has broadened substantially from large institutional investors to other investors such as small pension funds and high-net-worth individuals. A CDO equity investment program that purchases income notes from a select group of experienced CDO managers across various periods of time can be an effective way for investors to diversify their portfolios and improve risk-adjusted returns. We expect that continued growth in the CDO market will drive increased demand for CDO equity investments in the United States and in overseas markets, including Europe, the Middle East, and Asia.

CASE STUDY: DIVERSIFYING CREDIT RISK USING A CDO EQUITY FUND

The unrated CDO equity tranche can provide healthy returns if the credit fundamentals are strong. At the beginning of 2004, as spreads were low and prospects for credit were improving, a number of investors were looking at the CDO equity to pick up higher returns. The following case study details a simulation-based analysis of a hypothetical CDO equity fund, which pools the CDO equity tranches of a number of different CDOs and helps in diversifying credit risk across different underlying credit markets, CDO management styles, and CDO vintages.

Introduction

CDO equity is one class of the structured credit products that has the potential for high returns in the current environment.[4] CDO equity, which is typically unrated and represents the most subordinated part of the CDO capital structure, receives the residual interest cash flow remaining after payment of fees, rated note holder coupon, and the satisfaction of any asset maintenance tests. Targeted returns can range from the low to mid-teens but can be lower depending on (among other things) the level and correlation of defaults, the level and timing of recoveries, and the movement of interest rates. In practice, historical performance has differed depending on the underlying market that is referenced in the CDO. As a general matter, arbitrage cash flow CDOs backed by high-yield bonds (HY CBOs) and investment-grade bonds (IG CBOs) have been severely affected by the 2000–2003 bear credit market, whereas CDOs backed by structured finance assets (CDOs of ABS) and leveraged loans (CLOs) have, on a comparative basis, performed much better.[5]

Our study of 302 existing CDOs (spanning seven vintages from 2000 to 2005) starkly illustrates the disparity in performance among the different types of CDOs. The median projected equity internal rates of return (IRRs) for CLOs, mezzanine ABS CDOs, HG ABS CDOs, and CRE CDOs were 9.4, 9.7, 10.6, and 10.3 percent, respectively. However, the median projected equity IRRs for investment-grade CDOs and high-yield bond CBOs were 2.9 percent and 2.6 percent, respectively.[6] Investors are keenly aware of these differences, and as a consequence, the demand for CLOs and CDOs of ABS has increased dramatically in the past few years. As Figure 12.15 illustrates, CLOs and CDOs of ABS accounted for 54 percent of all U.S. transactions rated by S&P in 2003, up from 24 percent in 1998.[7] By contrast, high-yield CBO and investment-grade CBO issuance plummeted from approximately 35 percent in 1998 to just over 1 percent in 2003.

In addition to the recent trends vis-à-vis CLOs and CDOs of ABS, funds of CDO equity tranches have gained prominence. By pooling CDO equity tranches over time, these funds attempt to diversify across different interest rate and credit spread environments, underlying collateral types and CDO manager styles. The purpose of this article is to simulate and analyze the performance of a hypothetical fund that has a substantial allocation in CLO and CDO of ABS equity tranches. We believe this diversification across vintage, asset class, and manager reduces the probability of extreme outcomes, leading to more stable expected returns.

Modeling Assumptions and Analytical Techniques

We modeled a hypothetical CDO equity fund from the following types of deals (allocations indicated in parentheses): CLOs (40 percent), CDOs of ABS (40 percent), investment-grade CBOs (10 percent), and high-yield CBOs (10 percent).[8] The large allocation to CLOs and CDOs of ABS reflects their strong performance through the last credit cycle. Each deal was modeled beginning one year from its closing date to avoid ramp-up period complications and to reflect the first-year actual (i.e., historical) cash flow distributions and collateral changes. There was no additional leverage at the fund of CDO level, and fees at this level were assumed to be 50 basis points up front and zero thereafter.[9]

To project cash flow distributions to the fund of CDO notes, we used Monte Carlo simulations and modeled default correlation using the Gaussian copula function technique.[10] Default curves were constructed with Moody's historical data. In addition, our two-parameter model assumed a 15 percent interindustry and a 25 percent intraindustry correlation of default timing across all four CDO collateral pools. The resulting default scenarios were then run through the cash flow model to forecast payment distributions to the fund's notes. We then calculated the internal rate of return (IRR) for each simulation run and constructed IRR frequency distributions based on 20,000 runs. This approach allowed us to calculate

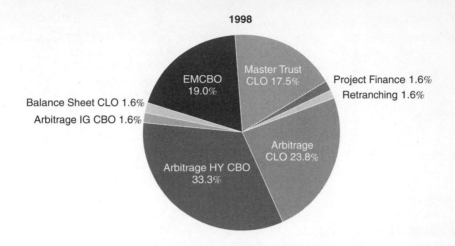

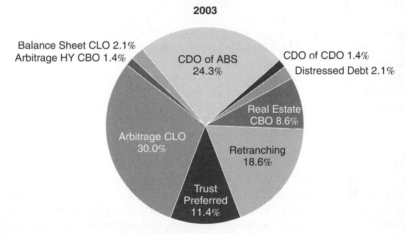

FIGURE 12.15 CDO Collateral—Historical Trends, 1998 versus 2003
Source: Standard & Poor's.

traditional, average performance statistics, as well as analyze extreme (tail) events consistent with the rest of the distribution.

Results

Figure 12.16 illustrates the frequency distribution of annualized IRRs for the fund of CDOs as compared with isolated investments in a high-yield CBO and an investment-grade CDO. With respect to the fund of CDOs, in 42 percent of the simulations IRRs were at or

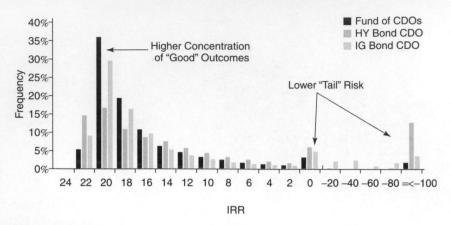

FIGURE 12.16   Fund of CDOs versus HY CBO and IG CBO—Frequency
Distribution of Annualized IRRs
Source: Citigroup.

above 18 percent, in 87 percent of the simulations IRRs were at or above 8 percent, and in only 6 percent of the simulations were the fund's shares unable to recover at least their initial amount invested. Despite the diversification within the fund of CDOs, its return distribution (as shown in Figure 12.16) still exhibits a right tail, as is common in fixed-income portfolios. However, this tail is less pronounced than the tails for the high-yield CBO and the investment-grade CBO.

In particular, the probability of achieving a negative IRR was much smaller for the fund of CDOs (6 percent) than it was for the high-yield CBO (20 percent) or the investment-grade CDO (17 percent). Despite the high volatility associated with high-yield and investment-grade CDOs, we believe that a fund of CDOs should have some limited flexibility to opportunistically invest in these asset classes because they can surprise on the upside. For example, while there is only a 5 percent probability that the IRR of the fund of CDOs exceeds 20 percent, the hypothetical high-yield CBO and investment-grade CDO (at 15 percent and 9 percent, respectively) have higher probabilities of extremely good outcomes.

In Figure 12.17 we compare the frequency distribution of annualized IRRs for the fund of CDOs with return distributions for the hypothetical CLO and CDO of ABS.

With respect to the CDO of ABS, it exhibited lower upside potential than the fund of CDOs, but similar stability of returns (the right tail of each distribution was similar). Finally, regarding the CLO simulations, they were very strong with respect to the average IRR (9.5 percent), median IRR (19.5 percent), and maximum IRR (20.3 percent). However, the maximum total loss (93.2 percent) and standard deviation of return (50.4 percent) were not as strong as the fund of CDOs results (see Table 12.4).

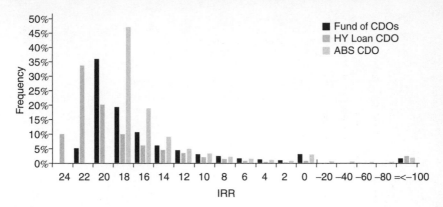

FIGURE 12.17 Fund of CDOs versus HY CLO and ABS CDO—Frequency Distribution of Annualized IRRs
Source: Citigroup.

TABLE 12.4 Return/Risk Profile

Performance Measure	Fund of CDOs (%)	HY CLO (%)	ABS CDO (%)	IG CBO (%)	HY CBO (%)
Average IRR	11.4	9.5	8.4	4.2	−3.9
Median IRR	17.3	19.5	15.8	16.8	14.3
Maximum IRR	20.3	22.6	17.8	20.0	21.8
Probability of loss	6.0	3.9	8.7	16.6	20.2
Maximum total loss	79.2	93.2	73.7	62.3	62.2
Standard deviation, IRR	25.1	50.4	26.1	32.6	44.2
Return/risk ratio	0.5	0.2	0.3	0.1	−0.1

Source: Citigroup.

Conclusion

A CDO equity fund allows diversification across three dimensions: vintage of origination, CDO collateral category, and CDO manager style. While any individual CDO transaction may outperform a diversified pool of CDO transactions, the diversification inherent in a fund of CDOs structure has the potential to reduce the probability of extreme events and deliver to investors a more stable risk-adjusted return (see the return/risk ratios in Table 12.4).[11]

CHAPTER 13

Commercial Real Estate CDOs

Darrell Wheeler
Ratul Roy

C ommercial real estate collateralized debt obligation (CRE CDO) issuance has surged as the interests of institutional investors and commercial real estate CDO issuers have converged. Institutional investors who lack the wherewithal to invest directly into subordinate real estate debt are now able to diversify their holdings into a managed commercial real estate pool at an attractive rating-adjusted spread. Conversely, CDO technology is revolutionizing the commercial real estate lending market by providing commercial mortgage-backed security (CMBS) investors and mortgage real estate investment trusts (REITs)[1] (now CRE CDO issuers) a low cost of funds and term financing without mark-to-market triggers. CRE CDO issuance is sure to accelerate as the pace of commercial real estate transaction execution increases, as the issuance of subordinate real estate debt booms, as more CRE market participants discover the benefits of using a CDO structure for stable financing, and as the market for CRE CDO debt continues to grow internationally.

CRE CDOs BY THE NUMBERS

Slow Start, but Growth Now Strong

Since the large commercial real estate losses of the early 1990s recession, real estate borrowers have been cautious not to overextend themselves, and lenders have been cautious not to provide too much leverage. Consequently, the commercial real estate market was initially slow to adopt CDO technology as many CMBS investors preferred to finance their real estate investments with reREMICs,[2] and as mortgage REITs utilized warehouse lines, lines of credit, and/or reverse-repo facilities. However, after the issuance of several CRE CDOs, subordinate CMBS investors realized that CDO technology could provide more management flexibility than reREMIC structures, which can only hold a static pool of CMBS certificates and bonds. Many CRE investors then developed their own CDO programs and turned to the CDO markets with a fresh supply of collateral to be securitized. A steady stream of CRE CDO issuance soon followed, and by 2005 the CRE CDO market had come into its own. The evolution of the CRE CDO market is discussed in detail in the section entitled "Key Events in the CRE CDO Market."

Approximately $16 billion of CRE CDO paper was issued for calendar year 2005,[3] a 170 percent increase over the 2004 number and 140 percent over the previous peak issued in 2002. Through 2005, approximately $41 billion of CRE CDO paper was issued across 83 transactions (see Figure 13.1).[4]

Three forces explain the explosive growth of CRE CDO issuance over the past year:

1. The realization by traditional commercial real estate loan investors and originators, such as mortgage REITS and opportunity funds, that the CDO market offers a useful, low-cost, term-funded financing source without troublesome mark-to-market triggers or reinvestment constraints.
2. Rising demand for securitized commercial real estate paper by the generalist institutional investor who sees commercial real estate (and its derivative products) as having attractive spreads, solid historical performance, and low correlation with many other asset-backed security (ABS) investments.

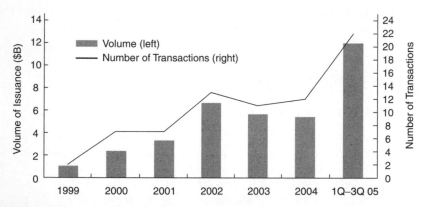

FIGURE 13.1   CRE CDO Issuance Surged in 2005
Source: Citigroup.

3. A surge in subordinate commercial real estate paper issuance, such as B-notes and mezzanine loans, and greater supply of CMBS transactions, issuance of which has increased by 80 percent in 2005 over 2004 issuance levels.

The need for term funding and flexible investment guidelines (force number one) also explains why so many recent CRE CDOs are issued for financing reasons as opposed to arbitrage reasons that are typical in the broader CDO market.[5]

Relative Value: Spread Pickup Often Gives CRE CDOs an Edge

For a given rating, CRE CDO spreads have historically been wider than the spreads of CMBSs (on a swaps basis or LIBOR basis), other ABSs, and some types of CDOs (see Figure 13.2). For example, depending on the collateral mix, triple-A CRE CDO paper can offer a 0 to 10 basis point pickup over comparably rated CMBS and CLO paper. Even greater spread pickup (25 bp or more) is obtained over credit card securitizations, RMBSs, and very high-quality corporates (not shown). The attractive yields combined with diversification benefits (and the possibility of countercyclical credit performance) make a compelling case for CRE CDO investing.

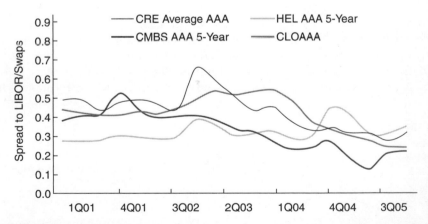

FIGURE 13.2 Triple-A Rated New Issue Structured Paper—Spread Comparison, 1Q 01–3Q 05
Source: Citigroup.

CRE CDO Performance Has Been Strong

CDO and traditional CMBS investors have been encouraged by the relatively strong credit and rating performance of early-vintage CRE CDOs. As of September 2, 2005, 14 CRE CDOs have been upgraded, while only four transactions have been downgraded (see Table 13.1). All four of the downgraded transactions[6] were issued in 2000 or 2001. Fitch cites exposure to manufactured housing securitizations (i.e., not the commercial real estate assets) as a reason for three of the four downgrades. Thus, investors should be mindful that the small buckets created for non-CRE assets can and do shape the performance of some CRE CDOs.

CRE CDO performance also stacks up favorably when compared to ABS CDOs. Figure 13.3 indicates the average annual gain (loss) of overcollateralization and weighted average rating factor (a measure of collateral quality) compliance/violation for 136 ABS CDOs and nine CRE CDOs issued between 1999 and 2004.[7] Most of the CRE CDOs are comfortably in the upper-right quadrant, which reflects improvements in the OC ratios and satisfactory or better average collateral ratings. Many ABS CDOs are similarly positioned, but the variation in performance seems much greater for ABS CDOs than for CRE CDOs; this is likely a reflection of the relative stability of commercial real estate collateral (historically REIT debt and CMBSs). Whether this characteristic is likely to continue into the future is less clear, especially as new and riskier (subordinate) securities are added to new CRE CDO collateral pools (see discussion in the next section) and as rating agencies ease their CMBS securitization criteria.

Strong CRE CDO performance is likely a result of the rating agencies' conservative rating approach for CMBS certificates, which has been guided by the 1991 to 1992 real estate recession and its impact on real estate loan performance. Because of this initially conservative approach to rating and sizing CMBS tranches, the agencies have had significant room to upgrade many pre-2000 certificates. This outperformance of the underlying CMBS certificates then drove much of the positive CRE CDO performance. It

TABLE 13.1 CRE CDO Upgrade/Downgrade Performance, as of September 30, 2005

	Number of Deals	Upgraded	Downgraded	Paid in Full
Moody's rated	63	2	2	5
S&P rated	66	1	0	5
Fitch rated	56	14	3	4
All CRE CDOs	71	14	4	5

Source: Citigroup.

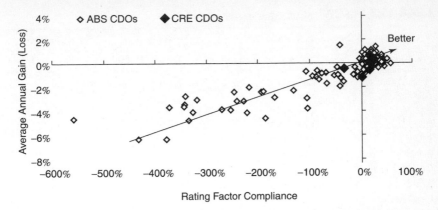

FIGURE 13.3 Performance of CRE and ABS CDOs from Moody's Deal Score Report, as of July 2005
Source: Moody's Investors Service and Citigroup.

should be noted, however, that credit enhancement levels on recent-vintage CMBS issues have decreased. Thus, we caution that some recent CMBS (and CRE CDO) rating upgrades might not be as frequent as the historical upgrade ratios that we show for CMBS certificates in Table 13.2. Nonetheless, the table does show a favorable upgrade-to-downgrade ratio, which should continue in the near term as some agencies have been slow to upgrade CMBS transactions. Many vintage subordination levels exceed new issuance levels by several percentage points and likely will be upgraded. To see this potential, we recommend that investors review our monthly triple-B and double-B projected subordination report, which lists every triple-B and double-B CMBS bond by issue date, and then liquidates each to compare projected subordination levels relative to recent credit levels issued by the rating agencies.[8]

Collateral Mix: Diverse and Evolving[9]

CRE CDO collateral composition and deal structures have evolved considerably over the past six years and especially over the past year and a half. In Figure 13.4, we summarize the evolution of CRE CDO collateral from 2000 to midyear 2005. Early CRE CDOs (1999 to 2003 vintage) were primarily backed by REIT debt, CMBS paper, or a mix of the two. Occasionally, RMBSs or whole loans were included in the collateral, but only in moderate amounts (typically less than 20 percent of the total pool size).

CRE CDO collateral pools changed dramatically in 2004 as real estate investors started to use CDOs to finance the acquisition of B-notes and

TABLE 13.2   CMBS Rating Actions, 2002–1H 05

Previous Rating	S&P			Fitch			Moody's		
	Up	Down	Default	Up	Down	Default	Up	Down	Default
AAA/Aaa	NA	6	—	NA	14	—	NA	33	—
AA/Aa2	278	10	—	409	10	—	292	37	—
A/A2	394	130	—	475	21	—	293	63	—
BBB/Baa2	330	97	5	423	77	—	281	149	—
BB/Ba2	133	132	—	227	65	—	69	114	—
B/B2	44	179	7	96	128	—	21	182	—
CCC/Caa1-Ca	11	27	24	9	97	15	4	63	—
Total	1,190	575		1,639	398		960	608	
Upgrade-to-downgrade ratio	2.07			4.12			1.58		

NA: Not available.
Source: Rating agencies and Citigroup.

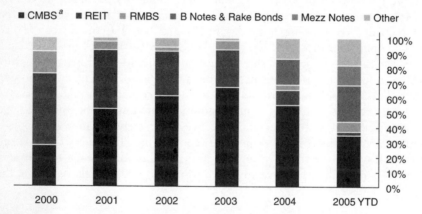

FIGURE 13.4   Collateral Evolution of CRE CDO
[a]Includes CMBS B-pieces. YTD through August 10, 2005.
Note: Excludes Taberna I and Taberna II, which are REIT trust preferred transactions.
Source: Citigroup.

rake bonds in significant amounts.[10] Other types of collateral, such as mezzanine loans, whole loans, credit tenant lease (CTL) loans, and trust preferred shares/securities, soon followed. CRE CDOs now contain a variety of products (slices of risk) available from a commercial real estate loan

TABLE 13.3 Range of Collateral Types in CRE CDOs Issued Through August 10, 2005

Collateral Type	Minimum (%)	Maximum (%)	Average (%)
CMBSs	0.0	82.8	30.4
B-notes and rake bonds	0.0	64.5	21.7
Mezzanine loans	0.0	56.7	11.7
REIT debt	0.0	12.4	3.6
RMBSs	0.0	49.0	5.9
Whole loans	0.0	49.3	7.1
Credit tenant lease loans	0.0	74.2	4.4
REIT trust preferreds	0.0	88.0	10.3

Source: Citigroup.

TABLE 13.4 CRE CDOs Notable for Their Unique Collateral Composition

Notable Transactions	Primary Collateral
Capital Trust RE CDO 2004-1	92% B-notes
Pure Mortgages 2004[a]	100% syndicated real estate term loans
Arbor Realty Mortgage Securities Series 2004-1	57% mezzanine loans
Caplease CDO 2005-1	74% credit tenant lease loans
Taberna Preferred Funding I	87% REIT trust preferreds

[a]Synthetic transaction.
Source: Citigroup.

financing, leading to considerable variation among CRE CDO collateral pools. In Table 13.3, we show the minimum, maximum, and average allocation to various collateral types for CRE CDOs closed between January 1, 2005, and August 15, 2005. Depending on the transaction, the bulk of the collateral pool could be any one of seven types of commercial real estate securities. We identify CRE CDOs notable for their unique collateral composition in Table 13.4. For example, Capital Trust RE CDO 2004-1 is almost exclusively backed by B-notes, while Caplease CDO 2005-1 is largely backed by CTLs.

BUILDING BLOCKS OF A CRE CDO

As the previous section highlighted, CRE CDOs are no longer backed just by CMBS certificates or REIT bonds, but now encompass the full spectrum of commercial loan risks. This evolution is coincident with the desire of CRE loan originators to parse a commercial real estate loan's risk and sell the slices to the most qualified buyers, who should also be the highest bidders. In this section we describe these CMBS by-products, as they are now a large part of CRE CDO collateral pools.

The road map for our collateral discussion is the stylized diagram in Figure 13.5 of the financing for Carolina Place Mall, a $235 million commercial property located in Pineville, North Carolina. At the top of the capital structure, the senior A-note was placed in a REMIC structure (CMBS transaction), while the junior A-note was set aside as an individual rake bond in the CMBS transaction and was later purchased by a CDO (Sorin Real Estate CDO I). Beneath the A-notes are two pari passu B-notes, one that was sold to another CDO and one that was sold to an insurance

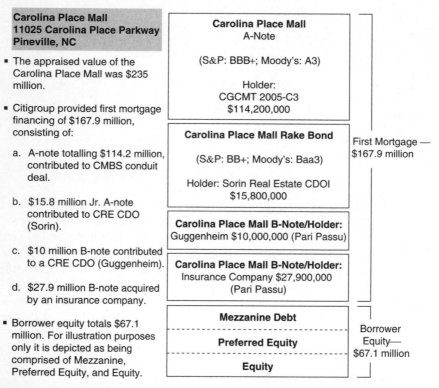

FIGURE 13.5   The Various Levels of Leverage: 11025 Carolina Place Parkway, Pineville, North Carolina
Source: Citigroup.

company. The rest of the property was financed from the borrower's equity, although it, too, could have been tranched into mezzanine debt, preferred shares, and equity if the borrower had required further financing. Each of these security types is discussed in the following subsections.

B-Notes and Rake Bonds

As Figure 13.5 illustrates, one of the most common ways to create subordinate debt is simply to sell junior portions of the secured mortgage loan. In this example, one junior position was sold into a REMIC for issuance as a rake bond, while two more junior loans were sold directly (outside of the REMIC) as B-notes. The subordinated positions of the secured mortgage may be structured as a participation in the first-loss portion of the loan, or they may be documented as a separate, subordinated note. Regardless, the division of the first mortgage is usually referred to as an A-note and a B-note (even when the subordinate position is via a participation without the separate, registered legal note) and offers the subordinate buyer the comfort of security in the property with attendant rights, although the position is subordinated to the A-note mortgage position. Several real estate players see value in having a secured mortgage interest as it has a direct secured claim to the underlying property even if the borrower files for bankruptcy.

This A/B note subordination method for dividing a credit interest has existed for many years and was first used in CMBS transactions in 1997 and 1998. At that time and in an event of default, the subordinate note buyer usually had no formalized input in the loan workout other than through its right to buy out the A-note for par plus accrued interest. Thus, B-note positions were truly subordinate interests in the loan position. But in recent years, these notes have developed substantial rights in directing the workout recovery efforts of the servicer in a defaulted loan situation. Subordinate positions now may have the right to approve workout actions of the servicer, to replace the servicer, or to receive servicer advances, or even the right to an exclusive buyout period at market levels or at traditional par plus interest.[11] The development of these extra rights has clearly broadened B-note investor appeal, as evidenced by their increased issuance, which is illustrated in Figure 13.6.

Recent subordinated note structures have become so complex that some designate losses within the notes themselves. These notes may still be placed in a CMBS REMIC structure or a CRE CDO, or privately placed outside the transaction. In the case where the note is placed within a CMBS REMIC trust, it may be entitled to advancing by the servicer but that right may be extinguished as soon as an event of default has occurred. We tend to refer to these positions as B-notes, although many industry participants refer to them as "rakes" or "legs" to signify that this part of the mortgage is usually

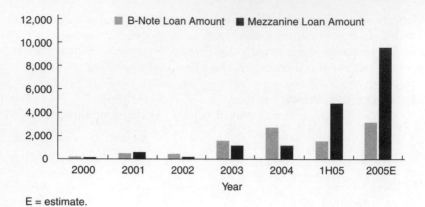

E = estimate.

FIGURE 13.6 Historical B-Note Amount and Mezzanine Loan Amounts in CMBS Transactions, 2000–2005E (Loans of $50 Million or More; $ millions)
E: Estimate.
Source: Intex Solutions and Citigroup.

not cross-collateralized with the rest of the trust. Many market participants call them B-notes when the participation is placed outside the trust and call the position a rake when it is still within the trust. The variation and room for confusion in the naming of subordinate positions means investors should always clarify the credit position and rights of each B-note that is being considered as an investment.

Second Lien Loans

Although not included in the example shown in Figure 13.5, second lien loans, or second mortgages, can also be placed against a property, but these are less common because the rating agencies tend to penalize the overall subordination levels of the first mortgage loan when there is a secured position behind the primary loan. Nonetheless, CDO investors should expect to see the occasional second mortgage loan within CRE CDOs. In those instances investors should ask for a summary of the intercreditor rights granted to the second mortgage position and ensure that the second lien holder has the expertise to work out what can be a very tricky secured but subordinated loan position.

Mezzanine Loans

The more common type of leverage in recent CRE CDO transactions comes from lenders funding a property loan secured by the equity interest of the borrower but unsecured as to the property itself. In this case, the loan has nothing to do with the mortgage position and is usually secured by the borrower's equity in the real estate property. Taking security in the property's equity is usually established by an intercreditor agreement between the mezzanine lender and the first mortgage. These mezzanine loans are also popular with some real estate investors that prefer to have direct recourse to the borrower, as they are not bothered with the first mortgage and its participations in an event of default. At the same time, these loans usually have the right to cure a default in the mortgage, and many now have the right to advise a special servicer or buy out the first mortgage. But even when these mortgages have few rights, sophisticated lenders can often assert their interests. In the case of the COMM 2001-FL4A transaction, a mezzanine loan on a defaulted hotel portfolio actually bought the B-note after the loan default, giving the mezzanine lender access to the B-note's workout direction rights and enabling that subordinate loan buyer to direct the special servicer to extend the loan. This was a rare and extraordinary instance, but the point is that an experienced and deep-pocketed CRE CDO manager can be very beneficial for the overall performance of the CDO.

Preferred Equity

Commercial properties can be leveraged further through the issuance of preferred shares, which entitle the lender to cash flow payments to the extent that the cash flow is available after payments to lenders. Preferred shares give the lender very little recourse other than to sit passively by during a loan default. This type of leverage usually is not well disclosed, because it does not require an intercreditor agreement and ranks last in the repayment schedule. Preferred equity can bring the total loan-to-value ratio to 90 percent or more.

Whole Loans

Having reviewed these potential leverage vehicles of a commercial loan, we see that each loan can be sliced in many different portions, which makes any given commercial real estate investment difficult to analyze. We should also note that a simple whole loan can be placed in a CRE CDO transaction, as can a construction loan that has future advancing obligations. Because simple (nonstructured) secured loans are relatively straightforward, we do not elaborate on them here.

CMBS First Loss Positions or B-Pieces

CMBS transactions are one of the few asset-backed securities in which the entire liability structure is sold to third parties, including the first-loss position (CDOs being the other notable exception). Sophisticated commercial real estate firms typically purchase the first-loss piece, which is unrated and can range from 1 to 2 percent of the overall pool balance. These firms have the personnel and resources to visit every asset in the pool to make their own (independent) assessments of its default likelihood. Should a particular loan seem too risky, these investors can often prevent the loan from entering the collateral pool (a "kick-out"). Thus, the B-piece buyer is positioned to *eliminate* collateral that could default rather than to assess the loans and attempt to extract a price that covers anticipated defaults. This is especially true when, as today, there are fewer than 10 first-loss piece buyers and the market power of each is strong—the individual asset opinion of one is usually sufficient to have the risky loan removed from the pool. As can be imagined, the negotiation between an issuer and the first-loss piece buyer can be heated as it can result in removal of 2 to 10 percent of a pool from the transaction.

All CMBS investors have benefited from this process. CMBS performance has been strong, and first-loss investors that originally thought their investments would be eliminated via delinquency in just three to five years have been surprised to see many of their 1997 to 2000 investments experience very few losses and earn excessive returns. Many of these original first-loss piece buyers have gone on to tap the CDO market with their seasoned collateral pools.

Traditional big first-loss buyers have been LNR Partners, Midland Loan Services, GMAC Commercial Mortgage, J. E. Robert Companies, Allied Capital, CW Capital, ARCap, Clarion Partners, Orix, and Criimi Mae. But this list has dwindled recently as CW Capital has purchased Criimi Mae and Allied Capital, and as Orix no longer actively buys B-piece paper. This mix of mortgage REITs and opportunity funds usually also buys the single-B certificates and some of the double-B certificates to make the underwriting exercise economical. These certificates typically have coupons set near the triple-A levels but sell for a deep discount.

First-loss buyers are usually also the special servicers for loans that become more than 60 days delinquent, and therefore they are in control in workout situations (subject to the CMBS transaction's pooling and servicing agreement).[12] Natural selection plays a role in which entity services CMBS pools as issuers do not select a first-loss buyer or servicer that the market views as being incapable of servicing and working out a pool since this negative perception affects the ability to sell all of the transactions' bonds. This investor/servicer arrangement has been effective for minimizing loan losses, but more importantly, it has helped CMBS transactions to avoid the inclusion of problem loans, as discussed earlier. Today, servicer quality is quite good and is not a distinguishing factor in CMBS transactions.

CRE CDO MANAGERS AND SPONSORS

Who's Who

CRE CDO collateral managers generally fall into one of three categories. The first category is asset manager—those managers who have large portfolios and actively manage funds in many debt and equity markets, including the commercial real estate market. These managers are typically interested in growing assets under management by leveraging existing infrastructure and market knowledge. However, asset managers have largely been absent from the CRE CDO market of late, in large part because CMBS spreads are quite tight and the CDO arbitrage is not sufficient to compel them to action. Should this condition change, investors should expect to see asset managers become active again. Instead, mortgage REITs and real estate loan investors, the other two categories of managers, have dominated recent issuance. The business rationale for CDO issuance for most of these managers, as stated, is to achieve term financing with a low cost of funds and no mark-to-market risks. Table 13.5 identifies all of the CRE CDO issuers through October 2005.

What to Look for in a CRE CDO Manager

As non-CUSIPed securities (a.k.a. uncertificated securities) are added to CRE CDO collateral pools, the role of collateral manager is becoming increasingly important. B-note and mezzanine loan investments require vigilant attention because of their subordinated positions, unrated status, and widely varying rights and obligations. Should the property supporting one of these loans become troubled, the subordinate lender often has the right to take corrective action to preserve its investment, but this takes time, adequate staffing, skill, and, sometimes, a lot of money. Hence, the skill and financial resources of the real estate investor (collateral manager) can have a material impact on recovery should a default occur.

We suggest that investors consider the following characteristics regarding CRE CDO collateral managers, in addition to their regular due diligence process (these criteria can be relaxed for static transactions provided that the investor is able to reunderwrite each of the securities):

- Does the manager have a track record in each of the security classes in which it intends to invest (or in which it is permitted to invest)?
- Does the manager have experience in the workout of defaulted assets?
- Does the manager have experience with the operation of commercial properties (for managers that plan to invest in the controlling classes of subordinate debt)?

TABLE 13.5   CRE CDO Collateral Managers/Sponsors

Asset Managers	Mortgage REITs	Real Estate Loan or Opportunity Investors
Babson Capital Management, LLC	Anthracite Capital, Inc. (BlackRock)	Brascan Real Estate Financial Partners
Ellington Management Group, LLC	ARCap REIT, Inc.	Five Mile Capital Partners
ING Baring (U.S.) Capital Corporation	Newcastle Investment Corp. (Fortress)	Guggenheim Structured Real Estate Advisors
MFS Investment Management	Capital Lease Funding, Inc.	CW Capital LLC (Allied)
Putnam Investments	CT Investment Management Co., LLC	Sorin Capital Management, LLC
Wells Fargo	Arbor Commercial Mortgage, LLC	HSH Nordbank AG
Alliance Capital Management L.P.	LNR Property Corp.	J. E. Robert Companies
Prima Capital Advisors	Gramercy Capital Corp.	Taberna Capital Management.
TIAA Advisory Services	NorthStar Realty Finance Corp.	GMAC Institutional Advisors, LLC
		G Funds Asset Management (GMAC)
		Structured Credit Partners

Source: Citigroup.

- If needed to maximize recovery, does the manager have the financial wherewithal or access to capital to buy out the senior note holders and obtain attendant rights?
- Is the manager adequately staffed to monitor the properties and respond to investor inquiries?

Naturally, there are many more questions that could, and should, be asked, but these alone will lead to a lengthy and informative discussion.

CRE CDO INVESTORS: A DIVERSE GROUP

To date, CRE CDO investors are a mixed group covering several continents and many lines of business. The general investor profile for Citigroup

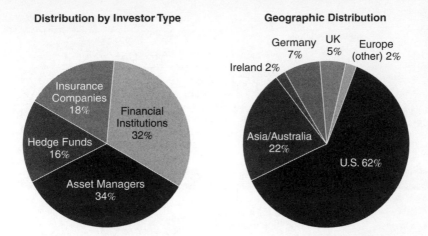

Distribution by Investor Type

Insurance Companies 18%
Financial Institutions 32%
Hedge Funds 16%
Asset Managers 34%

Geographic Distribution

Germany 7%
UK 5%
Europe (other) 2%
Ireland 2%
Asia/Australia 22%
U.S. 62%

Note: Data cover the trailing 12 months as of September 2005.

FIGURE 13.7   The Investor Base for CRE CDOs Is Broad
Note: Data cover the trailing 12 months as of September 2005.
Source: Citigroup.

CRE CDOs closed recently is shown in Figure 13.7. Hedge funds, financial institutions, asset managers, and insurance companies are all significant CRE CDO investors. Furthermore, many of these institutions are located outside of North America. This stands in contrast with CMBS issuance, which is sold almost entirely to North American insurance companies and asset managers, although the mix can vary significantly from deal to deal. Thus, CRE CDOs have broadened the investor base for commercial real estate dramatically.

KEY EVENTS IN THE CRE CDO MARKET

A Market Is Born

Many early CRE CDOs were viewed simply as sector-specific ABS CDOs, but as issuance grew and collateral pools evolved, it became clear that CRE CDOs were a segment of the CDO market unto themselves. The first commercial real estate CDO was Diversified REIT Trust 1999-1, a transaction supported by a static pool of senior unsecured debt issued by REITs and had no CMBS certificates. However, the second CRE CDO, Fortress CBO Investments I, did have CMBSs, and it showed the CRE market that CRE CDOs could be used to finance subordinate CRE debt.

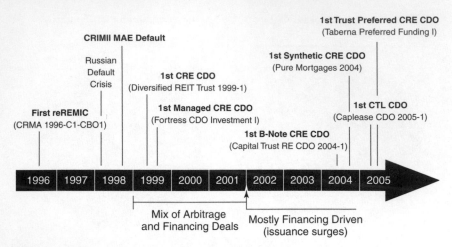

FIGURE 13.8 Key Events in the History of CRE CDOs
Source: Citigroup.

CMBSs soon became a CRE CDO collateral staple. Figure 13.8 illustrates the evolution from reREMICs (the precursor of CRE CDOs) to modern CRE CDOs, including key events that shaped the CRE CDO market and several CRE CDO firsts.

CRE CDOs closed before 2001 were issued for balance sheet/financing or arbitrage reasons and, thus, could be either static or lightly managed transactions. However, by 2001 most deals were executed for arbitrage reasons as asset managers such as Ellington Capital Management, ING Baring Capital Corporation, Alliance Capital Management, DL Babson, and others sought to build assets under management. Early investors were often traditional CDO investors, who viewed CRE CDOs simply as sector-specific CDOs, and traditional CMBS investors, who were eager to pick up excess spread on an asset class that they already knew and understood.[13]

This arrangement would have continued but for CDO investors' growing disenchantment with the performance of arbitrage CBOs during the spike in corporate default rates in 2001/2002. CDO equity of any type became very difficult to place as many traditional CBO investors (e.g., insurance companies) stopped buying. *Arbitrage* CRE CDO issuance plummeted, as did arbitrage CDO issuance in general.[14]

The Rise of CRE CDOs as a Source of Financing

CRE CDO issuance did not fall on the whole, however, as *financing* CRE CDO issuance surged in 2002 even as *arbitrage* CRE CDO issuance fell.

TABLE 13.6 Subordinate CRE Financing Alternatives (Assumes a Double-B Collateral Pool)

	Repo	Line of Credit	CRE CDO
Lender approval	Yes	None	None[a]
Margin requirements (mark-to-market)	Yes	Sort of[b]	None
Financing rate (spread over LIBOR)	85–150bp	110–150bp[c]	LIBOR + 40bp[d]
Leverage[e]	2–5×	2–5×	~10×
Tenor	Daily	Years	Matched to collateral
Recourse to borrower	Yes	Yes	No

[a]Manager discretion witHighn predefined limits.
[b]Advances may be limited by a borrowing base.
[c]Depends on financial strength of parent as well as the nature of the assets.
[d]Excluding up-front costs
[e]Defined as the amount of total capital divided by equity capital. Lower leverage for subordinated debt such as mezzanine loans and B-notes. Higher leverage for whole loans.
Source: Citigroup.

Mortgage REITs[15] aggressively began to tap the CDO market as a source of funding. The rationale was simple: CDO technology provided term funding, a low cost of funds, and no mark-to-market margin requirements. Few, if any, of these features were available from the banks (see Table 13.6), though they were sorely needed. We are certain that the lessons of Criimi Mae's bankruptcy in 1998, which was triggered by sharp mark-to-market volatility, were not (and still are not) far from many subordinate CMBS investors' minds.[16] Thus, many of these subordinate CMBS investors are now CRE CDO issuers.

Furthermore, because many subordinate CMBS investors were simply looking to replicate historical levels of leverage, they often held the equity and even mezzanine tranches of any CRE CDO they issued. As a result, placement of CRE CDO transactions was relatively easy (recall that arbitrage deals were hampered by the need to place CDO equity in 2001 and 2002), and issuance surged for financing-type CRE CDOs, while arbitrage-type issuance evaporated, save for a few transactions.

The use of CDOs as a financing tool has had an immediate and significant impact on the balance sheets of many real estate mortgage companies. Consider the source and maturity of debt for Anthracite Capital, Inc. (see Figure 13.9). This subordinate real estate investor primarily funded itself with repurchase agreements (repos) and lines of credit prior to 2002.

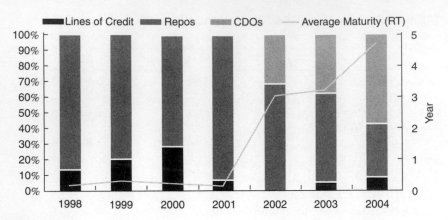

FIGURE 13.9 Funding Sources and Weighted Average Time to Maturity for a Prominent CRE Investor (Excluding Commercial Mortgage Loan Pools), 1998 to 2004
Source: Citigroup.

The average maturity of this debt was measured in weeks, while the average maturity of its assets was measured in years—a clear mismatch of assets and liabilities. In short, the investor was at the mercy of the banks and general economic conditions. With the advent of CDOs, the firm extended the average maturity of debt to nearly five years—much closer to the 8- to 10-year tenor of the assets—and eliminated margin requirements for a large portion of its funding.

Thus, CDOs provide an excellent asset/liability match for mortgage REITs as well as others. A passage from the 2003 annual report of LNR Property Corporation nicely summarizes the importance of CDO technology:

"[CDOs] have been an excellent means for us to further enhance the value of the securities we already own, better match our assets and liabilities, reduce our interest rate and refinancing risk, improve our liquidity position, and strengthen our overall financial condition."

The Push for Flexibility

Another structural shift also was taking place quietly. Many 2002 to 2003 vintage financing trades were executed in static form to achieve a low cost of funds. Furthermore, investors and especially traditional CMBS investors, who were becoming a large component of the CRE CDO investor universe, preferred to reunderwrite every credit and every security that backed the CRE CDO transaction. These investors simply were not comfortable with giving managers a great deal of investment flexibility and they preferred static deals. CDO underwriters and issuers were able to accommodate this preference because spreads were still generous, collateral was relatively long dated, and equity returns were a small concern (remember that the manager/sponsor often retained the equity). As a result, static financing transactions dominated issuance. Ultimately, however, restrictions imposed by static structures proved too constraining, and managed CRE CDOs reemerged in 2004, albeit in a modest form initially.

Managed CRE transactions reemerged for two reasons. First, the addition of subordinate debt, such as mezzanine loans and B-notes (see earlier discussion on the evolution of CRE CDO collateral pools, "Building Blocks of a CRE CDO"), has shortened the average lives of modern CRE CDO collateral pools. Thus, to avoid premature deleveraging of the transaction (which lowers CDO equity returns), managed transactions permit reinvestment of principal dollars. Second, traditional CDO investors, who are more comfortable with giving collateral managers trading discretion, returned to the CRE CDO market, and they seem to be more permissive than many traditional CMBS investors with respect to portfolio trading.

Still, most managed CRE CDOs only permit the sale of securities that are at risk. Thus, reinvestment of principal proceeds is limited to principal dollars from the sale of a credit-risk security, principal from prepayment, or principal from repayment due to maturity or amortization within a prescribed time frame. We call these "lightly managed" transactions. Only a few recent transactions permit the collateral manager to trade collateral at his or her discretion ("fully managed" transactions) and even then there are limits to the amount that can be traded in a given year (e.g., 15 percent of assets) (see Figure 13.10).

The Current State of the CRE CDO Market

The typical 2005-vintage CRE CDO is a fully managed or lightly managed transaction with a five-year reinvestment period and a three- to five-year no-call period. It is executed for financing purposes, and thus it includes a variety of collateral types, ranging from very subordinate mezzanine loans and preferred securities to whole loans and CMBSs. In addition, because of the financing nature of the transaction, collateral pools have become relatively chunky. It is not uncommon that the largest obligor represents 5 to 10 percent of the collateral pool, while the largest 10 obligors represent as much as 50 percent of the collateral pool.

The average collateral quality of CRE CDOs also varies significantly, from triple B to triple C, as does the leverage permitted in the CRE CDO transaction. For BBB- rated collateral, leverage of 18× can be achieved

■ Static Financing ■ Managed Financing*a* ■ Static Arbitrage ■ Managed Arbitrage*a*

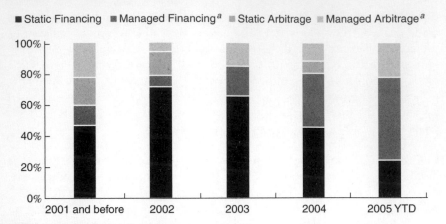

FIGURE 13.10 Evolution of Static versus Managed and Arbitrage versus Financing CRE CDOs, 2001 and Before to 2005 YTD

*a*Managed transactions are mostly lightly managed, which means that the manager is given the ability to reinvest principal proceeds for a certain amount of time and sell credit-risk credits. Discretionary trading ability was typically not granted. *Source:* Citigroup.

while 2× leverage may be achieved for triple-C collateral pools.[17] Collateral managers often retain all noninvestment-grade collateral and equity, although we expect more CRE CDO junior debt and equity to be available in the future.

INVESTOR ANALYSIS OF CRE CDOs

Proper analysis of a CRE CDO requires a unique blend of securitization and real estate knowledge, which is rare. Thus, investors generally approach the CRE CDO market from either a traditional CDO perspective or a traditional real estate investment perspective. Traditional CDO investors typically begin by analyzing the CDO structure itself: the leverage, the coverage tests and covenants, and the general characteristics of the collateral pool. By contrast, traditional real estate investors are likely to study each property in the transaction, building up to an opinion on the collateral pool as a whole. Only then will traditional real estate investors begin to consider the CDO tranching and tests. In our opinion, investors should strive to combine these two approaches, but in the meantime, we suggest resources and techniques that should help both types of investors begin their analysis process.

CRE CDO Analysis for Traditional CDO Investors

Traditional CDO investors (CLO, CBO, or ABS CDO investors) are familiar with CDO technology—the terminology, tests, structures, and so on—but are often at a loss when the discussion turns to the nuances of CRE collateral (e.g., the difference between a rake bond and a B-note). For these investors, we hope that our discussion of CRE collateral in the section "Building Blocks of a CRE CDO" has been helpful. Beyond that, we suggest that traditional CDO investors review the rating agency CDO criteria. Key papers are:

Moody's

Moody's Modeling Approach to Rating Structured Finance Cash Flow CDO Transactions, September 26, 2005.

U.S. CMBS: Emerging Trends in Commercial Real Estate CDOs, May 19, 2005.

Moody's Approach to Revolving Facilities in CDOs Backed by Commercial Real Estate Securities, July 29, 2004.

Moody's Approach to Rating Static CDOs Backed by Commercial Real Estate Securities, June 17, 2004.

Standard & Poor's

General Cash Flow Analytics for CDO Securitizations, August 25, 2004.

Global Cash Flow and Synthetic CDO Criteria, March 21, 2002.

Fitch Ratings

Rating Methodology for U.S. Revolving Commercial Real Estate Loan CDOs, September 28, 2005.

Global Rating Criteria for Collateralized Debt Obligations, September 13, 2004.

Cash Flow CDOs 101 for CMBS Investors, September 29, 2004.

Traditional CDO investors will note that the rating agency approaches to CRE CDOs are largely similar to the techniques employed for ABS CDOs (Moody's is the notable exception here, although most CDO investors will readily grasp its approach). Investors can then insert their own opinions regarding default, recovery, or correlation for each asset into these general analysis frameworks.

CRE CDO Analysis for Traditional Real Estate Investors

Many traditional real estate investors are skeptical of CRE CDOs, which convert a collection of lower-rated real estate positions into higher-rated

TABLE 13.7 North-Star III CDO Default Model

Collateral Piece[a]	Original Balance ($)	% of Pool	Rating	Loss Severity (%)						Weighted Loss Severity (% × Loss Severity)					
				B	BB	BBB	A	AA	AAA	B	BB	BBB	A	AA	AAA
Stanford Term Loan C	13,593,832	3.38	A2					15	20	0.00	0.00	0.00	0.00	0.51	0.68
WAMU Term Loan C	13,000,000	3.23	Aa2						15	0.00	0.00	0.00	0.00	0.00	0.48
GSMS 1998 C1	11,500,000	2.86	BB–		15	20	25	30	35	0.00	0.43	0.57	0.71	0.86	1.00
DLJCM 2000 CKP1	10,000,000	2.49	B+		15	20	25	30	35	0.00	0.37	0.50	0.62	0.75	0.87
Reckson Operating Prtshp	10,000,000	2.49	Baa3			15	20	25	30	0.00	0.00	0.37	0.50	0.62	0.75
SBM7 2000-C3	10,000,000	2.49	BB+			15	20	25	30	0.00	0.00	0.37	0.50	0.62	0.75
GSMS 2003-C1	9,085,000	2.26	BBB-			15	20	25	30	0.00	0.00	0.34	0.45	0.56	0.68
MLMI 1998-C1	8,765,000	2.18	Ba2			15	20	25	30	0.00	0.00	0.33	0.44	0.54	0.65
COMM 2003-FL8	8,000,000	1.99	Baa3			15	20	25	30	0.00	0.00	0.30	0.40	0.50	0.60
MLMI 1997-C1	8,000,000	1.99	B		15	20	25	30	35	0.00	0.30	0.40	0.50	0.60	0.70
GCCFC 2004-FL2A	8,000,000	1.99	Baa3			15	20	25	30	0.00	0.00	0.30	0.40	0.50	0.60
ISTAR Financial Inc.	8,000,000	1.99	Baa3			15	20	25	30	0.00	0.00	0.30	0.40	0.50	0.60
FUNBC 2001-C4	7,339,000	1.82	Ba3		15	20	25	30	35	0.00	0.27	0.36	0.46	0.55	0.64
General Growth Properties	6,982,500	1.74	Ba2			15	20	25	30	0.00	0.00	0.26	0.35	0.43	0.52

Deal	Balance		Rating	BB	BBB	A	AA	AAA	B	BB	BBB	A	AA	AAA[b]
AHR 2004-HY1A	6,745,000	1.68	BBB−		15	20	25	30	0.00	0.00	0.25	0.34	0.42	0.50
MLMI 1999-C1	6,735,000	1.67	BBB			15	20	25	0.00	0.00	0.00	0.25	0.33	0.42
MLMT 2005-MKB2	6,373,000	1.58	Baa2			15	20	25	0.00	0.00	0.00	0.24	0.32	0.40
CSFB 2004-HC1A	6,000,000	1.49	Baa2			15	20	25	0.00	0.00	0.00	0.22	0.30	0.37
COMM 2004-CNL	6,000,000	1.49	BBB−		15	20	25	30	0.00	0.00	0.22	0.30	0.37	0.45
MSC 1997-XL1	6,000,000	1.49	Caa2	20	25	30	35	40	0.22	0.30	0.37	0.45	0.52	0.60
GMACC 2004-C3	5,947,000	1.48	BBB			15	20	25	0.00	0.00	0.00	0.22	0.30	0.37
Aero 1 HQ Finance Trust	5,564,000	1.38	BBB−		15	20	25	30	0.00	0.00	0.21	0.28	0.35	0.42
GMACC 2000-C1	5,500,000	1.37	B1	15	20	25	30	35	0.00	0.21	0.27	0.34	0.41	0.48
AHR 2002-CIBA	5,500,000	1.37	Baa3		15	20	25	30	0.00	0.00	0.21	0.27	0.34	0.41
Total	402,141,548													

Model-Predicted Support (%)	B	BB	BBB	A	AA	AAA[b]
	0.22	2.35	11.79	18.29	23.40	28.86

Actual Credit Support (%)		BB	BBB	A−	AA	AAA[b]
		5.75	9.75	17.25	21.50	26.50

[a] Top collateral above $5.5 million is displayed.
[b] CDO tranche rating.
Source: Intex Solutions and Citigroup.

(and lower-rated) securities. Given the poor rating performance of many corporate bond–backed CDOs, this skepticism is understandable. Furthermore, CDOs seem to have a language unto themselves; terms such as WARF, OC and IC tests, and diversity score are just a few that seem to obfuscate the mechanics (and analysis) of CDOs.[18] So, with all of these unanswered questions, how would a traditional real estate investor begin to evaluate a potential CRE CDO investment?

We suggest that traditional real estate investors start with their expertise, which is the collateral. In fact, it is surprising how insightful a simple estimation of collateral losses for varying degrees of economic stress can be toward understanding the required amount of subordination for each CRE CDO tranche.[19] To get started, investors may consider a simple default and recovery matrix, which lists each asset in the left column and lists increasing rating levels from left to right along the top row. The rating levels correspond to the CDO tranche ratings and also to progressively higher severity rates (loss rates) for the collateral, which depend on the difference between the rating of the collateral item and the CDO tranche. Once the matrix is constructed, an expected loss can be calculated as the product of the notional amount times the loss severity for each rating category and the result placed in columns further to the right in the matrix. For this initial analysis we assume that *all* collateral will default; the only variable is the recovery amount, which varies depending on the CDO tranche being considered. This is severe, but it is also insightful when evaluating the subordination levels of the CDO.

The result of this analysis is shown in Table 13.7 for a recently issued real estate CDO, although we limit the collateral display to only the larger assets to simplify the presentation. For this initial review, every asset is assigned a loss severity, starting one level above its initial loan rating, which creates small initial expected losses that increases with each rating category to ensure that each level receives progressively stronger credit protection with its higher rating level. We assume that the starting severity rate is 15 percent for each certificate, which we have found usually makes for a close initial calibration with rating agency levels. The cumulative loss projection for all assets, which represents the total credit support one might expect for each asset rating of the pool, is shown at the bottom right of Table 13.7. For comparison, we have included the actual credit support levels of the CRE CDO transaction also. In this case, the back-of-the-envelope values are generally within a few percentage points of the actual subordination levels, and in our experience, this result is not atypical.

Beyond this initial simple analysis, investors should use the matrix for a targeted default analysis of specific credits by adding up the required subordination from the default of specific assets. To target specific assets, we add columns with key credit characteristics of each asset. These key characteristics can be as simple as the position in the credit stack, servicing control rights, overall leverage, and coverage. This simple listing of characteristics for each position creates a credit worksheet and usually leads us to believe that one asset or another could be more inclined to default and/or experience high loss rates.

For instance, in Table 13.8 we examine three different CDOs and default 5 percent of the triple-B certificates at a 50 percent loss, 10 percent of the double-B assets at an 80 percent loss rate, and 10 percent of the unrated assets at a 100 percent loss. Although the results do not match up as well as in the previous simple model exercise, we also do not come away feeling that any one of the three transactions lacks lower-rated credit enhancement to withstand our 10 percent single-B, 10 percent double-B, and 5 percent triple-B default scenario. (It should also be noted that we chose our scenario rather arbitrarily.) So again, it is also possible for a full credit analysis of these collateral pools to lead us to default more or less of a pool. This can quickly change our credit opinion in favor of one transaction over another.

TABLE 13.8 CDO Default Matrix Analysis

	B	BB	BBB–	BBB	A	AA	AAA
N-Star IIII							
Regular matrix scenario[a]	0.22	2.35	5.46	13.34	19.83	24.94	30.40
B/BB/BBB default scenario[b]	0.22	3.07	7.60	15.31	22.76	27.56	32.71
Credit support (%)		5.75		9.75	17.25	21.50	26.50
Newcastle CDO							
Regular matrix scenario	0.00	0.35	3.19	9.58	16.87	23.26	28.26
B/BB/BBB default scenario	0.00	0.52	4.13	10.45	18.64	24.82	29.61
Credit support (%)		5.00	5.00	9.10	13.10	17.70	22.40
Crest 2004							
Regular matrix scenario	0.00	5.73	13.74	19.11	24.34	29.03	34.65
B/BB/BBB default scenario	0.00	7.90	19.21	24.50	31.06	35.06	40.00
Credit support (%)		24.50	27.25	28.75	38.75	44.75	57.00

[a]Regular scenario marks 15 expected loss at rating above collateral rating, adding 5 for each rating above the previous.
[b] Default scenario takes 5 of BBB, 10 of BB, and 10 of unrated collateral and defaults at 50, 80, and 100 at each rating level, respectively.
Source: Citigroup.

Thus, if investors analyze and default just a few targeted assets in a CDO, a simple default matrix/worksheet created in Excel can provide a tool to quickly assess the credit protection of each CDO tranche. Overall, we think that traditional real estate credit types take comfort from an initial triage that can be performed in a spreadsheet format before delving deeper into the complexities of the CDO cash flow structure.

CDO investors will realize that these analyses are greatly simplified, as CDOs incorporate OC tests to preserve credit enhancement for the senior notes at the expense of junior debt and equity. Thus, the estimated credit support for the lower-rated classes under this simplified analysis tends to be lower than the actual credit support for the junior debt and vice versa for the senior tranches. Another very important factor that we did not consider is the correlation of collateral performance, which certainly will influence the subordination of each tranche. Thus, we suggest that non-AAA investors take their analysis to the next step by modeling individual defaults of the assets highlighted by their worksheet/matrix. Regardless of the amount of due diligence, the matrix forces one to pause and consider the credit rating and potential recovery that the agencies have attributed to each asset. This exercise can highlight assets that credit investors would consider misrated and worthy of further study.

In addition, we recommend *Cash Flow CDOs 101 for CMBS Investors*[20] as a good short read that explains most of what investors should understand.

ADDITIONAL SUGGESTED COLLATERAL ANALYSIS

The biggest challenge for CRE CDO investors is the evaluation of the default probability, default correlation, and recovery prospects for each item of collateral. This task can be especially difficult for traditional CDO investors who may be less familiar with the assets. Thus, in this section, we focus on the resources that are available to investors who want to estimate the prospective performance of the collateral. We first consider CMBS certificates and noncertificated assets second.

Analysis of CMBS Certificates

Unlike other ABS products, CMBS securities are not bought based on issuer name or servicer reputation, but based on each pool's loan content and leverage (subordination). As a result, a CMBS security backed by a high-quality (low-leverage) pool but with little credit support can be more risky than a CMBS security backed by a risky (high-leverage) pool but with extra subordinated bond classes. To help investors assess the risk/return trade-off of these two types of CMBS investments, we recommend that investors use customized default vectors such as the ones that we publish each month to predict future CMBS subordination levels and potential rating agency actions. We have written about this analysis in the past and stress that it can highlight CMBS certificates that could eventually take a loss or potentially have downgrades.[21]

In Table 13.9, we present a cutout of our monthly projected subordinate report, which liquidates all the fixed-rate triple-B and double-B certificates under a variety of higher stress levels that are intended to represent a realistic default scenario and some stress scenarios that the rating agencies consider. Effectively, this report translates specific troubled loans into defaults and then provides the resulting future projected subordination for each transaction. We feel that this marriage of current performance and current subordination provides the best-quality measure for any seasoned CMBS transaction. This type of projected collateral performance is relatively easy and can now be run in many programs like Trepp, Intex, or Yield Book.[22]

From a practical standpoint, we expect that most investors will use this analysis to flag troubled certificates that merit further investigation. Investors should also question whether the manager has realistically accounted for the potential loan losses from these troubled loans in their analysis. Our automated vectors use a simple 40 percent loss estimate.

The asset manager's specific knowledge of a troubled loan often suggests smaller losses, but not always. For example, in Table 13.9, we would be concerned about downgrades and future losses from the BACM 2001-1 and MSDW 2001-TOP1 BBBs and the CSFB 2001-CK1/CK3/CKN5/CKN6 and LBUBS 2001-C2/C3 BBs. Thus, many cash flow projection tools that have been developed to analyze CMBS pools can be helpful in considering CDO collateral.

Analysis of Uncertificated Securities

Analyzing other securities beyond the modeled CMBS collateral is more difficult. A large number of uncertificated securities (e.g., mezzanine loans, B-notes) are now included in CRE collateral pools. Often, these securities are not publicly rated by any of the agencies (though frequently shadow rated by the agencies for the purposes of the CDO), and so investors are left to assess the overall leverage of each position, along with the control rights of each, and to question the manager's expertise in selecting the position. For B-notes, mezzanine loans and preferred equity positions the exercise involves a full loan underwriting to determine the total leverage of the position and whether the property will be able to service that leverage throughout

TABLE 13.9 Monthly Subordination Report, MB823 ($ millions)

Vintage/Deal	Balance ($) Orig.	Special Curr.	Delinq. Srver (%)	Perform. (%)	Projected Deliq. Prob.	Subordination Pct. CDR Pct.	Triple-B Subordination Pct. Orig.	Pct. Curr.	Rel. Drop Expected	DelSSH	DSCRH	Expected 7 May 11	DelSSH 11 May 16	DSCRH 12 Jan 24	Double-B Subordination Orig.	Curr.	Expected	DelSSH	DSCRH	Expected 12 May 12	DelSSH 11 May 19	DSCRH 11 Jan 18
2001	36,703.20	33,881.00																				
BACM 2001-1	948.1	851.7	0.8	2.19	2.01	0.6	8.77	9.18	9.1	8.46	5.46	High	High	High	4.33	4.36	4.09	3.15	1.4	High	High	
BACM 2001-PB1	938.3	844.2	0.77	1.92	2.2	2.91	10.01	9.91	8.54	7.33	0	Med.	Med.	High	4.75	4.53	4.15	1.54	3.92	High	High	High
BAFU 2001-C3	1,136.70	1,075.60	0	2.33	1.88	0.73	9.5	9.81	9.75	9.3	3.63	High	Med.	Med.	4.75	5.19	4.78	3.45	4.53	High	High	Med.
BSCMS 2001-TOP2	1,006.60	921.4	3.62	0.34	1.81	1.11	10.13	10.08	9.92	9.47	7.56	High	High		5.5	5.19	4.78	4.31	1.71	Med.	Med.	Med.
BSCMS 2001-TOP4	902.5	849.3	0.39	0.5	1.71	0.18	6	6.42	6.42	5.56	2.01	Low	High	High	3.5	3.68	3.68	2.08	0.9	Low	High	High
CSFB 2001-CF2	1,127.80	997.2	0.1	2.61	2.43	0.1	6	6.38	6.38	6.29	4.64	Med.	High	High	3	3.19	3.19	3.04	4.16	Low	High	High
CSFB 2001-CK1	997.1	919	0.42	1.22	2.54	0.55	9.28	9.58	9.56	9.58	3.96	High	High	High	4.5	4.16	4.1	3.46	0	Med.	Med.	Low
CSFB 2001-CK3	1,127.00	1,070.60	0.03	1.83	2.05	0.19	11.02	11.87	11.87	11.64	5.65	High	High	High	4.75	4.07	5.05	4.55	0	Med.	Med.	High
CSFB 2001-CKN5	1,072.80	1,015.80	1.55	4.03	2.58	0.36	10	9.54	9.54	8.98	5.25	Low	Med.	High	4.8	4.78	4.04	3.36	0	Med.	Med.	High
CSFB 2001-CKN6	986.4	915.3	0.3	3.16	2.04	0.85	9.61	9.4	9.28	8.29	5.41	High	High	High	4.63	4.87	4.32	3.16	0	High	High	High
CSFB 2001-CP4	1,211.50	1,159.10	0.41	1.28	2.1	0.42	9.75	10.34	10.34	9.52	4.65	High	High	High	4.54	4.66	4.68	3.54	0	Low	High	High
FUBA 2001-C1	1,308.30	1,177.10	6.97	1.07	1.95	0.09	9	9.37	9.37	8.97	7.23	Low	Med.	Med.	4.5	4.66	4.66	3.87	1.69	Low	Med.	Med.
FUNB 2001-C1	1,001.50	947.6	1.58	0.86	2.02	0.08	9	9.1	9.1	8.79	5.26	Low	Med.	High	4.75	5.42	3.53	2.78	0	Low	High	High
FUNB 2001-C2	818.8	779.4		2.06	2.24	0.26	9.45	9.45	9.45	9.17	6.45	High	High	High	4.25	5.57	4.42	3.81	0	Low	Med.	High
FUNB 2001-C3	978.6	921.6	2.24	3.16	1.76	0.83	10.75	11.2	11.14	8.43	5.06	High	Med.	High	5.25	5.03	5.28	3.88	3.02	Med.	High	High
FUNB 2001-C4	1,128.90	1,080.30	0	2.44	2	0.48	10.5	10.35	10.29	9.82	9.19	Low	High	High	5.25	5.3	5.5	3.76	0	Low	High	High
GECCMC 2001-1	1,002.90	920.2	0.16	1.49	2.33	0.96	10	10.62	10.62	9.58	5.54	High	High	High	4.88	4.67	4.96	3.6	4.67	Med.	High	High
GECCMC 2001-2	963.8	911.8	0.18	2.34	1.98	0.42	9.88	10.58	10.45	10	6.27	Med.	High	High	4.75	5.56	4.99	4.51	2.79	Med.	Med.	High
GECCMC 2001-3	864.1	786	1.59	4.06	2.47	1.12	10.25	10.44	10.05	9.22	2.45	High	High	High	5.25	4.71	3.69	2.65	0.12	High	Med.	High
GMACC 2001-C1	754.9	708.8	1.84	0.12	2.12	1.19	10.5	11.02	11.02	11.02	9.42	Med.	Low	Med.	5.25	4.7	5.56	5.56	2.09	Med.	Low	High
GMACC 2001-C2	1,070.70	1,025.40	0.43	3.77	2.16	0.04	10.38	11.02	8.93	8.15	5.94	High	High	High	5.25	5.21	3.99	3.23	2.09	High	High	Med.
JPMC 2001-C1	867.5	830.9		1.07	1.85	1.61	8.75	9.15	8.87	8.61	6.96	High	Med.	High	4.5	5.11	4.69	4.33	0.12	Med.	Med.	High
JPMC 2001-CIBC3	1,014.80	909.1		3.92	2.03	0.27	8.5	8.87	8.87	8.61	6.96	Med.	Med.	High	4.5	4.7	4.69	4.33	2.09	High	Low	High
JPMC 2001-CIBC	961.7	911.6		1.54	2.23	1.15	10.25	11.07	10.85	9.62	7.65	High	High	High	5	5.21	4.59	3.02	0.4	High	High	Low
JPMC 2001-CIBC2	1,319.10	1,248.60		2.35	1.98	0.62	9.5	9.99	9.95	9.63	7.59	Med.	High	High	4.87	5.11	4.99	4.57	1.79	Med.	Med.	High
LBUBS 2001-C3	1,380.70	1,322.40	1.84	2.67	1.8	0.34	8.5	8.98	8.98	7.9	5.06	High	High	High	4.38	4.62	4.58	2.98		Med.	Med.	High
LBUBS 2001-C3	1,209.90	1,158.80	0.43	0.48	1.69	0.23	7	7.31	7.31	6.5	3.92	High	High	High	3.5	3.65	3.64	2.27	1.98	Med.	Med.	High
LBUBS 2001-C7	713	560.7		2.08	1.73	0.25	6.25	6.5	6.5	6.39	5.35	High	Low	High	3.25	3.37	3.34	3.18	0.56	Med.	Low	High
MSDW 2001-IQ	623.6	424.1	6.77	6.81	2.11	0.34	5.5	6.99	6.99	6.99	5.41	High	High	High	2.5	3.18	3.18	2.78		Med.	High	High
MSDW 2001-PPM	1,156.40	1,022.90	0	1.81	1.81	0.03	6.88	10.11	10.12	10.12	4.66	High	High		2.75	3.18	4.06	2.56		High	High	Med.
MSDW 2001-TOP1	1,028.10	965.8	0	0.58	1.7	1.56	5.87	6.55	6.45	4.64	0	High	High	High	2.63	2.88	1.94	2.7	2.88	High	High	
MSDW 2001-TOP3	1,042.00	955.4	0	0.13	1.27	0.11	6.25	6.58	6.58	6.54	5.63	High	Med.	High	3	3.12	3.12	3.27	1.45	Med.	Med.	High
MSDW 2001-TOP5						0.03	6.25	6.82	6.82	6.82	6.32	Med.	High	Med.	3	3.27	3.27		2.52	Med.	Med.	Med.

DelSSH: Liquidate all currently delinquent and specially serviced loans and run remaining pool at 0.5% constant default rate (half a point default rate).

DSCRH: Same as DelSSH except also liquidate all loans with debt-to-service coverage ratios less than one.

Source: Citigroup.

the loan term. This analysis covers the property's lease expirations, the surrounding real estate market, and potential future revenues.

Such a detailed underwriting analysis is likely unnecessary for triple-A investors, but should be performed by investors in the lower credits of the transaction. As a general rule, we suggest that investors start with the trailing-12-month cash flow and compare it to what the asset manager has underwritten for each loan to determine whether the asset manager's expectations are realistic. When the debt coverage for the entire loan looks more than sufficient, we would not be too worried. Yet, for floating-rate loans or higher-leverage fixed-rate loans, investors should consider whether a loan could service all of its debt if interest rates were to rise. Thus, any leverage underwriting should consider the full property leverage, with all of the subordinate debt, as that will most likely help decide the overall probability of a default. We suggest that investors amend the matrix in Table 13.8 to include the total debt and estimates for each asset's carry costs under a variety of stressed rates.

Once the investor has reached a comfort level as to the expectation of default, the next consideration is an assessment of recovery value should the loan default. For this calculation we suggest that investors consider using a property yield several percentage points higher than current property yields to assess the investment's vulnerability to loss given its position in the total debt stack. An underwriting process just for CMBS loans is described in the article titled *101 Ways to Overleverage a CMBS Loan.*[23] Again, this is the type of analysis that can build off of the asset matrix that we described in the subsection entitled "CRE CDO Analysis for Traditional Real Estate Investors."

Finally, once investors have firm asset default expectations, cash flow modeling software (e.g., Intex) gives investors the ability to time the default of assets with an overlay of the CDO structure.[24] Thus, the final step in any CDO analysis should be to take the credit default expectations and translate them into cash flows that potential investors can price. We highly recommend that any investor considering CDO investing subscribe to one of the analytic tools and learn to use the many features that they provide. This final step enables investors to take our simple listing of asset credit characteristics and translate those expectations into cash flows that reflect the CDO structure.

None of these steps is easy; subordinate commercial real estate investing requires hard work and a lot of consideration. But investing in a pool of subordinated high-leverage first-loss loans is not to be taken lightly. We expect that over time, the investment exercise will become easier as investors develop templates with which to examine transactions.

APPENDIX: LIST OF CRE CDOs

Closing Date	Deal Name	Manager/Sponsor	Size ($)
Sep. 29, 2005	Taberna Preferred Funding III, Ltd.	Taberna Capital Management, LLC	779,200,000
Sep. 22, 2005	N-Star Real Estate CDO V	North Star Advisors, LLC	500,000,000
Sep. 15, 2005	Carbon Capital II Real Estate CDO 2005-1	BlackRock Financial Management Inc.	455,000,000
Aug. 25, 2005	Guggenheim Structured RE Funding 2005-2	Guggenheim Investment Management	305,800,000
Aug. 4, 2005	Capital Trust CDO III	CT Investment Management	341,000,000
Aug.15, 2005	LNR CDO III Ltd.	LNR Partners, Inc.	1,103,000,000
Jul. 26, 2005	Anthracite 2005-HY2 Ltd.	Blackrock Financial Management, Inc.	478,100,000
Jul. 21, 2005	Sorin Real Estate CDO I Ltd.	Sorin Capital Management	403,000,000
Jul. 15, 2005	FMC Real Estate CDO 2005-1	Five Mile Capital Partners	439,419,000
Jul. 14, 2005	Gramercy Real Estate CDO 2005-1	Gramercy Capital Corp.	1,000,000,000
Jun. 28, 2005	Taberna Preferred Funding II, Ltd.	Taberna Capital Management, LLC	1,042,750,000
Jun. 1, 2005	NorthStar Real Estate CDO IV	NS Advisors (in market)	400,000,000

Closing Date	Deal Name	Manager/Sponsor	Size ($)
May 25, 2005	Guggenheim Structured RE Funding 2005-1	Geggenheim Structured Real Estate Advisors	501,214,176
May 1, 2005	Prima Cap- ital CDO Ltd., 2005-1	Prima Capital Advisors, LLC	409,400,000
May 1, 2005	CW Capital Cobalt I Ltd.	CW Capital LLC	451,000,000
Apr. 19, 2005	Newcastle CDO VI Ltd.	Newcastle Investment Corp.	500,000,000
Mar. 15, 2005	G-Star 2005-5 Ltd.	GMAC Institutional Advisors, LLC	600,000,000
Mar. 15, 2005	Capital Trust RE CDO 2005-1 Ltd.	CT Investment Management Co., LLC (Capital Trust, Inc.)	337,754,776
Mar. 15, 2005	Taberna Preferred Funding I	Taberna Capital Management LLC.	728,000,000
Mar. 5, 2005	Caplease CDO 2005-1	Capital Lease Funding Inc.	300,000,000
Mar. 1, 2005	NorthStar Real Estate CDO III	NS Advisors	400,000,000
Jan. 19, 2005	Arbor Realty Mortgage Securities Series 2004-1	Arbor Commercial Mortgage, LLC	481,000,000
Dec. 15, 2004	Fairfield Street Solar 2004-1	Massachusetts Financial Services Company	512,013,958
Nov. 24, 2004	Pure Mortgages 2004	HSH Nordbank AG	1,041,300,000
Nov. 1, 2004	Crest 2004-1	Structured Credit Partners, LLC	450,000,000

Closing Date	Deal Name	Manager/Sponsor	Size ($)
Nov. 1, 2004	Anthracite 2004-HY1	BlackRock Financial Management	346,059,175
Oct. 1, 2004	Brascan Real Estate CDO 2004-1	Brascan Real Estate Financial Partners LLC.	269,330,000
Sep. 30, 2004	Newcastle CDO V	Newcastle Investment Corp.	500,000,000
Jul. 20, 2004	Capital Trust RE CDO 2004-1 Ltd.	CT Investment Management Co., LLC	324,073,688
Jul. 1, 2004	N-Star Real Estate CDO II	NS Advisors LLC	400,000,000
Apr. 29, 2004	ARCap 2004-1	ARCap REIT, Inc.	340,912,558
Apr. 1, 2004	Crest Exeter Street Solar 2004-1	MFS Investment Management	350,000,000
Mar. 30, 2004	Newcastle CDO IV	NewCastle Investment Corp.	450,000,000
Mar. 25, 2004	Anthracite CDO III	BlackRock Financial Management, Inc.	435,621,017
Dec. 20, 2003	G-Force CDO 2003-1	G Funds Asset Management, LLC	615,666,135
Dec. 18, 2003	Crest 2003-2	Structured Credit Partners, LLC	325,000,000
Nov. 6, 2003	TIAA Real Estate CDO 2003-1	TIAA Advisory Services, LLC	300,000,000
Sep. 9, 2003	Newcastle CDO III	Newcastle Investment Corp.	500,000,000
Aug. 20, 2003	N-Star Real Estate CDO I	NS Advisors, LLC	402,000,000
Aug. 1, 2003	ARCap 2003-1	ARCap REIT, Inc.	414,380,000

Closing Date	Deal Name	Manager/Sponsor	Size ($)
Jul. 2, 2003	LNR 2003-1	Lennar Partners Inc	762,770,000
Apr. 10, 2003	Crest Dartmouth Street 2003-1	MFS Investment Management	350,000,000
Mar. 17, 2003	Crest 2003-1	Structured Credit Partners	600,000,000
Mar. 13, 2003	Newcastle CDO II, Limited	Newcastle Investment Corp	500,000,000
Mar. 13, 2003	G-Star 2003-3	GMAC Institutional Advisors, LLC	450,000,000
Dec. 10, 2003	Anthracite RE CBO II	Blackrock Financial Management, Inc.	363,420,670
Nov. 20, 2002	G-Star 2002-2 Ltd.	GMAC Institutional Advisors LLC ("GIA")	397,500,000
Sep. 19, 2002	JER CDO 2002-1	J.E. Robert Company Inc.	203,446,593
Sep. 19, 2002	Crest Clarendon Street 2002-1	MFS Investment Management	300,000,000
Jul. 9, 2002	Lennar CDO 2002-1		800,629,578
Jun. 1, 2002	G-Force CDO 2002-1 Ltd.	G Funds Asset Management LLC	1,104,991,254
May 29, 2002	Anthracite RE CBO I	BlackRock Financial Management, Inc	526,312,717
May 22, 2002	TIAA Real Estate CDO 2002-1	TIAA Advisory Services, LLC	500,000,000
May 16, 2002	Crest 2002-IG	Structured Credit Partners LLC	660,000,000
Apr. 25, 2002	G-Star 2002-1 Ltd.	GMAC Institutional Advisors, LLC	311,950,000

Closing Date	Deal Name	Manager/Sponsor	Size ($)
Apr. 25, 2002	Newcastle CDO I, Limited	Newcastle Investment Corp	500,000,000
Mar. 27, 2002	Crest 2002-1	Structured Credit Partners	500,000,000
Feb. 20, 2002	Storrs CDO Ltd.	David L. Babson	399,000,000
Dec. 18, 2001	Ctrdy G-STAR 2001-2	GMAC Institutional Advisors	350,000,000
Nov. 30, 2001	Putnam Structured Product CDO 2001-1	Putnam Investments	300,000,000
Sep. 6, 2001	Crest G-Star 2001-1	GMAC Institutional Advisors	500,000,000
Apr. 12, 2001	Pinstripe I CDO	Alliance Capital Management L.P.	483,750,000
Mar. 7, 2001	Crest 2001-1 Ltd	Wachovia Securities Inc.	500,000,000
Mar. 1, 2001	Ajax One, Ltd.	ING Baring (U.S.) Capital Corporation	375,000,000
Feb. 28, 2001	G-Force CDO 2001-1, Ltd.	G2 Opportunity GP, LLC	861,794,422
Dec. 14, 2000	Sutter Real Estate CBO 2000-1, Ltd	Wells Fargo	300,000,000
Nov. 15, 2000	Duke Funding I, Ltd.	Ellington Capital Management, L.L.C.	300,000,000
Nov. 2, 2000	Crest 2000-1, Ltd.	Structured Credit Partners, LLC	500,000,000
May 25, 2000	Mach One CDO, Series 2000-1		310,000,000

Closing Date	Deal Name	Manager/Sponsor	Size ($)
Apr. 13, 2000	Diversified REIT Trust 2000-1	Wells Fargo Bank (servicing agent)	287,150,000
Jul. 22, 1999	Fortress CBO Investments I, Limited	Fortress Investment Corp.	500,000,000
May 26, 1999	Diversified REIT Trust 1999-1		518,760,000

Source: Citigroup.

GLOSSARY

A-note The senior lien on a commercial property. It is generally rated investment grade and often securitized in CMBS transactions. There may be more than one pari passu A-note, with each piece sold to a different CMBS transaction. A-notes are sometimes called CMBS loans.

arbitrage CDO In its purest form, a CDO created and issued for the express purpose of creating excess returns for CDO equity investors and management fees for the collateral manager. When possible, the entire capital structure of an arbitrage CDO is sold to investors. (For contrast, see **financing CDO**.)

B-note Also a primary lien holder but with subordinate rights to the A-note holder via the intercreditor agreement. Increasingly, B-note holders are granted consultation or approval rights for loan workout options or the right to appoint or replace the loan's special servicer. B-notes are generally below investment grade and floating rate.

B-piece The junior or equity position in a CMBS transaction. It typically has a fixed rate.

capitalization rate Expected initial rate of return on investment. Cap rate is derived by dividing the asset's net operating income by the total purchase price or value. It can be quoted on a cash or GAAP basis. GAAP cap rates include straight-line rents.[25]

conduit loan A commercial real estate loan originated to meet the requirements for inclusion in a CMBS transaction.

coverage tests A CDO term that refers to the overcollateralization test and the interest coverage test.

credit risk security A security in a CDO collateral pool that is deemed by the manager to be at risk of downgrade or falling value. This definition varies from CDO transaction to CDO transaction.

credit tenant lease (CTL) loan A loan backed by the property's rent payments. Thus, the strength of the loan is intimately tied to the health of the tenant. Rent payments are set to equal the amount required to fully amortize the loan balance over the term of the lease plus tax payments, insurance payments and expected upkeep (maintenance). The property owner receives payments net of the agreed upon payments and the actual costs. Also see "Real Estate Operating Lease."

diversity score (DS)   A Moody's measure of the diversity of the collateral supporting the CDO.

equity REIT   A REIT that owns, manages, invests, or develops real property directly, generating rent payments, primarily from rental revenues.[26]

financing CDO   A CDO transaction created to provide a low-cost source of financing for the CDO sponsor (manager). While financing CDOs often have management fees and independent equity investors, the management fees are typically lower than arbitrage CDOs, and the sponsor retains much of the CDO equity.

fusion deal   A fixed-rate CMBS transaction in which the collateral pool comprises a few large loans and many smaller conduit loans. Usually, a CMBS pool is considered a fusion pool when the top 10 loans account for more than 42 percent of the collateral or the top three loans account for more than 18 percent. However, with recent pools growing in size, any pool that has more than three $50 million loans is commonly called a fusion CMBS pool.

hard lockbox   A preestablished bank account under the control of the servicer to which all property cash flows are placed before distribution (net of the mortgage payment) to the borrower. This advancing to the borrower can cease after certain preestablished triggers to effectively capture the cash flow for the lender.

interest coverage test (IC test)   A test of the debt servicing ability of the CDO. The interest coverage ratio is expressed as the amount of interest proceeds expected from the collateral divided by the interest due on the CDO liabilities. If the IC test fails, interest and/or principal proceeds from the CDO collateral are diverted away from CDO equity and potentially junior CDO tranches to repay senior CDO note holders until the test is brought back into compliance.

mezzanine loan   A loan secured by a pledge of equity in the mortgage borrower (property owner). A mezzanine loan is subordinate to the A-note and B-note, if one exists. Usually floating rate.

mortgage REIT   A REIT that invests in the underlying liens of a property. These investments serve as a source of funds or a loan to the REIT.[27]

non-CUSIPed securities   Typically unrated B-notes, mezzanine loans, or preferred equity bonds. These securities are then shadow rated for purposes of the CDO.

overcollateralization test (OC test)   Effectively a test of the loan-to-value (LTV) ratio of the CDO (generally expressed as the inverse of the LTV ratio). If the OC test fails, interest and/or principal proceeds from the CDO collateral are diverted away from CDO equity and, potentially, junior CDO tranches to repay senior CDO note holders until the test is brought back into compliance.

rake bond   A junior participation or B-note that is held inside of a REMIC structure for the benefit of a specific investor. (Other CMBS investors do not benefit from cross collateralization of this note.)

real estate investment trust (REIT)   A public corporation or trust that pools capital to acquire, develop, or finance real estate. As a public company, a REIT allows smaller investors to invest in commercial real estate through publicly traded stock, which typically trades on a major stock exchange.[28] REITs enjoy favorable tax status subject to certain constraints. Most notably, REITs are required to pay 90 percent of earnings to investors as dividends.

real estate mortgage investment conduit (REMIC) An onshore but tax-exempt securitization vehicle for real estate loans that became popular after the passing of the Tax Reform Act of 1986. REMICs are unmanaged (static) vehicles. For example, collateralized mortgage obligations (CMOs) are generally issued as REMICs.

real estate operating lease A loan backed by the property's rent payments, which are set to equal the amount required to fully amortize the loan balance over the term of the lease. Thus, the strength of the loan is intimately tied to the health of the tenant. Unlike a credit tenant lease, the owner is responsible for taxes, insurance, and maintenance costs.

reREMIC An onshore but tax-exempt securitization vehicle for CMBS and REMIC securities. See also **real estate mortgage investment conduit (REMIC)**.

springing lockbox An account (lockbox) that is originally under the control of the borrower but that reverts to lender control upon the breach of certain performance guidelines. See also **hard lockbox**.

waterfall The list of rules that govern the distribution of cash in a CDO.

weighted average rating factor (WARF) A measure of the average credit quality of a pool of assets. Lower values imply higher-quality pools.

whole loans A real estate loan that is not partitioned into A-notes and B-notes.

TERM SHEET

In this section, we have included a term sheet of a hypothetical commercial real estate CDO. The term sheet gives information on the CDO capital structure, portfolio information, investment guidelines, and CDO manager information.

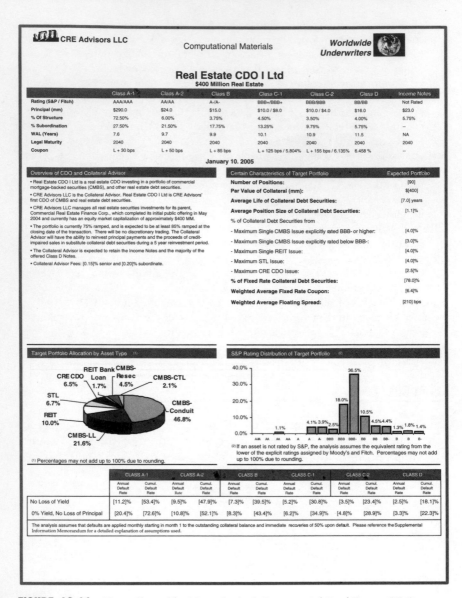

FIGURE 13.11   Term Sheet of a Hypothetical Commercial Real Estate CDO
Source: Citigroup.

CRE Advisors LLC   Computational Materials   *Worldwide Underwriters*

KEY PORTFOLIO CHARACTERISTICS OF COLLATERAL PURCHASED (as of February 16, 2005) (1)

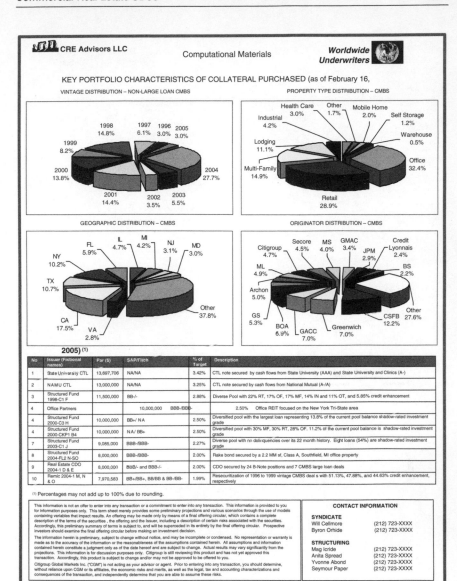

VINTAGE DISTRIBUTION – NON-LARGE LOAN CMBS

1998 14.8% · 1997 6.1% · 1996 3.0% · 2005 3.0% · 1999 8.2% · 2000 13.8% · 2004 27.7% · 2001 14.4% · 2002 3.5% · 2003 5.5%

PROPERTY TYPE DISTRIBUTION – CMBS

Health Care 3.0% · Other 1.7% · Mobile Home 2.0% · Self Storage 1.2% · Industrial 4.2% · Warehouse 0.5% · Lodging 11.1% · Office 32.4% · Multi-Family 14.9% · Retail 28.9%

GEOGRAPHIC DISTRIBUTION – CMBS

FL 5.9% · IL 4.7% · MI 4.2% · NJ 3.1% · MD 3.0% · NY 10.2% · TX 10.7% · Other 37.8% · CA 17.5% · VA 2.8%

ORIGINATOR DISTRIBUTION – CMBS

Secore 4.5% · MS 4.0% · GMAC 3.4% · Credit Lyonnais 2.4% · Citigroup 4.7% · JPM 2.9% · BS 2.2% · ML 4.9% · Archon 5.0% · Other 27.6% · GS 5.3% · BOA 6.9% · GACC 7.0% · Greenwich 7.0% · CSFB 12.2%

No	Issuer (Fictional names)	Par ($)	S&P/Fitch		% of Target	Description
1	State University CTL	13,697,706	NA/NA		3.42%	CTL note secured by cash flows from State University (AAA) and State University and Clinics (A-)
2	NAMU CTL	13,000,000	NA/NA		3.25%	CTL note secured by cash flows from National Mutual (A-/A)
3	Structured Fund 1998-C1 F	11,500,000	BB-/-		2.88%	Diverse Pool with 22% RT, 17% OF, 17% MF, 14% IN and 11% OT, and 5.85% credit enhancement
4	Office Partners		10,000,000	BBB-/BBB-	2.50%	Office REIT focused on the New York Tri-State area
4	Structured Fund 2000-C3 H	10,000,000	BB+/ N A		2.50%	Diversified pool with the largest loan representing 13.8% of the current pool balance shadow-rated investment grade
4	Structured Fund 2000-CKP1 B4	10,000,000	N A/ BB+		2.50%	Diversified pool with 30% MF, 30% RT, 28% OF, 11.2% of the current pool balance is shadow-rated investment grade
7	Structured Fund 2003-C1 J	9,085,000	BBB-/BBB-		2.27%	Diverse pool with no delinquencies over its 22 month history. Eight loans (54%) are shadow-rated investment grade
8	Structured Fund 2004-FL2 N-SQ	8,000,000	BBB-/BBB-		2.00%	Rake bond secured by a 2.2 MM sf, Class A, Southfield, MI office property
9	Real Estate CDO 2004-1 D & E	8,000,000	BBB-/- and BBB-/-		2.00%	CDO secured by 24 B-Note positions and 7 CMBS large loan deals
10	Remic 2004-1 M, N & O	7,970,583	BB+/BB+, BB/BB & BB-/BB-		1.99%	Resecuritization of 1996 to 1999 vintage CMBS deal s with 51.13%, 47.88%, and 44.63% credit enhancement, respectively

(1) Percentages may not add up to 100% due to rounding.

CONTACT INFORMATION

SYNDICATE
Will Cellmore   (212) 723-XXXX
Byron Orhide   (212) 723-XXXX

STRUCTURING
Mag Icride   (212) 723-XXXX
Anita Spread   (212) 723-XXXX
Yvonne Abond   (212) 723-XXXX
Seymour Paper   (212) 723-XXXX

FIGURE 13.11   *(continued)*

Notes

INTRODUCTION A Road Map of the New World of Structured Credit

1. The Code of Hammurabi (see http://www.constitution.org/ime/hammurabi. htm).

CHAPTER 1   A Primer on Credit Default Swaps

1. Typical credit events are described in the next subsection, on prerequisites.
2. www.isdadocs.org/index.html.
3. www.bba.org.uk.
4. This cash bond spread is also called the Z-spread, and it can be computed as the spread that when added to the spot swap curve (as a parallel shift) correctly prices the bond.
5. However, the protection seller will know that it will be the cheapest bond or loan that meets the criteria as he is short the delivery option. (If the buyer were long a different obligation other than the cheapest, she will sell that obligation, buy the cheapest one, and deliver it.)
6. At the time this case study was written, AT&T Wireless had not yet merged with Cingular.

CHAPTER 2   Credit Default Swaptions

1. To permit the comparison of CDS option liquidity between names that trade at much different spreads, traders often use prices as inputs to their model and infer the implied volatility of the spread. This volatility is then comparable from one credit to another. A "vol" is simply a 100bp move in the implied volatility.
2. To be more precise, the investor makes money if, upon expiry of the option, the CDS exceeds the strike plus the premium paid for the option.
3. Practically speaking, the profit and loss change is limited by the maximum potential credit improvement.
4. Corporate bond options are simply called *calls* and *puts*, and a call in dollar terms is the same as a call in terms of credit quality. A buyer of a call option on a corporate bond wants dollar price to go up and credit quality to improve. Similarly, a buyer of a put option on a corporate bond wants dollar price to go down, and credit quality to deteriorate. The seller has exactly the opposite payoff of the buyer.
5. For more details, see *Altman High Yield Default and Return Report, Second Quarter 2004 Update*, John Fenn and Gabriella Petrucci, Citigroup, July 20, 2004.
6. Citigroup High Yield Index.
7. Citigroup Broad Investment Grade Credit Index.

8. See *Implementing Credit Views Using CDS Swaptions*, Terry Benzschawel and Glen Taksler, Citigroup, April 13, 2004.

9. Butterfly trades may be used to express other views, such as mildly bullish views, as well. However, based on our thesis of a potential for slight spread widening, we present the trade as a tool for expressing a slightly bearish view.

CHAPTER 4   Credit Derivatives Indexes

1. It is not necessary for the single-name CDS market to be fully developed before the credit derivatives index starts trading. For example, the single-name HY CDS market had been relatively illiquid, but it started gaining in liquidity after the HY CDX index had been launched in 2003.

2. According to British Bankers' Association (BBA) Credit Derivatives Report 2003/2004, credit derivatives indexes have accounted for 9 percent market share in 2003 and are expected to reach 12 percent market share by 2006. Combined with index-linked tranches, the market share of full and tranched indexes was 11 percent in 2003 and is expected to reach 17 percent by 2006. BBA estimates that by 2006, credit derivatives indexes should become the second most used credit derivative product after single-name credit default swaps.

3. There was an exception in the roll between Series 3 and Series 4 (Table 4.3).

4. Dow Jones Indexes is part of Dow Jones & Company.

5. There are several differences between buying protection on an index and buying protection on a basket of reference credits. Those differences lead to index-intrinsic spread basis. We provide further description of the basis in the section "Index versus Intrinsics."

6. In most cases, investors use the Bloomberg CDSW page for calculating up-front payments, mark-to-market values, and durations (Risky PV01) for index trades.

7. Calculation is based on the recovery rate of 40 percent and a flat credit curve.

8. A deliverable obligation can be any obligation meeting a specified list of criteria from the confirmation agreement.

9. Tranche products can be settled using a physical or cash settlement. In a cash settlement, the protection seller simply pays the difference between the par value and the recovery value of the reference entity.

10. For more information about CDS Index Protocols, see www.isda.org.

11. For further explanation of duration-weighted (Risky PV01-weighted) average spread, see the Chapter 4 appendix.

12. Even though the index-intrinsics arbitrage could be difficult to execute, market players use index-intrinsics trends as an important signal for potential movements in credit markets.

13. It can be shown that most of the time the curve deformation can be reduced to its first three principal components. (parallel shift, curvature change and convexity change); a bucketing of the curve as 1 to 5 years, 5 to 10 years, and 10+ years effectively captures those three effects.

14. A Bund is a German government bond.

15. See *Credit Betas and Why You Should Be Using Them*, Etienne Varloot and Matt King, Citigroup, April 2004.
16. This can be justified by the historical fact that the credit market can be realistically reduced to a single market risk factor model. See *Empirical Analysis of Corporate Bond Spreads*, Terry L. Benzschawel and Dennis Adler, Citigroup, September 2002.
17. The intrinsic portfolio spread closely follows the market quote over time. Therefore, the two betas should be very close.
18. This a bit low compared to our first guess of 1.05 by looking at the ratio of the spread of the iTraxx, which was 43 bp as of the close on August 9, to the one of the EBIGC (41 bp). We have shown elsewhere that a good proxy of the beta is the ratio of the two spreads.
19. Some of this tracking error comes from the price resilience of the iTraxx note versus its underlying cash benchmark. Therefore, the *ex post* tracking error tends to overstate the residual risk of this hedge.
20. Even with only 125 issuers iTraxx achieves a better diversity score of 63 (as defined by Moody's binomial expansion technique) than the EBIGC with 248 issuers and a score of only around 46.
21. In the case of a hedging strategy, the maximum loss in case of default likewise is reduced from 180 bp (GM) to 120 bp (VW).
22. For further details about the CDX roll process, see "Guide to the Dow Jones CDX Indexes," Dow Jones Indexes, September 2005 (www.djindexes.com/mdsidx/downloads/credit_derivative/rules.pdf). For further details about the iTraxx roll process, see "iTraxx—Rules of Construction," IndexCo (www.indexco.com/download/Products/CDS/iTraxx.EUR.product.rules.pdf).
23. Risky PV01 divided by the notional and multiplied by 10,000 to estimate the "duration" in years.
24. For a more detailed description of credit risk models, please consult any of the standard textbooks on credit modeling.

CHAPTER 5 The Added Dimension of Credit

1. 10s30s slope = 30-year spread—10-year spread.
2. GM's perceived long-term average creditworthiness through time is more likely to be linked to its long-term rating rather than to the present idiosyncratic risk.
3. This implies that you are left with a positive cash position to start with.
4. That is, fewer euros are invested in the long end than are raised through short end selling, resulting in surplus cash in the portfolio.
5. Ford, for example, has a large number of bonds in dollars, sterling, and euros, with a steady issuance program across the curve.
6. A cross-currency asset swap can take many forms. One such form is to swap fixed cash flows in one currency for fixed cash flows in another currency. The cross-currency swap market is a floating-floating market; so intermediate steps involve fixed-for-floating asset swaps to make fixed cash flows into floating ones. Like regular asset swaps, the cross-currency asset swap does not terminate on the default of the name in question, and has to be honored until maturity

or unwound at the prevailing mark-to-market price. A perfect asset swap is an asset swap that does cease to exist on default, but it often costs more as a result.

7. A rough order of sensitivity for a 1 bp move in CDS spreads is as follows: On a CDS of notional €10 million, a 1 bp move in the CDS spread results in a €1,000 profit/loss whereas a 1 bp move in the interest rate swap spread results in only a €100 profit/loss.

8. FRNs have very little interest market rate risk as the coupons increase as market rates (Libor) increase.

9. Also known as cancelable asset swaps.

10. Lognormal distribution ensures that the firm value (debt + equity) never goes negative.

11. In practice, an out-of-the-money (OTM) put option on the (asset value/number of shares) with a strike equal to the net debt per share (which typically results in a 10 to 20 percent strike).

12. To be unwound on the maturity date of an equity put (typically a year or two).

13. In default, the stock price would be expected to go to zero, but to be conservative, let us assume a small value even in default.

14. iTraxx Europe, for example, now has a bid-offer spread of less than 1 bp, which is a fraction of the 5–10 bp spread in the previous indexes.

15. DV01 is the product of market value × duration.

16. On occasion, a large amount of issuance in lower-rated sectors can cause the opposite effect.

17. Protection buyer receives 1/125th of the notional on default of an underlying name.

18. Before credit default swaptions were introduced to the market, some investors used to strip the credit option from callable and puttable bonds to take advantage of poor pricing. The options they sold had the caveat that they would cease to exist if the bond defaulted. Hence, the convention for knock-outs in today's single-name market.

CHAPTER 6   Single-Tranche CDOs

1. This index was formerly referred to as the iBoxx index.

2. In a standard STCDO structure, it is easy to estimate the number of defaults in the underlying portfolio that will cause loss of payment by protection seller. As an example, assume that the tranche has 3 percent subordination, the reference portfolio has 100 names with $10 million size each, and the recovery rate is 40 percent for each credit. Five defaults can happen without affecting the tranche—five defaults will lead to $30 million loss on the portfolio: 5 × $10 million × (100%—40%)—and the losses associated with the sixth default will be covered by the protection seller.

3. See "Return of the Bull-Bear," Jure Skarabot, Ji Hoon Ryu, and Arvind Rajan, *Global Structured Credit Strategy*, Citigroup, February 15, 2005.

4. See *CDO Outlook 2005*, Arvind Rajan, Glen McDermott, et al., Citigroup, December 17, 2004.

5. See *A Primer on Single-Tranche CDOs*, David Li, Ratul Roy, and Jure Skarabot, Citigroup, April 27, 2004.
6. *Bull and Bear in a Boxx—Using Tranche Products to Express Credit Views*, Arvind Rajan, Graham Murphy, and Jure Skarabot, Citigroup, February 19, 2004.
7. We used the CDX IG 3 tranches (maturity March 2010/March 2015) to estimate the characteristics of the recommended trade. Trades with CDX IG 4 tranches will have different notional amounts and sensitivity than the presented analysis.
8. Although the 0 to 3 percent tranche has a low blowup mark-to-market to spread ratio, we did not consider the equity tranche for the long position. Even if the structure with the long equity position could be efficient from the blowup mark-to-market perspective, it will most likely have a significant net risk exposure to defaults.
9. See *Total Credit*, Matt King et al., Citigroup, July 2004. Another trade involves buying delta-hedged protection on a senior tranche.
10. This amount was chosen because it corresponds to the same jump-to-default risk as a $1 million hedged equity trade.
11. The trade proposed here is based on a bespoke portfolio and not on the iTraxx. However, it could be implemented on the iTraxx with similar results.
12. For extremely high levels of spreads, the equity hedge ratio starts to decrease as the marginal impact of a spread widening on a name that is almost sure to default becomes smaller.
13. For a discussion of the impact of correlations on tranches, refer to *Trading Credit Tranches: Taking Default Correlation out of the Black Box*, Ratul Roy and David Shelton, Citigroup, September 16, 2004.

CHAPTER 7   Trading Credit Tranches

1. While this is a simple measure, it does have limitations. By tracking only notionals of tranches and pools, a virtually riskless 97 to 100 percent tranche would appear to have the same leverage of 33 as a 0 to 3 percent tranche. It would be much better to track the changing marketwide Credit01, the tranche-specific spread sensitivity, which does differentiate between the 97 to 100 percent and 0 to 3 percent; however, we do not believe accurate industrywide data exists.
2. See, for example, "A Copula Function Approach to Credit Portfolio Modeling," David Li, Jerome Connor, and Alex Gu, *Quantitative Credit Analyst*, Citigroup, May 2003.
3. True default correlation measures the degree to which default of one asset makes the default of another asset more or less likely. These numbers, however, are the asset correlation inputs in a Gaussian copula framework for the construction of a joint distribution of survival times of credits in a portfolio and, although closely related, are not exactly the same. Nonetheless, we will follow the industry standard of calling these parameters default correlation.
4. We use a bisection method to perform this calibration. Unlike the multiple solutions seen in Figure 7.4 for mezzanine tranche correlation, the bootstrapping

method produces a unique correlation for each equity tranche attachment point given the monotonic relationship between tranche premium and correlation.

5. Predicted change in 3 to 6 percent tranche = change in iTraxx spread multiplied by Credit01 divided by tranche duration.

6. See *Bull and Bear in a Boxx*, Arvind Rajan et al., Citigroup, February 19, 2004.

7. See U.S. Europe 10-Year Correlation Trade, Matt King and Antoine Pain, Citigroup, July 29, 2004.

8. In its strategy publications, Citigroup recommended curve flatteners in the telecom sector (see "Relative Value—Cashing In on Curve Steepness in Telecom," Mathew Mish, Shuguang Mao, and Dennis Adler, *Global Structured Credit Strategy*, Citigroup, October 5, 2004), and we pointed out the curve flattening trade for the HVOL component of the CDX.NA.IG index (see the "Market Overview" section, Terry Benzschawel, Glen McDermott, Jure Skarabot, *Global Structured Credit Strategy*, Citigroup, August 10, 2004).

9. For example, compared to tranches on high-yield CDX or tranches on "Cross-Boxx" (combination of HVOL CDX and BB/B subsector indexes of high-yield CDX). Note that CDX/iTraxx tranches are not rated, but can be submitted to a rating process.

10. For further discussion and analysis of the recent roll, see "Roll of the Dow Jones CDX Indexes from September 2009 to March 2010," Richard Salditt, Jure Skarabot, and Dennis Adler, *Bond Market Roundup: Strategy*, Citigroup, September 17, 2004.

11. For further explanation of base correlation and its use as a relative value tool for tranche products, see *Trading Credit Tranches*, Ratul Roy and David Shelton, Citigroup, September 16, 2004, and "The Taming of the Skew," Matt King, *Global Structured Credit Strategy*, Citigroup, October 5, 2004.

CHAPTER 8   Understanding CDO-Squareds

1. Even though we have used the CDO^2 equity to make our point, the same argument holds for the CDO^2 mezzanine. If, following the loss of $60 million of the first inner CDO, that is, the entire equity plus a further $20 million of the inner tranche, a further $10 million was lost, the CDO^2 mezzanine would lose $10 million, representing 10/70 of its notional (larger than either the 10/1,000 or 10/60 ratios of the original notional of the CDO portfolio and inner tranche, respectively).

2. For more details of pricing and trading dynamics within tranches, see our previous research pieces: *The Single Tranche CDO Primer*, Citigroup, February 2004; *Trading Credit Tranches*, Citigroup, September 2004; and "The Taming of The Skew," *Global Structured Credit Strategy*, Citigroup, September 2004.

3. One reason for the low impact of the first default in a CDO^2 tranche is that the universe of credits potentially affecting the CDO^2 (i.e., all of the credits in the various inner CDO portfolios) is much higher. In the example of Figure 8.4, about 24 credits would need to default with zero recovery for the CDO^2 portfolio to be affected (assuming defaults were equally spread out among the five portfolios) compared with only five defaults for the inner CDO tranche

to be affected. Should defaults not be spread out and occur in only a few of the portfolios, however, the break-even number of defaults to affect the CDO^2 would drop.

4. Refer to Chapter 7 for details.

CHAPTER 9 CPPI: Leveraging and Deleveraging Credit

1. More details on the estimations and simulations are provided in the "Appendix: Our Methodology," at the end of this chapter.
2. Our assumption of rolling has two main consequences. First, the roll limits the number of defaults as credits downgraded to junk are removed from the index at each roll (hence a low default assumption would be reasonable). Second, the roll implies substituting cheap credits (the downgraded ones) for more expensive ones and therefore introduces a cost. We argue the medium default assumption implicitly takes this cost of rolling into account.
3. For an introduction to CMCDS, refer to Chapter 3 of this book.
4. Setting RM very high would lead to a structure with constant leverage.

CHAPTER 10 Collateralized Loan Obligations

1. Since 1993, the compound annual growth rate of institutional tranches has been 48 percent.
2. Prime rate funds are mutual funds that buy portions of corporate loans from banks and pass along interest designed to approximate the prime rate to shareholders.
3. For more details, see Chapter 12.
4. S&P estimated that about 56 percent of new issuance in the first three quarters of 2003 was placed into CLOs.
5. The S&P studies agree with the Moody's findings. In fact, S&P did not downgrade a single CLO tranche in 2003.
6. We consider a tranche downgraded if its current rating is lower than its initial rating. If a tranche was downgraded and subsequently upgraded to a rating equal to or higher than the original rating, we do not consider this a downgraded tranche.
7. Middle-market loans and leveraged loans have many characteristics in common. A general description of middle market loan characteristics can be found in Appendix A later in this chapter.
8. In the event of an issuer's default, debt holders often receive only some fraction of the original value of their loans or bonds. Usually, debt recovery value is realized through either sale of the debt in the secondary market or repayment of debt by the issuer in a workout process. The position of a debt instrument in the firm's capital structure and the degree to which debt is backed by liquid assets are important indicators of expected recovery rates.
9. See Appendix B for a brief description of CLO mechanics.

10. There is no guarantee that a market will develop for any particular CLO, nor is there any guarantee, if one exists, that a market will continue to be made.

11. *Middle Market CLO Performance Update: 2003*, Elizabeth Russotto, Ashleigh Bischoff, and Alla Zaydman, Fitch Ratings, March 1, 2004.

12. We consider a tranche downgraded if its current rating is lower than its initial rating. If a tranche was downgraded and subsequently upgraded to a rating equal to or higher than the original rating, we would not count this as a downgraded tranche. We treat upgrades similarly.

13. S&P claims even higher accuracy with its CreditModel.

14. Only a certain percentage of credit-impaired loans may be replaced. The replaced loan must not lead to a downgrade of CLO liabilities, either outright (lower perceived quality or recovery rate) or as a result of increased default correlation within the collateral pool.

15. A complete description of CLO structures and mechanics can be found in the second half of this chapter.

16. This test statistic is similar to the inverse of loan-to-value for the tranche.

17. For more details, see "Diversifying Credit Risk Using a CDO Equity Fund," Glen McDermott and Alexei Kroujiline, *Global Structured Credit Strategy*, Citigroup, March 2, 2004.

18. For a detailed discussion of CDO combination securities, see *CDO Combination Securities: Putting the Pieces Together*, Glen McDermott and Terry Benzschawel, Citigroup, February 4, 2002.

19. The approximately 100 bp deterioration in the tranche's IRR is driven by changes in the amortization schedule of the tranche under different stress scenarios. The tranche amortizes sooner under higher CDRs because of the payment waterfall structure, and hence, the interest coupon payments are calculated off the reduced balance of the tranche, leading to a moderate reduction in the IRR values. Once the default rate exceeds 13 percent, the tranche's cash flows would be compromised and the resulting IRR would deteriorate rapidly, passing a zero yield point along the way at a 15.5 percent CDR and going further into a negative yield territory as the default rate increases.

20. For more information on this technique, see "A Copula Function Approach to Credit Portfolio Modeling," *Quantitative Credit Analyst*, Citigroup, May 2003.

21. The fact that the graph in Figure 10.47 shows returns above 14 percent is artificial and was caused by the graphical smoothing routine. In fact, as the table in Figure 10.47 indicates, the maximum observed return was approximately 13.8 percent. The histogram graph was constructed with the graphical smoothing routine rather than discrete vertical bars to approximate the whole distribution of returns.

22. For simplification purposes, the loss values in Figure 10.47 were calculated on cash-on-cash basis, ignoring the time value of money.

23. In general, the CVAR values can be constructed at any percentile point of the distribution. For example, a 5th percentile CVAR would correspond to the average loss assuming that the loss exceeds the 5th percentile value. Although

the loss distribution is closer to normal than that of the returns, the CVAR measure still suffers from the nonnormality of the underlying distribution. Computing CVAR values at different percentile breaks may help in detailed analysis of the distribution tails.

24. Each combination security was analyzed assuming a LIBOR flat coupon. We analyzed a CLO transaction that closed in 2003 and was backed by a pool of leveraged loans. During the course of the deal's life, the collateral par decreased by approximately $1.4 million from its original volume of $300 million. The transaction was originally structured with 8 percent leverage for the income notes and approximately 23 percent subordination for the most senior tranche.

25. See *The CLO Handbook*, Glen McDermott et al., Citigroup, February 2004, and "Diversifying Credit Risk Using a CDO Equity Fund," Glen McDermott and Alexei Kroujiline, *Global Structured Credit Strategy*, Citigroup, March 2, 2004.

26. We define expected loss as a simple average of all tranche losses across 20,000 simulations and CVAR as the average tranche loss across those simulations where there was at least one dollar of loss.

CHAPTER 11 ABS CDOs

1. We use the term *SFS* as a broad umbrella term that covers three main subsectors: residential mortgage-backed securities, commercial mortgage-backed securities, and asset-backed securities. *ABS* is also used to cover only non–real estate SFS.

2. Figure 11.3 does not include agency or government-sponsored enterprise (GSE) mortgages.

3. Structured Finance Rating Transitions: 1983 to 2003, Moody's Investors Service.

4. Broadly speaking, a D rating occurs whenever a structured finance security either misses a timely interest payment or sustains an ultimate loss of principal.

5. Neither study includes collateralized debt obligations.

6. These asset classes include manufactured housing, franchise loans, and 12b-1 fees.

7. Performance data does not include collateralized debt obligations.

8. See Chapter 12 of this book.

9. The data have not been adjusted for withdrawn ratings.

10. CDOs of SFSs often contain an investment bucket for other CDOs (e.g., a synthetic CDO of SFS will usually contain a 15 to 20 percent bucket for synthetic corporate arbitrage CDOs). As can be seen from the figure, recent performance has varied considerably depending on the underlying asset type.

11. The relative brevity of the existence of the CDOs of SFSs can be seen from a comparison of the number of years of data available for the various CDO types and the lower number of data points compared to CLOs and CBOs.

12. In some cases, the senior tranche in a high-grade SF CDO can be funded 40 bp (or more) more cheaply than 85 percent of all term liabilities issued by traditional SF CDOs.

13. More details on these collateral asset types can be found elsewhere in this chapter.
14. For details, see Chapter 10 of this book.
15. When high-grade SF CDO tranches are assigned new issuance ratings, the rating agencies usually run cash flow analysis under the assumption that the put is exercised at the beginning of the CDO life.
16. Assuming 55 percent recovery rate.
17. Values are approximate and are based on corporate default studies.
18. Excluded sectors often include franchise loans, manufactured housing, 12b-1 mutual fund fees, high-yield CBOs, and aircraft securitizations.
19. To account for the senior note coupon uncertainty, we run two sets of cash flow scenarios with different coupon spread values. The first scenario (no-put scenario) assumes that the put option is not exercised and the senior note holders receive flat LIBOR coupon until the end of the deal. The second scenario (put scenario) assumes that the put option is exercised at the closing date and the senior note holders receive LIBOR + 40 bp.
20. CDR analysis is a simple and quick way to characterize the quality of a CDO tranche, but the method has serious limitations. Defaults do not occur uniformly over time, but instead are clustered or correlated. The impact of correlated default rates on CDO tranche returns will be amplified by an obligor position size and CDO leverage. To capture these risks we employed an alternative probabilistic approach based on Monte Carlo simulations and copula technique.
21. To project the cash flow distributions, we employed Monte Carlo simulations and modeled default correlation using the Gaussian copula function technique. Default curves were constructed with Moody's historical data on corporate defaults. In addition, our two-parameter model assumed a 30 percent interindustry and a 40 percent intraindustry correlation of default timing in the underlying collateral pool of the CDO. We applied a 55 percent constant recovery rate for all defaults in the underlying collateral. The resulting loss scenarios were then run through the cash flow model to forecast payment distributions to the mezzanine tranche.
22. The particular tranche view on correlation can vary from transaction to transaction. These are very rough generalizations that should not be considered true for all structured transactions.

CHAPTER 12   CDO Equity

1. Readers should look at *CDO Equity—A Correlation Study*, J. Prince, A. Kroujiline, and G. McDermott, Citigroup, September 9, 2004.
2. "Recovering Your Money: Insights into Losses from Defaults," Karen Van de Castle and David Keisman, *Standard & Poor's CreditWeek*, June 15, 1999; and *Debt Recoveries for Corporate Bankruptcies*, David T. Hamilton, Global Credit Research, Moody's Investors Service, June 1999.

3. *Management of CBOs/CLOs*, Robert J. Grossman, Fitch IBCA, December 8, 1997.
4. For an in-depth discussion of CDO equity, see *The ABCs of CDO Equity*, Glen McDermott, Citigroup, July 2000.
5. See *Diversifying Credit Risk Using a Fund of Funds Structure*, Glen McDermott and Alexei Kroujiline, Citigroup, February 20, 2004.
6. For more details, see *An Analysis of CDO Equity Returns—Update No. 3*, David Park and Jeff Prince, Citigroup, April 19, 2006.
7. In fact, CDOs of ABS did not exist as a CDO asset class until late 1999.
8. The CDOs were randomly selected from Citigroup-originated cash flow arbitrage CDOs.
9. For more details on the modeling assumptions supporting this analysis, see the appendix of *Diversifying Credit Risk Using a Fund of Funds Structure*, Glen McDermott and Alexei Kroujiline, Citigroup, February 20, 2004.
10. For more information on this technique, see "A Copula Function Approach to Credit Portfolio Modeling," David Li, Jerome Connor, and Alex Gu, *Quantitative Credit Analyst*, Citigroup, May 2003.
11. Investors should exercise caution when using standard deviation as a measure of return volatility in nonnormal distributions. The return/risk ratios in Table 12.4 were calculated by dividing the average IRR by the standard deviation of IRR. The return/risk ratio is not a Sharpe ratio because (1) our ratio is not historical, but simulated, and (2) we made no adjustment for the risk-free rate.

CHAPTER 13   Commercial Real Estate CDOs

1. See the glossary at the end of this chapter for a list of commonly used CRE CDO terms.
2. Criimi Mae Commercial Mortgage Trust 1998-C1 is a classic example of how CMBSs can be securitized using a reREMIC structure.
3. By way of comparison, global ABS CDO issuance will likely reach $50 billion for 2005.
4. Including RE CDOs backed solely or primarily by REIT trust preferred securities. For our readers' convenience, we include a list of closed cash flow CRE CDOs in the appendix at the end of the chapter.
5. In 2001, more than 50 percent of CRE CDO issuance was arbitrage motivate the a. For the year to date, arbitrage considerations have prompted less than 10 percent of CRE CDO issuance (excluding CRE CDOs backed primarily by trust preferred securities).
6. Ingress I, Crest 2000-1, Duke Funding I, and Putnam Structured Product CDO 2001-1 have been downgraded.
7. This represents the total number of ABS CDOs and CRE CDOs included in Moody's Deal Score Report as of July 2005.
8. Please see *Monthly Subordination Report, MB823*, Darrell Wheeler and Jeffrey Berenbaum, Citigroup, October 7, 2005.
9. Also see our description of various commercial real estate securities in the next section, titled "Building Blocks of a CRE CDO."

10. To our knowledge, the first CRE CDO to include a significant allocation (~10 percent) to B-notes is G-Force 2003-1, which was issued on December 20, 2003.

11. Investors interested in a full discussion of these B-notes and their rights should review our CMBS article on subordinated debt, *A Review of B-Notes, Mezzanine Loans, and Other Secondary Debt Structures*, Darrell Wheeler, Citigroup, October 8, 2004.

12. For a discussion of the pooling and servicing agreement, see *What's in the Pooling and Servicing Agreement and How It Can Affect CMBS Investors*, Darrell Wheeler, Citigroup, April 23, 2004.

13. New-issue AAA-rated CRE CDO paper was issued at LIBOR plus 50 bp at the end of 2000, while triple-A CLO paper was issued around LIBOR plus 44 bp. Meanwhile, seven-year triple-A CMBS paper traded at swaps plus 33 bp and 10-year triple-A CMBS paper traded at swaps plus 45 bp.

14. Nonetheless, a couple of established arbitrage CRE CDO managers did get deals done in the 2002 to 2003 time frame. These managers include MFS Investment Management and GMAC Institutional Advisors.

15. Examples include CT Investment Management, Newcastle Investment Corp., Lennar Partners, Aries (Structured Credit Partners), and Blackrock Financial Management.

16. Criimi Mae was a major subordinate CMBS investor until filing for bankruptcy in the fall of 1998 when it was unable to meet margin calls from its lenders. The value of Criimi Mae's collateral, which was largely B-piece CMBSs, fell considerably during the flight to quality that was triggered by the Russian crisis earlier that year.

17. In this instance, leverage is defined as the total amount of debt and equity issued by the CDO divided by the debt and equity rated below investment grade.

18. See our glossary of terms later in the chapter for a more detailed explanation of these terms.

19. The agencies run sophisticated annual default models against the collateral and account for diversity (or lack thereof) within the collateral pool and various cash flow allocation mechanisms within a CDO transaction. Our analysis is only intended to be a "reasonability test."

20. *Cash Flow CDOs 101 for CMBS Investors*, Alexis Kim, Mia Koo, Jennifer Story, and Susan S. Merrick, Fitch Ratings, September 29, 2004.

21. "June CMBS Delinquency Looks Good, So We Reduce the Universal CDR for Our Projected Credit Subordination Levels," Darrell Wheeler and Jeffrey S. Berenbaum, *Bond Market Roundup: Strategy*, Citigroup. July 8, 2005.

22. In Yield Book, this projected subordination report is in a global template called "G Subord" and can be found on page 4.2 in the "Report" section and run against a portfolio of securities.

23. *101 Ways to Overleverage a CMBS Loan*, Darrell Wheeler and Lauren Moskovitz, Citigroup, April 2005.

24. Underwriters generally release their Intex models after the transaction closes.

25. Definition supplied by *REITs 101*, Jonathan Litt et al., Citigroup, September 29, 2004.

26. Definition supplied by *REITs 101*, Jonathan Litt et al., Citigroup, September 29, 2004.
27. Definition supplied by *REITs 101*, Jonathan Litt et al., Citigroup, September 29, 2004.
28. Definition supplied by *REITs 101*, by Jonathan Litt et al., Citigroup, September 29, 2004.

Index